THE FUTURE OF LEARNING

The Michel Thomas Method

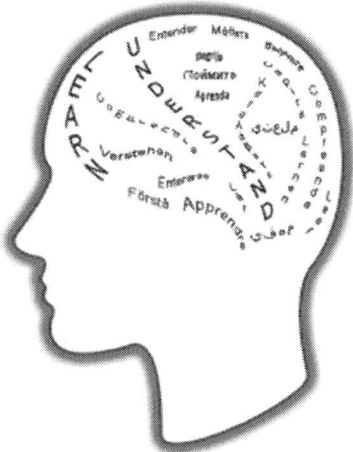

Freeing Minds One Person at a Time...

Marilyne Woodsmall, Ph.M.
Wyatt Woodsmall, Ph.D.

A selection of other works also by

Marilyne Woodsmall
&
Wyatt Woodsmall

*People Pattern™ Power:
The Nine Keys to Business Success*

*Red Alert: The Culture Crisis -
Implications of the General Developmental Model*

*Learning How to Learn™:
Cultivating our Children for the Future*

Motive: The Secret Key to Influence

The Secrets to Motivation in the Workplace

*Behavioral Assessment Tools:
Profiling Plus™ - Hiring Right
The Value Culture™ Profile
The People Pattern™ Profile*

THE FUTURE OF LEARNING

The Michel Thomas Method

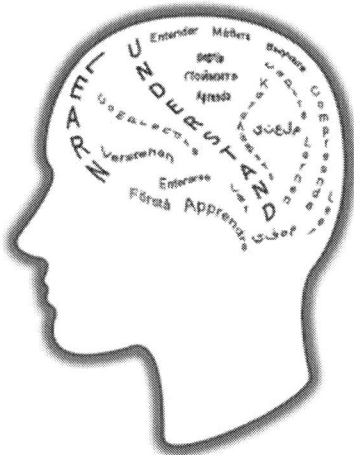

Freeing Minds One Person at a Time...

Marilyne Woodsmall, Ph.M.
Wyatt Woodsmall, Ph.D.

Next Step Press

THE FUTURE OF LEARNING
THE MICHEL THOMAS METHOD
FREEING MINDS ONE PERSON AT A TIME...
COPYRIGHT © 2008
By Marilyne Woodsmall, Ph.M., and Wyatt Woodsmall, Ph.D. All rights reserved.
No part of this book may be reproduced or transmitted in any form or by any
means, electronic or mechanical, including photocopying, recording or by any
information storage and retrieval system, without written permission from the
publisher. For information contact Next Step Press, P.O. Box 642, Great Falls, VA 22066.

Printed in the United States of America

Cover design by James Davidson
Typeset in Arial

ISBN 1-892876-11-6

DEDICATION

We dedicate this book to the life, work and memory of
our dear friend, Michel Thomas,
with love and gratitude for being in our lives, for his invaluable contribution to this book, and for his steadfast commitment to engender our fundamental right to "*Freedom of Mind*."

As Michel had requested, we also dedicate this book to his "two mothers," Freida, his biological mother, and his aunt Idessa, both of whom were his "*Master Teachers of Life*." It was their wisdom and love which inspired and molded Michel into the remarkable man that he was.

ACKNOWLEDGEMENT

We would like to convey our gratitude to our wonderful friends and students around the world for their continuing support of our work and research. We would also like to express a special thank you to particular friends for their involvement with this project: to Gail Levine, for her enthusiastic and dedicated contribution to the editing of the manuscript; to Shelly Wooldridge for her technical expertise and help with the formatting of the manuscript; and to James Davidson, for his assistance in preparing the manuscript and for the beautiful design for the front and back covers of this book, which reflect the essence of Michel's ground-breaking method, and capture the intensity of a young Michel Thomas, as well as the wisdom and dignity of the man he was to become.

Most of all, our profound and heartfelt gratitude goes to Michel Thomas for his treasured friendship, for his unwavering support of and commitment to the success of this project, for his trust and for his candidly sharing both the secrets of his revolutionary teaching method, as well as the very depth of his being, to make this book what it is, a legacy of Michel's magnificent and unparalleled contribution to our world, one which represents the future of learning and the reality of freeing minds one person at a time to make this a much better world for all.

THE FUTURE OF LEARNING   THE MICHEL THOMAS METHOD
Freeing Minds One Person at a Time

CONTENTS

DEDICATION... v

ACKNOWLEDGEMENT

CONTENTS x

Forward 1

Chapter One

    MICHEL THOMAS: A REMARKABLE MAN
    WITH A GRAND MISSION 9

Chapter Two

    THE MESSAGE: THOSE WHO "GET IT" AND THOSE
    WHO DON'T AND THOSE WHO NEVER WILL… 13

Chapter Three

    MICHEL THOMAS: A BIOGRAPHICAL VIGNETTE..................... 23

Chapter Four

    EDUCATION AND DEMOCRACY: THE DELICATE LINK 37

Chapter Five

    THE *MIND PRISON*™: THE FAILURE OF OUR CURRENT
    DIS-EDUCATIONAL SYSTEM™ 61

Chapter Six

    THE *MICHEL THOMAS METHOD*:
    THE *MASTER TEACHER'S* MODEL 93

Chapter Seven

    THEORY AND PRACTICE:
    THE WAR BETWEEN THE TWO 261

Chapter Eight

    PRACTICAL APPLICATIONS OF
    THE *MICHEL THOMAS METHOD* 297

Chapter Nine

    MICHEL THOMAS: A UNIQUE PROFILE
    THE DIFFERENCE THAT MADE THE DIFFERENCE................. 317

Chapter Ten

   MICHEL'S MODEL SCHOOLS: DREAM OR REALITY 361

Chapter Eleven

   MICHEL THOMAS' TEACHING TRIUMPHS:
   THE RULE RATHER THAN THE EXCEPTION............................ 377

Chapter Twelve

   CONCLUSION 415

APPENDIX A

   ADVANCED BEHAVIORAL MODELING™ TECHNOLOGY........ 421

APPENDIX B

   MICHEL'S LANGUAGE COURSES 425

APPENDIX C

   PHOTOGRAPHS AND DOCUMENTS 431

ABOUT THE AUTHORS... 437

INDEX 441

Forward

HOW THIS BOOK CAME ABOUT

This book is about a magnificent journey that began in 1997. At that time, a mutual acquaintance, who attended one of the modeling trainings we had conducted several years previously began talking to us about an incredible educator named Michel Thomas, who was able to teach a foreign language in three days. Of course, it sounded too good to be true. After all, within our current educational system, it takes years to learn a foreign language. In fact, most people never achieve an acceptable level of proficiency. Our mutual acquaintance, Harold Goodman, D.O., was aware of the diverse modeling projects that we had been working on in different fields and of our particular interest in and research on learning. He thought that it would be a great idea for us to "capture" Michel's revolutionary teaching method by means of our proprietary *Advanced Behavioral Modeling™ Technology* (Appendix A).

We were obviously intrigued by all that we were hearing and wanted to know more. It seemed so outside of the realm of consensual reality that someone could actually teach a person to speak a foreign language proficiently in what seemed to be nanoseconds in the grand scheme of things, that we agreed it would be a fascinating modeling project on which to work. Being open-minded and always in search of that which is unique and different, we truly believe that anything is possible with extraordinary individuals in extraordinary situations. This is particularly true when certain elements synchronistically come together, even if the world at large may not think in such a manner at this point in time. Also, the two of us had been planning to write our own book on what we refer to in our teachings as our *"dis-educational system"*™. So why not do it now and write about the man who has made such a magnificent and lasting contribution to education and to our world in general.

We have spent years modeling *how* different experts in their respective fields do what they do. Being the *"Experts on Experts"*™, we figured that it would be enriching and captivating to model an expert who seemed to have come up with an extraordinary teaching method, one that could help revolutionize the educational system, which we, too, believed needed a major overhaul. Later, as we worked with Michel, we realized that we shared Michel's passion for learning and knowledge. We also felt the same great urgency to change an ineffectual system, and to shed light on the dire circumstances surrounding education. Furthermore, we shared his passion to help transform a culture of ignorance into a culture of enlightenment before it was too late. Besides, Michel the man was quite intriguing in his own right; and we were delighted to have the opportunity to meet this expert, who was more than unique in the field of education.

In our work all over the world, we have met some incredible *"experts,"* exceptional in the execution of their craft or skill, as well as some wonderful human beings. Yet, Michel stands alone, even among them. He was truly in a league of his own in all respects. His amazing life story of untold horrors, of great courage and determination and of superhuman escapes may appear to be fiction to many. And we, as well as all those who had come to know him, realize that his entire life could not be more real than reality itself. It is too bad for those few who have chosen to dismiss his story and his teachings, for they are the losers in all of this. They truly have no clue as to what they are missing. Still another reason for us to work with Michel — to help open the eyes of many who have chosen to remain blind to his message and to his priceless gift to humanity.

In any case, the process of connecting with Michel Thomas was a long one, given the challenges of his myriad life experiences, all of which go far beyond the experiences most of us will ever witness in our lifetime. Michel was a cautious man, and one who simply did not jump precipitously into any situation without careful thought to his course of action. He did not know us, and we did not know him. It was natural for him to wonder what we were going to do with the information he would give us, since he had not yet met with us. It seems that over the years, Michel had been reluctant to share the secrets of his method with anyone, for fear of having others steal them. In fact, he had mentioned to us on several occasions that there were individuals who had attempted to learn his secrets and then announce them to the world as their own. Meanwhile, academia was not reacting in a favorable way, insisting that what Michel was doing was outright impossible.

Whether out of skepticism, jealousy or ego, the list of critics persists to this day, and a few continue to question both the believability of his life, as well as the success of his teaching. In spite of students lauding him all over the globe, in spite of the plethora of documents, files and photographs to back up his claims, in spite of the list of his past and present ecstatic students who make up what could pass for the "*Who's Who of Hollywood, Business and Politics,*" the critics remained unbelievers. It is certainly their loss.

In spite of meetings put off and other missed connections, our mutual acquaintance remained persistent, very persistent, in fact. We were often on the road engaged in modeling projects and conducting trainings, and Michel was quite a busy man who was also constantly on the go. So very often our intermediary was not able to reach him. Whenever he did, though, our mutual acquaintance would continue to talk to Michel about our unique expertise and track record in behavioral modeling using our proprietary technology, and about our modeling him and his teaching method. Both sides thought that if Michel's method was so phenomenal, it could really revolutionize the manner in which everything is taught, and not just languages. We all knew that it was of utmost importance to "capture" his method while he was still here with us. A sense of urgency had taken over. Finally, in 2001, after many wonderful phone conversations, we had the pleasure of meeting Michel; and the wonderfully intriguing and enriching journey through Michel's mind began.

The timing of our meeting was no accident, for we truly believe that all things happen for a reason and at the time when they are meant to happen. Up until then, Michel was not ready to reveal his method. Then suddenly, it was obvious that a similar sense of urgency had come over Michel as well. He realized that the time had come to share his cherished method, that he could no longer keep this invaluable gift to himself. The time had come to share his brilliant method with the world.

Michel's gifted mind worked in fascinating ways, beautifully integrating critical thinking and keen, intuitive abilities. As we shall later see, this sense of inner knowing had served him well throughout his life. In meeting with us, it set the tone for what lay ahead. Michel somehow "knew" that by our modeling him, we would precisely *capture* his actual method. Michel was definitely a stickler for words, a trait fortunately shared by us, and one which facilitated our collaboration and resulted in a wonderful exchange on so many levels. Furthermore, as a reflection of his method, every word and explanation of this manuscript had to be clear and precise in his own mind to create *understanding*. In this light, unlike many other experts, Michel had a keen awareness of process.

Michel was also a man who knew exactly what he wanted. On more than one occasion, Michel stated to us that he was not interested in some academician's opinion or theory about what his method was, and that is one of the reasons that he chose to work with the two of us. From the onset of our project, Michel stated that he did not want his method presented as an academic treatise because paradoxically, such a structure represented the very thing that he abhorred and had worked so passionately and assiduously to change his entire life — the rigid templates of traditional teaching which serve to reinforce the bureaucratic stranglehold on learning. In addition, after all the rejections he had experienced in the halls of academia, Michel remained cautious.

At the same time, Michel loved giving interviews of all kinds because the media attention, mostly with the foreign press, afforded him the vehicle to communicate his message about his work. It also gave him the opportunity to discuss how his revolutionary teaching method reawakens what he referred to as the "*innate drive for learning*" which has been crushed by traditional schooling. Still, Michel was not interested in sharing the true secrets of his method with the dozens of journalists, teachers and others who were anxious to present their scoop, or their version of the *Michel Thomas Method*. In the course of interviews, he would always provide interesting and stimulating bits of information about the obvious, external elements of his method (for example, that there is no note taking, no memorization, no homework, no "*trying to remember,*" etc.), to inspire the listeners and viewers, yet Michel would never disclose the underlying mental processes involved, or the hidden keys behind his method.

Finally, Michel stated on several occasions that he wanted to avoid having his revolutionary method reduced to being someone's global platitudes about what they thought he was doing, when, in fact, they could not know "how" his mind had created the method. He also realized that someone simply observing him in action or listening to him teach would not provide the real, behind-the-scene answers. That is why we are honored that Michel, a man of great intensity and discretion, put his trust in us to "*decode*" and to decipher the inner workings of his remarkable mind, using our modeling process as well as our expertise in training and human typological studies. The boundless access to his expertise that he afforded us in all aspects of our modeling process is simply priceless, as he revealed with such meticulous precision and depth, the closely-guarded and previously undisclosed "internal" processes and elements of his learning masterpiece.

As professional behavioral modelers, we examine and then synthesize the various components of what we as modelers refer to as "*unconscious competency,*" (Appendix A) and what is known in the new school of pedagogy as "*wisdom of practice.*" We take this *wisdom of practice* to a deeper level of understanding through our modeling process, by analyzing the intricacies of Michel's *unconscious competency*, which we present in the Method Chapter. And, in alignment with Michel's wishes, we chose to do so in a user-friendly manner that reaches people in a personally meaningful way.

We have also provided a typological (behavioral) profile of Michel that explains how his particular personality traits and what we refer to as his "*model of the world*" provided the foundation for the creation of his method and for what he was to become in life. In addition, we will show in Chapter Seven how, contrary to the critics, Michel's method is not only based on sound pedagogical principles, it was also decades ahead of what is happening today in the so-called new school. Furthermore, we will discuss how Michel's results can be explained by modern theories of learning and teaching.

And now, after hours and hours of elicitation as part of our proprietary modeling process, after days and days of questions and answers, after the joyous experience of being a student of Michel's in order to go through a personalized learning experience with him (also to have the experience from another perspective, as professional modelers), after weeks of synthesis and after reviewing hundreds of pages of notes, after listening to our audio recordings and watching videos of our elicitations of Michel, and after all the quality interactions with him, we created the model of the *Michel Thomas Method*.

Finally, we now have the great privilege of presenting Michel's incredible method to the world at the exact time that it was meant to be revealed. It has been three years since the initial and revised manuscripts were completed with Michel's wholehearted collaboration and his enthusiastic stamp of approval the year before his passing. And we are grateful that he was then still with us to endorse the result, and to see, firsthand, how our modeling process had captured his expertise and *wisdom of practice*. As a pioneer in education, and, as an exceptional resource of *"life wisdom,"* Michel Thomas was, in all ways, what we refer to as the *"Master Teacher,"* for present and future generations. In our follow-up book, the content of which Michel was aware and supported, we will shed more light on specific aspects of Michel's genius. We will also present additional learning templates and specific ways of revamping our current *dis-educational system*™.

The whole journey has been richly rewarding on many levels, and for that, we are extremely thankful. We are very appreciative of Harold for his tenacity in making the initial introduction, as well as for his initial participation in the project. And, of course, we are so grateful to Michel for his generosity of time and resources, his boundless energy, his unyielding support, his complete openness and candor, his warm kindness, his uncanny wisdom, his unselfish sharing of personal documents, letters, photos, articles, and papers, his true friendship and, most of all, for his sharing of his spirit, his entire being with us. Michel so graciously, excitedly, willingly and completely opened up to us as we modeled him and his method

In allowing us to translate his method to the world, Michel has given us the opportunity to share his timely and powerful, personal message of truth about the dire state of affairs in education, a message which impacts all of us, particularly our children, and thus, the future of our world. Although he is no longer with us in the physical realm, his memory, his vision and his legacy will further his quest of freeing minds for generations to come.

Michel became our trusted friend with whom we exchanged thoughts and ideas on a myriad of subjects, in addition to his sharing of his expert knowledge from his fifty plus years of successful teaching. What began as a firm handshake years ago had been transformed into a firm hug of respect, friendship and love.

Thank you so very much, Michel, for who you were and for your part in helping to make this a better world. We should all be grateful to you for having been a shining light among us. We will do our part in making certain that your light remains a beacon of hope and of meaningful change in the manner in which you so desired.

>	Marilyne Woodsmall and Wyatt Woodsmall
>	January 2004
>	(Updated January 2007 as a posthumous tribute
>	to Michel Thomas)

Chapter One

MICHEL THOMAS: A REMARKABLE MAN WITH A GRAND MISSION

"My intention in creating my method was not to teach languages quickly. I created it to change the world."

— *Michel Thomas*

Every so often an extraordinary soul appears on our planet, a soul who is meant to accomplish wondrous things, a soul who is to live an extraordinary life, a soul who is to escape the grips of death many times over, a soul who is to touch the lives of all those who are blessed to cross his path, a soul who is to effect major change in the fabric of mankind. That extraordinary soul was a man with a grand and noble mission. That extraordinary soul, that man, was Michel Thomas.

The above accolades may appear to be exaggerated to those who have never had the privilege of knowing Michel Thomas — the magnetic personality, the brilliant educator, the wonderful human being, the devoted father, the captivating storyteller, the skillful interrogator, the great survivor of an evil, moral pestilence that almost destroyed our world during one of its darkest hours. No one could ever bestow enough laurels on this extraordinary man who appeared among humankind to accomplish a very special mission that only he could realize.

Only an incredible human being with exceptional courage, great determination and with a powerful drive to survive, when others could not or did not, could achieve that which Michel Thomas had in his long and prodigious life. Michel Thomas — a man of deep convictions, a man of unrelenting courage, a fighter for a noble cause, a man whose brilliance and wisdom will continue to shine as a beacon beyond his passing, to lead his fellow man out of the darkness of ignorance to a new way of thinking, of teaching and of being. The *Master Teacher*, with his unique teaching method and his singular thinking will help to engender what Michel referred to as true *"freedom of mind"* and dignity of self in an era of increasing mindlessness, confusion and even terror.

So who was this man, Michel Thomas, and what was he all about? From the very first moment that we met Michel, we realized that we were in the presence of someone very special indeed. Someone truly unique in our day and age, Michel was part of a rare breed still known to some today as a "gentleman," and a gentleman in every sense of the word. He was also a gentle man on the outside who exuded that old-world European charm, which, as many know, is more the exception than the rule in our present day society. Beware however, for that polite and gentle exterior belied something much bigger and more powerful at work here. Behind that poised, mild-mannered exterior lay a cauldron ready to explode into unbridled anger at any moment, given the proper provocation. If one did not know Michel the man, and understand his perspective on the world, or know about the many death defying incidents in his life, his outbursts would have truly frightened some. And they most certainly have on more than one occasion.

What immediately struck one about Michel was his powerful presence. Some may have called it *charisma*, a meaningless term in Michel's mind. Such a description is much too superficial for the likes of a man of his stature. Instead, we prefer to describe his personal appeal as a tremendous sense of self-confidence, natural charm, intensity of being, profound wisdom, heightened awareness of everything within him and around him and an extraordinarily contagious and ebullient energy, all impeccably blended together and bursting forth as a shining light while he was among us. He had the most amazing, penetrating gaze and soft blue eyes that could literally see right through you and often did.

We have named it the *"Michel look,"* one that was undeniably his and his alone. It was a look that is visible early on in photos of Michel in his teens and twenties, when he was already engaged in life and death struggles during World War II. It intensely communicates a profoundly etched memory of unheard torment and humiliation that few will hopefully ever have to experience: living a "hell on earth" in concentration and deportation camps, miraculously escaping the hands of death to join forces with the Secret Army of the French Resistance for two years, then to fight bravely with the First Combat Intelligence Unit during and after the war for three years in all, and after the war, working with US Counter Intelligence as a special agent to track and capture Nazis war criminals.

All of these larger than life experiences, the kind from which the threads of fiction are woven, created an intricately designed puzzle of events, people, images and emotions, tragedies and triumphs, each contributing to that *look* and to the making of Michel, the unique man and illustrious educator. The *Michel look* was often mesmerizing to those around him, especially to those caught by surprise. One can only wonder if it was that *look* which somehow swayed the Gestapo, Klaus Barbie, whom Michel called *"the model of evil,"* to release Michel after their confrontation in Lyon. The *Michel look* immediately took hold whenever a topic was broached that recalled the horrors of the past which Michel personally witnessed.

Although Michel was born of the Jewish faith, he was certainly more like what we would call a *"Universalist."* He understood and appreciated all people, all races and all religions. For this he thanked his "two mothers" who imparted this wisdom to him when he was a child. Michel had a better understanding of Christianity than most Christians, and he had studied the other world religions as well. He raised his own children to appreciate the value of all human life and of all life, for that matter.

Interestingly, both in spite of and because of his extraordinary life, Michel was at the same time both grounded and, in a sense, above it all, a quality which enabled him to understand nuances and to see things in people and situations that most others certainly could not and perhaps would not. More important, it was the inexplicable sense of knowing deep within himself, of knowing that he had led such an astonishing life, in order to accomplish a very special mission for humankind, which fed that mighty power, that unwavering self-confidence and unstoppable drive, all of which contributed to making Michel Thomas the remarkable man that he was.

It was this same inner knowing which created a sense of mystery around Michel Thomas that sparked a certain curiosity among anyone who was near him, to want to learn more. That inner knowing combined with an almost ethereal and authoritative bearing, resulted in one's having what was essentially a feeling of standing in the presence of one very powerful and exceptional human being.

Chapter Two

THE MESSAGE: THOSE WHO "GET IT" AND THOSE WHO DON'T AND THOSE WHO NEVER WILL...

Michel Thomas, whom we have named the *"Master Teacher,"* had a very deliberate and specific message for the world. His message is about the need to wake up to what is really happening around us: the proliferation of programmed minds created and fostered by an educational system that destroys the *innate drive for learning* and our ability to engage in critical thinking. Michel's message goes even further. His message serves as a word of warning about the ominous consequences of nonaction. The time has come to end what Michel referred to as *"thought control"* before it is too late (We explore these ideas further in Chapter Four.).

There is more to his message. Michel wanted people everywhere to know that there is a way to bring back *freedom of mind* and the joy of learning. He paved the way and provided a powerful template for this freedom — the *Michel Thomas Method*. Let it be known that the *Michel Thomas Method* is both a revolutionary template for learning which, at the same time, provides a powerful blueprint for changing the world. Those who get it know that his method and his message are two powerful parts of an even more powerful whole.

As with all things in life, there are those who get it; and there are always others who don't get the message, and, of course, there are those who never will. Some will immediately see the connection between Michel's method, his philosophy of life and his mission to "change the world." From a learning perspective, those who experienced Michel's teaching firsthand, of course, get it. They personally experienced the rekindling of the passion for learning. The genuine gratitude and great excitement as well as the countless support of Michel's enthusiastic students continued to pour forth from many different directions right up to the final days of his life.

In spite of Michel's overwhelming successes around the world, there have been a few skeptics and critics over the years who have attempted to dismiss Michel as a charlatan or a phony. Some of the skepticism stemmed from the fact that for so long Michel had been unwilling to disclose his method, for fear that others might steal it, claim it to be their own or distort it in some way.

They are, nevertheless, among those who don't get it. Because of our love and support of Michel and of our promise to him to get his method and message out into the world in a significant way, we would like to place his work and his life into the proper perspective it deserves from the start, before we even delve into his philosophy of education and into the *Michel Thomas Method*.

We certainly understand that skepticism is a healthy attitude to have, especially in the face of what might otherwise appear to be an impossible or very challenging task. From a behavioral perspective, there are some people who need facts, data and tangible proof that something exists or has occurred in order to believe it or to acknowledge it (Chapter Nine). For these prospective unbelievers, let it be known that Michel had decades of tangible successes with students from all walks of life and all social classes — from the affluent and elite to the poor and underprivileged. With each and every success, Michel would teach his students in the face of great odds — teaching those who had had horrible memories of school and bad feelings about learning in general, especially when it came to learning a foreign language.

In spite of these odds, the outcome would be spectacular each and every time. Michel always managed to inspire his students and reawaken their *innate drive for learning*. Because of these odds, Michel was inspired all the more to make a difference in the lives of his students. Failure was not part of Michel's vocabulary. His teaching success was a given in his mind. Michel knew that with each success, he was profoundly and positively impacting his students' learning, as well as their personal lives in significant ways.

In spite of Michel's countless successes, the skeptics stood firm in their disbelief of the *Master Teacher* and his method. Some critics have even suggested that the success of his method was a direct result of his charismatic personality, a notion which is total nonsense. As we mention elsewhere in this book, Michel's genius went so far beyond a simplistic reduction to charisma, for he was truly a deeply nuanced being on many interconnected levels. An academic once referred to the results Michel obtained with his students as impossible and "a menace to the lay public." Other detractors have even suggested that Michel used hypnotic techniques to achieve his success. Again, this is total nonsense. What Michel achieved was far too "*layered*" and profound to be explained away by simple hypnosis. Others tried to reduce his method to the use of cognates, which, Michel considered insulting to him. As we shall examine in the Method Chapter, the use of cognates is certainly not a method on its own, nor does it represent in any manner, shape or form, the essence of the *Michel Thomas Method*.

Curiously, among Michel's critics, no one had the courage to come forth to challenge Michel personally regarding his method. In light of this, Michel proudly expressed the following to us:

> In three days, in less than three days, I achieve in teaching what takes several years in the language department of any university. If you ask the language department of any university how long it would take just to cover but not to achieve, but to cover, they will gladly tell you that it will take two to three years, not including the years in high school. What I do in three days is more. It is not to cover it, but to know it. I challenge any university. Nobody takes me up on it. It only takes three days to prove it or to disprove it. In all these years, nobody took me up on it. No university, no college.

What we find interesting is that this very ignorance on the part of critics to spread misinformation about his method, was directly connected to Michel's message about the terrible state of affairs in the world at the present time and throughout history. More than ever, we witness how the powers that be continue to thrive and create fear by maintaining control over the uneducated masses. The misinformation and lies they pour forth, their blatant disregard of the truth, their rejection of expertise and the ease of their deception — these are exactly what Michel cautioned us to be aware of regarding certain people and attitudes in today's world. He warned us to be aware of those in our present day societies who speak out of ignorance and/or who conceal the truth under a veil of self-importance and clever words.

Furthermore, Michel was well aware that mind control, or thought control is nothing new and had existed even in ancient times (We will come back to this topic of controlling the minds of the masses in Chapter Four.). Fortunately for the rest of us, there are many who can and do see beyond this veil. And to understand the message of this book, one needs to shed this veil in whatever manner it manifests, so that one can take in Michel's message and actually act upon it. This means doing one's part in changing what we call the current "*dis-educational system*"™.

Let it be known that this book is just one of the ways that the two of us are taking action — by honoring Michel, the Master Teacher and revealing his authentic method that reawakens the joy of learning — and by spreading his message of warning to all those who are ready to listen — regarding what is happening in our world at the present time and about the consequences of nonaction.

First and foremost, this book is about the *Michel Thomas Method,* which, in itself, was Michel's powerful vehicle for the change that he championed throughout his life. Both the message and the method go hand in hand. In fact, Michel wanted this book about his method to also communicate his message to the world. Of course, we additionally want to celebrate all that Michel was and still is, as his legacy lives on. Any other approach would not have done justice to his life and work... For this Michel graciously expressed his heartfelt gratitude.

We would like to iterate that this book is not a critique of all teachers because there are obviously good teachers out there who are making the best of a bad system. Many of them are not in the spotlight either by choice or by circumstance. At the present time, there are also wonderful home-school teachers around the country, as well as individuals who are creating their own schools and/or programs because they are disenchanted with the inadequate system now in place. Like Michel and like the two of us, they are among those who also want to change the world by adopting a new educational system that creates joy rather than fear, and that stimulates learning rather than stifles it.

In the past decade, increasing numbers of people have been stepping up to make a difference in the world within their respective fields all over the globe. Many have wonderful missions and have created organizations to help foster efforts to improve the quality of life, to save our planet's resources, to enhance our well-being, to create special programs for children, and much more.

In 1998, as part of a personal mission, we were inspired to create *The Children of Light and Wisdom Foundation, Inc.* Michel was delighted when asked to be a member of our Board of Directors during what turned out to be the last months of his life. He sadly passed on before this could officially occur, yet his spirit and legacy lives on with us. Our mission is to help transform the world and uplift humanity by developing enlightened global leaders, using a synthesis of cutting-edge educational models and unique teachings. Through *The CLWF Institute for Global Leadership* we are bringing together those who get it — including pioneering thinkers, leading experts and innovative business people — to raise consciousness and to train and develop children and adults to become competent, exemplary leaders of Light and Wisdom, equipped as critical and creative thinkers to solve the diverse and complex challenges of our rapidly changing, interconnected world. (http://www.theclwf.org)

Michel would be happy to know that those who get it and who want to help change the world are finally coming together *en masse,* uniting people with no prior connection from around the globe, as they engage in their respective projects and missions. Curiously, in spite of what is happening around us in the world, there are, nevertheless, people who don't get it. In some cases, it is because these individuals are still focused on ego, greed and/or self-aggrandizement, either personally or on behalf of corporate entities. In other cases, it is due to outright ignorance. And in others it is about fear — the fear of change and/or the fear of taking action to effect much needed change. Later, in Chapter Four, we will discuss Michel's perspective on the consequences of such nonaction.

As far as Michel's method is concerned, there are still those who truly don't get it. These individuals are interested in his method as an academic exercise, yet are not concerned about the state of education, or, lack thereof, in the world. We have even come across those (from abroad) who are quite content with the way things are done in their country. In fact, they thought that the book would insult their teachers, a reaction that did not sit at all well with Michel: "Good teachers will welcome this book," he stated. These individuals are the ones who fail to see beyond the "veil." They fail to see that this book reveals the very truth which Michel had spent his entire life exposing about what is tragically happening within the entire educational system worldwide. The time has come to remove the dust of stagnancy and to replace it with the energy of change. Michel's method provides a powerful template for meaningful change that gives parents, teachers, students and anyone, for that matter, a way to create a better world, a better future, their future, your future, our global future.

> Michel's message is directed to all those who care about the future of our children, and hence, the future of our world.

The fact that some people may interpret the message to be one that is directed at teachers is quite revelatory, in that it demonstrates to what extent these individuals are missing the point of Michel's message entirely. Michel's message was not about any one group or any country's system versus another. His message was truly universal and directed to anyone astute enough to realize that we face great global challenges for which we must, together as a world, unite to fight the hypocrisy and thought control that destroys our very freedom before it is too late. His message serves as a wake-up call to parents and to all those who continue to allow their children to *serve time* in school, with their minds enslaved, as Michel always said.

Michel had had enough of people who simply didn't care about the detrimental effects of the educational system on students. He had had enough of people who were incapable of understanding his position. He had had enough of the idiocy.

His annoyance was not about others disagreeing with him, but rather about the fact that their reaction confirmed what he had been saying all along: that their minds were still unable to "*see*" what was happening all around them, that they, too, were victims of thought control. Furthermore, he intuitively knew that those who didn't appreciate his philosophy and his beliefs were obviously more comfortable with things staying the same because "they, too, were part of the conspiracy between parents and teachers" that supported the bad educational system in place.

From a behavioral perspective, we realize that what we refer to as the "*value culture*"™ or set of values out of which given individuals operate, will, to a large degree, predict their reaction to this book. Either people will get the message or they will not. Either they will know that the current system is in dire need of drastic change or they will not. Either they will feel personally threatened by Michel's method or they will welcome it. Then there are those who will consciously choose to ignore it or who are, themselves, deeply entrenched in ignorance that they cannot move beyond it. Of course, there are also those who have already achieved such a state of mindless conformity that they are incapable of seeing it or acknowledging it.

Bureaucrats (such as those who work within a traditional system) usually don't get it because they are too ensconced in a dichotomized mind-set. Bureaucratic structures will typically prefer to avoid change and will be adverse to critiques of an established system, whether educational, governmental or otherwise. They like to follow set rules and are uncomfortable with anyone or anything that doesn't fit their mold or traditional modes of operation. These individuals are especially uncomfortable with models that get to the truth. And anyone who knew Michel was well aware of his disdain of rigid, bureaucratic systems. The bottom line is that this book is not a critique of teachers *per se*, but rather a critique of an ineffective educational system and the bureaucrats who maintain it. It is this very system which, according to Michel, does not teach teachers how to teach. Instead it encourages poor teaching and stifles the *innate drive for learning* in students.

Michel truly despised the current system and was never afraid or reluctant to express his adamant views about it. On the contrary, he was one of the few people in his time that actually had the courage to do something to change the system. And he did so with great passion, confidence and dignity. Michel deplored the fact that the traditional system continues to support the *status quo* which engenders conformity rather than creative thinking and problem solving abilities in students, as we shall discuss further in Chapter Four.

What is the message here? The message is to consider and then act upon Michel's vision of rekindling the *innate drive for learning* for all. Those who get it will take action and will work with other like-minded individuals who understand what is at stake. Those who don't will continue to "vegetate" through life, content with their imposed reality. Furthermore, Michel's message is a wake-up call to take action on the part of teachers, students, parents and officials who, in some way, know what is going on and realize the need to change a system that *chokes* the students' learning. Michel provided the way. It is time to embrace it.

In short, this book goes beyond a critique of our current *dis-educational system*™. This book goes beyond a critique to present Michel's solution — his masterful template for freeing minds and for bringing back the great excitement and thrill of real learning. Michel's method provides the solution that parents and their children can welcome with excitement, the very excitement for learning that Michel espoused. Michel's method and message, together, provide a powerful, effective and joyous way to eliminate a system which he would always refer to as "a *criminal institution* that slams the door shut to learning," and replace it with fresh minds, that are free, happy, excited to learn and to live life to its fullest.

What Michel Thomas achieved was far more than to open the doors to learning. His life experiences, his expertise, his *wisdom of practice*, his unique perspectives, his passion for learning and his respect for the value of all life, each represents an integral part of his message to the world. With these treasures, Michel Thomas has laid out the path to the future of learning, and to a new way of thinking about ourselves and about the human potential, which he believed, when channeled appropriately, could inspire other individuals to higher levels, and eventually could help to change the world and create *freedom of mind* for all. Let us hope that people everywhere, from all walks of life, begin to get Michel's powerful message and begin to engage in the process of freeing minds one person at a time.

Chapter Three

MICHEL THOMAS: A BIOGRAPHICAL VIGNETTE

Who was Michel Thomas and why did we write a book on his teaching method? There are some people for whom *Michel Thomas* is not a household word, at least not yet. So a brief, biographical sketch of his life is in order to help readers understand how his personal life experiences became the driving forces behind his breakthroughs in learning and his eventual teaching masterpiece. Michel was so delighted that we had included this biographical vignette in this book about his method because he knew better than anyone, how the many personal challenges he had overcome had set the stage for what was to follow in the development of the *Michel Thomas Method.* Furthermore, he especially wanted readers in the United States and elsewhere to be aware of these details of his life so that they could understand how his personal journey was so closely and specifically linked to his passion to "change the world" for the better by creating a unique teaching method.

Michel's life story was quite extraordinary and many might find it unbelievable except for the fact that every aspect of it is so well documented. In fact, it almost reads like fiction, and it is nevertheless true from every perspective. The interested reader is advised to read Christopher Robbins' wonderful biography of Michel Thomas, called *The Test of Courage*. The famous spy novelist, John Le Carre, once described Michel as "One of the bravest men you will ever read about." In fact, there is so much more than one could ever imagine possible in a given lifetime.

So who was Michel Thomas? Michel was born Moniek Kroskof in Lodz, Poland to financially comfortable Jewish parents who were associated with a family-owned textile manufacturing business. Although he suffered from a severe case of rickets as a child during World War I, which resulted in a temporary leg deformity, Michel was able to overcome it due to great diet and doctors, so much so that he later developed into an elite athlete.

Not all was rosy in his childhood, however, for his parents divorced and then he lived with his mother Frieda, whom Michel adored and she him. Later, at age six he went to live with his aunt Idessa in Germany. Throughout his life, Michel referred to them as his "two mothers." They are responsible, he said, for the wonderful relationships that he had developed with women over the years as well as for teaching him the meaning of respect and mental wealth, among many other wonderful life lessons. He always described himself as *"his mother's son."* Michel quickly learned German at the age of seven as a reaction against the Poland he wanted to erase from his memory. While in school he became an avid skier, swimmer and rower and an overall first-rate athlete who preferred to excel in individual, rather than in team sports. Michel was a good student and because of his physical strength, he was always the class leader.

In high school, Michel, as a non-German, always wanted to excel in the German language and did. He also had a voracious appetite for knowledge in spite of the educational system and he was a quick learner (At this time in his life, Michel was already aware of the fact that those in power did not want an educated proletariat, but instead an educated elite.). This was an observation that was to become a driving force in the creation of his teaching method later on, as we shall see in Chapter Six. It certainly was not the existing educational system that triggered his desire for learning. On the contrary, Michel wanted to accelerate his own learning in order to get out of the traditional system as quickly as possible, so he quit school and persuaded a local, famous music critic/teacher who was known as *"the walking encyclopedia"* to personally tutor him.

When the Nazis came to power in Germany in 1933, the situation became perilous and at the age of nineteen, Michel left Germany for France. He traveled to Paris and then to Bordeaux, where Michel found freelance work as a photographer and later as an artist. Michel attended the University of Bordeaux, where he took classes in philology, philosophy, archaeology and the history of art. Of course, he totally devoured the information. Unlike most students, he was there to pursue knowledge for the sake of knowledge. He was not there to prepare for a profession in order to earn a living, which Michel believed is still often the case today. Michel always stressed his love of learning for learning's sake. Such a mind-set was, and still is, in stark contrast to what motivates most students to attend college.

Michel also acquired a life-long interest in psychology which took him to Vienna to study. He eventually was forced to escape to France after the arrival of the German Army and the annexation of Austria. Michel sadly described to us how during this period he became "*stateless.*" With no official state, he was considered "*fair game*" without any protection. After eight months, he escaped again to France when World War II erupted in Europe.

France quickly succumbed to the evil grip of the Nazis, and Michel then found himself in quite a perilous position in Vichy-Controlled France. The entrance of this evil force onto the European stage coincided with a whole series of highly improbable events that began to unfold over the course of several years. Michel's life story is that of an explosive and action packed play or thriller of its own. While in Nice, Michel faced his first incarceration, enduring four months of solitary confinement, on false charges of influence peddling.

According to Michel, the truth was that he was using his influence as part of French Army Intelligence in order to save Jews, and he did not earn a penny from his actions. He was able to help a large number of Jewish families to avoid being sent to camps. Michel was finally acquitted and moved to Monaco upon the recommendation of his attorney. At the time, the Vichy government was persecuting all Jews, particularly Jewish refugees. On one particular night he decided to stay in Nice, and he was arrested and sent to the French Concentration Camp at Le Vernet, where he almost starved to death amidst the most lurid conditions. Michel survived by virtue of his inner conviction and his drive to survive against all odds (with some help from Providence mixed in as well).

With each event, each escape, another page was written in the journal of Michel's life mission which was already playing out in a grand manner. Fortunately, all of these extraordinary events in his life are very well documented. In fact, throughout the years, right up to his passing, Michel had kept every letter, document and paper relating to these events, all of which substantiate him in everything to the very last detail.

Michel was then sent to a punishment camp that serviced a coal mine where he was forced to endure slave labor in the dark underground abysses of filth and stifling heat. After awhile he escaped with the help of a friend. He was recaptured and sent to *Les Milles*, another camp which was a logging operation. While in the camp he was warned by the Resistance that all Jews in camps were going to be deported and killed (already in 1942) and that he should try to escape. By the time Michel got word, it was already too late; and he was shipped off, this time, to a deportation camp. In the camp he managed to avoid deportation several times by once hiding between the ceiling beams of a building and another time under a field cot where French guards would play cards. He miraculously managed to escape on both occasions.

Both incidents were dramatic examples of perhaps some miraculous power at work to keep him alive. Was it Providence at work aiding Michel on his mission, making certain that he experienced the worst possible crimes against humanity in order to spur him on with even greater determination? Finally, one night Michel managed to carry out a dramatic escape from the deportation camp. This certainly tinged his resolve to survive with an even greater passion.

Michel then joined the French Resistance and began a new life in the French Secret Army. On February 9, 1943, while on his way to a meeting at 9 rue Sainte Catherine in Lyon to recruit Jewish refugees into the Resistance, Michel was caught by the Gestapo under the command of Klaus Barbie who became known as the Butcher of Lyon. Upon reaching the top of the stairs, Michel was first grabbed by German soldiers, who dragged him into a room where they kept asking him questions in German. Of course, Michel kept on responding in French, "I must have made a mistake." Finally, getting nowhere with Michel, the soldiers brought him into the room to see their boss, Klaus Barbie, who immediately addressed Michel in German as well. Once again, Michel answered in French, knowing all too well that the slightest indication of his understanding the Gestapo meant certain death for him.

Michel continued to speak French knowing that his interrogators did not understand him. At one point, one of the soldiers shouted to Barbie near Michel's left ear, "Let's get rid of him. How should I kill him? Shall I shoot him in the neck or in the temple?" Michel had to absolutely maintain his *sang-froid,* otherwise they would have known that he understood German, which would have probably triggered his immediate execution. If he had reacted in any way whatsoever, he would have been eliminated. At that point, Barbie suddenly jumped up from his seat, raised his arms and said in German *"identitätspapiere"* (identity papers) which, of course, resembled the words *"pièces d'identité"* in French. At that moment, Michel purposefully expressed a welcome sigh of relief, as would any "innocent," unknowing person in his shoes: *"Ah! Vous voulez mes pièces d'identité. Bien sûre. Les voilà!"* ("Oh, you want my identity papers. Of course! Here they are!") He had to show the great relief of finally understanding what his interrogators had wanted from him this entire time.

What a relief seemingly to finally understand what they wanted! Michel immediately took out a whole pack of his false papers, identifying him as a Frenchman, Michel Sberro. In the end, he managed to convince Barbie that he was a French artist who was in the building to show his artwork. Barbie let him go. Michel found out afterwards that all eighty men and women, captives in that room, were deported to Auschwitz and put to death (including the father of Badinter, the French Minister of Justice).

Something surely happened within Michel prior to and during those hours of questioning by Barbie, something of which he was not totally aware at the time. As he was walking up the stairs to the Resistance meeting before his capture, on three occasions he decided not to listen to an inner voice warning him not to proceed. The final one told him that the Gestapo was in there, and that he should not go in. Even though a foreboding feeling came over him, he continued up the stairs; and the rest of the story, as we have seen, is amazing history.

At that time, it was difficult for Michel to believe anything that he could not explain rationally. Michel realized that he should have listened to that inner voice. The incident turned out to be a good lesson for him to follow his own instincts and intuitive ability from then on. During the war and during combat situations, that inner voice would occasionally come to him; and he would take heed. He pointed out that he never waited for the voice to appear, nor did he try to listen for it. It would just happen and he would act accordingly...with each intuitive message.

The incident with Barbie is revelatory in another way. It reveals the tremendous self-control which Michel was able to access whenever need be. For example, once he got into the room and was face to face with Barbie, the incredible scenario described above put this ability to the test under the most challenging circumstances imaginable. Michel pretended not to understand a single word of German. If he had reacted in any manner that would have revealed that he understood what was being said to him, it would have meant certain death.

Was it the *Michel look* that took over and caught Barbie unaware, or was it simply that Michel was such a good actor to not let on that he understood every word regarding his potential execution? With a gun pointed at his temples and around his head and neck at different times, Michel had to consciously control his every gesture, motion and breathing, as well as all of his emotions. Any physiological change instantly would have given him away to the Gestapo, who was all too ready to catch Michel in the act. Michel maintained almost super-human control of his reactions. It is this ability which saved his life during his encounter with Barbie, and also served him well at other times during the war.

While working with us, Michel often pondered, "How was I able to convince Barbie?" Those who knew Michel will recognize what we are saying about his *look*, a powerful trait which probably affected the outcome of their interaction in some way. In 1985, past and present curiously merged, when Michel, the lone survivor of the Lyon incident, was asked to identify Barbie at his trial for crimes against humanity. Even then, Barbie continued to feign ignorance of French. In the meeting that Michel had with Barbie, there was an attorney, the judge and a court interpreter since Barbie would only speak in German. Not until after the trial, did Barbie make a statement in French, a detail which never escaped Michel's innate astuteness during their initial encounter.

About two months after the Barbie incident, Michel was captured by the French Milice in Grenoble and was tortured for six and one half hours. Later the French Resistance managed to free him. He was moved to the French Alps and was given a new set of false documents and a new name — *Michel Thomas*, which is the name that he had kept from then on. He chose the name *Michel Thomas* because as he explained to us, "It was a name that could blend into any country and one with which I could easily remain obscure and hide." Michel chose a name that was popular in several different countries and one which would allow him to remain rather inconspicuous and not stand out in any way.

Michel was very active in fighting with the Resistance in guerilla warfare and commando activities in the Alps, for which Michel has full documentation. On June 5, 1944 the long awaited coded message from the BBC revealed that the allied invasion of France at Normandy was at hand. The invasion in the south of France followed about two months later. Finally, Michel's commando unit became a Special Police Group for the investigation and the arrest of war criminals. Michel remained with them for a short while, and then was assigned to the American Army as a liaison officer. He was attached to the combat intelligence section of the First Battalion, 180th Infantry, of the 45th Division (The Thunderbirds). Michel's extraordinary abilities quickly earned him the respect of combat intelligence, and his knowledge of the country and of local Resistance agents made him invaluable on reconnaissance patrols. Michel also quickly developed a stellar reputation for his questioning of German Prisoners, a gift which he had refined even more over the years. The American and British Intelligence Agencies could well have used Michel's incredible interrogation skills in recent years to fight terrorism.

In September 1944 in the vicinity of Autry, Michel was recommended by his commanding officer for a Silver Star, one of the American Military's highest honors, for acts of bravery and heroism that helped remove an imminent threat to maintaining an important military position. We are delighted to report that after sixty long years, Michel was finally awarded his well-deserved Silver Star on May 25, 2004 (Michel did not personally pursue it at any time in his life.). Michel led patrol units and in some cases he would go alone, as he did when two patrol units did not return. On Dec 15, the Thunderbirds entered Germany at which time Michel was later transferred to CIC,

Counter Intelligence Corps in which he remained a very active and formidable agent during the war and where he continued until 1947. He was in Dachau with combat troops on the day of its liberation. Michel then captured and interrogated the man in charge of the crematorium — Emil Mahl the "Hangman of Dachau," another vile human monster with whom Michel showed great courage in his interactions with him.

This is not the last of Michel's remarkable feats during the war. Yet another amazing turn of events was to take shape a matter of months later. On May 1, 1945, the day the American 45th Division broke into Munich, Michel had already established informant nets behind German lines through which he would receive intelligence reports about noteworthy occurrences and developments. It so happened that one of his best informants reported that a convoy of large covered trucks with SS troops had been seen moving in the vicinity of a large paper mill in the Munich suburb of Freimann around the end of April into the first week of May. Michel had their exact location and ordered the surveillance of these trucks, so he knew that they were unloading something. At first Michel thought that they might be transporting gold or some other valuable commodity. He had just gotten to Munich and went immediately to the site. With help from his informant net, Michel was able to enter the paper mill without breaking in, where he discovered "mountains and mountains of documents" which turned out to be sixty-six thousand kilos of original Nazi Party records left by the SS to be pulped and destroyed. Incredibly, among the records were over ten million worldwide original Nazi membership cards!

Michel's discovery of these records has been fully documented by Robert Wolfe, of the National Archives of the United States and historian of German war records, who said, "... Michel Thomas was the original discoverer of the Nazi Party's Master file of worldwide members." In a declaration made at a special session conducted by the University of California's School of Law and of Journalism, at Berkeley in April 2003, Robert Wolfe also stated: "These records were the most important documentation of the war; if they had been pulped in that paper mill, we would not have been able to prove, in spite of the deniers, that the Holocaust and other victimizations occurred...and the deniers would be having even more of a field day today..." He added: "...if any one of us could make such a contribution in our lifetime, it would be enough." These are quite powerful words from the man who is an advisor to the National Archives Nazi War Criminal Records Interagency Working Group. So the records discovered by Michel proved to be invaluable in the post war denazification program and in the search for war criminals. Moreover, Michel's discovery became an important basis of what was to become the entire Berlin Document Center.

The war ended on May 8, 1945. At that time, because of his astounding track record, Michel was asked by CSC Headquarters to take charge of the mission to capture war criminals, in particular, a top priority, SS Major Gustav Knittel. Michel accepted the mission on the condition that he would be the only person involved in the mission, and that no one would know about it. Up until that point, all attempts to capture Knittel had failed, until Michel took over the mission, that is. Although Knittel had disfigured his face with acid to elude capture by agents, Michel found the SS tattoo on his arm and knew that he had found his man. So he captured and interrogated Gustav Knittel who happened to be the most wanted SS war criminal on the American war crimes list at that time for his execution of American prisoners of war.

Michel also masterminded a sting operation to infiltrate a postwar underground terrorist organization of thousands of former SS members. He personally posed as SS Officer Dr. Frundsberg, and as astonishing as it may seem, he actually persuaded its members to accept him as *Kommandant* of a group of four thousand former SS terrorists! When the whole organization was turned over to him — Michel told us that he expected it and was prepared for it! However, Michel admitted that for one second, probably the only second of his entire life, he was unprepared for one thing which he did not expect. What he didn't expect was "a total switch," he recounted to us. By "a total switch" Michel was referring to that single second when the entire organization was turned over to him, which triggered an obvious physical change in the members of the organization. Michel would frequently come back to this specific detail of an immediate and dramatic physiological shift that he perceived in everyone. The SS officer with whom he was interacting quickly straightened his posture into obedience mode, and with a stiff facial expression and compliant voice asked Michel: "And now, what do you order us to do?" In no way did Michel anticipate that there would be an instantaneous expectation of orders on the faces of the former SS terrorists.

"To give orders immediately is what I didn't expect." explained Michel to us. "That instant of change, I didn't expect it, especially the way it happened. Here I was playing with life and death. What do I do now?" he recalled with a tone of surprise in his voice even years later. Michel was so uncharacteristically taken by surprise during this split second that he would linger on these details every time that he would talk about this incident, about just how much he didn't expect the entire former SS terrorist organization to be turned over to him.

That was the one moment for Michel to give an order. Suddenly there was no time for transition which meant that Michel didn't have time to think. "To give orders at that instant was what I didn't expect. Oh my God! I have to give an order right away!" he said years later. There was an immediate expectation of orders from Michel at which point he instantly took control and gave the necessary order with a sense of great authority. Once again, just as in his interaction with Klaus Barbie, Michel managed to take control of himself and of the situation at hand. Remarkably, this sting operation led to the arrest and conviction of the organization's leaders in a US Military Court in Germany. It was shortly thereafter, having spent three years with the US Army that Michel decided to leave and go to the United States. The move in itself was to mark a major transition in Michel's life, setting into motion the next step of his life mission.

In July 1947 Michel left Europe to come to America accompanied by his dog Barry, his faithful friend and constant companion, the beautiful and strong SS trained Landseer Newfoundland whom he had gotten from an SS prisoner. Michel had to reteach Barry how to interact in a peaceful and non threatening environment once in the States. Barry acclimated very well to his new home, although the sight of uniformed police and mail carriers always triggered his prior war time aggression. Michel settled in southern California and rented a house in Beverly Hills. There Michel decided to teach languages, the very same man who never wanted to be a teacher in the first place. Michel realized that education was the key to attaining *freedom of mind* and the way to prevent a reoccurrence of the horrors he had just witnessed and experienced during the war.

As we shall see in Chapter Four, Michel was ready to engage in his own war, although this time, it was to be a war against the darkness of ignorance. He would shed light on the world by changing an ineffective educational system that "chokes" learning instead of stimulating it. Michel believed that the rise of the Nazi party in Germany had been linked to an elitist educational system that did not want an educated proletariat. He also held that a free society needed an educated citizenry, a concept that was to become the philosophical foundation upon which his pedagogical method was created.

Furthermore, as we shall later see, he was intrigued by a remark made years previously by one of his professors at the Sorbonne in France who had said, "Nobody knows anything about the learning process of the human mind." As a result of hearing this statement, Michel made the exploration of this learning process a lifelong pursuit. He chose as his subject the most foreign subject that a person could ever learn — which was foreign languages. This would immediately allow him to assess the process of learning and to reach achievement levels that were heretofore seemingly impossible — at first teaching a foreign language in a matter of weeks and eventually in just three days. He was going to achieve what many believed to be inconceivable. After all, Michel was born to accept and to overcome all challenges as he had done successfully to that point. This challenge was one he relished and which reverberated in every cell of his being.

In September 1947 Michel opened the *Polyglot Institute* on Rodeo Drive in Beverly Hills, California. Michel immediately developed a reputation as a language wizard. His school gradually began to attract the rich and famous as celebrities from all walks of life and the glitterati of Hollywood came to learn different languages for acting roles, for jet-setting, for sheer fun or for whatever reasons their hearts desired. Michel changed the name to the *Michel Thomas Learning Center* when he realized that people did not know what the word "*polyglot*" meant. Michel considered his school (and life for that matter) to be a practical laboratory, so he assiduously began to explore the learning process of the human mind. He developed a system that promised a high level of language achievement in just twelve weeks. Michel continued to refine this method over the next twenty five years to create the method that he used until his passing in January 2005. Michel described his updated method as follows:

> In three days students are now guaranteed a comprehensive knowledge of a western language's grammar, together with a functional vocabulary, enabling them to write, read and converse in all tenses — without the need to memorize by rote, to take notes or to do homework.

For many people this statement seems more incredible than Michel's exploits and adventures during the war. Courage is something that people can at least imagine to one degree or another, but few can imagine that anyone can gain language proficiency in just three days. Yet Michel had been achieving these astounding results for over twenty-five years and had been teaching languages for the last sixty years of his life.

In recent years Michel continued to attract the privileged, and his client list was like a veritable *Who's Who in Hollywood* along with the higher echelons of political and corporate circles. Among a handful of the celebrities past and present to learn with Michel are: Natalie Wood, Doris Day, Jayne Mansfield, Lucille Ball, Yves Montand, Barbra Streisand, Candice Bergen, Warren Beatty, François Truffaut, the Carl Reiners, Diana Ross, Emma Thompson, Mel Gibson, Melanie Griffith, Kelly Preston, Bob Dylan, Bill Murray, John Cardinal O'Connor, Cardinal Bevilaqua, the Duchess of York, Texas Governor John Connelly and his wife Nellie Connelly, Hope Lange, Jill St. John, Woody Allen, Ann-Margret, Donald Sutherland, Dyan Cannon, Raquel Welsh, Priscilla Presley, Sophia Coppola, and Pierce Brosnan.

Over the last half century, Michel had tried on several occasions to create a model school and what he called a *"supra-national university"* as an international showcase for his remarkable method to show what real schooling should be, including how to teach teachers how to teach. He also had a plan to create an International University in Monaco with the support of his former student, Grace Kelly, who wanted to learn French quickly before her marriage to Prince Rainier. Tragically neither of these projects had come to fruition, and Michel would often tell the two of us just how deeply this hurt him. He said that he had done so much, that he had tried so many things to change the established system, but to no avail.

Michel continued to express these same thoughts during the years we modeled his method and shared a multitude of conversations with him. He would often explain to us how for decades he had to fight an educational system that was so absolute in its structure that it tragically closed the minds of students to the joys of learning. In his heart Michel was acutely aware of the immense human learning potential, and he was anxious to reveal how easily anyone, yes anyone, could learn and have fun doing so. By changing the system, he knew that he could "change the world." These powerful words certainly capture the inner driving force behind Michel's innovative teaching method.

During his last years Michel continued to travel the world teaching languages and demonstrating his remarkable method. He never slowed down at all and showed no visible signs of wear and tear. In fact, we had often joked with him that our next project was to model his perpetual vitality and sustained energy level. On the contrary, Michel seemed even more energized and more committed than ever to "change the world," particularly at this time in our history when a frightening mind-set was and still is spreading seeds around the globe with the vision of destroying our very freedom.

Michel constantly reminded us that certain tragic events of recent years have hit too close to home and are too reminiscent of the past evils which he witnessed firsthand in many forms. Thus, to the very end of his life, he continued to teach, to explore the learning process of the human mind and to further refine his remarkable method so that many more could be illuminated.

This is what Michel Thomas was all about. This was Michel Thomas, the man, and Michel Thomas, the *Master Teacher*. And this is just a brief summary of what he has accomplished in his fascinating, dramatic life. What becomes clear is that Michel was a complex figure with a mind that welcomed complexity in order to simplify it for others. Although hesitant for years to do so, he had finally consented to share his remarkable method with the world. We are blessed that Michel chose to work with us and to reveal his *wisdom of practice* in order to create a model legacy of his method.

That is what this book is all about. It is Michel's testament to humanity. Here you will discover *how* and *why* Michel's method really works. Here you will discover what the potential for learning really is within each of us. Although he is no longer with us in the physical realm, his spirit remains will the two of us and with all who knew him. It can only be hoped that this book further contributes to Michel's mission to "change the world," and that finally others will honor his brilliance and heed his warning about the future.

Chapter Four

EDUCATION AND DEMOCRACY: THE DELICATE LINK

"You can't have a free and democratic society without an educated citizenry."

— Michel Thomas

The personal philosophy of Michel Thomas regarding education was about as unique as the man himself. Indeed, it was totally linked to Michel the man and to the whole of his extraordinary life experiences. His philosophy is particularly connected to certain events which led to the annihilation of millions of his fellow man during that dreadful period in history over sixty years ago.

An understanding of his philosophy of education is an important prerequisite to an appreciation of the incredible drive, the intensity and the passion within this genius of a man which led to the creation of his own phenomenal teaching method. This teaching method would become in his own mind, and, then, in reality itself, a means to an end. What was this end? As Michel would so often tell us, designing such a unique and effective teaching method was his means to a specific end — to "change the world."

It would be unjust to Michel, therefore, to write a book about the *Michel Thomas Method* without providing an understanding of its intimate connection to the philosophical cornerstone at the heart of this highly refined and multi-faceted learning masterpiece, which he had so expertly designed. Michel was extremely gratified to know that we had immediately understood these behind the scenes nuances regarding the creation of his method. Furthermore, he was delighted that we had actually taken the time to write about this facet of his work to complement our model-based presentation of the method. This is because Michel knew deep within, just as we had understood from the start, that both are two vital parts of an inseparable whole.

The *Michel Thomas Method* was much more than a better way to teach a foreign language, or any subject for that matter. On a deeper level, for Michel, his teaching method was about "changing the world." In Michel's own words, his method was a means "to guarantee our very future" at a time when there are forces at work ready to obliterate that which we take for granted each and every day: Our very right to be, our very right to live. Michel so eloquently expressed his sentiments about this very issue:

> "....we are living in a Tower of Babel — with the chances of survival diminishing every day because we are not able to make ourselves understood nor are we able to understand our neighbor."

What is at stake? Specifically what is at stake, to use Michel's own expression, is our very *"freedom of mind."* For Michel Thomas, *freedom of mind* refers to our right to think independently as individuals, rather than as conformists who are carried along by the swift tides of public opinion. Michel knew full well, that our ability to think critically and to communicate effectively with each other has been terribly compromised by an ineffectual educational system which enslaves our minds.

This enslavement is the result of thought control. The time has come to begin freeing minds one person at a time. Michel was all too well aware of the massive thought control methods that have been imposed on society at large for centuries. Schools and place of learning are the major centers of thought control, and for this reason, Michel referred to these establishments as *"criminal institutions."* Now with advances in technology these methods have become even more insidious. To make matters worse, the so-called masses have remained quite oblivious to the perpetuation of this sinister "crime" by the elite, who want to maintain their domination over them.

As we worked with Michel over the years, and during the course of our myriad personal conversations with him, we could sense his outrage over this "crime" intensify. Whenever he spoke about these "criminal institutions," his rage would transform into a profound sadness. No one had taken heed of his warnings. No one had given him the opportunity to realize his dream of creating *freedom of mind* with his learning masterpiece. In light of Michel's powerful descriptions of these centers of learning as "criminal institutions," and in light of what is truly happening in our world, we decided to refer to the educational establishment as the *"Mind Prison"*™, both in this book and in our teachings. We further discuss the concept of the *Mind Prison*™ and its manifestations within our *dis-educational system*™ in Chapter Five.

For Michel, the consequences of the educational system's shortcomings and outright "crimes" are tragically connected to the downfall of any so-called democracy. At first glance, the fragile connection between education and democracy may appear to be a bit curious, or out of the reach of comprehension for many. In order to grasp the significance and relevance of this connection, Michel believed that it was important to have a basic knowledge of certain circumstances and events in world history. Such knowledge would serve as a backdrop for what is to come.

Such knowledge would also allow one to understand better the interconnectedness and the consequences of this unfamiliar association between education and so-called democracy. It would also allow one to place this interplay into a contextual understanding of past, present and future events affecting humankind. Michel believed that equipped with an understanding of what is really happening in the world, one would be better able to understand the inherent repercussions of this unfamiliar association.

One can begin to grasp this atypical connection through Michel's own eyes — through his unique perspective of world history and his in-the-trenches experience of events, along with his way of interconnecting seemingly unrelated events. All of these elements taken together greatly facilitate one's understanding of his position regarding a relationship between two disparate concepts which may not be obvious to all at first glance. Given this point of view, we can begin to comprehend in what manner Michel's life experiences and personal philosophy were such driving forces behind the creation of his remarkable teaching method.

Nine months before his passing, Michel became incensed when he realized that there were certain individuals in the publishing industry who did not think it was necessary to write a chapter about "Education and Democracy" in a book about his method: "They obviously don't understand what I am about or why I created my method!" So it was with Michel's full approval and encouragement that we wrote this chapter to show how his personal philosophy and his historical perspective on education are so closely linked to the creation of his method. Furthermore, we have found that those who are really interested in learning his teaching secrets are just as eager to discover the entire picture, and in particular, his motivation to create his masterwork. In honor of who Michel was and of why he created his method in the first place, this chapter thus unfolds.

Finally, to place Michel's beliefs into perspective, we would like to quote the great American President, and genius in his own right, Thomas Jefferson, who said that it is impossible for a nation to be "ignorant and free" and still survive. And so thought Michel Thomas as well, so much so that he was driven to change the shape of education as we know it by creating a teaching method that he believed would bring *freedom of mind* to all, and thus help "democracy flourish."

THE UNEDUCATED MASSES

In order to grasp the meaning and nuances of Michel's historical perspective, it would be helpful to consider briefly the place education held in humankind's history. First, throughout history, education was a privilege reserved for a chosen few and quite deliberately so. With the striking *Michel look* laser-printed in his fired up blue eyes, Michel vehemently explained in his own words that there was one and only one reason for this situation:

> "To rule the masses, the ignorant masses."

For centuries it was a given that the masses were not to be educated. Moreover, the masses had no recourse, for they were meant to remain at the station of life into which they were born. Education in whatever form was only reserved for the relatively few, so-called elite. No one even bothered to challenge this notion. This was the way to guarantee that those at the top could remain there while the disparity between the privileged few and the unfortunate multitudes could continue to grow.

What was the means chosen of sustaining this hierarchy? Michel explained that the means used to achieve this was humankind's major means of communication — language itself. Historically in order to insure that the *status quo* of ignorance remained intact, the powers that be ordered that all learning be conducted, not in the language of the people, but rather in a language that was literally foreign to them. That language was Latin. The language of the people was considered vulgar in the sense of commonplace, and this so-called ordinary language of the inferior classes was meant to keep them there.

So before one could even attend school or any place of learning, one would have to learn Latin, an erudite language which literally would be the key to opening the door to an education. For several centuries, Latin remained the requisite language to gain entrance into a place of higher learning or to gain access to a university.

What did an education do for those born in a position to acquire one? Education was and is still supposed to be the key to a better life (although in today's world a superior education does not necessarily equate with higher earning potential). Having an education allowed those at the top to stay in control of their destinies. It also allowed them to take hold of the important governing positions in order to keep the masses at their mercy in all ways.

A vicious cycle ensued because the educated elite were those who could earn a good living and could afford to have their descendants follow in their footsteps, while their unfortunate counterparts, i.e., the masses, were forced by the nature of the rules, to continue surviving in total ignorance. According to Michel, that was not even living. It is what Michel referred to as *"vegetating through life."*

In his historical perspective of education, Michel also emphasized the importance of remembering the huge role played by the Church centuries ago. The Church was the

Authority both in matters of state and in the context of life in general. It was only through clashes with others in a position of authority of another kind that the power of the Church began to dwindle. Since the Church represented a major power center and place of influence, it made sense that Latin be its official language. The Bible used by the Roman Catholic Church, considered by many to be the source of the laws of life and a masterpiece of wisdom, was written, of course, in Latin. The masses could only learn about the Bible by means of stories related through oral tradition. Otherwise, the only other way that people at large could learn anything, was through the arts. Learning occurred particularly through stories related by paintings and sculpture. This approach may appear to be harmless, and yet stories can be used as a powerful mechanism of mind control.

These art forms told the stories that would facilitate the control of the masses even more. Thus, with everything in the elite language of Latin, an entire world of humankind's knowledge was completely inaccessible to the people at large. Michel described how for centuries these masses had been doomed to struggle in ignorance, until a very timely event occurred in the seventeenth century.

This timely and significant event was the translation of the Bible into the common language of English. Michel invited those of us in today's world to ponder the following: "Can you imagine what it would be like to have all books, newspapers, etc., all written material in this information age available to you only in a language you do not know?" Michel would have asked today's world to imagine the reaction of the people at large, centuries ago, when the Bible was finally accessible to them. The masses of the seventeenth century were ecstatic and anxious to get their hands on this new wonder — a book written in a language that they could actually understand.

From his astute historical perspective, Michel described how the translated Bible had a transformational effect on the people. Everyone wanted to know it and be able to read it and to have it. It became quite obvious to the man at the throne at that time, King James, that people everywhere wanted the English version. He had the great sense to make the English edition official. We all know that it became known as the King James

Version, to which it is still referred today several centuries later. And, as most people know, the King James Version has held its ground all these years.

With this huge development, people began to get in touch with information in a new way. Did this mean that the masses suddenly became the equivalent of the privileged elite? Of course not, far from it. Even with the accessibility of information, the masses still lagged economically and socially far behind the elite, who continued to thrive as they always had. The masses still were unable to think for themselves or to establish opinions because the educational system would not permit them to do so. As often happens, "*Plus ça change, plus c'est la même chose,*" ("The more things change, the more things remain the same.") even in our present-day information age, as we shall later see.

Michel continued his historical perspective by explaining that after several thousand years, humankind finally arrived at a period in history when something called *"democracy"* began to take shape. As we all know, the word "democracy" is from the Greek meaning "rule of the people." And as Michel correctly and not so subtly remarked, "not the people being ruled." The truth is that humankind "has always been ruled." With the onset of so-called democracy, circumstances were supposed to change. "Did the onset of democracy bring about great change in the educational system?" Michel asked. "No." In fact, even from the perspective of teaching languages, ineffective models dating back to the Greeks are still in use in the traditional system, as we shall point out in Chapter Six, where we present the *Michel Thomas Method*.

IS IT DIFFERENT TODAY?

Michel would often remind us with an expression of utter disgust and dismay on his face, "that sadly, no tragically, the situation has not changed much even to this day." Michel believed that the consequences of not taking action to revamp the educational system would be catastrophic to society, just as it had been in the past, when the elite maintained their control over the masses. Michel also held that the consequences of nonaction would be even greater in the near future and beyond, if they are not already, given modern day technological advances. Michel's thoughts are reminiscent of the celebrated cynic H.L. Mencken who wrote in the 1920's that the goal of public education was not to provide our youth with knowledge or intelligence:

> ... Nothing could be farther from the truth. The aim...is simply to reduce as many individuals as possible to the same, safe level, to breed and train a standardized citizenry, to put down dissent and originality. That is its aim in the United States...and...everywhere else.

Michel believed that in our so-called democracies, no matter where they are, we continue to support an educational system that still keeps the masses in their place — in total ignorance. Michel presented the case that people today are little more elevated in learning in what we call "democracy" than they used to be centuries ago.

> "How is it that in a democracy we have institutions called *schools* which are merely a conspiracy between parents (in some ways, nonthinking parents, because they have to follow the law) and the laws of the state, the laws of a democracy?"

Michel continued by asking if this is really democracy "where parents are forced to send children to an institution where by law, yes, by law, they have to serve time. This is what we call democracy?" This reflection would always trigger deep-rooted anger within Michel, whenever he talked about these institutions called schools, institutions "where children are condemned to serve time." Many found his words about school to be quite harsh, to say the least, and yet Michel steadfastly held this belief in the very core of his being.

Michel went on to say in a rather acerbic tone: "I think that in our democracy one has to serve time whether one wants to or not." He felt that realistically, one does not have a choice in the matter; and that this is certainly not what democracy is supposed to be about. "How can it be a democracy if one is institutionalized without free will, until the age of eighteen?" Michel would explain that no matter where you attend school, no matter what institution of which you are part, you will only be released "when you reach that magic number eighteen." Even worse, is that beyond the age of eighteen, the same negative patterns remain imprinted upon the students when they supposedly reach adulthood. They continue to "vegetate," as Michel would say, by wasting countless hours of mindless viewing in front of the TV, DVDs, by playing video games and by engaging in countless other diversions of no educational value.

Michel contended that while "in a state of vegetation" it is easier for the elite to maintain their grip on others, and to ensure the uninterrupted engendering of mediocre minds and obedient citizens. Conformity is the key to maintaining control of the masses and conformity, in turn, breeds obedience. According to Michel, "That is exactly what we are doing." His words may seem harsh and perhaps exaggerated to some, yet they ring so true. To truly grasp what he so fervently believed, it is important to understand the historical context and the personal circumstances which triggered his life-long drive to change the educational system.

Meanwhile, as Michel would explain in disgust, the situation in education is even worse than at first glance because "even when the children are released from their forced bondage," it is almost impossible for them to eliminate all the bad feelings they experienced in the learning process during the years they spent in a mental "straightjacket." Michel believed their "*innate drive for learning* has already been choked, and at worst, killed entirely," so that their great potential for learning has disappeared for all practical purposes. The end result, he said, was "that they live out the rest of their lives in a state of vegetation because when they die, their own immense potentials have not been touched." With a face ruddy with rage and a tonality of voice that reflected what he felt so deeply within his being, Michel forcefully declared,

> "If I want to let myself go, I will call what they are doing a crime, a major crime."

This thought may surprise and even shock some people, particularly those who are stuck in the ways of the past and who prefer to maintain the *status quo*. Bureaucratic institutions reflect this mind-set. The reaction of some to his belief angered and hurt Michel a great deal. He experienced deep hurt because he knew better than most, what were the present-day consequences of perpetrating such a "crime." Furthermore, Michel was quite aware of what the future repercussions would be if the so-called world's democracies continue to allow such a "crime" to persist. This was quite an indictment of the current *dis-educational system*™, from a man who had passionately devoted the last fifty plus years of his life to effect meaningful change to no avail.

Michel argued for decades that there seemed to be another sub-conspiracy at work to make sure that the system in place remained that way, endorsed and supported financially by those who wanted to maintain control over the masses and encourage their mindless conformity. Of course, as Michel pointed out from the annals of history, and as we know, this is the best way to maintain control of the minds of the masses because conformity breeds weakness while individuality engenders strength. On another level, Michel strongly espoused the great power of the individual, a belief that he held and expressed in every fiber of his being in all that he did throughout his entire life. This was just another reflection of his complex and multi-faceted mind.

Why keep the system the same? Michel's answer was simple: "To keep the ignorant in a state of ignorance." Kids grow into adults who haven't learned anything in school. They just repeat or imitate what they are told. As such, these nonthinking minds are even more easily manipulated. This does not represent *freedom of mind* because they are not free, not free to think on their own, even though, as Michel eloquently affirmed,

> "Man's mind must be free.
> This is the Alpha and Omega of everything.
> This is no slogan, but a creed —
> a deep and irrefragable conviction."

Michel would take his own message to heart to teach his own children not to accept everything that they heard, not even from their own father. He shared with us a charming little story about his son, Guri, who at the age of five or six was having a discussion with his father. At one point Guri said to Michel: "Did I make my point, Daddy?" Michel, of course, was delighted to see that his little son did not agree with him. In essence, what Michel was doing was opening up the mind of his child to critical thinking. In so doing, he would ensure that no one could ever impose his or her ideas upon his son. Michel pointed out that later in life, as an adult, his son would know how to vote based on his own decisions, rather than based on the will or opinion of others. Still today, many people make decisions based on polls, on what TV pundits say, and on popular opinions rather than based on their own criteria for making decisions (Chapter Nine). To this day, Guri, as well as his sister, Mishie, have remained quite the independent thinkers whose minds absorb knowledge like a sponge.

Michel deplored the fact that simple thinking was not encouraged in the traditional system, so how can one expect students to engage in critical thinking? And if they have nonthinking parents, they don't have the resources to develop their minds. This merely exacerbates the situation. For Michel, the consequences of nonthinking will be disastrous and in this regard, Michel declared in a tone of despair,

> "I am deeply concerned about the survival of democracy."

This was an intense conviction which Michel held dearly within the depths of his very heart and soul. He reminded us to "beware of he who screams and shouts with the loudest voice." For it is he who screams and shouts the loudest who is heard in the final analysis, and it is he who becomes the great master of the weak minds. And, as Michel pointed out, "The words and the thoughts which one usually shouts the loudest become the driving force behind public opinion."

What is the effect of public opinion? In Michel's mind, public opinion can be a huge threat to *freedom of mind*. Public opinion, whether it be the reflection of good or evil, has the potential to be deadly and can spread lies and misinformation with the speed and force of uncontrollable wildfires. Michel was quite disturbed by the effect of public opinion among the masses, even more so in this day and age than earlier on. The reason is that today public opinion is more often than not, triggered and fostered by the media and the internet.

Public opinion about a particular issue can, and often is, created within minutes, aided by the combined power of visual images and audio content broadcast with lightening speed around the globe. Whether they are serious issues like global warming and ethnic cleansing or else irrelevant news items such as Paris Hilton's latest escapades or what some celebrity wore to go shopping or to some event, public opinion is not far behind. "All you need is to make one statement and repeat it and it becomes public opinion," Michel admonished. Once public opinion sets in, it is harder for the nonthinkers created by Michel's "criminal institutions" to know the truth. "Because," as Michel expressed, "even now we don't seem to be able to even reach those prisoners in school." Michel argued that the truth does not reach students in the traditional system because the doors to learning within them remain tightly shut with no means of escape from "condemnation." Then as adults they remain clueless to the truth, believing what the news reporters and pundits say about issues and events in the world. We elaborate on this notion further in the next chapter, *The Mind Prison*™.

Michel greatly feared a repeat of history if significant action was not taken soon to revamp the system. He would constantly emphasize that by preserving the current system as is, it becomes so very easy once again, as in earlier history, to rule the masses, and more specifically, the "uneducated, ignorant masses" even today. The current system is the perfect vehicle in which to control minds. Nowadays, we see all around us that thought control is rampant. In fact, we would often discuss how much easier than ever it is to control minds because of technological advances. Ironically, technology has made thought control more dangerous than ever.

Mind control is nothing new but at least in earlier periods of history, the so-called masses were not nearly as large in number as today. *Freedom of mind* was also an issue in ancient times as it is now. For example, even during the times of ancient Greece and Rome, by way of superstition and the powerful priests, minds were enchained to the beliefs thrust upon them by those in positions of power.

Michel believed that little has changed since ancient times regarding *freedom of mind*, despite the veil of so-called democracy draped over parts of the world. According to Michel, the consequences of this reality go far beyond the possibility of devastation. With a look of grave concern and tormented sadness, he declared, "To be nice about it, the reason [to rule the ignorant masses] is to make democracy vulnerable and very easy to knock over, very easy!" And whenever Michel would talk about the horrors he witnessed during the war years or in recent times during 9/11, one had a sense of just how deeply he was pained by what he saw happening around him.

The extraordinary whole of his life experiences serve as backdrop to the scenes unraveling before our very eyes today. Michel often insisted that unless something was going to be done "with urgency, great urgency," the heavy curtain would fall upon the final act of humankind's existence sooner rather than later. Michel painfully witnessed several so-called democracies fall like a house of cards one by one. He often recalled with a heavy heart, how for a time, even the United States and its allies refused to intervene in the brutal destruction and sheer, unconscionable devastation of life occurring all around them before World War II erupted. Imagine witnessing the fall of several democracies around him within a short period of time. Michel vowed to do all that he could to prevent anything like that from happening again. He would do so by creating his masterful teaching method so that nonthinking minds would become a thing of the past, and no one could ever again be manipulated by those in power. This was the ultimate driving force that impassioned and compelled Michel to move ahead right up until his last days.

MICHEL'S GERMANY

One simply has to be reminded of Michel's childhood growing up in what was then known as the Weimar Republic (Germany) to understand his pain, and how his grand mission of creating his powerful teaching method came about. With great detail, Michel described how at that time, Germany basked in the spotlight as a highly-cultured society. Its worldwide reputation was that of a rich culture, endowed with great minds in the arts and sciences that created masterpieces of literature, art, music, physics and the like. Whenever Michel looked back at this period in German history, he would lament the fact that people simply did not realize what was really happening in their country.

Even in erudite circles, people didn't recognize the fact that, despite its reputation of having highly educated people and highly cultured individuals, in reality, Germany was, indeed in a sad state of affairs. The reason for this was that education, as in the past, had remained strictly elitist. With his usual look of disgust, Michel explained: "Education was not available to the masses. I repeat — not available. The masses had no access to higher education." They were not even allowed to go to what could be considered the equivalent of high school. The populace was relegated to attending what Michel called "people schools" known in German as "*volkschule*," where they learned only how to read and write.

He explained that at that time for the most part, what the masses learned was known as Gothic writing and only very elementary and simple math. This was basically the extent of their education. After that, a few would go into various vocational training of some sort. The bottom line was that the masses were expected to learn how to do all the physical and manual labor. "Is this truly democracy?" he would ask time and time again, always in a voice of sheer repugnance. The masses were still left in the dark, unable to think for themselves, incapable of having their own opinions. Meanwhile, the economic situation at the time provided the perfect ingredients for an unspeakable tragedy waiting to happen.

Michel fervently believed that the existing educational system had set the stage for what was to come. In addition, both the economic and educational state of affairs provided the ideal mélange of elements for one particular individual with "evil" in his veins to make his arrogant entrance onto the world's center stage, albeit, at first, unnoticed by the majority — the human monster known as Adolph Hitler.

One may ask how it is possible that in a supposedly civilized and highly cultured country, as was Germany at that time, that an uneducated nobody could precipitously rise to uncontested power and infamous notoriety from beneath the shadows of ignorance and catapult himself into the role of *Fuhrer*. According to Michel, the answer was quite simple. First, when the elite received Hitler with open arms, the masses, who respected those with advanced degrees, followed suit. Second, by maintaining a blanket of ignorance over the masses, Hitler, a man who couldn't even get into art school (although, according to Michel, rumor had spread that he had some talent as an artist), was able to easily manipulate their minds. It seems that Hitler was simply an uneducated, unremarkable guy from Austria, with one trait that launched his entire rise to infamy and beyond: he knew exactly how to appeal to the masses.

MIND CONTROL — APPEALING TO THE MASSES

According to Michel, Hitler knew how to appeal to people who were just like him, the uneducated. Hitler knew how to tap into the weak minds of those without schooling. He knew how to mesmerize those who had not acquired any knowledge whatsoever and thus, could not engage in critical thinking of any kind. How easy it was, indeed, to manipulate these malleable minds that could not think on their own. Michel sadly explained that Hitler simply had to tell them that he was the answer to their woes. With automaton-like reflexes, they immediately believed him without a single forethought or afterthought. This was because they were incapable of exercising their God-given cognitive power, their personal will. Hitler knew exactly how to entreat these unknowing souls. Instead of becoming the laughing stock of the country, he was elected to lead the people.

Michel recounted how Hitler was quite adroit in avoiding meetings because he realized that he could not think and really did not have knowledge about anything of import. He, did, however, know enough to attend meetings only when a script of questions had been prepared in advance, just as an actor would study for a given role. Michel described Hitler to be like an actor or a puppet mind leading all the other puppets around him because the masses did not know any better. As history revealed, together they ended up creating a real life play of human horror.

Michel would constantly remind us how the unspeakable horrors of World War II were born out of an ineffective educational system, and of the ignorance engendered among the unenlightened masses. The trauma, the untold grief and suffering, the outright expunging of human dignity, the huge toll of death and destruction he witnessed each and every day, all of this and the scores of horrific memories as each so-called democracy fell to the Nazis, triggered a fervent and powerful drive, not a desire, but rather an intense drive in Michel "to bring about some significant change in our educational system."

Michel noted that two centuries of history had still not made a difference. Michel insisted that these democracies, supposedly free societies, the Weimar Republic, France and Austria (where Michel witnessed firsthand the triumphant arrival and welcome of Hitler) were totally "knocked down" as a direct result of a poor educational system that catered to the elite. And this realization was a constant source of great distress for Michel, who so poignantly expressed his sentiments to us,

"I have not been able to in fifty years of work, to even make a dent into our educational system. I'm not trying to be critical, but it hurts me deeply, what I experienced. And I am not even making conclusions about my experiences."

Indeed, throughout his ninety years of life, Michel bore the mental scars of what he personally endured and even more so, of what he had no choice but to witness — the pain and degradation that his fellow man had born. These fallen democracies were supposed to be strong and powerful. They were not supposed to succumb and crumble when a breeze of "hot air" blew their way. They were not supposed to fall under the pressures of economic crisis. Democracies are supposed to stand strong. And yet, this mediocre, quotidian man appeared out of nowhere and began, individual mind by individual mind, group by group, region by region, country by country, to take control of an entire continent with the malevolent intention to master the minds of the entire world at large.

There is another factor to consider in this discussion of education and democracy which is directly linked to the rise of Hitler and about which Michel would often speak. It has to do with human emotions and the fact that one may much more readily manipulate the emotional tenor of another when that individual (in this case, the masses) has no ability to engage in critical thinking of any kind. Hitler and others like him who succeed in inciting others to commit evil acts, somehow know the power of uniting people in hatred. With respect to these emotions, Michel had specific beliefs:

> "It is so very difficult to unite people with the appeal of love...hate is active, love is not."

Hitler manipulated the minds of the masses to believe that in the name of hatred, they could somehow become the super race. Hitler actually fabricated a racial category which he decided to call the "Aryan race," one which would be able to rule the world. Michel was always quick to point out that there are only Aryan languages and that there was no such thing as an Aryan race.

And so the masses willingly listened and followed that voice, believing all the way that they, the supposed Aryan race, were to take over the world. Michel described that up until that time, the Jews were the ones who were successful in their chosen fields as bankers, doctors, teachers, lawyers, etc. Then, suddenly, they became the *"untermensch"* (subhuman): "Jews were like vermin and were exterminated with the blessing of the so-called civilized world."

"It was so easy, much too easy, to topple these democracies," Michel declared. All one had to do was to instill hatred and to unite people in a common cause of hatred, an invented one no less, that would unite people who were incapable of independent thought or action. As such, "You could convince them to engage in any evil, destructive or horrendous act possible, all in the name of hatred." He painfully remarked that the same thing was happening today. Michel also reminded us how much easier it is to unite the masses *against* something rather than *for* a cause.

Michel remembered all too well how the dominos of freedom began to tumble one by one. He once remarked: "If there hadn't been any Jews in Germany when Hitler took over, Hitler would have had to invent them too." Michel said that most people don't realize that there were fewer than six hundred thousand Jews living in the country when Hitler rose to power. Inventing hatred served the purpose, however, a hatred that was enough to topple what had been considered up until that moment, solid democracies.

THE CONSEQUENCES OF NONACTION

"Always the world has been under the tyranny of thought control, but until now, the world has been big. Now it is small, very small. Millions are in the thralldom of a few. These few can determine the destiny of all. And do."
— *Michel Thomas*

Because we live in an age of global openness and increased global travel, Michel sensed that we are even more vulnerable to the spread of what he called "evil" at this time in history than during World War II, when this evil was contained within the confines of Europe and Great Britain. He remarked that for about thirty or forty years, its spread was relatively contained for the most part. On several occasions Michel pointed out that in this day and age, we are "globally wide open," more so than during the Nazi/Hitlerian spread of evil in Germany and later in German occupied Europe. Michel described the circumstances as follows: "At that time, it was still confined mostly to the borders of Europe and had not yet poisoned the rest of the world, a situation not unlike what we are experiencing now."

From Michel's point of view, the spread of evil is a rapid process especially among the nonthinking minds of the masses. Once it happens, it spreads like wildfire in places where borders and "defenses against evil are down" and easily penetrable. With a look of grave concern he warned: "To me they [the defenses] are down globally now, and, therefore, are a greater threat than at the time of Nazi Germany, a greater, much greater threat." Without an effective educational system to teach people how to think, Michel believed that democracies are in grave danger at the present time.

It disturbed Michel deeply that no one seemed to want to talk about the threat whenever he would broach the subject. Within ten years (of 2003) he feared that people would say with regret: "We never knew that would happen." Michel believed that it would be more correct to say: "We never wanted to know." For this very reason, Michel's deep convictions imprinted his very being at deeper and deeper levels with each year that passed. Even the last year of his life, he was very certain of one thing, that there was a reason that he was still alive: "There is a reason why I am far from feeling the chronological age which I am supposed to carry." Michel repeatedly told us that he was ready for his message to get out. Right up until the very end of his life, he faced that mission with great dignity, unyielding determination and boundless courage each and every day.

Michel believed that the greatest challenge we face today is to create a solid and effective educational system so we don't have a repeat performance of history. Yet, he felt that nothing was being done to educate the masses. Michel would often cite the example of seven million undocumented illegal aliens who are going to be given legal status in the United States. This was a very sore subject to him. He believed that most of them are not going to be interested in getting an education. Michel realized that most of them are forced, like the masses of before, to take jobs involving manual labor. He also believed that the government doesn't really care about educating them. In Michel's view, it is simply "a political game," nothing more.

He asserted that the politicians merely want to get votes wherever they can, from whomever they can, regardless of the consequences. Michel would often lament to us,

> Where are we going as a country? The press, the politicians, always talk about this huge national problem we have — this enormous political

problem — what to do about education and how to improve the system. Yet, what are they doing about it? Absolutely nothing.

The irony, according to Michel, is that they would not even know what to do about it, even if they did choose to do something. He staunchly believed that although many in the system do not want to face the truth, the educational system is a bad one and one that keeps the masses in check, pure and simple. Moreover, from his perspective, the system is a self-sustaining entity that continues to reject reform that would effect any real and meaningful change on a large scale.

Government creates the laws and forces children to go to what Michel referred to as a *"criminal institution"* and raises the taxes of its citizens in order to pay the salaries of bad teachers. "Imagine," asserted Michel, "we are paying higher taxes to pay bad teachers more money." And the teachers unions are behind them all the way. It is often suggested to cut down the size of classes as a way to improve the quality of our educational system. Michel pointed out that doing so will not change anything at all, since the students will still be exposed to the same bad teachers. "If teachers don't know how to teach, they shouldn't be teaching... We need more money for what? Not one mention of how to teach, or of finding better ways of teaching."

According to Michel, it is not by increasing the salaries of teachers that you somehow create better teachers or improve the educational system. The teachers would continue to be supported by the unions representing them. Also, we have seen that with the "publish or perish" rule at the university level, there may be competent teachers who are not awarded tenure, while inadequate ones have sometimes managed to squeeze through the cracks by publishing in the right places. The latter often remain in their positions for years gloating in their own self-importance with no desire to really teach and to connect with the students in a meaningful way, and this further infuriated Michel.

Since the early part of the twentieth century, for many years (and to some extent even now) education meant acquiring certain basic skills, the three Rs: reading, writing, arithmetic. There was literally no critical thinking involved in the process.

Students were expected to memorize facts, and were not taught to "think" or express their opinions in the very same way as the masses of the past. The times are changing at such a rapid pace that we must keep up or be lost in the shuffle of ignorance. Illiteracy is still embarrassingly and tragically high in the United States and in many areas around the globe. We are living in a world that is becoming smaller and smaller, with information spreading faster than the speed of light. We are living in a world in which complex global issues have taken a front row seat. More than any other time in our history, we need people competent to deal with this growing complexity. For the most part, trivial factual recall is not particularly relevant, except in the context of game show entertainment.

In short, we must come up with learning processes that teach *understanding* which leads to *knowledge*. This is precisely what Michel Thomas accomplished every time he taught his courses. How he achieved success is part of the genius that was Michel Thomas. Now that you have had a glimpse of Michel's philosophy of education and of his historical perspective on education, you will have hopefully acquired a greater appreciation of the intimate connection between his method and his beliefs regarding the importance of educating people everywhere as a way of ensuring the survival of the free world and the very survival of what he referred to as "*freedom of mind.*"

Finally, Michel was here to remind us of all that needs to be done to insure that our so-called democracy does not topple as did others before. We must take charge of educating our people in order to avoid another catastrophe, a tragic consequence of inaction, indifference and ignorance. Still, there is no effective action being taken, as Michel observed so well:

> "Education has become such a big national issue and I haven't seen one single thing done that would really improve our educational system. Nowhere, nowhere, is there an indication that we should look at the way we teach, or to find an innovative way to teach."

As we shall also see in other chapters, the current educational system does not encourage critical thinking. This conflicts with the very essence of *freedom of mind*. The ability to think critically engenders individuality and is a threat to conformity, which is the backbone of the existing educational system. In Michel's view, incompetent teachers remain rigid fixtures in the system, reinforcing the process of mind enslavement. And little or no money is given to teacher education to bring in new and innovative perspectives and ways of thinking.

The fact is that we must develop young citizens who will be the future leaders of the world, and teach them how to engage in critical thinking to solve global challenges. This can only happen by re-vamping the entire educational system. Michel believed that if the system continues on its same ineffectual path, we will not succeed in this endeavor. Michel was the first to ask: "So where is the difference between Nazi education and what we are doing now?" It deeply pained Michel to observe what was happening in the world and he had been warning of the dire consequences of taking no action for decades. So far, no one has taken heed. Michel very eloquently reminded us of the dangers of capitulation:

> "The inclination is to give up, surrender, and yield to the master nearest at hand, the voice that is loudest, and the pressure that is most imminent."

Perhaps the time has come to take action finally, to realize the importance of educating the people of our planet, of understanding that fragile link between education and democracy, so that we don't find ourselves at the mercy of evil once again. As we shall see throughout this book, Michel has taken many giant steps in leading the way to *freedom of mind* by creating his wonderful method, by having freed the minds of his students, one person at a time, and by having the great courage to speak out amidst deaf and often indifferent and disinterested ears, his words echoing unheard in the unwelcome corridors of academia, at least until now. For Michel, the choice before us is between darkness and light. Michel constantly reminded us that we need to act before it is too late...and the time has come to listen finally to what he had to say...

Chapter Five

THE *MIND PRISON*™: THE FAILURE OF OUR CURRENT *DIS-EDUCATIONAL SYSTEM*™

"There are no bad students, just incompetent teachers."
— Michel Thomas

What we have always referred to in our teaching and other writings as our current *"dis-educational system"*™ sadly leaves much to be desired. We now live in a world of what we like to call "the ignorant educated," who, for the most part, are asked to regurgitate meaningless information which neither enhances the quality of life nor is connected to the acquisition of *knowledge*. The result is that this *dis-educational system*™ merely keeps us in a stranglehold of mindless ignorance. Instead of attempting to improve the teaching system, we are simply reinforcing a bad system that is deeply embedded into our human psyche.

Michel Thomas had always been aware of these and other tragic shortcomings of the traditional educational system. So fifty years ago, Michel decided to break away from what he considered to be an ineffective and worthless system. Throughout his life, he would always make unique choices and would take the route less traveled with great passion. Doing so had always been powerful drivers for Michel throughout his amazing, multi-faceted life. As we have seen in the prior chapter, Michel was quite distressed by what he considered to be improper and inadequate teaching amidst growing ignorance among the masses. For this reason he decided that it was time to take action and to leave his mark on our educational system before it was too late, even if there were those who simply did not understand his mission. The time has come to start freeing minds one person at a time.

Early on in his life Michel began cleverly assimilating bits of wisdom and guidelines he had acquired from several influential mentors and teachers. To these he would add his singular perspectives on the world that he developed in his childhood and combine them with his own brilliant insights born from what he called his "probing of the learning process of the human mind." After years of empirical research and the practical experience of trial and error, seeing what worked and what did not work, the result was the creation and refinement of his personal and unparalleled teaching method. This unique method now stands alone above all others as his great gift and legacy to those he left behind. His brilliant *magnum opus* stands in stark contrast to what we find in our current *dis-educational system*™.

SENTENCING OUR CHILDREN TO THE *MIND PRISON*™

Always with great indignation in his voice and reflected in a look of sheer disgust, Michel would refer to our traditional educational system as a *"criminal institution"* in which children are sentenced to serve time by law." Michel's description may appear to be extreme to some parents and teachers, and yet, he believed that even these words were not strong enough to depict what he considered to be the deplorable state of our educational system that enslaves the learning process of our children. For this reason, we decided to refer to the traditional educational system as the *Mind Prison*™ in this book about Michel and his method and elsewhere in our work. Michel thought that our description of what he called a *"criminal institution,"* known as schools, was quite appropriate.

Just the mere mention of the word "school" would infuriate Michel. Whenever he would speak of this "prison," his penetrating blue eyes took on a tinge of sadness combined with the intensity of resolve to leave his own mark and legacy in education. Michel considered traditional education to be a total failure, "a tragic institution in which children and students of all ages are forced to serve in bondage against their will, with inept teachers and ignorant parents who subject them to hours and hours, days and days and years and years of joyless schooling," in some form or another within the confines of this *Mind Prison*™.

According to Michel, children are forced to "serve time" in an unjust institution called *school*, the latter word, which he thought to be a complete and utter misnomer. Michel believed that our educational institutions are more like prisons which strangle our children on all levels:

> "Our children are sentenced to serve time."

The above became Michel's powerful mantram. "By law they have to serve time, and as a parent, I am forced to deliver my children to an institution which I consider a prison," he continued.

> "Children are caught in a conspiracy between their parents and the government which makes them enter into a prison from the age of five until they have completed the contract at age sixteen or eighteen. It is a crime! A horror story!"

He explained that people talk about their personal goals of having families and children, and then what do they do with their children? "They condemn them to prison," he angrily declared.

From Michel's perspective, the situation nowadays is even worse because schools have become nothing more than custodial institutions for parents who can leave their kids and go off to engage in their own activities. He believed that children are "locked up" so that the parents can do whatever they please. Furthermore, children are sentenced very early on with pre-school, where they will still not learn anything. It simply takes them away from their family at an earlier age.

> "Children are like inmates except that they don't have voices to speak out as do inmates."

With great indignation in his voice, Michel asked: "Where is the outcry? Where is the outrage? Parents encourage the prison time. Why bother to have children if one is not going to allow them to have a life, a God-given life with their innate God-given gift, meaning the gift for learning?" From Michel's point of view, this gift for learning turns into a drive for learning which is accompanied by great excitement and fulfillment. So why bring children into the world and deprive them of these natural gifts?

According to Michel, there are two basic differences between serving time in school and serving time in prison. The first difference is that those who serve time in jail actually do have a voice and have people to represent them in the form of advocates. Children, on the other hand, don't have anyone to represent them. For Michel they are just there to obey the rules of a worthless system in which it is not a question of learning at all, but rather a question of performing a chore. The children simply do not have a voice.

Michel considered them to be powerless souls "sentenced to drudgery and ignorance without a voice to speak out for them." The second difference is that we, as a nation, spend so much more money on jails and on our prison system than we do on our educational system:

> "Evidently, our jails are more important to us than education."

He also had ideas for improving our prison system, and that was to be the subject of another book.

Michel was first to say that he was not surprised by the amount of violence that is increasing in schools, even among girls. Children are forced by law to physically serve time in an institution which stifles their *innate drive for learning*, so why are people surprised? He asserted that serving time in any institution has the potential to break out in violence. From Michel's standpoint, one simply cannot be forced to study or be forced to learn, and that is exactly what we are doing in our schools. It was no surprise to him that children become violent and rebel against their own "condemnation." "I don't blame them if they rebel," he said, "those who still have the motivation, if not the motivation to learn, then the motivation to rebel."

According to Michel, the joy of learning is being wrenched out of them bit by bit, a joy of learning which would otherwise give them a sense of integrity, of pride and a sense of personal goals which they can set for themselves. Michel believed that children don't have to run away to escape. They simply turn to violence as a means of expressing their anger and rebel against those who keep them in those terrible institutions.

The political debate rages on as politicians and pundits alike place the blame on the lack of sufficient funding for education. "Money for what? To create smaller classrooms with fewer students in each? The size of a class matters not if there are incompetent teachers," Michel angrily asserted. His position was that any increased funding merely perpetuates a bad system. Michel believed that as long as the children remain *"sentenced to prison,"* the rebelling will continue. Then teachers feel that they have to use some form of discipline to retake control of the classroom, much to the disapproval of many parents who often *choose* to remain blind to their own child's behavior. How often does one hear, *"My little Johnny would never do that."*

Michel recommended that we spend more money on our educational system worldwide by finding another approach to teaching —- an innovative approach. In the years that we knew Michel, he would often pose the following rhetorical question:

> "Is anything being done anywhere to teach teachers how to teach?"

"No" would be his resounding answer every time. Teachers are thrown into the classroom to oversee the operation that keeps children "in strait jackets," as he would say. Teachers are told to "make the best of it" or "see what you can do with them." Michel contended that the teachers don't know "what to do with them." He would ask time and again, "When does a teacher become a teacher? Just because one has a B.A. or an M.A. or Ph.D. in education should not automatically qualify the person to be a teacher." Does supposedly knowing a given subject suddenly make a person a teacher who can actually teach? Of course not. Furthermore, Michel felt that knowing a given subject may lead one to want to lecture. And, as we shall later see in the Method Chapter, his view was that lecturing was not teaching.

What is it exactly that makes a person a teacher? Michel would argue that without a high quality teaching program that actually teaches one about the learning process of the mind and that teaches one a method that has been proven to work, how can we have effective teachers? He would often lament the fact that this is the very situation which we find everywhere in the world and not just in the United States.

Meanwhile, the torture in the *Mind Prison*™ continues. As Michel explained, in our present system, children are forced to attend school by their parents and are then admonished by them whenever they get the chance:

- "You have to pay attention to the teacher."
- "You have to *try* hard."
- "You have to be a good student."
- "You have to bring home good grades."
- "You have to make me proud of you."

Students end up having demand after demand placed upon them. Such statements may appear to be innocuous to most parents, yet this could not be farther from the truth. Placing demands upon children merely creates pressure on them to live up to some standard imposed upon them by their parents and teachers.

They are not allowed to open their inner channels to what would otherwise be a source of joyous learning. Instead of stimulating and encouraging the learning process by making it fun and truly exciting, they are actively halting the flow of energy to learn. Also, parents place the responsibility for learning on their children, as do teachers on their students, on the learners. For Michel, this is not only wrong, it is criminal. Every association with learning is tied to *tension*. Parents and teachers tell the students to *work* hard, to *try* hard, to do home *work*. The entire immediate association with learning is always *tension* day in and day out.

Interestingly, Michel's teaching experience has confirmed many times over that the more university degrees a person has, the more difficult and challenging it is to open the doors of their minds to learning in a new way. In fact, the more "successful" these people have been in school in terms of passing the requisite tests to get their respective degrees within the existing system, the more resistant they are to giving up old patterns and to opening up to new ways of learning. The result is that it took Michel a little longer to teach them using his method because his approach was so antithetical to the one used in the traditional system. Those within the system who are most successful are very proud of their success and of their ability to "learn" by following the rules of that system.

The other interesting phenomenon regarding these "successful" students is that they were always the ones among his students who blamed themselves when they made a mistake. Michel is quick to tell them not to blame themselves because he is the one who accepted total responsibility for their learning. The responsibility for remembering is the responsibility of the teacher. If they make a mistake, it is his problem, not theirs. It is up to the teacher to determine why the mistake was made in the first place and to do something about it. This unique concept of the teacher taking complete responsibility for learning and for remembering rather than placing it on the student is a major key to the *Michel Thomas Method.* We will cover this concept more thoroughly in Chapter Six, where we discuss the specific components of his method.

PRACTICE WHAT YOU PREACH

By the way, Michel practiced what he preached in his inner circle with his own children. Early on when his children became of school age, Michel decided that he would not send them "to serve time in an institution" like the *Mind Prison*™. Instead he chose to begin home-schooling them. At that time, home schooling was illegal and was quite a revolutionary concept. "I was ready to fight," Michel always said with pride. "It is illegal to do anything that will hurt my children. I will not let my children be sentenced to prison!" he boasted when describing his decision. In spite of possible legal challenges, Michel did it anyway and over the years he remained curiously surprised that the authorities never confronted him about his stance. Nowadays home-schooling is becoming more and more tolerated as a viable option to parents for their children and is even accepted in some states. As for parents teaching their children, Michel had strong opinions about this subject as well: "It becomes a gamble whatever they [parents] can do, but at least they are not putting their children into prison. Of course, it becomes a question of luck. What do parents know about teaching?"

Later in Chapter Eight of this book, we will talk about specific recommendations for parents regarding how to teach their own children. It is interesting to note that some of the great forefathers of the United States such as Thomas Jefferson, George Washington, Benjamin Franklin, and Abraham Lincoln never officially finished secondary school. And somehow they learned along the way what it took to be a leader, a great leader for that matter. Perhaps they knew something that modern educators refuse to acknowledge about what it means to be educated versus being "*put through school.*" And their wisdom was not a product of the traditional system. In truth, the compulsory *dis-educational system*™ does not create leaders, but followers, the type that fall into the category of "employee," one who is told what to do and one who is often incapable of taking one's own initiatives.

Unlike Michel, most parents force their children to slave away at a given *Mind Prison*™ on a daily basis, only to continue the painful grind in the form of homework assignments after normal classroom hours. Michel viewed this as a kind of evil social contract between the school system and parents that literally kills all the joy of learning. He argued that this educational bondage actually serves to instill hatred of learning into our children, a destructive emotion which remains within us throughout adulthood, and penetrates into other realms of thought and behaviors which affect our choices later on in life. He also added that hatred does not magically appear out of the sky.

Michel indeed had very specific thoughts about hatred. He believed that hatred could be injected into a person rather deliberately. It can be taught and sometimes taught by parents who don't understand the process. Michel contended that hatred is not innate. It can be taught to our children and then completely takes hold within them with hatred itself growing, as the children grow into adulthood. He believed that later, as adults, one could invent rationales for hatred. It can also be self-taught, acquired as a reaction to certain situations and experiences. In his mind, even worse was that hatred could easily be transformed into evil, whereby evil then takes control of one's life and spreads like a cancerous cell. According to Michel, tragically, hatred is not something that can be physically destroyed because it is mental and emotional in nature, and not physical.

And who better than Michel Thomas, knew the destructive, evil power of hatred that can take control of the souls of humankind when such seeds are planted in the minds of the masses. In the previous chapter, we saw how these seeds of hatred and lack of education have contributed to the demise of democracy. We have also seen how these bad seeds do not bode well for the future either. Just as in his language teaching, Michel realized the importance of stressing the positive and of planting "good seeds" in the teaching and upbringing of his children. He often explained to us the way in which he developed in his children a respect for life, all life whether human, animal or plant. And he was delighted that we chose to include in this chapter the following anecdotes about how he taught his own children. He had educated them in a way that was in marked contrast to approaches taken in the *Mind Prison*™.

On several occasions over the years he would relate to us the story of his daughter, Mishie, who at the age of six, picked a flower and threw it away. Michel immediately said to her: "What you just did — that is life and you don't throw away life. Now that you picked the flower you are responsible for this one flower. You now have to take it home, put it in water and take care of it." And she very diligently did so with tender, loving care. This incident helped his daughter to understand the importance of cherishing life and of correcting one's mistakes. It also reveals how Michel applied several of the principles of his method (as we shall see throughout the book) in teaching his own children:

1) The first is to cherish learning and to respect all life.

2) The second is not to place blame on children.

3) The third is to take personal responsibility for one's actions.

4) The fourth is to learn how to correct one's own mistakes.

Both Mishie and her brother, Guri ended up collecting boxes of insects during their childhood years in Larchmont, New York, a suburban town in Westchester County, north of Manhattan. One day his daughter found a cockroach, put it in a coffee can and began to take care of it. The little cockroach, an unlikely pet, became just that, a beloved pet of Mishie's. She would go almost everywhere with it, even take it on the train into the city. There she was, this precious little girl walking up and down the aisles of the train, proudly showing off her dear, pet cockroach to her fellow commuters. One can only imagine their reaction at seeing an insect that more often than not, elicits shrieks of disgust rather than expressions of tender care or love. To this day Mishie (and her brother, as did their father) cherishes all of her current "*babies*" (her pets) and establishes amazing communication with all of them and with those of other people as well.

These stories are revelatory in that they open a door into Michel's perspective on life and on teaching. From these stories we learn that Michel always emphasized the positive and never blamed a child for what may be perceived to be a mistake or a wrong. Michel adopted the same perspective in his teaching. Unlike the traditional educational system which places blame on the learner, Michel would not place blame on the student or on the person learning the lessons of life, in this case, his children (or any children for that matter). In so doing, he encouraged the learner to grow, to cherish learning and to desire to learn more rather than to squelch his or her learning potential. We will talk more about the concept of blame in Chapter Six, in the context of the *Michel Thomas Method*.

Michel spoke also of another lesson, that of taking personal responsibility for one's actions, this time while relating to us a childhood incident involving his son, Guri. It is a story about little Guri which is quite revelatory on several levels. It gives us a touching glimpse into both Michel's personal philosophy about life and his *Universalist* perspective. At the same time, it provides another powerful lesson in how to teach our children to become responsible adults in an ever more complex and interconnected world. At age six, Guri was already a highly intelligent and inquisitive child. One evening, as Michel sat at his desk in his study in their Larchmont home, Guri approached his father and immediately noticed an open drawer with an SS dagger sticking out of it. The desk was usually locked, and it was quite rare for Michel to leave the desk drawer unlocked and open. So he was literally taken by surprise when little Guri walked in and said to his father: "There is a sword in your drawer. Where does it come from? Where did you get it?" At his young age Guri thought that the dagger was a sword.

Although Michel had an impressive collection of weapons, his children had never seen any of them; and he made sure that there were no war toys such as guns, soldiers, and the like in the house among the many other toys the children had to play with. As Michel described it, "I was caught and I was uncomfortable." During his father's brief silence, Guri then said, "You got it in a fight with a bad guy and you took it away. Who did you fight?" Michel was taken by surprise and did not know what to say, and it was so unlike Michel to be at a loss for words. Once again, Guri answered his own question by exclaiming, "I know. You fought with the Assyrians."

The child had learned about the Assyrians in Bible study. Michel knew that if he had said, "the Germans," then Guri would have thought that all Germans were bad. That wouldn't have worked. If he had said, "Yes, the Assyrians," that wouldn't have been right either because then Guri would have thought that the Assyrians, then the Syrians, then the Arabs were bad, and Michel did not want to teach his children hatred. Doing so would have clashed with his own beliefs and with his teaching. Something popped into Michel's head and he replied, "I fought with the Nazis and took the dagger from a Nazi bad guy."

Although it was the first time that Guri had heard the word "Nazi," he accepted his father's answer. The next night, however, Guri had more questions after he had thought about his father's comment. "You fought with the Nazis, Dad? If they come back, I want to fight them with you." In spite of the fact that the Nazis were evil incarnate, in spite of having lived with the extreme pain of having had his entire family annihilated by them, Michel still refused to instill seeds of hatred into his son: "I talked to him a long time because I did not want to create hate in him, not even towards the Nazis." As we learned earlier in this chapter, Michel had definite views with respect to emotions: "Although one is not born with hatred, one can be taught hatred. And the great danger arises when we instill hatred into our children. What that means is that hatred is passed down from generation to generation and lives on forever in them as adults."

The next night, the conversation turned to big questions about God. Guri, the contemplative child that he was, remarked, "Aren't we all created by God? All life is created by God. What about the Nazis and other bad people, are they created by God too?" Of course, Michel taught his children to respect all life; and he went on to explain, "Yes, we are all created by God, but we are not puppets of God. We have responsibilities given to us by God. Good seeds and bad seeds are within all of us, and it is up to us to decide what we chose to do."

Michel taught his children that each of us has God-given ingredients, both good and bad. Furthermore, we are the ones who decide what to make of them. The manner in which we select these ingredients and how they blend and develop within us is our personal responsibility. Michel believed that we are responsible for our own actions, not God. Michel wanted his children to know not to count on Divine action because Divine action is within all of us. What we do or fail to do is what matters, and what we don't do is much more important than what we do.

He also explained to his son that we each have a variety of seeds within us. Those with bad seeds chose evil and become the bad guys. Sometimes the bad seeds take over and grow even more. Sometimes the good seeds take over and good prevails over evil. What is important is to not let the bad seeds interfere with the growth of the good seeds. Let the good seeds become strong so that one develops into a strong, good person. There are also people who are weak and they let the bad seeds, the evil seeds, grow more. Michel asserted that these bad seeds come forth due to "bad influences, bad teachers and bad injections."

What happens in this case is that these bad seeds become more powerful than the good ones and will cover up or push away whatever good seeds may be left. Then there are also people who somehow let both seeds sprout — the good and the bad. And people such as this are capable at any time of switching from one to another. Michel cautioned that these are the people whom you cannot trust because they cannot trust themselves. A similar thing occurs with multiple personalities in which there are multiple seeds, so that one cannot trust these people to know who they really are. According to Michel, in today's world there are those with multiple seeds thriving in places high and low. He always affirmed that the bad seeds are ready to take control at any time within those with weak minds and will.

Michel went on to tell Guri, "It is important not to let the bad seeds develop, and to only develop the good seeds and strengthen them so that one grows up to become a good person." Learning to develop the good seeds is what we have to do, and not to give in to the bad seeds, for there may be situations and circumstances in which we are forced to choose between the two. Michel reminded us that with strong seeds, it is easier to choose the right side.

There were also good and bad seeds in nations as well, and that history reflected the choices made by nations. Michel also explained that we are responsible for our own lives, and there is one God for everyone. Guri then asked, "What about the Jewish God?" and Michel responded, "There is no Jewish God or Christian God or Moslem God… We are all brothers and sisters and we are all children of God." For Michel, there was only the oneness of the universal God. No matter what race, religion or ethnicity, we all come under the one God. As we mentioned, Michel was a *Universalist* in all ways.

Moreover, he believed in the equality of all life, not only human life, but all life. The lesson of the story is that we must take personal responsibility for what we are and for who we become and that we must respect all life. That lesson must be taught to our children by their parents. To do so, parents must accept responsibility for their own actions, before they can plant good seeds into their children. Michel sadly contemplated that in our present society, we are witnessing indifference in some people. He also pointed out that increasingly, in some places, we are also seeing the seeds of hatred planted into unknowing, young minds that have the potential to turn into modern monsters of evil.

For Michel, the notion of taking personal responsibility developed early on into what he referred to as his *"Two Commandments,"* which he personally added to the original *Ten Commandments*. The first one is his so-called *Eleventh Commandment*. This commandment is a good example of what we call the *Internal Evaluation People Pattern*™, which determines how an individual makes decisions. Michel never needed the approval of others to validate anything that he said or did. This pattern is also the reason why he couldn't understand how people could be so influenced by the stupidity of others (Chapter Nine). Michel's *Eleventh Commandment* is:

> THOU SHALT NOT FOLLOW THE MULTITUDE TO COMMIT EVIL

In the context of teaching children, this means to teach them never to use an excuse to engage in bad or evil or to commit any unkind acts or to engage in behavior that is harmful to any living being, just because others are doing so. Michel taught his children, Guri and Mishie, not to follow the crowd; and he recommended that today's parents take heed of this lesson. He firmly believed that children should be taught to be individuals who make decisions based on what they know to be true and right. He thought that children should not be told to imitate others or to act in a particular way, simply because their peers are doing so. Michel must have taken this commandment so literally that he could never stand in line for anything, not even for a movie, because for him it became an issue of not following the crowd.

This is the opposite of what millions do every day around the globe. We live in a society in which children are encouraged, at a younger and younger age, to be part of the crowd and emulate in dress, language and mores certain pop stars and entertainers, whose typical conduct often exudes narcissism, superficiality and vulgarity. From little girls and boys to teens and to college students, all too many want to look and act like these celebrities whose images are artificially created and endorsed by the media. Tragically, these children and young adults who follow such individuals have already become part of the "ignorant masses" who are brainwashed by the press which spotlights scandals and stupidity.

Parents and teachers must take an active role in steering children onto a path of healthy self-expression rather than mindless adoration of inappropriate role models who have placed self-aggrandizement and money ahead of self-enlightenment and knowledge. And, as we mentioned earlier, the *Mind Prison*™ by its very nature of stifling the excitement for learning in children, pushes them *en masse* towards what they perceive to be other sources of pleasure which, in turn, contribute to idiocy. "Let's all be like so and so" conformity takes hold and closes the door to healthy self-expression and critical thinking.

Michel's *Twelfth Commandment* (the second of his personal two) is connected to the one previously discussed above. For those who are aware of a typology which we have been teaching, writing about and applying for several decades, this commandment reflects the mind-set of a particular *Enneagram* type we refer to as the "*Venge*," for vengeance. In Chapter Nine we discuss this typology in the context of Michel's behavioral profile. Michel's *Twelfth Commandment* is:

> THOU SHALT NOT STAND OR SIT IDLY BY

In other words, if you witness something that is wrong, it is important to stand up and to act and not deny that you were a witness to a wrongdoing. Michel maintained that to witness a wrong and then to stand idly by is "to acquiesce." Such a stance makes you, in essence, an accessory to that "crime." In Michel's eyes, this is exactly what many parents, teachers, school boards, academicians, and politicians are doing with regard to the *Mind Prison*™. They sit or stand idly by as, in Michel's words, "children are condemned to serve time in institutions called schools."

Michel wanted to know how was it possible that no one seemed to stand up to this "major crime." Is it that most people readily accept the *status quo* because they themselves are products of the *Mind Prison*™? Is it because they have been programmed to be complacent citizens? Why is it that so many parents don't take the time to educate their children? He also wondered why politicians cry out for change and then pass legislation that keeps things the same. Those who refuse to take action are like sleepwalking passers-by who wander along without conviction for anything. Remember that what we don't do is much more significant than what we do. Michel strongly cautioned that it is time to move into proactive mode before our children, our hope for the future, totally relinquish their minds to the control of others.

Fortunately, we had someone like Michel who truly understood what is happening around us. The values and wisdom that Michel has passed onto his children are light years ahead of the mind-set promulgated by most parents today: that of placing their children in the guardianship of mindless TV programs, cell phones, computer and video games which discourage real communication and deprive our children of meaningfulness in the context of their precious lives. And, of course, the marketing moguls out there are doing everything in their power to make certain that this dire and appalling situation continues ahead at light speed.

THE *INNATE DRIVE FOR LEARNING*

Another major shortcoming of traditional education, according to Michel, is that ironically, it stifles learning, the very thing that education is supposed to encourage. Michel contended that this horrible *Mind Prison*™ in which students find themselves, smothers the *innate drive for learning* so that people "live" without really living, and die without tapping into their great learning potential. So many people go through life without having realized even a small fraction of their potential. With a look that conveyed his disdain for the current system, Michel explained:

> "Learning is crippled and smothered, usually in the home, and finished off in our school system,"

For Michel, too many schools are simply "institutional straight-jackets" when they should really be places of inspiration and excitement.

Thus, the individual basically spends year after year in a vegetative state in which no real learning occurs. Quite frankly, if one stops learning, one realistically stops living and evolving to higher levels of being. Our wise father always said, "If you think that you know it all, then you might as well be in a coffin." Learning is what life is all about. Without it, we vegetate through existence, rarely, if ever, experiencing the great heights and immense joy of learning that we, as living beings are meant to experience. All learning should be associated with a high degree of enjoyment. The *innate drive for learning*, the inner fire, never dies. It simply dwindles, as if it didn't exist, until it is rekindled. Michel was the master rekindler, as we shall see.

First, let us discover what this *innate drive for learning* is all about and of which Michel Thomas would constantly speak. We will come back to this principle in the Method Chapter. This *innate drive for learning* happens to be one of the most important concepts to understanding Michel's method and is paramount to understanding Michel's philosophy of learning. For Michel, it is the powerful drive that is in every living being. Notice that Michel said "living being" and not human being because for Michel, even what are considered by science to be lower life forms, all have the *innate drive for learning*. "From the tiny ant to the big elephant, the *innate drive for learning* is there." "Take ants," he said. "Ants organize armies to fight each other. They are the only other living beings who do what humans do — fight each other, fight their own kind." According to Michel,

> "The innate drive for learning is stronger than the sex drive and is as great as and can be even more powerful than the drive for living and the drive for survival itself."

Michel contended that given free reign, the *innate drive for learning* goes beyond the drive for living in some cases, because there are people for whom the drive for survival is not very strong. Some people may, for whatever reason, give up their drive to survive, yet the drive for learning never leaves us. And, it is a powerful drive, not merely a desire. This drive for learning far surpasses the notion of desire. Every living being has the drive to grow, to learn to explore, to discover new things and new perspectives on things. Michel believed that the *innate drive for learning* is always within us: "The drive for learning, if not blocked, is always there looking for satisfaction." he said. This drive is a natural one, and not one that is somehow artificially generated. By the way, Michel even equated sending a dog to training school to sending a child to the *"prison called school."* They are two sides of the same coin. In both cases, we are smothering this innate drive found in every living being. In fact, as a child, Michel had a strong dislike for the circus because he deeply resented witnessing the training of animals at the circus, a bitter distaste which he still felt to the very end of his life.

It is important to make a distinction here between what Michel called the *innate drive for learning* and motivation. In the traditional system, educators often say: "This student is learning because he is motivated." That is meaningless. According to Michel, the motivation for learning is innate in everyone because in his words, "motivation is the product of one's *innate drive for learning.*" One does not learn because one is motivated to do so. Motivation has merely become a catch word of the educational system. One may often hear a parent or teacher say to a child or student, "You have to be motivated!" That is their standard answer to everything, and as Michel always said, "It is their answer to bad teaching." When students do poorly, the classic response is that the teacher has a class in which no one is motivated, so that there is nothing that he or she can do about it. That couldn't be farther from the truth because motivation for learning is part of an innate process.

> "Motivation is an outcome, an outcome of the innate drive for learning."

Michel argued that motivation is a natural outcome of the *innate drive for learning* that is completely ignored in our educational system, so completely ignored, as though it did not even exist. No one ever discusses the drive for learning, a situation which Michel considered to be almost criminal. This drive for learning is not some minor little drive. It is one of major importance that needs to be addressed. In this light, motivation is redundant. Motivation is innate and it goes together with the drive for learning. It is an innate by-product of the drive for learning and is not something separate. Motivation is an integral part of the drive for learning. Without that drive, one cannot be motivated.

Michel contended that we, as a society, merely stand by and witness the willful suppression of this natural drive, which could otherwise bring immeasurable joy and fulfillment. We end up stifling the very drive that could bring us the greatest joy. Michel expressed this thought in the following manner:

> "Learning is and should be the fulfillment of a very powerful, innate drive that leads to and creates a high degree of excitement."

An aura of sorrow surrounded Michel each and every time he discussed how "the drive for learning, if not killed, is being choked, slammed shut by our educational system." Such was Michel's sad commentary on the present state of education where the acquisition of *knowledge* is being suppressed in every way possible.

FROM ZERO POINT TO OVERWHELMING SUCCESS

Since this book is about Michel's method of teaching and the learning process, let us give as an example of the *innate drive for learning*, using the most foreign subject of learning, which is a foreign language. To teach a foreign language implies starting with a student who has zero knowledge of the subject matter. Given this context, it was quite remarkable that Michel achieved what he did in just a few days. He was able to do so because of what he called *"proper" or "real teaching."* Such a foreign subject as a foreign language would usually take years of high school and college studies with memorizing and learning by rote, and with very unsatisfactory results, if any results at best. Very few people would come out of it with any tangible or even somewhat satisfactory results, after having been subjected to spending a lot of time and effort memorizing and cramming and so on. Anyone who has taken a foreign language in the *Mind Prison™* has experienced this horror and knows firsthand what is involved and how ineffectual traditional language teaching really is. Yet with *Michel,* what was achieved was nothing short of a learning miracle.

What Michel achieved was outright remarkable! In a two phase, five day program which included a first phase involving three days of learning with Michel, followed by two days of working with another teacher, the student or students came out with more than proficiency in a foreign language. Within the first three days or first phase, the student acquired a solid and comprehensive *knowledge* (and the emphasis is on *knowledge* and not on what is covered) of the entire grammar, of the entire structure of the language. This comprised all the tenses, including the subjunctive, everything. And all of this was achieved without memorizing. In fact, there is never anything to memorize, and there are no drills whatsoever. There was absolutely no homework allowed, or what Michel referred to as *"no mental homework,"* something which he strongly recommended not to do. There were no textbooks, and note taking was not permitted. Michel did not allow any of these in his method for the reasons he described as follows: "In my method, homework and note taking have been found to impede the learning, to break the continuity of the process which stimulates the learning potential."

Given this unorthodox scenario, Michel enabled the student after just three days of his teaching the target language, to use the language in speaking and in reading and writing. The next two days develop proficiency and the students are able to read newspapers, magazine articles and even literature. They also begin to have discussions in the target language. All this in what is, for all practical purposes, a five day program that allows one to use the newly acquired language with exceptional facility and great enjoyment (Chapter Six).

Moreover, the students will not need further instruction, as impossible as this may seem. Michel accomplished this unlikely feat in just five days, when everywhere else developing such a skill would take years, if at all! Even more impressive, is that what the students understand, what they know, what they acquire as *knowledge*, they will never forget. This notion is a critical element of Michel's method which we cover in depth in Chapter Six. Finally, each and every time Michel taught another student or students, he achieved the same improbable results, results which could never occur in the current *dis-educational system*™. With each mounting success, year after year, Michel totally debunked the learning myths which continue to thrive in the traditional educational system, that institution in which, as Michel would say, "the drive for learning is choked."

THE MYTHS OF LANGUAGE LEARNING

The teaching methods of the *Mind Prison*™ not only contribute to creating *tension* in students, they also lead to a loss of self-esteem in many. That is not all. A consequence of ineffective teaching methods also results in the proliferation of myths around learning, specifically around the learning of a foreign language. According to Michel, each one is exactly that: a myth. And from his point of view, each one of these myths is simply an excuse for bad teachers and their inability to teach. Of course, human beings readily believe in myths, yet for Michel these myths of learning were totally unacceptable.

So what exactly are these myths of learning? The first myth is the one which we briefly mentioned above. It is the myth which promulgates the falsity that only a person with a so-called ear for languages or gift for languages can actually learn another language. There is no such thing as an ear for languages or a gift of languages.

Michel contended that everyone who can speak his native language has already proven his gift for languages. Everyone who can speak his native tongue is certainly capable of learning one or more different languages, unless, of course, this "innate desire" has been killed off by faulty teaching. There are increasing numbers of individuals who give up on language learning because they are convinced by the educational system that only those who have a gift for languages or an ear for languages are capable of learning another language. The tragedy is that they harbor negative beliefs about their abilities which filter into other aspects of their lives. They readily throw in the towel instead of pursuing their goal because they end up buying into this absurd learning myth which the current system deliberately preserves.

Even people who believe that they have no ear for languages came through with shining colors as students of Michel, such as filmmaker, Woody Allen, who said: "I am a poor student, particularly in languages. I had years of Spanish in school and could never speak a word. In several days, he had me speaking French and I learned it in a way I've never forgotten and it was painless. A tremendous experience."

There was also the case of French film director, François Truffaut, who went to Michel because he desperately wanted to learn English, even though he was one who bought into the myth that it would be an almost impossible task for him to learn another language. When asked why he had traveled six thousand miles to study English he responded, "Because you have a very famous language teacher here — Michel Thomas." Michel explained to us that it was out of frustration and difficulty in learning English that Truffaut created his film masterpiece, *L'Enfant Sauvage (The Wild Child)*. In this film, Truffaut teaches a child who was raised by animals in the wilds how to speak French. Until learning with Michel, none of the language courses Truffaut had taken had ever worked. He had even gone to England to study with no success.

Truffaut had taken Michel's English course at the time of the Watergate hearings and expressed the following on a signed photograph to Michel: "At first, I learned from you the word: impeachment and four weeks later, I was able to have a meeting in English at the Warner Bros. Headquarters. Thank you, Michel." Elsewhere Truffaut wrote to Michel from Bel Air: "You are definitely the best teacher. I am unfortunately the worst pupil... For the first time tonight I understood some phrases, few sentences in Watergate Hearing on TV... I was very happy about that and I know that I couldn't have done it without you. Fondest and Warmest Regards, François Truffaut." And who said that François Truffaut had no ear for languages.

Michel often got looks of astonishment and incredulity from students who personally had this disempowering belief about not having an ear for languages. Because of the ease and speed at which learning with Michel occurred, even students who accepted the myth were immediately transformed into confident speakers of the new language.

The second myth about learning maintains that the learning of a foreign language is a painful process which is associated with anxiety, mental torture, and even worse, with the mistaken belief that learning another language is an arduous and almost impossible task for most people. This is all nonsense except in the world of Michel Thomas, where learning a foreign language was actually an incredibly enjoyable experience of heightened excitement that boosted self-confidence rather than tearing it down. Michel explained that it is only because children as well as adults want to avoid reaccessing painful or embarrassing moments from their pasts where they found themselves in distasteful and uncomfortable learning situations, that they begin to associate all learning with mental torture.

It is difficult for people to accept the reality of the excitement of learning. To learn something practically in no time, and then to learn a subject that is totally foreign to boot, and to learn in a matter of days that which is not usually achieved in years is more than remarkable. This is unheard of in the current *dis-educational system*™. Yet it was a wondrous reality in the world of Michel Thomas! His method is a powerful demonstration of what can and should be done in education.

Michel's method also came in handy in a variety of situations and for different objectives. Michel described what he considered to be the rather amusing case of actress Jayne Mansfield, who had asked Michel to teach her French so that she could communicate with her boyfriend at the time who was a famous director. Michel recounted the rather amusing story that Ms. Mansfield had learned the language in a few days so that she could travel to New York, as she and her boyfriend had decided, meeting halfway between LA and Paris, where the two would have dinner at which time she could finally converse with her companion in his native tongue. When she called Michel the next day as promised, he assumed that she was calling from New York. Not at all. She had taken the first plane back to LA without even finishing dinner. It seems that when she was finally able to communicate with her director friend in his native tongue, she found him so boring that she immediately left. She couldn't stand a second more of his company. So much for the language of diplomacy.

In any case, everyone knows that traditional language learning usually takes years and with Michel's method, something that would normally take years was actually accomplished in just a matter of a few days. Michel had proven his case time and time again. Every time he would teach his course, it took only days to prove the validity of his method. In fact, for years he had been challenging any college, any university to take him up on it, to no avail. Up until his passing, no college or university had taken Michel up on his challenge to prove what he could do.

The third myth about language learning is not valid either. This third myth is that Europeans have greater facility in learning languages than do Americans, due to the geographical proximity of their countries. Michel contended that it is simply not true that Europeans somehow have a miraculous ability to learn other languages. Anyone familiar with language schools throughout Europe (whether Germany, Switzerland, France, Italy, Belgium, and the list goes on) as well as with individual public classrooms at all levels, knows that European children and adults experience the same difficulties that Americans do in learning another language. Michel was fond of citing as an example the Swiss who, he pointed out, are exposed to the study of languages and yet they do not come out with a true knowledge of the foreign language.

He explained that in Switzerland there are multiple national languages, whereas, as hard as it is to believe, "there is tragically no national language in the United States." Michel vehemently thought that the national language for America should be English. In any case, Michel argued that for the most part, contrary to popular belief, the Swiss are neither bilingual nor multilingual. According to him, most of them are monolingual, which means that they cannot communicate with another Swiss once they have crossed one language border into another. The exceptions are the educational and professional elite, who learn the languages by visiting other countries.

Michel also thought that in general, Europeans who work in the hotel or restaurant business learn just enough of a language to deal with and to receive foreign tourists, although they are not what he considered "fluent." He would add that in the United States, there are millions of documented citizens born here who do not even speak English, not to mention the undocumented ones. From Michel's standpoint, the big problem is that bilingualism as it exists in the current system "simply does not work." We will come back to the subject of Michel's views on bilingual education in the Method Chapter. In any case, whatever the myth circulating among the corridors of the *Mind Prison*™, other institutions or homes, they are totally false and serve to destroy self-confidence by installing negative belief systems about one's ability to learn, therefore blocking the road to fulfillment and joy which Michel considered to be a God-given right for all.

SPECIAL, INFLUENTIAL TEACHERS: MAKING A DIFFERENCE

Fulfillment comes with learning that is exciting, and Michel constantly argued that it is precisely excitement that is lacking in traditional education or the *Mind Prison*™.

> "All learning should begin or lead into sensations of, feelings of excitement, of great excitement because learning should be fulfillment."

And fulfillment is not possible without excitement. As we will discuss in detail in the Method Chapter, the whole learning process in the *Mind Prison™* is based on work and *tension*, on concentration, on paying attention and on memorization. And, as Michel expressed, "Even what is acquired as memorized knowledge rarely becomes *knowledge*." Without *understanding*, there is no true learning. Without *understanding*, there is no acquisition of *knowledge*.

Michel believed that in destroying, or at best, in arresting the learning process, the entire educational system of the *Mind Prison™* ends up turning off people and especially young people to knowledge. It deeply bothered Michel that the learning experience of most children and adults is not a happy one, and certainly not a good experience. In fact, it angered him that people carry these bad memories as heavy baggage throughout their lives. Michel would often put forth the question, "How many among you can honestly say that you were fulfilled as a student? How many among you can remember a teacher who greatly influenced you in a positive way?"

He contended that if you ask people if they remember any one teacher in all of their experiences of school, from pre-school to high school to university, to graduate school, that if they come up with one particular teacher who stands out among the rest, they are among the fortunate few. And usually, that teacher will have influenced the person tremendously. Michel would ask others, "Can you reel off an entire ten person list of wonderfully exciting teachers you have had?" Then Michel would argue, "If a person can recall even two people who have positively affected them, it is by pure luck." Rarely did he hear a person mention more than two teachers. "That is very rare," he emphasized.

Just take a minute. How many of you have children who are so enthralled about getting on the school bus each morning that you never have to prod them into going to school? Not many probably. What Michel referred to as "great excitement" is not particularly prevalent in the *Mind Prison™*, with some exceptions, of course. Certainly there are those of you who have had wonderful teachers or who know of them.

Michel, too, was quite fortunate to have had several great teachers, tutors and mentors in his early years and at the University of Bordeaux as well as at the Sorbonne. He would always describe the affect they had on him with both gratitude and joy. These special people and teachers taught him things that made a lasting mark in his mind. And it was these "pearls of wisdom" which had a great influence upon what was later to become his own masterful teaching method.

For example, much to the surprise of his mother, when Michel quit high school, he personally asked a special man who, at the time, was nationally recognized as a first class music and literary critic to become his private tutor for all subjects. Michel was so passionate about learning with his tutor, who was known as "*the walking encyclopedia*," that he would at times have to travel to other countries in order to be with the tutor.

Of significance is that Michel's tutor did something for him which Michel had never thought possible. He helped Michel discover the joy of mathematics and turned a perceived weakness into a great strength. Michel felt that in learning there was one subject in particular in which he was weak. And for a long time he believed that he simply had to live with it. In the past, just to pass this subject made him happy. The subject was math. Although every other subject was fine, in math, he felt weak. Michel's tutor taught him everything including math, and turned his study of math into something truly exciting. Math suddenly became a challenge and Michel relished the challenge.

More important, what had been perceived as a weakness by Michel, an accepted weakness for which nothing could be done, had become a strength of his. Over time, this strength increased in intensity, so much so that it led Michel into studying both physics and chemistry. He was so excited that he even built an in-home laboratory which provided Michel the wonderful opportunity to create — to create in chemistry — conducting experiments that were fun and exciting, even if they did cause explosions and gas fumes in his house. In relating this story to us, Michel wanted to make the point that it was because of good teaching that his weak subject was magically transformed into a forte.

Another major influence on Michel happened to come from a math teacher, Dr. Fleishmann, who had a certain favorite utterance. According to Michel, it wasn't that this teacher was so great, but rather that he had a unique way of formulating a particular conclusion about things and loved to frequently demonstrate his conclusion. Michel described how this teacher would go to the blackboard and put up a mathematical problem. "Take your time and just solve the problem," he would say to the class. One had all the time in the world, whatever it took; and the students would fill up the entire blackboard from top to bottom with the final result, the solution at the bottom. Once the students had finished, the teacher would turn around, face the blackboard and say, "Here is the problem. Here is the result. You were lucky." Of course, the class didn't understand his reaction. Why lucky? He would go on to explain that as the student or class meticulously wrote the solution, step by step, down the blackboard, any mistake made along the way, even a tiny one, would have made the whole thing wrong.

At first Dr. Fleishmann called it lucky. "But now let's look at it again," he said. "Here is the problem. Here is the formula. Here is the solution. It took me just a few minutes and I got the same solution!" he boasted. Then he would do his favorite thing by shaking his head and would say: "There is nothing so simple that it can't be made *very* complicated." This is exactly how it usually happens and this one sentence set Michel's thinking gears quickly into motion, something that did not end until his passing. So here was Michel, a young boy of sixteen, ruminating over his math teacher's iteration which so influenced him at the time, that he came up with his own clever rendition by turning it around: "If it is true that there is nothing so simple that it can't be made *very* complicated," then Michel reasoned,

"There is nothing so complicated that it can't be made *very* simple!"

With this incident, we have a glimpse into the early stages of Michel's strategies behind his eventual amazing teaching method. Here, then, Michel began to reduce things to simplicity within his own mind, everything. As we shall see in the Method Chapter, this casual iteration of Michel's math teacher had such a huge impact upon his young mind that it eventually became an integral part of Michel's teaching philosophy and teaching method later in life.

Since we are speaking of influential people in Michel's life, without a doubt, the teacher who exerted the most lasting and strongest influence upon Michel was his mother and also his aunt, whom he referred to as his *"second mother."* Although Michel's mother taught him so much and impacted him on so many levels, we would like to mention one particular pearl of wisdom of which Michel was particularly fond, which she passed onto her son. It is important because it was a lesson which later influenced his teaching philosophy and teaching method. That special pearl of wisdom was about wealth and it is one which many parents in our entitlement society would do well to pass on to their own children. Michel's mother told him not to count on material wealth and not to place value on the acquisition of material wealth because it meant very little in life. Although wealth was something good to have, one should not cherish it because one could lose it at any time. He explained that one could be deprived of material wealth in a split second by robbery, ill fortune, etc.

However, there was one type of wealth that was everlasting — and it is the only wealth you should acquire: it is the wealth that you put in your head (in your mind). Your most prized possession is your mental wealth, your *knowledge*. The acquisition of *knowledge* is man's greatest source of wealth. That is something that can never be taken from you. It is a personal treasure that can never be lost. Michel's mother would tell him about the Greek myths, about King Midas who hoarded gold, and other stories. These myths made such an impression upon Michel that they stayed in his mind his entire life. He realized that living life frivolously was a total waste. Furthermore, Michel realized that the *knowledge* you could acquire could never be taken from you. So he was determined to afford others the opportunity to acquire this most precious gift of mental wealth. As we shall see in Chapter Six, the concept of the acquisition of *knowledge* is a cornerstone of the *Michel Thomas Method*.

Finally, there was also another person who greatly influenced Michel's own teaching. It was a psychology professor at the Sorbonne whom Michel heard to say, "that nobody knew anything about the learning process of the human mind." It was this one remark which set something off in Michel's own mind. "How could it be possible that humans don't know anything about this?" he asked himself. So Michel began his own journey of self-discovery and research to "probe the learning process of the human mind" which, in turn, led to creation of his magnificent method. Not bad for someone who never ever wanted to be a teacher in the first place, and especially not a language teacher.

In fact, Michel was turned off to teaching very early on as a child. He recalled with amusement how, as a child, he often had the experience of people asking him questions. Much to their surprise, he would answer them with what were considered to be long explanations by a child his age. He remembered being called "*precocious*" without knowing at the time what the word meant. In any case, these adults would react in turn by saying, "Ah, what a great teacher you would be." Michel hated to hear that. In fact, he despised it. "I hated teachers. I was angry and this is something, therefore, that I never wanted to be, and definitely not a language teacher." When Michel made the decision to teach languages, it was only "to probe the learning process of the human mind." And again, this was largely due to the influence of the psychology professor at the Sorbonne.

Michel carried this excitement of learning and his mother's pearl of wisdom regarding wealth with him to the University of Bordeaux, where his first courses were in archeology, philosophy and philology. People were always asking him what he was going to do in life with such subjects. Michel couldn't understand their questions because for him attending the university was not a means to earn a living. He did not equate the kinds of classes he had chosen with his future money-making potential. It was a way to gain another form of wealth about which his mother had taught him: *knowledge*, that wonderful resource of mental wealth which no one could ever take from him!

Michel was blessed to have a loving and wise mother/teacher at home. He was also fortunate to have several remarkable and influential teachers who knew how to create excitement in him, and who knew how to trigger confidence and joy instead of doubt and frustration as in the *Mind Prison™*. Michel was blessed with certain teachers who managed to transform a disempowering belief system about his ability to succeed in a particular subject into a wonderfully empowering one. He was blessed with teachers who had opened his eyes to new and innovative ways of learning and thinking and with teachers who ignited great excitement about learning deep within his heart and soul. The end result was that Michel would become over time, all the more outraged at the shortcomings and weaknesses he witnessed around him in the traditional educational system, the *Mind Prison™*.

As a consequence, he had no choice but to do something about it. That inner fire within his very being enveloped him once again, igniting that profound desire to make a difference. Michel would choose to act, not in some discreet manner, but in keeping with the events and situations of his life, he would choose to act in spectacular fashion, lighting the way to a new and innovative way of teaching and learning. The result was the *Michel Thomas Method*.

The contrast we find here is rather striking. On one hand, we have parents, teachers, the school system and all those who are willing or unwilling participants in this contractual *Mind Prison™*, and who have successfully stifled this *innate drive for learning* in their children by creating and promoting an atmosphere of *tension*, that in Michel's words, "chokes the drive for learning, and it is then slammed shut by the system." And then, on the other hand, there is Michel Thomas, the *Master Teacher*, the master rekindler of the *innate drive for learning*.

Michel personally endorsed the inclusion of the chapters leading up to our presentation of his method. Each puts forth Michel's message to the world. In them, we have presented his personal philosophy of education, its connection to democracy and what he believed to be the key to the future. We have also examined his fervent views regarding the shortcomings of the traditional educational system which keeps children in learning "straightjackets" while they "serve time in prison." We have explored the lessons he taught his own children as well as the specific, positive influences that certain of his own teachers had upon him. All of these factors and events in some way, have powerfully influenced the creation of his teaching method later on.

With the above background, we will now reveal the secrets of the *Michel Thomas Method* which he disclosed to us. Let us discover how Michel Thomas, the *Master Teacher* and teaching genius, so brilliantly, so effortlessly, quite naturally and unpretentiously triggered our *innate drive for learning* by eliminating all *tension* in his teaching. Let us explore how he unlocked the keys of "the learning process of the mind" to create a revolutionary method — one that results in freeing minds one person at a time, and one that truly embodies the future of learning. With this, let us discover how Michel Thomas achieved consistent, lasting, memorable successes where the *Mind Prison*™ has failed so miserably time and time again.

Chapter Six

THE *MICHEL THOMAS METHOD*: THE *MASTER TEACHER'S* MODEL

Michel Thomas was unquestionably one of the world's greatest educators. He was the leading expert in his field who made amazing breakthroughs in learning. His methodology undeniably lays a solid and proven foundation for the future of learning. That is why we refer to Michel as the "*Master Teacher.*" Michel was truly a learning wizard on so many levels who created his own teaching method. How was this possible? How did he achieve such unbelievable success in teaching?

Both critics and skeptics alike have said that what Michel did was unique to him and that it couldn't be replicated. They are wrong, very wrong. In this chapter we will explain the "magic" behind the *Michel Thomas Method*. Michel spent his life probing the learning process of the human mind, and he discovered many things about this process which allow people to learn at a rate previously considered impossible. And even more incredibly, he accomplished this without using traditional methods. Furthermore, the *Master Teacher* did it in a way that makes the learning process *easy*, *effortless* and *exciting* as well as *effective*.

We will see how the *Master Teacher* had streamlined and accelerated the learning process. We will explore how he used his ingenious mind, the great lessons learned from his own life as well as his personal wisdom to create tools of wonder to magically transform the learning process into a truly exciting and pleasurable experience. Michel managed to shatter many existing beliefs that have been linked to the traditional learning process for centuries. We shall trace, step by step, what Michel did when he taught his courses. We will also give many explanations of why what Michel did worked so well. And, most important of all, we shall show how Michel's method provides a powerful and effective blueprint for others to follow.

WHAT IS A METHOD?

First, it would be helpful to understand what we mean by a method. What exactly is a method? It is a way of doing something in accordance to a definite plan. An educational method is a way of teaching and learning that occurs according to a deliberate and systematic plan. It does not happen by accident or by chance. Rather, a method is a planned, orderly, logical, systematic and deliberate way of proceeding. Michel clearly explained this as follows:

> "My method has been designed to teach rule-governed syntactical, morphological and phonological constructs of the language, using examples and illustrations as the grammar and the rules are being learned."

Michel's method teaches the mechanics and tools of the language, and how to use them with a continuous process of student response and feedback. And most critical of all, as we will see, Michel's method places the responsibility for learning and for remembering on the teacher and not on the student.

Michel's methods contrast with the methods used in most language programs, which are often too lengthy and rarely achieve the expected results. These other language programs are based on grammar exercises, tedious memorizing, on fragmentary and ineffectual conversations, and use tools such as textbooks, drills and reading exercises which require more time than any busy person can afford to take. Most important of all, these other language programs differ from Michel's method in that they are totally reliant on the student's individual ability to learn; and contrary to Michel's method, these programs place the responsibility for learning totally on the student.

The *Master Teacher* carefully worked out and refined his method of language teaching and learning over years of trial and error. His language teaching method included both what he taught (the content of the language including the grammar and vocabulary) and how he taught (the process). Although Michel developed his method specifically to teach foreign languages, it can be applied to teaching any subject matter. It is a general method of teaching and learning and is not just specifically applicable to teaching languages. What is really exciting is that Michel's method can be applied to other subject areas to produce equally amazing results.

For purposes of analysis and as a brief, initial overview, we shall see that Michel's method of teaching and learning languages can be broken into several elements:

1) The learning environment
2) The content
3) The delivery of the material

The first element begins with the learning environment and the initial frames that Michel would lay out at the start of his course. The next part deals with the content of the learning sessions. This involves breaking the material to be covered into particular units or chunks and then *sequencing* these units in an appropriate fashion. The last element has to do with the actual delivery of the material. Before we get into the actual details of the method, however, let us look at the bigger picture of what Michel accomplished in his teaching.

Below is an overview of some of the more important elements of Michel's method. We will elaborate on all of these elements and on others as well in this chapter. We must emphasize that the method includes all of the elements organized in a particular way. Critics have often tried to simplify what Michel did. For example, they take one small element out of context and then say that it is the key to the method. They make absurd statements which base Michel's method on his use of cognates or on his use of helping verbs. This demonstrates a complete misunderstanding of the process. Explanations like these always annoyed Michel because no one element on its own is the method. All elements are necessary. In the past people tried to copy some of what Michel did and then wondered why it wouldn't work. The answer is simple. All of the elements together have a synergistic effect. All are vital parts of the whole and none can be left out.

OVERVIEW OF METHOD ELEMENTS

- Course objectives
- Create incentive based learning environment
- Initial teaching and learning frames
- *Tension* and anxiety free ambiance
- *Understanding* and *knowledge*
- Memory
- *A sharpened awareness of one's own language*
- "Memory Mechanisms"™*
- Explanations
- *Heuristics* and "*Meaningful Memory Associations*"™*
- Anchors
- *Imprints*
- *Generalizations*
- *Layering*
- *Chunking and Sequencing*
- *Self-Correcting*
- *Dialogical teaching*
- *Block teaching*
- Group dynamics and *esprit de classe*

*Terms we created to describe particular aspects of the method

OVERVIEW: STRUCTURE OF COURSE CONTENT

In all of Michel's language courses three things occurred. First, the learner was taught the structure of the language. In his complete courses, the *Master Teacher* taught the entire structure (grammar) of the language and all of the tenses including the subjunctive. Michel called the tenses "*the tools of the language*," and he taught how to use them correctly. He referred to grammar as "*the structure or mechanics of the language.*" He explained the process metaphorically as follows:

> "You learn the strokes of how to *swim*. Once you learn the structure, it becomes self-sufficient."

Michel strongly emphasized that any further instruction would only undo what was previously learned.

Second, the learner was taught a complete, practical and functional vocabulary. In his audio courses, Michel provided sufficient vocabulary to enable the learner to begin to converse in the language. The students were encouraged to spend ten minutes a day reading the newspaper, magazines or interviews of interest to them. Continuing this process daily was very important in itself because it would build up vocabulary (The student would notice words that tend to reoccur and would then learn them.). It is interesting to note, that although the grammar presented in the introductory audio course is limited, even with that limitation, Michel explained further,

> "It is still enough for you to *swim* in the language. I wouldn't recommend for you to jump into the deep ocean, which you can do after my complete course."

With the initial audio course you will be comfortable *swimming* in a "deep pool or lake." As we have said, Michel would teach the students how to *swim* — how deeply they plunge and how fast they do so is up to them. After the five day course, there was no need for further instruction. The student learned how to swim and then he or she would *swim*. To use Michel's metaphor, "The style and speed of *swimming* come from practice."

Third, the learner was given the confidence which came from "swimming in the language" to use the language in actual conversations. During the entire learning process, Michel would continue to reassure his students of their progress, which, in turn, boosted their self-esteem as well. Moreover, his students ended up carrying their confidence with them into other contexts of their personal and professional lives. Michel may have been arguably the best confidence builder around!

No matter whether it was in the context of personalized one-on-one teaching or with his tapes, Michel's focus would always be on developing the practical understanding necessary to actually use the language correctly. He would teach correct grammar and a practical and functional vocabulary. He accomplished this without using grammatical terms other than *noun* and *verb* and *adjective* and without memorizing grammatical rules. Correct grammar was taught in the context of learning to speak the language correctly. It was not enough for Michel that his students just be understood in the language. Michel was a perfectionist for structure and insisted on correct grammar. We will discuss this concept further on in this chapter.

Michel would constantly remind us of the following truth,

> "What one knows based on *understanding*, one will never forget."

And in Michel's eyes, the goal of education should be to create *understanding* which in turn leads to the acquisition of *knowledge*. So how does one develop *understanding* and *knowledge* of the language? Michel would teach the language by using explanations, examples and illustrations as the students were learning the grammar and the rules. This provided the initial mental exposure. He would then reinforce this through practice, which meant that he would have the student use the new *knowledge* in a variety of sentences. Michel would come back to the initial exposure and deepen the *understanding* until it became permanent. *Understanding* was demonstrated by the ability to apply the new *knowledge* in a variety of other circumstances. The concepts of *understanding* and *knowledge* were a critical component of Michel's method, and we shall discuss them more extensively later in this chapter.

Michel would continually monitor what the student was saying for anything that indicated a lack of *understanding*. When this happened, Michel would go back to what the student already knew and would then refresh what was not understood. At that point he would reinforce it with numerous examples until it was learned.

The student was encouraged, in Michel's words, to always *"think things out."* With Michel, guessing was not permitted. And from his perspective, guessing right is just an accident. In fact for Michel, guessing right was wrong. If the student understood and knew what Michel was explaining, then he or she could think out the concept and then didn't need to guess. Michel could tell if the student was thinking it out because he would have the student translate a long, complex sentence composed of different phrases as he or she thought out, step by step, each element of the sentence. If the students made mistakes because they didn't take their time to think it out, then Michel would know that they were guessing.

COURSE OBJECTIVES

Michel would start all of his courses by covering the course objectives. As we have said, Michel demanded precision in word usage and expression; and he always insisted on specifically stating the course objectives in the following manner:

> "In three days you will acquire a solid comprehensive working knowledge of the entire structure and grammar of the language together with a solid, practical and functional vocabulary which will enable you to converse, read and write in all tenses — without the need to memorize by rote, take notes or complete homework."

After three days with Michel, the student would spend two additional days with one of Michel's instructors, practicing reading and speaking.

MICHEL MAGIC IN THE ROOM

The *Michel Thomas Learning Session* differed dramatically from the way in which language courses are traditionally taught. In fact, Michel went out of his way to insist that there be no physical, mental or spatial reminders of what we have referred to earlier as the *Mind Prison*™. He created his own process of effortless and fun learning without using any tools, props or concepts from the traditional *dis-educational system*™. Let's see how the *Master Teacher* accomplished his magic.

Before the students arrived, they already had an idea of what they were in for with Michel. They knew that they would learn a language in three days and they knew that Michel had taught thousands of students successfully. Of course, the students did not know how he achieved his outcomes. Nevertheless, they had decided to make the necessary investment in time and money to take his course. The students wanted to master a foreign language quickly, and they expected that Michel would deliver as promised. Most of them arrived both excited and curious as to how the actual process worked. Thus began the wonderful learning journey with the *Master Teacher*.

Before Michel even uttered his first word, there was already a sense of calm and trust that permeated the atmosphere of the room, which was reinforced by his charming smile and gentle manner. As an observer on the outside looking in, one immediately had a sense of a deep connection already being established between teacher and student, unlike anything experienced in the traditional *dis-educational system*™. There is a kind of *je ne sais quoi* element of almost unreal surrender of one's mind to join that of Michel's without any hesitation whatsoever on the part of the student or students. Michel, with an air of reassuring self-confidence in both his voice and physiology, seemed to have already set the tone between him and his student (or students). This, in turn, laid the groundwork for three days of sheer delight and great excitement and astonishingly all of this in the context of language learning. "I always give more than is expected, never less. And it is not being generous. This is who I am," he said. And this applies to everything that Michel did in his personal life as well.

Now the real fun began. Michel would not waste time with small talk. He would make immediate eye contact with the student or students. As we shall later see, this detail is quite a significant part of the magic and mystery surrounding the method. When the *Master Teacher* started his language course, he would immediately lay out the course objectives followed by a set of ground rules for the course which we will refer to as a series of *"initial or introductory frames."* Michel's initial frames already marked a complete break from tradition — they completely defied the traditional "school rules" and modalities which are written in stone as part of the current *dis-educational system*™.

Because his frames were so diametrically opposed to the expectations of anyone who has gone through the *Mind Prison*™, the students already had relieved looks on their faces when he addressed them at the beginning of each course. By then they were sitting comfortably in their armchairs as he began by telling them what they were going to achieve:

> "You are here to learn, and what you will achieve in a matter of a few days, three days, is that you will have acquired a solid, comprehensive *knowledge* of the entire structure and grammar of the target language, including all tenses including the subjunctive and a practical and functional vocabulary."

Much to their amazement, Michel would go on to tell them that all this would be accomplished without doing the following:

- Without memorization - There is never anything to memorize.
- Without learning by rote
- Without the use of textbooks
- Without taking notes - Notes are not allowed.
- Without homework - Homework is absolutely not allowed — not even mental homework.
- Without ever *trying to remember* anything.

Because as Michel added,

> "The full responsibility for your remembering will be in the teaching — my teaching."

At this point the students were really curious and excited. They didn't know how they could learn this way because they had never done so before. They were used to traditional educational methods. What Michel had just said was contrary to all of their previous learning experiences. They were about to take a journey to a new kind of learning experience — a magical one — and they were ready to discover how it worked. And in order to discover how it worked, we need to explore these initial frames we just summarized more closely.

INITIAL FRAMES

One of the unique aspects of Michel's method has to do with the initial frames that he laid out at the very beginning of the learning session. A *"frame"* is a way of providing context for information in order to clarify the meaning of the content presented. If you change the frame, you will change the meaning of the content. The first frames he would set were intended to explain the contents of the course, and to describe what the objectives were and how they would be achieved. Michel would also present the time frames and the logistics of the course at the start. For Michel's complete courses, the course would begin with three days with Michel followed by two days with his instructors. The objective, as we have indicated, was for the learner to develop

> "...a solid and comprehensive *knowledge* (the emphasis is on *knowledge*) of the entire structure of the language, meaning the entire grammar in all tenses, and a practical and functional vocabulary enabling the learner to use the language after that in speaking, reading and writing."

In the course of our modeling Michel, he would often repeat this objective and was quite adamant about the precise wording of it. One learned all the tenses including the subjunctive.

INITIAL FRAMES

- Course objectives
- What you will accomplish
- How this will be done
- Make yourself comfortable
- Let go of all *tension*
- Do not write or take notes.
- Do not *try* to remember.
- Remembering is the teacher's and not the learner's responsibility
- Give yourself time to think.
- Never get annoyed at yourself if you make a mistake.
- Let go of all expectations
- Learning should be accompanied by a feeling of great joy

All of this was achieved without the traditional modalities — without drills, memorizing, learning by rote, taking notes and homework, not even mental homework (which Michel said was absolutely not allowed). There were no textbooks and there was nothing to read during the initial three days. One would certainly not be allowed to take notes. Every one of the traditional modalities mentioned here creates a great deal of *tension* in the learner, and Michel realized that *tension* is one of the greatest enemies of learning. For this reason he wanted no part of these negative associations incorporated into his learning process. Hence, Michel would go to great lengths to remove any possible source of *tension* in the learner from the very beginning. Although we will elaborate on this further in this chapter, we will briefly mention that Michel would inform his students from the start, that he, as their teacher, would be taking full responsibility for their learning and for their remembering.

One may ask how it is possible to learn to speak, read and write a language without textbooks, without rote memorization and without taking notes. This is what was so amazing about Michel's method. During the learning process where one doesn't take notes, and one doesn't have textbooks, one learns how to pronounce and how to spell correctly. He explained this as follows:

> "If you know how to spell, then you will also know how to write. And if you know how to write, then you will know how to read. It is exciting to see that after three days students who started with zero knowledge of the language will be able to read. And they will also be able to pronounce correctly what they are reading. They will know where to put the stress on words."

Students were always surprised to learn that there was no note taking in Michel's courses and that it should be of no concern. About being concerned, a former student, a medical journalist said: "Not at all because part of Michel's genius — he's a real systems person — is the built-in redundancy."

After three days with Michel, the learner would spend another two days with Michel's instructors reading and discussing. In this two day period, the learner would develop further proficiency. Here the students were given short contemporary passages to read and discuss. This helped to build up vocabulary and started the student in the process of reading the language. Discussion took place in the target language.

After these two days, the learner would be encouraged to spend only ten minutes a day on a daily basis reading a newspaper, magazine or interview of interest to him or her in the newly acquired language. According to Michel, spending ten minutes a day was much more important and more effective than spending a few hours a week doing the same thing. Also, Michel preferred that the reading be done without the use of a dictionary. The key was to be consistent.

LEARNING ENVIRONMENT — EASE OF LEARNING

Early on Michel realized the importance of appropriate settings or learning environments that support and nurture learning and the acquisition of *knowledge*. He created a specific physical and mental environment that supports the entire learning process from its very inception. The result was a self-sustaining system that maintained a *tension*-free atmosphere which enhanced the entire learning process from start to finish, even deepening it as the session continued. The ambiance that Michel created served to help unleash at a deep level, one's vast learning potential. The physical structure he created to support the learning process complemented the clever structuring of the mental associations of his subject matter. These elements are two parts of the same whole. Further in this chapter, we will discuss the latter in more detail.

Why did Michel take such great care over the orchestration of the learning milieu? Michel discovered that within everyone there is an innate potential for learning. He also realized that the degree of this potential can vary depending on the individual and on the learning milieu. Michel did not base his method on any sensitivity or feeling for languages on the part of the student. His method was designed to teach even those learners who believe that they are incapable of learning a foreign language. Furthermore, certain conditions are necessary to actualize the *innate drive for learning* which Michel believed to be the most important thing that every student possesses. At a very deep level, Michel knew that this innate drive was still undiscovered and ignored by the traditional educational system, in which he said that teachers choke the drive "through misuse and ignorance."

Michel further explained his insistence on creating a particular ambience that is conducive to learning:

> I think that it is self-evident that these inner potentials require the right environment in order to take off and soar. If not, they will remain just that, potentials, dormant perhaps, as they so frequently are in students within traditional classroom settings. This is why I am insistent upon a particular kind of milieu. I look for an environment defined by years of examined experience, because I look for the break-through that leads to tapping the learning potentials within each student. Now this is a tenet of my method: with a carefully wrought system administered under replicable conditions, a breakthrough will occur and stimulate those innate potentials.

The potentials of students are immense because of this drive. This is why Michel took such great care in the creation and maintenance of both the physical and psychological elements of the learning environment to reawaken this *innate drive*.

Moreover, Michel realized that once one taps into the learning potential and once the breakthrough occurs, it is necessary to sustain and to deepen it. He also had a method in which to do this, as we shall see later in this chapter. Michel's method was based on the development of self-worth in the student. Michel was aware of the psychological principle "that each successive interaction in one's environment generates important feelings of personal efficacy and self-worth." Michel also realized the following:

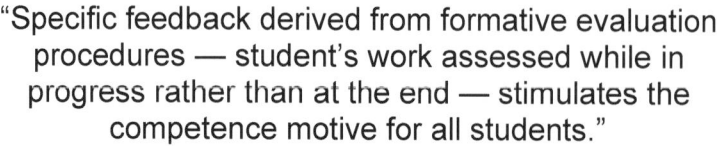

"Specific feedback derived from formative evaluation procedures — student's work assessed while in progress rather than at the end — stimulates the competence motive for all students."

This is why Michel would use constant reinforcement as part of his method. It allows the student to monitor his or her own progress and to experience immediately the immense joy and excitement that it generates. This is the key to sustaining and enhancing the innate learning potential.

A UNIQUE LEARNING AMBIANCE

So how would Michel create the special physical and psychological ambiance that enhances learning? First, let us describe the physical setting. Michel taught his live course in his office or in a comfortable setting elsewhere. The room always included comfortable arm chairs. In Michel's office, there were comfortable leather arm chairs for both Michel and the learner. There were plants, a table and a lamp. Plants and/or flowers were an important ingredient in this ambiance. Michel believed that it was not necessary to have a table or desk on which to write, for the simple reason that the student had no need to write anything or to take notes. Also, the room should be neat and clean and there should be no distractions. Ideally, rooms should have windows otherwise the students are enclosed in a windowless space which will trigger an unconscious feeling of entrapment and the negative *tension*-creating associations that are connected to the *Mind Prison*™.

In creating his carefully constructed learning environment, Michel went to great lengths to erase all previous negative associations with learning. Michel's learning environment was as far removed from a classroom, physically and psychologically, as one could get. In it we found no visual, no auditory, no kinesthetic or olfactory reminders of the traditional classroom. For example, in his ideal learning environment there were no desks and no blackboards or flip charts or overhead projectors. There was no smell of chalk or erasers or of magic markers. There were no school bells and no class schedules. Rather, it was a physical space where traditional belief systems had been replaced by Michel's unique perspective on the learning process of the human mind which created and reinforced new beliefs about learning.

We have just discussed the elements of the physical learning environment which the *Master Teacher* intentionally designed. There is another aspect of the learning environment to consider: How did Michel create the concomitant psychological environment for learning? Let us assume a scenario in which there was one learner taking the course in Michel's learning space. The student was ushered into a comfortable room as previously described.

The learner was already comfortable when Michel entered the room. Michel would greet the learner, would shake the person's hand and would then sit down right across from the learner. With his approachable yet confident manner and warm smile, Michel would always immediately put the learner at ease. Michel's demeanor was gentle and non-threatening. His voice was calm and steady, yet subtly tinged with a hint of excitement. He would not waste time on small talk, but jumped right into the task at hand, doing what he did best with great passion.

Michel did not believe in authoritarian teaching nor did he believe that the teacher should be put on a pedestal, as in the traditional *dis-educational system*™. Over the years, Michel had witnessed the typical teacher/student interaction in the current *dis-educational system*™. He would always get quite upset whenever he spoke about the lack of communication between teacher and student. Even worse, he said, "is that teachers love to get in front of a class to lecture for hours merely to show off what they think they know."

REAL TEACHING VERSUS LECTURING

Michel was not fond of lecturing. From his perspective, lecturing does not constitute what he called "*proper*" or "*real teaching.*" He thought that in some cases lecturing may be about showing off on the part of certain teachers, and at the same time he acknowledged that there were some good teachers who are not about showing off. He believed that in certain cases lecturing could be an acceptable means of teaching when done effectively. However, with lecturing there is the issue of connecting with students. For Michel, this connection was a vital aspect of proper or real teaching and represented a core issue. As Michel explained,

> "When teachers lecture, they usually do not connect with their students. They do not know what their students are thinking."

Michel stressed that lecturing *per se,* was not the problem. Instead, it is a matter of how it is done. In this vein, Michel explained that teachers should know "how to receive." In the rare moments when Michel would lecture, he was "the receiver." If teachers don't connect with their students, then how are they to know whether or not the students understand the subject matter? Lecturing makes it very difficult to do. Michel thought that teachers who lecture cannot decipher a student's needs, and if they cannot read their students, then they should not be lecturing.

The usual purpose of most lectures is to reel off lots of data which is to be regurgitated back in the form of tests. We know that tests do not assess understanding. In some, although not in all cases, tests can be a way to simply feed the lecturer's narcissism by mirroring back the information presented. It's often another way of placing the teacher on a pedestal.

Michel, on the other hand, believed that the teacher and student are on an equal level. From his perspective, teachers who lecture are often expressing the needs of their ego to stand out among the crowd and show of their perceived superiority over their students. Often they simply want to hear themselves talk. In Michel's world, there was no sense of superiority on his part. He did not feel the need to engage in power plays or in ego games nor did he believe that they should ever be part of proper or real teaching. The process here is all about collaborative learning. Real teaching is interactive and is not lecturing, according to Michel. Unfortunately, lecturing is something which has been done for centuries. As we mentioned in Chapter Four, even worse was that in the past, lectures were conducted in Latin, and not in the language of the people. Michel was always emphatic:

> "A teacher does not lecture."

For Michel, the essence of real teaching is "*interchange*." Teaching is an *interchange* involving explaining and responding, which leads to *understanding* and *knowledge*. Michel, the *Master Teacher* in every way, would always be aware of students' emotional states, blocks, prior traumatic learning experiences, etc. that could interfere or create *tension* and therefore negatively impact learning. Furthermore, he would be quick to remedy the situation. Michel was able to do this because he didn't lecture. Instead, he would connect with his students on a deep level. He would achieve this in a deliberate manner, as we shall see later in this chapter in our discussion of group dynamics. The students were like cherished flowers. Michel did not merely water the flowers. He would nurture them as well.

As we have said, once the student was comfortably seated in his learning environment, Michel would lay out the course outcomes and the initial learning frames. He would begin by telling the student exactly what the course consisted of and what to expect. This was followed by the learning frames which further enhanced the psychological environment for learning to occur. The learning frames involved the "do's" and the "don'ts." The "do's" included letting go of all *tension* and being comfortable.

THE ELIMINATION OF ALL *TENSION*

There are three critically important concepts to understanding the *Master Teacher*'s method. These involve:

1) The eliminaton of all *tension*,
2) Remembering
3) The relation between *understanding* and *knowledge*.

These three concepts help to explain how Michel's method differed from traditional methods. We need to discuss each one in turn in order to provide a basis for a deeper understanding of the *Michel Thomas Method*. We will begin with Michel's ideas on the elimination of *tension*.

Educators often place an emphasis on relaxation. For Michel, this is to put the cart before the horse. Instead, for Michel, the important thing is to eliminate any form of *tension*. Then relaxation will naturally follow. Michel clarified the *tension*/relaxation dichotomy in this way:

> "To relax and to try to relax are not so important. To me what I am watching for is not to have any form of *tension*. And once you remove *tension*, relaxation will come automatically. You can be comfortable and relaxed and still build up a lot of *tension*. Again, we are talking here about important concepts."

As trainers, we know that holding *tension* in the mind/body inhibits the rate at which students learn, while *tension*-free students will find the doors to learning wide open within them.

Michel tried to remove all *tension* before he even started the language learning process. He did this immediately, as soon as he uttered his first word about his objectives. Michel explained it as follows:

> They are listening to me and in listening to me, I am not telling them to relax really. I don't use the word "relax." They are in comfortable chairs, so I don't need to tell them *to relax*. I tell them that they will be exposed to a method where they are not to *try to remember* anything. The emphasis is on *trying*. Remembering is one thing, but don't *try*. Whatever you do, don't *try to remember* and I will tell them why. Because the responsibility for your remembering is with me. It is my job. Remembering is not your job. Not *trying to remember* immediately removes *tension* and brings about relaxation. So don't *try*. If I say that, then that immediately removes *tension*.

Thus, all the remembering on the part of the students was Michel's responsibility. How can they be anything but relaxed!

This emphasis on the removal of *tension* is surprisingly new to all of his students. He described his interaction with his students in the following way:

> I don't want to call it shock. It is not a shock because the word 'shock' creates *tension*. It is instead, amazement. So they say, you don't want me to *try* so I won't *try*. That is easier for them than to talk about remembering. I don't want you to *try*. Because the responsibility for your remembering is my job. Don't *try* to take my job away from me. If you don't remember something, it is up to me to know why you don't remember. It is up to me to know why you don't remember and to know what to do about it. So that process, what to do about your remembering is my job. Don't *try* to do it yourself. With this, I remove already all *tension* before I even start.

Imagine learning between eighteen and twenty-two tenses in three days and having the responsibility for remembering them all placed on the shoulders of the teacher! That is precisely what Michel was so delighted to do every time he taught a course. In the traditional *Mind Prison*™, remembering is equated with memorizing. The student has to work at it, has to do homework, has to work hard and has to get good grades. By contrast, Michel was assuming full responsibility for remembering and taking away from the student the anxiety created by the burden of memorizing and cramming.

Michel explained further:

> Another important thing that comes up with the distinction between relaxation and removal of *tension*…I usually succeed in removing all *tension* before I even start with what I just explained. That is already done. On some occasions, some learners may tense up, and that will register in me if they do it. I notice it immediately and do something to remove the source of the *tension*.

Often learners, themselves, are carriers of anxiety and *tension*. They bring in the baggage of *tension* with them because this is what they have learned to do in the traditional educational system. Others may maintain *tension* in their bodies due to personal or professional problems. They have learned how to increase their *tension* levels by memorizing and by cramming and their *tension* is only released by testing. Then they can forget everything and begin the process again. For many learners forgetting is actually the release of their *tension*, i.e., the *tension* of cramming and memorizing. This is a mental release. Michel's method was designed to dispel this *tension* from the beginning by removing its source. The method completely removes any form of *tension* or any form of anxiety that will interfere with learning. Relaxation is a by-product of this effort.

So Michel succeeded in breaking down the traditional belief systems around learning and especially in respect to language learning — belief systems that have been passed from one generation to the next. He succeeded in completely eliminating the negative associations attached to the traditional learning process listed below:

TRADITIONAL DEMANDS OF LEARNING

- Learning Means Hard Work
- Learning Means *Trying* Hard
- Learning Creates Pain
- Learning Requires Concentrated Effort
- Learning Demands Study
- Learning Generates *Tension*
- Learning Requires Homework
- Learning Creates Anxiety
- Learning Requires Memorizing and Learning by Rote
- Learning Requires Cramming for Tests

Let us summarize how Michel's method differs from traditional teaching methods. First, there is no need to write or to take notes. With Michel's learning process, learning is easy, a source of immense pleasure and creates great excitement. There is no hard work, no *trying* hard, no pain, no concentrated effort required, no study, no *tension*, no homework and no anxiety. Furthermore, there are no black boards or visual aids and there are no text books. There will be no lectures and tests. Real teaching is not lecturing. As Michel always emphasized,

> "Learning will take place without memorization, without drills, without learning by rote, without taking notes which is not allowed, without textbooks and without homework, which is absolutely not allowed."

All of these frames do two things. First, they remove all associations with previous learning situations about which the student may feel negatively. Second, they remove all sources of *tension* associated with traditional learning methods.

What are some of the things that produce *tension*? First, is an authoritarian teacher. Second, is a teacher who lectures, and a student furiously trying to take notes to keep up with what the teacher is saying. Third, are homework assignments which fill up the time outside of class and achieve little. Fourth, are textbooks which must be studied and remembered. Fifth, are papers and reports which take time to write and often students are simply regurgitating information with no real *understanding* or acquisition of *knowledge*. Underlying all of these things is the element that is the greatest source of *tension* — testing and grading — and the anxiety and *tension* associated with them. In Michel's method, as we have seen, all of these are eliminated!

Why does the removal of *tension* facilitate learning? In our own work as trainers and coaches, we have discovered that *tension* exists in the mind and in the body. Both physical and mental *tensions* are unconscious responses to stress and anxiety. Human beings don't consciously tense. They unconsciously tense. Telling people to relax does not remove the *tension*. They may be able to consciously control physical *tension* temporarily, but as soon as they go unconscious, the *tension* will return. *Tension* distracts attention from the here and now and focuses it on the future. Mental *tension* occupies the mind with worry and stress-producing anxiety. All of this interferes with learning which can only occur in what we call "*in the now*," or the present moment. Thinking out can only occur in the now. So all *tension*, mental and physical interferes with learning. *Tension* drains attention and the ability to focus. And physical *tension* drains energy. Anything that diverts attention and energy will adversely affect learning.

So how does one get rid of physical and mental *tension*? Michel had the simple answer. Eliminate the source and cause of the *tension* from the beginning. *Tension* is an unconscious response to a stressful environment. Remove the stress in the environment and the *tension* will disappear. This is why Michel so carefully crafted his initial frames to eliminate all stress and anxiety from the beginning. Michel realized that even if he placed no stress on the students, the students can still manufacture it themselves. So Michel also had to prevent the students from producing stress for themselves. He did this in two ways. First is by removing all responsibility for learning from the students. Second is by giving the students a continual series of positive reinforcements which continually build their feelings of personal efficacy and self-worth. With all responsibility for learning gone and with no anxiety and with continual success, all *tension* quickly drops away and learning is free to occur.

THE PARADOX OF *TRYING*

As we have just explained, the notion of *tension* was an interesting one in the world of Michel Thomas. He was quite adamant in asserting that *tension* within the traditional system is based on certain learning modalities which are inherent in the system: on cramming for tests, on memorizing, on rote learning and on home work. In this light, it is important to understand the distinction that Michel made between *tension* and relaxation. First of all, in Michel's world, unlike in the traditional system, *tension* does not exist. As we have seen, from the very beginning frame he would lay out, Michel's goal was the *total removal of all tension*, and not relaxation.

An interesting paradox of sorts exists here: in order to create relaxation, you have to *try* to relax. And *trying* produces *tension*. A student may say: "I am going to *try* to relax." That merely generates *tension*. Instead, Michel was a master of completely removing *tension*, as we pointed out earlier. Furthermore, within the traditional *dis-educational system*™, students come to class with *tension*, with expectations and with anxieties, all of which create more *tension*. There is an immediate association created of "I'll *try*." or "I don't know if it will work, but I'll *try* anyway." Thus, with expectation and anxiety there is *tension*, made more intense by *trying*; and the *tension* is saying "not to relax." According to Michel,

> "The *tension* has to be totally, and I mean totally, removed in order to create the receptivity for *real learning*."

Creating *tension* merely serves to block the mind.

> When tense, the student is basically learning only with his conscious mind (although minimally), when, in fact, learning should occur ideally with a balance of using both the conscious and subconscious minds.

What a waste to simply tap into only part of the potential of the human mind! The wonder of the subconscious mind is that it acts like an eternal sponge, soaking in everything, encoding it in the mind forever. Any *tension*, however, will close rather quickly the doors to the subconscious mind.

So why should it be surprising that Michel conferred the rather dubious description of "*prison*" to our present educational system. Instead of sparking excitement in students, as did Michel's personal method with his own students, the traditional system uses a learning process that "turns most people off." Why? Because, as Michel beautifully expressed, "it is based on *work, tension*, on paying attention, on *cramming*, on *memorization, and* on *concentration*," all words which, in themselves, unconsciously create *tension* in the mind as well as in the body.

Cramming, memorization and learning by rote have no place in Michel's world. The current educational *dis-educational system*™ is based on these ineffective learning methods. Cramming all night and day for a test does not accomplish anything. One ends up having to take a meaningless multiple-choice test where one is presented with four or five choices. From the start, one can eliminate at least two of the options because they do not make sense. More often than not, one is in a situation of guessing between two possible answers. Success or failure on a test comes down, then to correct guessing. One may be fortunate or lucky enough to be able to pass a test without knowing anything, simply by guessing the correct answer. The whole process is insane. Even if one were to remember what one learned in cramming for a test, we all know that one will not be able to retake the test just five days later with the same results. We will discuss further the concepts of memorization, guessing, cramming for tests, etc. later in this chapter.

In our work as professional behavioral modelers and trainers, we are well aware of the profound mind/body connection, and over the years we have witnessed firsthand, how *tension* created in the mind is necessarily linked to the physical body where it creates real muscle *tension*. Muscle *tension*, in turn, creates fatigue. All of our work and research on learning and training has shown that learning is blocked when the mind/body connection is stressed and tense. Moreover, the mind/body connection affects attitude. The end result is an unpleasant learning experience for the student in which his mind, body and spirit have been poisoned by *tension* (and attention).

We would also like to take note of the notion of fatigue because in the context of learning, fatigue is an interesting concept. First, it is important to know what one means by fatigue. For example, there is both mental and physical fatigue and they do not necessarily go together. Indeed, a person may be extremely physically fatigued, but it will not prevent the person from receiving messages from the teacher or from understanding and absorbing what is being taught because the person is not mentally fatigued. In fact, the excitement of learning can actually help the person to forget the physical fatigue.

The same goes for teachers, and Michel easily attested to this fact based on a personal experience about a year before his passing. At the end of 2003, Michel was hit by a car while crossing the street in front of his home. And, as we indicated in his biographical vignette, Michel had an amazing history of experiencing larger-than-life situations. Nothing had changed after all these years. He was not just hit by some little vehicle. No, it was a stretch limousine! Fortunately for all of us, Michel's split second, lightning-quick reflexes saved him from real serious injury or death at that time.

The point is that even after being badly bruised and in the hospital on IVs, Michel was nevertheless determined to teach his class two days after the accident, and once again, achieved his usual phenomenal results in spite of his less than perfect physical condition. The student was never even aware of what had happened to him. Being struck by a stretch limousine could not even squelch Michel's innate drive! Here was the perfect example of how Michel's excitement of teaching spurred him to do what many others might think impossible.

The very excitement of teaching helped him to forget the physical pain and discomfort he was experiencing as a result of his accident. How many teachers or students do you know who would have reacted in such a way? Very few, because as Michel would frequently point out: "The excitement for learning does not exist in them." He believed that more often than not, students will find some lame excuse to not attend school for just a little cold because their *innate drive for learning* still remains dormant and their excitement has been stifled.

From day one, the child goes to school with *tension* and comes home only to be exposed to additional *tension* by parents who ask, "What did you learn in school today?" The *tension* is once again reinforced on an even higher level, so that the child walks around carrying *tension* in his entire body. The parent then admonishes the child for not answering the question as the parent would like. This is exactly the opposite of what learning should be. "All learning," asserted Michel, "should begin or lead into a tremendous feeling of excitement, of high excitement." Mere excitement is not enough. Learning must engender "great, great excitement" otherwise it cannot be legitimately called learning in Michel's view.

In some circles, *tension* is actually expected because it has become so assimilated into the system that it, quite frankly, appears to be the norm. It is as though if you don't feel tense when learning, then something is wrong with you. Children then carry their mental and physical *tension* into adulthood. Both adults and children bring negative expectations about learning with them wherever they go. Michel would recall many times in conversations just how many adults he had seen over the years, who literally breathe *tension* daily when he met them for the first time. They, however, are the fortunate ones who had crossed Michel's path. Thanks to Michel's brilliant method and reassuring manner, these lucky individuals were effortlessly transformed into *tension*-free students who came away having learned an additional valuable tool they had otherwise never thought possible — proficiency in a foreign language in three days!

Interestingly, Michel's teaching experience had confirmed many times over that the more university degrees a person has, the more difficult and challenging it is to open the doors of their minds to learning in a new way. In fact, the more "successful" these people have been in school, in terms of passing the requisite tests to get their respective degrees within the existing system, the more resistant they are to giving up old patterns and to opening up to new ways of learning. The result was that it took Michel a little longer to teach them using his method because his approach was so antithetical to the one used in the traditional system.

He found that those within the system who are most successful are very proud of their success and of their ability to "learn" by following the rules of the traditional system. The other interesting phenomenon with these so-called successful students is that they were always the ones among Michel's students who blamed themselves when they made a mistake. Michel was quick to tell them not to blame themselves because he was the one who accepted total responsibility for their learning.

As we shall see in the next section, in Michel's world, the responsibility for remembering is the responsibility of the teacher. If students made a mistake, it was his problem, not theirs. It is up to the teacher to determine why the mistake was made in the first place and to do something about it. This unique concept of the teacher taking complete responsibility for learning and for remembering rather than the student is a major key to the *Michel Thomas Method*, as we will now explain.

THE SECRET OF REMEMBERING

Michel's initial frames or ground rules did not stop with his ideas on *tension* and on *trying*. The next frames deal with what we call the *"Secret of Remembering."* These frames serve to refine Michel's concept of not *"trying to remember."* In the previous section, we discussed this component of the method in relation to the notion of *tension*. We would now like to consider this component of not *trying to remember* from the perspective of what we have named *"memory mechanisms."*™ Michel specifically explained to us his concept of not *trying to remember* as follows:

> What I expect from you, and this is very important, is that you never *try to remember*. And I emphasize never to *try to remember* because the *trying*, not the remembering, is *tension-producing* and will interfere with learning. I want to make it clear, that when I say 'never *try to remember*' it doesn't mean 'not to remember,' but it means not to *try*. Never *try to remember* because this is a method where the responsibility for your remembering lies with the teacher and not with the learner. *All of your remembering is my responsibility.* Your responsibility is not to *try*. This means that at any point, if you don't remember anything whatsoever, then you don't have to *try*. It is not your responsibility. It is my responsibility. And it is up to me and it will always be up to me to know why you don't remember and what to do about it. That is my job and don't try to take it away from me.

As one can see, Michel was quite precise with his wording of the concept of not *trying to remember* for it is such a critical part of his method. And he will frequently come back to it in his teaching, just as he did during our modeling process.

Michel would assume full responsibility for what was happening at every moment: for remembering, for learning and for retention of content. Just saying this produced the immediate effect of removing any sense of self-consciousness on the part of the students which would otherwise inhibit their learning process. The students knew that Michel was the "*giver*" and they, as learners, were the "*receivers.*" They simply had to sit back and accept the gifts of *understanding*, *knowledge* and joy which Michel would offer them.

True learning lies in good teaching and in his teaching Michel welcomed the responsibility for the students' learning with open arms. There was no need for the students to feel guilty or to lose confidence. Any mistakes were transformed into *understanding*. The students end up *understanding* what they did and why they made the mistake. And they appreciated their individual progress all the more. "At times you may get annoyed with yourself and say, 'Oh, I should know it.' Don't. It is up to me," declared Michel.

The Oscar-winning British actress, Emma Thompson, learned Spanish from Michel in 1997 and is an outspoken fan of both the man and his method. In an article which appeared in the Guardian several years later, she recalled an incident which made a lasting impression upon her: "I couldn't remember something simple and I started to cry, because I was frustrated with myself. He said, 'You don't understand — it's my fault.' And the effect of that is remarkable, it forces you to relax." This is precisely what Michel accomplished every time he taught. Michel would lift the burden of responsibility off of the student, and in so doing released the *tension* associated with it. By the way, if anyone had ever tried to take the responsibility of learning away from Michel, they would have wondered what hit them.

This concept of not *trying to remember* is a critical component of Michel's method and he would often purposefully repeat himself in order to drive in the point. That is the reason why we often come back to this concept as we proceed in the discussion of his method. Michel wanted to stress the importance of not *trying to remember* and in explaining his approach to us, he made a very clear distinction between *trying to remember* and "*remembering.*" He insisted that the two should not be confused.

Remembering occurs when one does not *try*. *Trying*, as we have said, is *tension*-producing while remembering is not. When a student didn't remember something, it may have been that he/she did not quite understand. It is certainly not because the student did not *try* hard enough. It was up to Michel, the teacher, to determine why the student did not understand a particular concept in the first place, which is a far cry from traditional education.

Michel believed that the effort to remember creates two problems. First it doesn't work. *Trying to remember*, cramming, or rote learning may lead to short-term recall; and it is just as quickly forgotten. In fact, forgetting is often the mental release of the *tension* of cramming and *trying to remember*. Cramming, in the sense of cramming to pass a test, is a complete waste of time because one is simply not able to repeat the same test five days later. As Michel rightfully pointed out, "You may be a good student who passes tests. So what!" Memorization is merely recollection and is not learning. He added that memorization is a forced process which blocks the natural learning channels of the mind. Crammed knowledge and memorized knowledge do not represent real *knowledge* because real *knowledge* is based on *understanding*

The second problem is that *trying* to do anything produces *tension*. "*Trying to remember*" produces even greater *tension*. Michel's method was designed to eliminate all *tension*. With the concept of the teacher assuming the entire responsibility for remembering, Michel made an important distinction.

> He was not taking over the responsibility of the students' memory. Rather, he was taking charge of their remembering.

And remembering has to be based on *understanding*. Michel stated this well:

> "Remembering without *understanding* is memorizing."

In summary, Michel's frames were as follows:

- There is nothing to memorize.
- Don't *try to remember* anything
- There is no memorization or rote learning.
- There is no *trying*.
- There is no making any effort to remember.
- One should not *try to remember* from one second to the next.
- There is no *trying to remember* anything.
- Simply put, there is no *trying*.

These are the essence of our *memory mechanisms*™ (Michel thought that our choice of expression was a perfect description for what he did as part of his method.).

When Michel would introduce a new concept, the tendency for many people was to *try* to grasp it and hold onto it. The reaction is like, "Oh, that is something new, and I have to remember it." The "have to" erases it and makes it difficult to come back to it. While the student is *trying to remember* it, he or she is stuck in the past. The very act of *trying* to hold on to it causes the student to lose it. Michel's point was to let it go because he would come back and reinforce it. It was not necessary to grasp it completely the first time because Michel deliberately built redundancy into his teaching and would reinforce a concept until it became natural. It may seem arbitrary the first time, but after several times it would become natural. So when Michel would make what he called an "*initial imprint,*" it was important to leave it alone, not to hold onto it. If you left it alone, then it was there for you. In fact, Michel always would find it to be an interesting process to come back to it.

When Michel returned to it, the student would either immediately know it or he or she would have had what Michel called the "*aha experience*" or "*aha reaction.*" This aha experience would, in turn, deepen the *imprint* and then the student would know it. If they didn't have the experience, Michel would reinforce it once again. He said that it was rare for him to come back to it a second time without an immediate reaction from the student. Michel found this to be an interesting phenomenon from a learning perspective. We will come back to Michel's concept of *imprints* later in the chapter.

So why did what we named Michel's "*memory mechanisms*"™ and remembering instructions work so well? We have found that there are two key points in answer to this. First, is to eliminate anything that will interfere with memory. The primary thing that needs to be eliminated is any *tension* from stress, anxiety or expectation. Michel accomplished this by placing the responsibility for remembering on himself and not on the student.

Second, is the memory process itself. Remembering is largely an unconscious process. It occurs automatically. *Trying*, on the other hand, is a conscious process. Conscious *trying* interferes with unconscious remembering. Holding on to the moment is a conscious process. As soon as we *try* to hold on to the moment, that moment is in the past and we are no longer in the now or the present moment.

> We can't emphasize enough the fact that learning and remembering occur *in the now*.

By not *trying* to hold on, we are able to stay in the now and to allow the automatic memory process to function.

THE TRUTH ABOUT MEMORY

In our own research on learning over the years (which we incorporated into our *Learning How to Learn Technology*™ in the early 1990's and into our trainings ever since), we discovered several important truths regarding memory which will shed light on why Michel's approach was so effective. We found that memory is a three-way process.

1) First one must capture the information in short term memory from the start.

2) Second one must place it in storage in long term memory.

3) Third one must be able to recall it out of long term memory.

These processes all occur automatically as well as unconsciously with no effort on our part. We remember many things without ever having *tried* either to remember them or to recall them. The process just happens unconsciously.

There is a great deal of research on memory. This research indicates that there is a correlation between the time spent studying and the amount recalled. The same research indicates, however, that the study methods are more important than the time spent studying. Research concludes that it is very difficult to remember nonsense syllables, but it is easy to remember information that is organized and interconnected.

> In other words, it is easiest to remember things that are clearly explained and that can fit easily into our previously existing understanding.

It is difficult to remember anything that is confusing or anything out of which one cannot make sense.

This is why clear explanations are so important. They connect up what we are learning to what we already know. *Trying* harder to remember what is confusing is not the answer. "Garbage in, garbage out," as the saying goes. The solution to memory is not to put more effort into it. In fact this has the opposite effect. The solution is to provide clear explanations that lead to automatic and unconscious recall.

Michel brilliantly devised a component of his method which we have chosen to name "*meaningful memory associations*"™ which are, in essence, powerful *heuristic* devices to assist memory. We will discuss this element of the *Michel Thomas Method* in more detail in a later section. For the purpose of the present discussion, we would like to stress that memory research shows that a powerful association to something that we already know is one of the best ways to remember. Research also shows, as Michel often pointed out, that it is easy to remember the lyrics to a song or the words to a poem that one sings. Research indicates that the use of mnemonics and singing or chanting is also a powerful way to remember. For example, opera singers always remember what they sing. They are capable of singing an aria at any time. Average people can also often remember lyrics to a song that they particularly like.

The real issue here is: Why do we forget? We forget because of interference. We remember what is unique but we can't remember what is indistinguishable from everything else. This is another reason why clear explanations are so important. They enable us to fit new information into our existing knowledge base. Explanations allow us to take in and to connect up with what we already know. Memorization and cramming are conscious processes involving repetition. They focus on remembering rather than on connecting.

Memorization and cramming are problematic in two ways. First, is the fact that what is memorized is quickly forgotten because it is not connected to something we know. Second is that simply parroting back information does not produce the *understanding* which is critical to *knowing*. This leads us to Michel's next critically important component of his method, which is the concept of *understanding*. Also, as we will see in the next chapter on "Theory and Practice," this issue lies at the heart of one of the major shifts in modern pedagogical thinking. We will also see that Michel was far ahead of today's new school of thought.

THE KEY TO *UNDERSTANDING*

We have already mentioned the importance of the *Master Teacher's* beliefs about learning and *understanding* and memory. Let us summarize them briefly.

- Learning is based on *understanding* and knowing.
- What one *knows*, which is based on *understanding*, one will never forget.
- *Understanding* means that the *knowledge* is organized and interconnected.

> The key to education is to transfer *understanding* which leads to the acquisition of *knowledge*.

THE *MICHEL THOMAS METHOD*: THE *MASTER TEACHER'S* MODEL

The evidence of *understanding* is the ability to *generalize* and to apply the *knowledge* to solve problems in different situations. You can memorize a set of formulas, which students often do, but this does not mean that you will be able to apply the formulas in the real world to solve problems. This requires *understanding* and *knowledge* and critical thinking. Michel emphasized that everything is understood in the moment. Learning is what we call in our terminology an "*in time*" process, one that occurs in the present moment, in the now. Learning does not occur in the past or in the future. Michel wanted learners not to *try* to hold on to the moment of *understanding* because he would come back to it and deepen it until it became permanent. In short, *understanding* and *knowledge*, and not rote memory, are the key to learning. Regarding this distinction, Michel often iterated a personal mantram of sorts:

> "You can't forget what you know and understand. What one knows, one will never forget."

You may block it for a moment, but you can't forget it. You may block what you know, as, for example, with the tip of the tongue phenomenon, but you can't forget it.

There is an interesting twist about remembering and blocking which we will touch upon. How often do you hear someone say, "Don't forget!" One first has to know something in order to forget it. So to say, "Don't forget" means nothing unless you already knew something about what you are told not to forget. If a person is referring to an event or situation which one has never experienced, then one is incapable of remembering the event or situation in the first place. Sometimes people would like to forget what they know, or they may not like to remind themselves of something, someone or some event that became knowledge to them. The truth of the matter is that they really have not forgotten what they know. They are simply blocking it and have merely chosen to not pay attention to it or to not refer to it in their own minds.

Moreover, they may be successful in blocking what they know, but they are not forgetting even if they think that they are. There is a huge difference between blocking and forgetting. To forget refers to something one actually really didn't know in the first place. However, when you acquire that which Michel referred to as *knowledge*, you don't forget. If it is true that "what you know, you will not forget," then you don't have to worry about remembering!

Blocking is different. Michel gave the example of a person who temporarily can't recall his or her own telephone number. What happens is that this makes people think that they are forgetful. It means nothing, however, according to Michel; and he explained it as normal because for a moment one is blocking one's own telephone number. It doesn't mean that the person has actually forgotten his or her own number. In such a case, it doesn't mean forgetting, it means blocking. Then the person begins to think badly about himself or herself: "What is the matter with me?" he or she may ask. That serves to create *tension*, of course. And the harder we *try to remember* that name or number, the more tense we become.

In our terminology, blocking means that you know the information, but at that given moment it is not in your conscious awareness. What we mean by this is that the information is in the subconscious mind and can be retrieved under appropriate circumstances.

> The subconscious does not respond well to *trying*, which is a conscious activity.

This just further blocks the subconscious mind. Once we stop making a conscious effort and allow the subconscious mind to function on its own, the information will just pop up automatically.

Another example of blocking occurs in everyday conversation. One may be talking to someone else and say: "It's on the tip of my tongue." This is the same phenomenon as the example of the telephone number. It is not forgetting. Once again, it is blocking. What you end up doing once again is telling your body to tense up on a subconscious level. It is almost impossible to find that name or number in the mind when it is blocked. The more you *try*, the more you block. It's that simple. Michel explains blocking to mean that "something is submerged." He described this to us as follows:

"You put it down, it disappears from the surface and you are unable to find it. It is no longer on the surface and the more you look for it, the more you 'push down', the deeper it goes and the more you end up blocking it."

Such blocks happen to everyone and Michel's advice was simply not to worry about it. He suggested to: "Release the pressure of the push and let it pop up!" What he meant is that we simply let go of the block by thinking of another word or set of words instead. As for the phone number, the more that you are *trying to remember* it, the deeper that you are pushing it down, the more you are "submerging" it. In essence, what he was saying is that if you *try* to think about the word at the tip of your tongue, the deeper it goes into the subconscious mind.

Michel's advice was to just forget the word and to use another word or even a sentence in its place. Then the word for which you were searching which was "submerged" will immediately pop up. Also, if you know it, you will expect it to pop up. How many times have you been in a situation in which you tried to remember the title of a song or the name of a character in a book? The more you tried to remember the more difficult the task became. Then, suddenly when you release the pressure of *trying to remember*, the word pops up in an instant! Thus, simply put, blocking is not forgetting.

> "What you *understand* becomes *knowledge* and what you *know* becomes part of you. It becomes a permanent part of you, and what you *know*, you don't forget.
> What you *know*, you will never forget.
> You may block, but you will not forget."

UNDERSTANDING

The word *"understanding"* was an important concept for the *Master Teacher*. There is a danger, however, of misunderstanding what he meant by it, so it is important to take a moment here to clarify what Michel meant when he used the word. The problem arises because the word "understanding" is ambiguous and is often used in two different senses in English. One sense is "to know thoroughly; to grasp or perceive clearly and fully the nature, character and functioning of a thing." This is the sense in which Michel used the word.

Another sense of understanding is "to comprehend; to get or perceive the meaning of." Understanding and comprehension are often used interchangeably, but more precisely, understanding stresses the full awareness of *knowledge* arrived at, while *comprehension* is the process of grasping something mentally. The critical point is that in this sense one may "comprehend" the words in a statement without *understanding* at all what is meant by them.

> Whenever we refer to "*understanding*" here
> in the context of Michel's method,
> we will mean *knowledge* and not comprehension.

As Michel would often declare:

> "The objective of learning is to gain *knowledge*."

Now we would like to make some distinctions which will clarify further the notion of *understanding* to which we refer. In order to do this, let us consider what are known as "*facts.*" Facts are isolated and learned one at a time. How do facts relate to *understanding*?

> *Understanding* involves connecting and integrating
> the facts together so that they form a whole
> which is greater than the sum of the parts.

A focus on remembering the parts obscures the vision of the whole. It is the whole that counts. You can't make applications or solve problems from the parts alone. It is only the organized whole which shows how the pieces fit together that allows you to solve problems or to make applications. Michel's goal was the practical use of a foreign language. He knew full well that one does not learn to speak a language by memorizing grammatical rules and vocabulary and verb conjugations. Instead, one learns to speak a language by *understanding* the connections and by practice.

Michel's original impulse to teach languages was to "probe the learning process of the human mind." In the process of this exploration, Michel made some interesting discoveries about how the learning process works, which he described as follows:

> Let me explain something which is very important. What I expect from any student, to me it's always the same, whether it's one student or the whole class. All learners know and I emphasize this that what I expect and what I want is that when I explain something for them, they need to fully *understand* it. But *understanding* to me means *understanding* just for the moment. When I explain something, I want it fully understood at that moment.

And, he added that if something is not fully understood at that moment, then the student needs to ask questions to make sure that it is fully understood.

To be fully understood means that it makes sense in terms of what the student already knows and that it does not contradict or conflict with existing knowledge. At that moment of first exposure all of the connections are not necessarily clear. And once again, it is important not to *try* to figure out the implications at that moment. They will be revealed as the learning session goes on. If it is unclear, then it needs to be clarified. But if it is clear, then the student should let go of it and move on because the implications will be discovered through using it.

Michel also explained that it is also important that once something is understood, the student should not *try* to hold on to it. And that process of *understanding* has to be very, very clear for each individual. "I don't want them to just have a general idea of *understanding*, of just to be nice and say 'Yes, it is clear.' No! Again, it is very important just for the moment to be completely understood for that moment."

By *trying* to hold on, the student is making a conscious effort and is trapped in the past. At the moment of first exposure, a student is not aware of all of the ramifications and uses. These are not to be figured out *a priori*. They will become apparent later in practice. Practice serves to fill in and connect up the unknowns.

IMPRINTING

In short, the student doesn't have to worry about remembering something, but only to focus on *understanding* it because Michel could come back to that moment and deepen it at any time. He referred to this aspect of his method as an *imprint* and explained it to us in this manner:

> It is the moment of what I call an *imprint*. The moment of *understanding*, of full *understanding*, is the moment of initial *imprint*. One doesn't *try* to hold onto it. I may at some point come back to it. They may or may not remember when I come back to it. If they don't remember it immediately, I will reinforce it and they will say 'aha.' They will have the aha reaction, and they will have a deepening of the initial *imprint*. If they *try* to hold onto it, however, the *imprint* is gone.

According to Michel, an *imprint* may be something very specific. It may be an idiomatic expression or the idiomatic use of something or an important vocabulary word. An *imprint* is not just a question of explaining. "You see, explanations are not *imprints*," he went on to say. "Therefore, if I give something which doesn't fit, then you say: 'How am I going to remember it?' And the point is that you don't need to *try to remember* it. It is very important for you not to *try to remember* it." Michel added:

> "*Trying to remember* it and holding on to it is what I call throwing sand on the *imprint*."

He continued to explain: "Personally, I find *imprints* interesting, what I call *imprints*, because of how it [the process] works. There is something new which is not a rule. Now how will they remember it since they are not supposed to *try to remember* it? I will do something to help them to remember it, whether by an important vocabulary word or by an idiom or whatever. But somehow, in different sentences and in different ways, at some point, not immediately, it will be used again."

One of two things will happen. Either the student will remember it and have the aha reaction or else the student may look for it and may not find it in which case that was fine according to Michel. He refined his explanation of *imprints* as follows:

> So I will come back to it [the *imprint*] and it will be there again and I will deepen it. It is interesting to me that it works that way. If they remember it, they will have the aha reaction. The aha reaction means 'I am right there.' So I deepen it once and I may do it still another time. It will be there. Once I deepen it twice, it is there. It is also interesting to me because whenever one tries to remember, then it is gone.

If Michel didn't get the aha reaction, he would know that the *imprint* was not there; and then he would have to create a new *imprint*. Michel found the concept of *imprints* rather intriguing because of what it revealed to him about the learning process of the human mind: "All this is just interesting to me. To me these are interesting discoveries about the mind."

It needs to be stated explicitly that the *Master Teacher* instinctively knew the importance of memory. In fact, with his understanding of the memory puzzle and also in creating his method with its parts/whole synergy, Michel was, in essence, a *"systems builder."* What he said was that an understanding of the whole is more than simply memorizing its parts. An understanding of the whole allows the parts to fit together so that they make sense. Without this understanding everything is an isolated piece, and it is simply too much work to chase after a thousand pieces. Understanding creates an integrated whole which then deepens into *knowledge*.

As we previously mentioned, there is another problem with *trying to remember*. Simply stated, *trying to remember* involves conscious effort, and this creates *tension*. The *tension* is there because there is always the effort to remember. Paradoxically, this *tension* makes it even harder to remember. Memory should be an effortless process. Michel early on discovered that in a state devoid of *tension* and anxiety, students had incredible memories for what he taught them. This was an amazing revelation sixty years ago. They recalled without either *trying to remember* or *trying* to recall. He was delighted to see that his students were able to recall without having to *try to remember*. This is a consequence of the natural process of reinforcement and of the connectivity of understanding. Once again, the *Master Teacher* revealed his genius.

WHY THE DISTINCTION OF KNOWLEDGE BASED ON UNDERSTANDING WORKS IN THE MICHEL THOMAS METHOD

Why does Michel's method of *knowledge* based on *understanding* work? As we have said, *understanding* is a process of connecting new information to what we already know so that it becomes *knowledge*. It is essentially an integration process. When we are first exposed to new information, the first checks we make are to ask whether it makes sense (Is it internally coherent?) and also whether it corresponds to or contradicts what we already know. If it corresponds to what we already know, then we can connect it into our previous understanding. If it contradicts what we already know, then it calls for further examination. We are faced with two options. We can either reject it or we can readjust our previous understanding to include it.

When we are first exposed to new information that makes sense and that is not incompatible with our previous understanding, we often unconsciously give it a provisional status. We will check it out to see if it holds up. We do this through practice. Also, all of the connections and implications of the new knowledge may not be clear at first. We accept the new information but it has yet to be integrated into our prior knowledge base. As we continue to use the new information, we make more and more connections, and it becomes more and more deeply integrated into what we know. Once assimilated, the new information becomes part of our *knowledge.* Once it is part of our *knowledge* we will never forget it.

The important point in our discussion is that the door to *knowledge* is through *understanding* and not through cramming and memorizing. As we stressed before, these activities neither produce *understanding* nor do they lead to long term recall. As we will see in the next chapter, a major issue in education today is the conflict between the old *dis-educational systems*™ that enforce cramming and memorizing and the new systems that stress the critical importance of understanding and problem solving. The former leads to uniformity and mindless obedience while the latter leads to critical thinking which is absolutely necessary for democracy. It is vital that we now take charge in shifting from the ineffective, antiquated system to an entirely revamped educational system. As Michel would so often reiterate in the course of our modeling him and in private conversation, "Critical thinking is essential to the survival of true democracy."

NO PERFORMANCE ANXIETY

One of the greatest sources of *tension* is the pressure to perform. Given the nature of our present "driven to succeed" and performance-based society, this type of *tension* is much more prevalent than ever and at younger ages. This is a *tension* that every student usually places upon himself or herself in the desire to succeed. In the traditional educational system, success and performance are notions that are incessantly being reinforced or triggered by both teachers and parents. Students are constantly told that they are responsible for their learning. The teacher is just there to help, but ultimately the students must do the work. They must work hard and study hard and be accountable. At some point, they will be tested on what they know. Moreover, to succeed in life you must *work hard* to get good grades; and having good grades means getting into college to prepare for a successful career. It is simply not acceptable to go through life ignorant and stupid. Ironically, that is precisely what Michel saw happening in today's world. Needless to say, all of this creates incredible pressure, anxiety, and *tension* in the learner.

Michel realized that the final *tension* which had to be released is the *tension* of expectations. In order to deal with this, Michel did quite a remarkable thing which we mention once again, this time in the context of performance. Remarkably, he took complete responsibility for the students' learning. The students are told that they are not to *try to remember*. It is simply not their responsibility. It was up to Michel to present the material in a way that the student would remember it. And if the student didn't remember, Michel would figure out why and would make the necessary adjustments.

MICHEL'S PROBLEMS

- Eliminating mistakes is Michel's problem and not the students'.
- Responsibility for learning is Michel's problem and not the student's.
- Learning and remembering are Michel's responsibility — don't try to take them away from him.
- Michel is at fault, never the student.

Michel's doing this took tremendous pressure off of the student. We cannot overstate the fact that the responsibility for learning and remembering was up to Michel. If the students made a mistake, Michel would never correct it. Instead he would "recycle" until the students *thought it out* and corrected it themselves. Michel would not directly correct his students and instead he would teach the students how to correct for themselves. Since they had been taught how, the students would continue to think things through and correct themselves. This is an important point because once the students left the learning session, they didn't have a teacher around to correct their mistakes. To be successful, they needed to be able to think things through, to discover their own mistakes and to correct themselves. And this is precisely what Michel skillfully taught his students to do.

Michel would do nothing at all to put pressure on the student. For Michel, pressure simply did not exist. He would never tense up or raise his voice or reveal any annoyance to the student. He told us that he would never reveal annoyance because he personally never experienced annoyance in the first place. The only thing that the student needed to do was to respond. If the students made a mistake, Michel would make no fuss about it. He would simply lead the students back to a similar situation so that they could go back and think it out and correct themselves.

In short, Michel had two rules: First, was that the student was never at fault. Second, the corollary of rule one, was that learning and remembering were Michel's responsibility. The student should let him do his job and never try to take it away from him. If the student didn't remember something, then it would be up to Michel to know why and to figure out what to do about it.

> Students' problems — None!

These frames were designed to get the student to let go of all *tension* and performance anxiety they might experience. With no performance anxiety, the student would be free to just respond. In fact, learning in this way would end up creating an immense excitement because Michel was triggering that powerful *innate drive for learning* that is in all living beings. Such concepts are unheard of in the traditional educational system. It is much easier on teachers to place the blame for lack of learning on their students. By washing their hands of all responsibility, teachers are freeing themselves of *tension* and placing it in their students.

With Michel's system, the students felt no undue stress or anxiety in the context of learning. Because he put the responsibility of learning completely on his shoulders, he was literally able to remove every atom of *tension*, even if a person walked into his course already carrying some *tension*. With the fast-paced, sound bite society in which we live, most students arrived at his learning center breathing *tension* in every cell of their bodies. Michel would quickly and masterfully calibrate who was tense and why, and would then immediately wave his magic *tension*-releasing wand to eliminate any stress and anxiety caused by external factors (not to mention the *tension* anchored in all who had had bad experiences in school, particularly in the context of language learning, which was the majority of people.).

There was another important by-product of learning with the *Master Teacher*. Michel, in eliminating *tension* from his students, brought them an additional benefit — a gift of self-confidence as learners. Once students had gone through his course, they could control and monitor their own progress. They were able to go off on their own to speak, read and write in the newly acquired target language. What he was doing was empowering his students to move ahead on their own. At the same time, he was instilling confidence within them in the context of their personal lives. By tapping into their immense learning potential, Michel was helping to guide them to an appreciation of life, to living a richer, fuller life and enhancing its overall quality. His teaching would often help them to remove *tension* in both their personal and professional lives. The students would go back to their lives with renewed confidence and not just in the context of learning. Michel's teaching literally opened the door to a new way of being as well.

THE ANNOYANCE FACTOR NOT ALLOWED

In the *Master Teacher*'s presence, the students were never permitted to get annoyed at themselves. Many students have been conditioned by parents and teachers to get irritated at themselves when they are not successful. There are some who may even hit themselves because they have been punished as children. As we have seen, conditioning creates a great deal of *tension* within the students and *tension* is something that Michel did not permit under any circumstances. In fact, Michel would stop the students right away if he perceived the slightest bit of self-directed anger or frustration. He would then tell them that there was no room to get annoyed at themselves in his presence. Why? Because annoyance produces *tension* and Michel would eliminate the *tension* so that learning could continue unimpeded.

There is another twist regarding annoyance in Michel's learning environment. He would tell the students that it was fine for them to get annoyed as long as they were getting annoyed at him, and not at themselves:

> If you have to get annoyed, then get annoyed at me because I am doing it to you. You are not doing it to yourself. And I mean it. If you make a mistake, it is not your fault. It is up to me. If you miss something, if you want to get annoyed, it is perfectly alright. I accept it. Just get annoyed at me. Externalize your annoyance, but never get annoyed at yourself. It's like *trying* to drive a car while at the same time pushing on the accelerator and the brakes. It's not good for the car. It's not good for driving. You cannot do both at the same time.

This made complete sense and saying this would usually suffice to snap the student out of any *tension*-producing self-annoyance.

There is another problem with expressing annoyance which the *Master Teacher* described this way: "I will tell them that they are getting annoyed at themselves and that is producing *tension*." He would tell the students that there was no reason for them to get annoyed. Furthermore, he would point out that it is very important to know that people who get easily annoyed at themselves while learning also easily get annoyed at themselves in many ways in other contexts of life. They place great expectations upon themselves and they often punish themselves when they don't meet their own expectations in life. There is an inseparable connection between learning and life which Michel observed over the years with one necessarily influencing the other (From our work as modelers and as trainers, we know that negative attitudes and emotional stances from life can have a detrimental effect on learning and on performance.). Like annoyance, anything that gets in the way of learning is bad. Michel described the link between bad attitudes in life and learning as follows:

> That is interference with living. Anything that interferes with learning also interferes with what I call living. It's like *trying* to drive a car by pressing on the accelerator and the brake pedal at the same time. The same brakes that interfere with learning also interfere with living. If you remove what interferes with learning, you also remove what interferes with living.

Michel preferred to see his students experience the joy and excitement of exceeding their own expectations, and he would always derive great personal joy from assisting them in the process.

Michel learned another valuable lesson. Over the years he had seen many students walk into the learning session with their individual problems so he would tell them, "If you want to get annoyed, fine, but externalize it. Get annoyed at me! And I mean it because I caused it. It is my responsibility, not yours. Never get annoyed at yourself." This was quite a revelation for his students. Michel went on to say:

> Many had gone through their lives never realizing what they were doing to themselves, especially those who had problems... They say that now they are living. They are talking about my course saving their lives. Suddenly, they feel like they are living. They are experiencing something for the first time. They call it life-saving. I don't say that to turn myself into a lifesaver. I want only to show the close connection between learning and life. Allow people to learn properly and you open up the doors to living, the same doors.

For the *Master Teacher*, removing the annoyance factor from his students' shoulders created great excitement and served to enhance the learning process by triggering one's *innate drive for learning*.

THE *INNATE DRIVE FOR LEARNING*

As we have mentioned in our chapter on the *Mind Prison*™, the *Master Teacher* believed that the *innate drive for learning* is a powerful drive found in every living being. From his perspective, it may even be stronger than the sex drive and may be equal to the drive for living and for survival itself. He witnessed that true learning produces a high state of excitement and a deep feeling of joy. As the students build on a ladder of previous successes, they become more and more energized and excited. This motivates them to accomplish great things.

As the learning process proceeds, the students experience the joy of exceeding their own expectations. Michel continually encouraged his students to take their time in answering and to think things out. Michel's approach emphasized *understanding* and not memorization. The students were told to take their time in answering or in solving or resolving problems. The students were encouraged to think everything out, step by step, and to express what they knew based on what they had learned. Students were told not to make guesses about grammar or to try to sound things out. Instead, Michel would tell them to express what they knew based on what they had learned (The only time that Michel permitted guessing was with vocabulary, and even then, usually towards the end of the course, when the students had already developed a sense of the target language.).

The *Master Teacher* would present the material in a way that the students could understand what he was saying and in a way that made sense to them. He would constantly build upon what they already knew. Remember Michel's mantram: "You can't forget what you *understand* and what you *know*." Once the students *understand* something, it makes sense to them and they know it. You may sometimes block what you know, but you don't forget. What you *understand* you can think out. Michel would ask the students to translate a long, complex sentence such as: "I can't come to visit you now because my mother called and I have to get some medicine and deliver it to her before she leaves to go on her trip." In order to think it out, the students would break it up into clauses and then translate a clause at a time. The students were encouraged to take their time. Michel emphasized that time is relative and what seems long to the speaker is not long to the listener.

Moreover, the students came to realize that even the most complex sentences are made up of simpler parts. Once you know the parts, you can combine them in many different ways. There is a valuable secret here. The secret is simplicity and happens to be another major element of Michel's method. Michel reduced the complexity of grammatical structures to simple parts which were then put together as an interlocking of these simple parts. It is an interesting interplay between complexity and simplicity which results in complete *understanding* and *knowledge* of the working of the parts to create the whole. This was a vital piece of Michel's method and part of the magic of the *Master Teacher*.

EXCITEMENT

Michel would keep going without breaks or pauses. If the students needed to excuse themselves, then they would have to request a short break. Amazingly, Michel could go on for hours even later in life — for eight to ten hours or more a day and he would usually skip lunch. When in a learning session with Michel, it was like reading a good novel that you simply couldn't put down. Michel created such incredible excitement about learning that you didn't want to stop, even to eat.

The excitement that he triggered within drove you forward. You wanted to keep going. In short, he proved that real learning is exciting, so much so that the student does not want to stop or even to delay the process. Michel would teach a language in three days, going from 10 a.m. to 6 p.m. This would give the student a greater feeling of accomplishment than to learn something in ten days or in two weeks. Michel pointed out that the shorter learning format was more "dramatically efficient." And he expressed his feelings about this with great pride etched into his face:

> "I like the excitement of achieving in three days what is not achieved in two to three years at any college."

He liked to deliver much more than the students ever expected and always achieved his goal with grand panache.

Michel believed that intensity was alright, yet he always insisted that his method did not depend on it. The intensity was a by-product of the excitement of true learning and the desire to continue the excitement without pausing or stopping. Michel liked the feeling of accomplishment that occurred when the student learned the language in three days, but this was not critical. Students could stop and come back days later and pick up just where they had left off. They would think that all that they learned had gone because they hadn't thought about it for awhile. Yet, it was not gone. This couldn't be farther from the truth. What they had learned to that point was still all there when they resumed the learning session from where they left off. The same is true with Michel's language tapes (Appendix B). A student may listen to four tapes and then stop for several weeks. When he or she comes back to them, the person may think it necessary to start over from the beginning of the tapes, but the person can take up just where he or she left off. Once again, it is like putting down a book for awhile. You start where you left off. You don't go back and reread the book from the beginning.

As we mentioned in a prior section, Michel discovered that learning occurs through forming an initial *imprint* and then letting go of it. Michel would come back to the initial *imprint* at some point and reinforce it. There was built-in redundancy in his method which added to its effectiveness. After a short while, new material could be introduced while old material was at the same time being reinforced. We call this process *"layering."* In a teaching or training context, *layering* means doing multiple things at once. We will return to this concept in the next section.

FRAMES AT THE END OF THE DAY

At the end of each day, students might expect some admonition to spend the evening reviewing the material in their mind and perhaps to do some homework. At this point, anxiety may begin to creep in based on patterns from the traditional *dis-educational system*™, particularly as the students begin to wonder how they will remember any of what they had just learned and be able to recall it the following day. Once again, Michel would do everything he could to alleviate this *tension*-producing anxiety. The students were told that there was no homework.

Furthermore, they were not to review in their own mind what they had learned during the session that day. In fact, they should do whatever they felt like doing except review what Michel had taught them. Of course, if you don't think about it, there will be no anxiety. It was possible that things might spontaneously pop up in the students' minds during the evening. If this happened, Michel would recommend:

> "Make no conscious effort to review. Just accept it. But it is important that you never go beyond it."

Yet this was not enough. Michel realized that expectations are usually sources of *tension* that interfere with learning. So Michel would tell his students that there was no reason to worry. Worry is *tension*-producing. In fact, he would tell them: "You aren't expected to know the language yet. In fact, when we meet again, I expect you to tell me that you forgot everything, but you will experience that nothing is forgotten." So the students were relieved of all pressure since nothing was expected or required of them.

> **FRAMES AT THE END OF THE DAY**
>
> No homework — it is absolutely not allowed.
> No mentally reviewing what you have learned.
> "When we meet again, I don't expect you to remember anything."

Of course, the next day the students were often shocked to realize that they remembered quite a bit of what they had learned, and sometimes everything, much to their amazement. The next day Michel would resume exactly from the point where he had left off the day before. Michel immediately would reassure the student by saying:

> "I don't expect you to remember anything. Remembering is my problem and not yours. Just let go of any *tension* and anxiety and be relaxed and make yourself comfortable and we will continue."

By the third day, this was automatic and Michel would not need to say anything more about it. Michel would start where he left off the previous day with some easy constructions that the student could understand. He then would begin to introduce new material as he continually reinforced what the student had already learned.

CONTENT

The initial frames are critical to produce an optimal atmosphere for learning. As part of our research in learning over the years, we know that learning involves a relationship among three things. These are:

1) The teacher
2) The student and
3) The content.

It is up to the teacher to present the content in such a way that it is understood by the student and then easily applied. Content has to be taught in a linear fashion. It would be nice to be able to teach it holographically or all at once, but this cannot be done. So content must be broken into parts or chunks and these parts must be taught in a certain order or sequence.

HOW TO TEACH CONTENT

- Start with what the student already knows.
- Have *a sharpened awareness of one's own language*.
- Learn how to speak using correct grammar.
- Learn it right the first time.
- The heart of the language is the verbs.
- Build "*meaningful memory associations*"™ based on familiarity.
- Simplify.
- Build a success ladder beginning with what the student already knows.
- Teach for *understanding* and not for memorization.
- Teach for acquisition of *knowledge*.

First, we will focus on the way in which the *Master Teacher* ordered his material. Obviously, Michel would not explain what the parts and sequence were to his students. Michel would simply proceed with the learning. To understand how Michel would organize the material, it is necessary to listen to and to analyze the actual content of his learning process. When we do this, we discover several key elements.

As Michel would remind during the modeling process, "There is nothing so complicated that it can't be made very simple." Unfortunately, as Michel also realized, "There is nothing so simple that it can't be made very complicated." Michel took the former approach, whereas from his point of view, some so-called educators may like to take the latter approach. Some of the keys to understanding Michel's method are as follows:

START WITH WHAT THE STUDENT ALREADY KNOWS

Let us see how Michel put these principles into action. In teaching languages, there are many cognates between French,

Spanish, Italian, German and English. Part of his method was his ability to incorporate quite effortlessly the connections between English and the target language. Michel described why he used cognates: "I want to show you right from the beginning that we are going to get acquainted with a language that is not entirely foreign or alien to English." Michel would explain that there is a broad common basis of familiarity between English and French (or Spanish, Italian, or German).

In fact, over sixty percent of the English vocabulary comes from the French (Michel would humorously suggest that English is really badly-pronounced French.). English is a mixture of Anglo-Saxon German and French. "You will have a starting vocabulary of well over three thousand words." he would tell his students. The same holds true for Spanish and Italian. In German, the similarity is in the grammar and in the vocabulary. Michel would point out that "essentially and structurally English is Anglo–Saxon, meaning a Germanic language. And in German there are a lot of similarities which I am going to point out right from the beginning."

So Michel would start by stressing the commonality between the languages. In other words, there are already a large number of words that the student could easily figure out. Michel would begin with easy vocabulary and built upon this easy foundation. In so doing he was able to create a recognizable comfort zone. Students immediately knew how to put words into sentences, first short sentences, then long sentences. Also, it is possible to say something in many different ways in a language. Michel would relate the target language back to specific English constructions which the student already knew.

Here is another secret that Michel revealed to us. He Michel focused on how native speakers speak their own language. Native speakers are listening for certain cues that let them know the tense and other important features of the language. Michel was well aware of what the native speaker was listening for, and he would teach his students how to speak so that they would be both understood and grammatically correct.

It is important to remember that Michel's method consists of several key components. All of them work together synergistically in a well-designed system in which all the elements smoothly flow together, with different elements taking center stage at given points in the learning session. However, when taken in isolation, these individual elements do not have the same power. Some people have said that Michel's method works because he started with cognates. Their simplistic analysis infuriated Michel. To say that his method was based on cognates is totally absurd. Cognates may lead into the method because they immediately allow students to create sentences which they understand. Cognates also serve to create a comfort zone of familiarity for the students at the very beginning that naturally overrides any feeling of overwhelm regarding what is traditionally considered to be a daunting task — learning a foreign language.

So cognates serve a specific purpose in the *Michel Thomas Method*, but they are certainly not the method, even with any stretch of the imagination. People who say this don't understand the method at all, nor do they have a clue as to the way Michel's mind worked. Michel referred to his use of cognates as an "effective gimmick to get started, but it is not the method." His secret here was that his "effective gimmicks" helped in the formation of sentences.

As far as the method is concerned, we mentioned earlier that no one piece in isolation is the key. The method is, instead, about all the pieces and the way in which they fit together synergistically to create a highly effective system. That is the real key. Again, Michel would start with what the student already knew, but this was only the beginning of the brilliantly master work which bears Michel's genius. To say that his method was based on cognates is completely ludicrous on the part of some educators.

Also, we would like to point out that Michel would mention cognates for another reason. The *Master Teacher* described the process as follows:

> I do refer to many French and English words having the same roots, but I do so in the introductory sections of our educational encounter, the moments spent before the method really begins. This is about the time the student is shown that he or she really knows a lot more French than

imagined. It has to do with establishing the climate of the setting. It has nothing to do with the instructional materials. It is neither a tenet, nor a basis, nor a strategy, nor even a point of reference. It is affective, peripheral, reassuring and true.

Finally, cognates were another way in which Michel used simplicity to create *understanding* which leads to *knowledge*. His approach of using cognates initially as simple building blocks to build more and more complex grammatical structures in a target language was brilliant. Applying his own teacher's lesson in reverse, "There is nothing so complicated that it can't be made simple," Michel used cognates at the start of his learning session to create simplicity out of the complexity of language. Once again, we have a glimpse of the workings of the *Master Teacher,* whose complex mind always found a way to simplify for his students — by reducing the complexity of the larger whole to the easily assimilated simplicity of parts only to come full circle back to the complexity of the whole — teaching his students the ability to communicate with proficiency in a language other than their own while using correct grammatical structures.

HAVE *A SHARPENED AWARENESS* OF ONE'S OWN LANGUAGE

Usually one learns to speak one's own language before being taught the grammar. Traditionally, grammar comes later, if at all. Often a speaker of a language learns grammar inductively from speaking and hearing the language. He or she does not normally begin with the grammar. The result is that many people do not know the grammar of their own language, so that they are not aware of what they are trying to express. Thus, starting with what the student already knows can be a double-edged sword. The positive side which we just saw is that one can begin with a rather large vocabulary. The downside is that many people don't even understand the grammar of their own language.

Michel explained that these people lack what he called "*a sharpened awareness of one's own language.*" This makes it more challenging to learn the correct grammar of another language. Such was the case of French actor, Yves Montand, who didn't know the grammar of his native language. Michel ended up teaching him how to speak correct English and while doing this, he taught him how to speak French using correct grammar.

Without *a sharpened awareness* of their own language, learners will impose the same misunderstanding of grammar that they have about their own language onto the language they are learning. This notion of having *a sharpened awareness of one's own language* was an important one for Michel. He believed that this was essential to learning a language correctly, and to being able to communicate properly in that language: "Once you know the language, and you know how to use the language, it is important to think, 'What am I trying to say?'" Although the notion of *a sharpened awareness* was not part of the actual teaching process *per se*, it always would come up in the context of Michel's teaching.

Having *a sharpened awareness of one's own language* involves an awareness of a fundamental usage of verbs and of grammatical concepts, and Michel would very often make the point that one does not learn these correctly, if at all, in the traditional educational system. Michel believed that having *a sharpened awareness of one's own language* was one of the most important factors in establishing an understanding of another language. Tragically, it is a concept that is rarely taught or retained in the *Mind Prison*™.

Most native English speakers have absolutely no clue as to what certain expressions and verb forms really mean. Michel had witnessed time and time again that students in the traditional system were never taught to make distinctions grammatical or otherwise. He would also lament the fact that students in the traditional system were unaware of subtle nuances, of which there are many in any given language, and which may drastically alter the meaning of a translation, if misunderstood and misused.

Michel was fond of giving the recurring example in English, of students' inability to make the simple distinction between the expressions "will" and "will you please." As any educated person should know, the word "will" expresses the future tense in English, although not always.

"Will you wait for us?"

The above phrase expresses the future. The phrase below:

"Will you please wait for us?"

does not express the future tense, but rather is the expression of a polite request. It was shocking for us to learn from Michel just how few students understand the difference between the two phrases.

Take another example. In English, we have the expression "*to have to.*" When one says "You *have to* do this today," it means "You *must* do it today." In line with this, when Michel typically would, then, ask his students to explain the meaning of, "You *don't have to* do it today," they would respond by saying that it meant, "You *mustn't* do it today." This is totally incorrect. In their minds, the students were thinking that if "*you have to*" means "*must*," therefore, "you *don't have to*" means "you *mustn't*." This is wrong. What "you *don't have to*" really means is "you *don't need to.*" This is the kind of subtle distinction to which Michel referred — the type of subtly that is usually not properly taught in the traditional school system so that the majority of the population neither makes nor understands the distinction. The above examples illustrate what Michel referred to when he spoke of having *a sharpened awareness of one's own language*. There is such a huge difference in meaning between "You *have to* do it," and "You *don't have to* do it". Much to his dismay, so many educated people don't get it at all!

Michel explained that having this *sharpened awareness of one's own language* greatly facilitates what you will understand and what you will say in another language that is not your native tongue. Because of these deficiencies on the part of his students, Michel was, more often than not, obliged to teach them these basic distinctions within his course. By Michel teaching them these fundamentals, the students could at least begin to acquire this *sharpened awareness* while learning a new language. Otherwise, students would transfer the same mistakes and misconceptions to the target language.

We should note in passing that although this realization was difficult on Michel, in that it merely reinforced the ineptitude of the current system, one would never know it based on his facial expressions, body language and tonality. His whole persona continued to exude the same charm, grace and enthusiasm at all times. When he would teach, students appeared to take in new information by osmosis, and did so with no sign of concern, anxiety, fear or *tension*.

LEARN TO SPEAK GRAMMATICALLY CORRECTLY

Often people use understanding as a test of language fluency. One can say things that are grammatically incorrect and the listener may be able to figure out what you mean. However, this in no way means that what you are saying is correct. It just means that you were lucky. This can lead to the mistaken view that close is good enough, and that you don't have to be grammatically correct to be understood. From the *Master Teacher's* perspective, this is an unfortunate attitude to develop and one which he did not accept.

Correct grammar is important and Michel would make a point to teach correct grammar. In fact, he was quite adamant about it. However, Michel approached this aspect of teaching correct grammar in a different way than most language teachers and grammarians. Anyone who has learned a foreign language in high school or college remembers being filled with grammatical terminology, rules and the seemingly endless exceptions to the rules. Traditionally, every lesson would accompany the textbook, and each would include a dialogue, an accompanying set of vocabulary and a grammar section full of rules.

No wonder it takes forever to gain proficiency in a language in this traditional way. Michel would teach the full, complete grammar in three days (which takes years in high school or college), yet he achieved this "in a way where one learns it, one absorbs it and one knows it." In so doing, Michel demystified traditional grammatical structure by creating one that he presented more simply and elegantly.

The *Master Teacher* would teach correct grammar with effortless ease, without having the students memorize grammatical rules, and without having them use grammatical terms. He would teach all of the tenses of the language, even the subjunctive, but without labeling the tenses. "I may put other labels on them, and they are understandable labels, not grammatical labels," he would say. Michel emphasized that the label itself was not important. What was important is how to say something correctly in the target language.

Michel would only use three grammatical terms. They were *noun*, *verb* and *adjective*. He found that most people were confused, even about these basic terms because of the way in which they are taught in the traditional system. So Michel would never assume that students knew what these words meant. He would take nothing for granted, and he defined his terms very carefully.

One would assume that an educated person would know what a noun, adjective or a verb is in his or her native language. Surprisingly, this is not the case. In his fifty plus years of teaching, Michel made a disheartening discovery:

> "Close to ninety percent of so-called educated people, and even highly educated people, do not know what a noun, an adjective or a verb is."

As Michel explained, their answers to the question, "What is a noun, adjective, and verb?" will be based on what they remember from school, which is usually incorrect. As you may remember from your own schooling early on, one is taught that a noun is *a person, place or thing*. This definition is meaningless, according to Michel.

For years, children have had to memorize the definition of a noun, which meant nothing to them. In short, they simply memorized the definition, but they didn't *understand* it. This is demonstrated by their inability to use the definition to properly categorize or classify words. To prove this point, Michel would tell his students that he was going to give them words in

English, and that he would like them to identify whether they were nouns, adjectives or verbs.

For example he would ask students what the word *"happiness"* is. Is it a noun, verb or adjective? Students would think to themselves, "It is not a person, place or thing, therefore it is an adjective." They simply were unable to categorize correctly the word *"happiness"* because they never understood the meaning of a noun in the first place. According to Michel, the students would think in their minds, "It is not a person, place or thing; therefore it cannot be a noun by definition. Without a clear understanding of the definition, they are going to guess wrong each and every time." Of course, we all know that *happiness* is a noun.

When Michel would ask: "What is an adjective?" Most of the time he would get the answer that "an adjective is a word that modifies a noun." Again, this is a definition which one learns in the traditional system and does not mean anything to students in Michel's view. Fortunately, in recent years prior to his passing, he was happy to hear some students defining an adjective as a word that "explains" a noun, a definition which makes more sense. This change from using the word "explain" rather than the word "modify" is already quite an improvement. Still confusion exists. When Michel would ask students, "What is the word *'proud'*? They would think, Um, it's a noun. In their minds they would be thinking: Um. A proud chair. No. A proud door. No. Therefore the word *'proud'* cannot be an adjective, so, therefore, it has to be a noun." As unbelievable as these answers sound, Michel continued to get them very often in the course of his teaching over the years. Obviously, the students were merely guessing incorrectly because they did not have an understanding of the meaning of the grammatical terms.

Next, when he would ask students, "What is a verb?" the immediate answer was that "a verb is action." It is something related to action. So Michel would proceed to ask: "What is "to have"? What is "to be"?" Students simply did not know the answer even in this day and age. Michel sensed that they were asking themselves, "What could they be? They cannot be a verb because there is no action involved. For it to be a verb, action has to come from somewhere, so it is not a verb."

One would think that everyone who has gone through our school system would have a basic grasp and understanding of these fundamental concepts. These are simple definitions of a noun, adjective and verb which students simply do not know. The point of this is that Michel was obliged to start his lessons with a clear explanation of terms which the students should have known in the first place. He would have to spend time explaining all of these grammatical terms to his students. What was the point of his talking about a noun or a verb or an adjective if the students couldn't comprehend what he was saying?

Thus, the *Master Teacher* would teach correct grammar and in so doing, he would never use grammatical terms. After all, grammatical terms are just meaningless labels for the features of the language. As we have seen, students didn't understand basic grammatical terms, let alone advanced grammatical terms like the "pluperfect subjunctive" and the "future progressive tense." Michel also used labels which were his own unique brand of labels. As Michel explained,

"I put other labels on it, understandable labels, but not grammatical labels. Once you know it I can put a label on it. The label is not important. It is important to know how to say it correctly in the language."

To illustrate this, Michel gave the following example and said:

If I had seen it, I would have bought it, but I couldn't go there last night because I was very busy. These are all different tenses. And in order to express such a sentence correctly, one can't just do it by implication or not, or just guess whether it is 'I was' or '*not.*' What kind of tense is 'I wasn't doing it'? or 'When did you see it?' or 'Did you see it'? I saw it (By implication one should say, 'I saw it not.'). 'I didn't see it.'

Grasping all of these is not an easy task, yet Michel would masterfully explain all of these tenses with great ease and simplicity.

In traditional language courses, too much time is spent presenting grammatical labels which the students are asked to memorize. It's bad enough that rote memorization does not lead to *understanding*, and to make matters worse, there is the additional problem that most of the time, even the labels don't mean anything in the students' minds. Of course, the need to memorize the labels puts added pressure on the students, increasing their *tension* all the more. Meanwhile, the students have not gained *understanding*. Concentrating on the labels takes their focus away from learning as well.

As with anything that one learns, correct grammar has to be based on understanding. It has to become *knowledge*. One has to know that it is correct to say, "I didn't see it," and that it is incorrect to say, "I saw it not." If one says, "I saw it not," one will know that a mistake has been made because one knows what is correct,

> The beauty of understanding the grammar is that the students can self-correct their own mistakes, because in their minds they understand the difference between correct grammar and incorrect grammar.

As Michel emphatically stated to us over and over again:

> That is what grammar is for. And it is correct grammar, not guessing grammar, and not learning how to communicate in some form of spoken grammar to make oneself understood. And to think that not everyone speaks grammatically correctly. My students learn correct grammar and how to use it correctly.

Michel gave us another example in French. He would ask his students how to say in French: "I didn't understand you because you didn't tell it to me."

Je ne vous ai pas compris, parce que vous ne me l'avez pas dit.

According to Michel, this is a sentence that, unfortunately, most students who have studied high school French or college French very often get wrong. Even people who have been living in France for years, who one would assume would be fluent in French, will get it wrong. It is correct to say:

Je ne vous ai pas compris, and *Vous ne me l'avez pas dit.*

According to Michel, most people will say incorrectly:

Je n'ai vous compris pas, and *Vous ne me l'avez dit pas.*

If you say this, most French people will understand you. The speaker thinks "Okay. They understand me. I can make myself understood." What is the problem? The problem is that once students start making these mistakes and once they accept speaking in a way that is grammatically incorrect, it becomes very difficult to correct. It is important to learn it right from the start and to insist on correct grammar. Michel said that at times students may even start carrying the mistakes over into English, and he actually witnessed this. For example, they will start saying, "I have understood not." It becomes set in their minds. Moreover, as Michel pointed out:

"It is very difficult to unteach."

Indeed. Michel was proud to say that he always taught correct grammar. In three days students learned to speak correctly using twenty to twenty-two tenses which gave them the ability to understand literature and to read magazines. As Michel explained, "If you don't have a good understanding of grammar, you will not be able to read. You will read children's books, maybe."

Several times over the years Michel had offered the following powerful challenge to language departments:

> In three days I achieve in teaching what it takes years to learn in high school or college. Ask any language department how long it would take just to cover, not to achieve, but to cover what I spell out. This does not mean that one will know it, but that one will have gone through all the textbooks and courses. If you ask any language department how long it would take to cover, not to learn, but to cover what I spell out, they will gladly tell you that it will take two to three years. What I do in three days is more than they achieve in two to three years. Because in my course I don't just cover it...my students know it. For years I have challenged any language department to prove me wrong. Nobody has taken me up on the challenge. It only takes three days to prove it or to disprove it. In all these years, nobody has taken me up on it. No university and no college will accept the challenge.

In March 2004, Michel offered a worldwide challenge in an article about him that appeared in *The Financial Times*: "I publicly challenge any university language department to do this. I will show that I achieve more in three days than they cover in two to three years. They never take me up on this! But it takes only three days to call my bluff — they could blow me out of existence!"

Grammatical rules go back to the Greeks and Romans and even before. People have been teaching grammar the same way for over two thousand years. Each generation inherits from the previous generation. No one seems to have questioned if this is the best way to teach it. Until Michel, that is.

Michel simplified grammar by discovering
the patterns hidden under the grammar.

Let us take a familiar example in English. In learning to conjugate regular verbs in the present tense in English, one is taught to memorize "I think, you think, he, she or it thinks, we think, you think, and they think." There are books with conjugations of five hundred verbs that go through this for every verb. This is ridiculous! There are only two endings to know! One is the infinitive and the other is the infinitive with an "s" on the end of it. There are only two categories. One is "I, you (sing), we, you (plural), and they think" and the other is "he, she, and it thinks." The simple rule for the present tense of regular verbs in English is that for the third person singular, one adds an "s" to the infinitive and for everything else, just use the infinitive.

If one looks for the patterns in the language instead of mindlessly parroting the grammatical categories, one will often find that there are simple rules.

> In our terminology we call this looking at the language "*logically*" as opposed to "*grammatically*."
> Michel called it "*simplifying*."

Discovering these simple, logical patterns makes it easier to teach the language and it also makes it easier to learn the language. The problem with grammatical rules is that they usually seem arbitrary and they don't make sense. This makes them difficult to learn and places an emphasis on mindless rote memorization without *understanding*. How can you understand and know something that does not make sense? All you can do is mimic back the material without understanding what you are saying. The result is that you are parroting the subject matter rather than learning it.

The *Master Teacher* discovered *generalizations* that make sense and he came up with explanations that explain why things are the way that they are. Now they are no longer arbitrary. Furthermore, now they make sense and now they are user friendly. This was a major part of Michel's magic. This is exactly what Michel did and it happens to be another of the secrets to his success. He would find the simple, logical patterns that are hidden by what appears to be complicated grammar and this is what he would teach his students. It streamlines the whole process by cutting out meaningless jargon and superfluous conjugations and transforms the arbitrary and idiosyncratic into something that finally makes sense.

Let us take another example from French where Michel simplified the grammar by creating a distinction between what he called the "*long box*" and the "*short box.*" Michel explained this distinction to us by saying that *nous* and *vous* are always in the same box, the long box, and that whatever isn't "we" and "you," one cuts short: "In French, all verbs, all forms, all conjugations, I put in two boxes. One is a long box. The other is cut short. It becomes the short box." Michel would explain that nothing else fits into the long box except these two verb forms: *nous (we)* and *vous (you)*. For example, with the verb *parler* (to speak), there are two forms in the long box, *nous* and *vous*:

Nous parlons (We speak)
Vous parlez (You speak)

Then he would explain the fact that in French, there is only one single exception for *nous* (we), which is *sommes* (are):

Nous sommes. (We are)

Once he laid out his explanation, he then would give examples: *Nous sommes fatigués.* (We are tired.) *Nous sommes occupés.* (We are busy.) The student quickly grasps the use of *nous sommes (we are)*.

Michel would then give other examples of an *"er"* verb:

Aller (to go)
Nous allons. (We are going.)
Vous allez. (You are going.)

Remember that *nous* and *vous* forms are found in the long box.

Where: *Où*
Where are you going?: *Où allez-vous?*
Tonight: Ce soir

Where are you going tonight?:
Où allez-vous ce soir?

Let us take another "*er*" verb: *arriver* (to arrive).

Nous and *vous* are again in the long box.

Nous arrivons. (We are arriving.)
Vous arrivez. (You are arriving.)

Tonight: *Ce soir*
We are arriving tonight:
Nous arrivons ce soir.

Michel would then ask the student to say:

You are arriving tonight.
Vous arrivez ce soir.

Again, *vous* and *nous* go in the long box.

Amazingly, in practically no time at all, the student is able to use and to understand these sentences. In the traditional *dis-educational system*™ it often takes months to learn the correct use of these verb forms.

Once Michel explained what is contained in the long box, he would tell the students:

> "Everything else you cut short. You cut off the ending. These go into the short box. So, for example, with the verb *parler* you cut off the last '*r*,' and you pronounce *parle* and that applies to I, you, he, she, it, everybody, nobody, who, they, etc."

Then, when he would ask the students how to say, for example, "Everyone speaks English here," they immediately knew how to say it correctly:

Everybody: *Tout le monde.* Here: *Ici*

Tout le monde parle anglais ici.

Michel reinforced his explanation by reminding them of the rule for his box distinction: "The same box, you cut it off, so you don't have to think, oh gee, what is 'They are arriving.' So, 'My friends are arriving tonight.' is: *Mes amis arrivent ce soir.*" Michel jokingly remarked that if one were to teach these verbs the traditional way as tedious memorization, "By the time that the students go down the traditional lists of I, you, he, she, it, we, etc., they [my friends] would have arrived and left already!"

This is the way to teach grammar, according to Michel's method. And, he reminded us, "They [the students] know how to spell it!" Here, once again, he managed to reduce complexity to simple patterns. Moreover, whenever he did this, the students knew how to spell what they were saying! And very quickly they learned that ninety percent of the French verbs end in *"er."*

The students also learn that other verbs may end in *"ir"* like *partir* (to leave) or in *"re,"* like *attendre* (to wait). The long box rules still applies: *nous* and *vous* forms for these verbs are still found in Michel's long box. Thus, the same thing applies with the *"ir"* and *"re"* verbs as with the *"er"* verbs: *vous* and *nous* go in the long box.

For example, take a verb ending in *"ir"* – *partir (to leave):*

> *Nous partons (*We are leaving.)
> *Vous partez* (You are leaving.)

Then a verb ending in *"re": vendre* (to sell):

> *Nous vendons (*We are selling.)
> *Vous vendez* (You are selling.)

These verb forms for *nous* and *vous* are also found in the long box.

Once again *nous* and *vous* are in the same box, the long box. The rest goes into Michel's short box. It is not the length of the list of verbs that determines whether it is the long box or the short box, but rather, whether the ending is cut short or not.

Michel would go on to refine his explanation one step further:

> But in the short box, if there is not an *'er'* verb, if you cut off the ending, the *'r,'* (*attendre*) you already know in spelling that you don't have an *'e'* there, therefore, you don't sound the consonant. So immediately you know if it is either an *'er'* verb or not an *'er'* verb. If it is an *'er'* verb in what I call *'the short box,'* you sound the consonant, and you understand why. Or if it is not an *'er'* verb, you don't sound the consonant. You also understand why. It is not because I say so! They will know how to say 'Everyone is waiting.' *Tout le monde attend*. They will know that *attendre* is used in the sense of 'to wait.' In no time, they will know how to say: 'Everyone is waiting for you.' *Tout le monde vous attend*.

Michel remarked on several occasions that as unbelievable as it seems, most students of French don't know how to say this simple little phrase correctly. Again, in the traditional system, they are taught memorization in the place of *understanding*.

By contrast, instead of wasting time on the normal "I, you, he, she, it, we, you, they" conjugations, Michel was able to detect a simple pattern that facilitated *understanding* and made it easy to learn. Instead of committing to memory endless conjugations which usually don't make sense, all one has to remember is to fit the verb into Michel's long box or short box. Then everything becomes automatic and that *knowledge* remains with the students forever.

Let us give another example of how the *Master Teacher* was able to simplify grammar. It happens to be a brilliant example of Michel's genius at work once again. Michel explained to us the brilliant and rapid way in which he taught the entire future tense in French as follows:

> In all textbooks you have practically hundreds of pages of grammar, with rules and regulations and conjugations and tenses and tenses and tenses, those books of five hundred verb

conjugations. It's endless. Let's take the future tense, for example, in French of *'er,'* *'ir,'* and *'re'* verbs. It's endless. We have the books which give the future tense of the verbs, which means you have to memorize all the future endings of all those verbs. This is done by cramming and memorizing. I will teach you the future tense of all those verbs in less than fifteen minutes! I am talking about all verbs: *'er,'* *'ir,'* *'re,'* and regular and irregular verbs. Imagine learning the entire future tense of all verbs in record time!

By the time that Michel would teach the future tense, his students would have already learned how to say in the present tense: "I have," "He has," "They have," which corresponds to: *j'ai, il a, ils ont*. And *Ai, a* and *ont* will be endings used with the future tense.

To explain the future tense in French, Michel would tell a clever little story which students always remember:

> I will say, you know, in French for the future, that originally, in the beginning of the French language, to say 'I will leave tomorrow.' one would say: 'I – to leave – have – tomorrow.' or *'Je partir ai demain'*. *Je* is 'I.' *Partir* is 'to leave': *Ai* is 'have'; (*demain* is 'tomorrow') 'I to leave have tomorrow' is *'je partir ai demain.'* For 'he to leave has tomorrow.' is *'Il partir a demain.'* They have' is *'ils ont.'* 'They to leave have tomorrow.' *'Ils partir ont demain.'* All of this becomes *'Je partirai.'* Why not contract it in spelling since it was already contracted in speaking. The grammarians got together and hooked on the endings to the verb, and it became the future tense. They got used to using it and began to contract it so we now have: *'Je partirai, Il partira, Ils partiront.'* [I will leave, He will leave, They will leave.)] Those endings become *rai — ra — ront*. They are the universal endings for all French future tense verbs. Period! Regular or irregular verbs, it matters not.

It didn't even matter whether the little story was true or not. What is important is that it facilitated the learning process. It made sense to Michel and he would teach the future tense in French this way. That is all that matters. And it was yet another example of Michel's innovative and brilliant mind. Imagine reducing the entire future tense of all French verbs into a clever little formula that really works and simplifies the whole learning process at the same time! Complexity again reduced to simplicity. Michel's process was truly original and exciting.

Of course, teachers in the traditional system never tell you this because students are supposed to painstakingly memorize it all. And you have those books of hundreds of pages of conjugations that students feel obliged to buy. Michel felt that these books were major rip-offs. He would often lament the following: "Teachers never point out that the endings of all the verbs are the same in French. Take any verb. And you understand it and tune into the ending. You will know that it is the future tense."

LEARN IT CORRECTLY THE FIRST TIME

As the *Master Teacher* would always emphasize, it is hard to *unlearn* something. Everyone knows how difficult it is to break a bad habit. The same applies to learning. Once you learn something incorrectly, you may continue doing it even though you are corrected hundreds of times. You may even realize that it is wrong, and you may still keep on doing it. In education and in life, there is a false belief that we learn from our mistakes. We usually don't, and in education the process of correction often leads to a loss of self-esteem. What is the solution?

> The solution is to learn something correctly the first time.
> It is important to arrange learning so that
> the probability of mistakes is minimized.

Learning should be accompanied by getting things right wherever possible rather than getting them wrong and having to *unlearn*. We call this "*building on a ladder of previous successes.*"

Michel would not take students for one-on-one sessions who had already taken a course in the language they wanted to learn. This may seem strange. There was a good reason behind it. The reason was that if the student had already learned mistakes, it would have taken a long time to correct them. If they had succeeded in learning the language, then they would have claimed that they had already known it. A crucial part of Michel's method was giving students the ability to detect and correct their own mistakes. If the mistakes had gone uncorrected until now, it would have taken longer to erase the set mistakes than to teach the language properly from the start.

There is an important principle in education which helps to explain some of how the Master Teacher's methods differ from traditional methods. It is called the 80/20 rule, or Pareto's Principle; and it applies to the traditional system. What it says in this context is that twenty percent of the total number of mistakes that a student will make will occur eighty percent of the time. What this means is that there are a small number of common mistakes that most students make. When we explained the 80/20 rule to Michel, he told us that this rule only applied elsewhere because students were not taught correctly in the first place. And the 80/20 rule did not apply to Michel. He was quick to point out that in the case of students in the traditional system:

> They only make common mistakes because they haven't been taught properly. Teaching can only lead to mistakes if it is not done properly. I don't do that. People may individually make mistakes in my class. If they do, then it is up to me to know why they made the mistake and to know what to do about it. I teach them so that they are able to detect and correct their own mistakes. Some students may make a mistake twice, but only very rarely do they do it a third time.

Common mistakes wouldn't happen in Michel's teaching and mistakes were simply not an issue for him. Often, when students realized that they had made a mistake, they would usually end up by correcting their own mistake. If they were not able to do so, Michel would lead them into correcting their own mistakes. If they made a nonthinking mistake, Michel may have asked them to repeat it. In repeating it, the students would naturally slow down and think. If they did not, Michel would lead them into correcting the mistake. The result was that when they occasionally "*derailed,*" the students would be able to quickly get back on track. He would always lead them back. In doing so, Michel was literally taking them back on track to learning, to the experience of *understanding*.

The best way to eliminate mistakes is never to make them. The best way to clear up a misunderstanding is to avoid it before it can ever arise. Michel would build simple explanations and distinctions into his teaching which were designed to eliminate these potential problems before they could arise. There was no 80/20 rule for Michel.

> The 80/20 rule applies in traditional education and in the business world, but not in Michel's world for one very important reason: because in his world he created *understanding*, and *understanding* which led to *knowledge*.

Michel pointed out that the 80/20 rule applies in traditional education because there is no teaching, only lecturing. As we mentioned earlier, in true teaching, there is no lecturing. There is a huge difference between being lectured and being taught. Michel would not lecture. He would engage in real teaching and he would teach things correctly from the start.

The bottom line is this: Learn it right the first time. If you don't learn to make mistakes, then there will be nothing to correct. Michel would start with a *tabula rasa*, a blank slate. He would teach the students how to speak grammatically correctly from the very beginning. And if they did make a mistake, they were immediately aware of it and then would correct it themselves. When we get to the next chapter on Theory we will see that this is a big problem in education today. Students start with many preconceived ideas that are entirely wrong. It is the job of the teacher to detect and correct these misconceptions. Otherwise the students will be confused and will make mistakes. We will come back to this point later.

There are several other problems with learning from mistakes, besides the fact that students usually don't learn from them. The first is that mistakes throw students into a performance mode, where they often become overly cautious and more concerned with avoiding mistakes than with learning. This also is a major source of *tension* and further interferes with the learning process. The second is that mistakes capture valuable attention.

> Research indicates that we only have seven plus or minus two chunks of attention.

This means that we can only consciously pay attention to five to nine things at once. It would be desirable that all of the chunks of a student's attention be focused on learning. If the students are concerned about making mistakes, then they will expend valuable and limited attention checking and monitoring to make sure that they are avoiding errors and mistakes. This short circuits the learning process. Michel would teach his students to think things out. They were automatically aware of mistakes and were able to self-correct without wasting attention on *trying* (that word again) to avoid mistakes.

VERB TENSES ARE THE HEART OF THE LANGUAGE

As we have indicated several times, in his complete courses, the *Master Teacher* would teach his students a comprehensive, working knowledge of the entire grammar of the language. This would include all of the tenses of the language including the subjunctive. Remember that Michel considered the grammar to be the structure of the language and the tenses to be the tools. Depending on the language, the number of tenses is between eighteen and twenty-two tenses. Michel's students comfortably knew these tenses and were able to use them with ease. Michel would accomplish this feat in just three days! This was quite remarkable! Just as remarkable was the fact that Michel never named the tenses during the entire course. What he would do was teach the student how to use the tenses correctly. In the traditional *dis-educational system*™, students will spend years and years studying a language and never know a quarter of the tenses, if that many.

For Michel, verbs were the heart of the language. Different tenses denote different time orientations and conditions. Michel would arrange his sequence around the tenses. First, one learned to speak in the present tense. Also, one began with regular verbs. Irregular verbs would be slotted in when Michel would deem it appropriate to do so. Although the student was not aware of it, Michel's plan was to teach the student all of the tenses of the language (eighteen to twenty-two) in just three days. So Michel would begin with the present tense and then would move to the past tense and to the future and so on.

Michel usually worked in complete sentences. He would ask something like:

"I must talk to you now because I have to leave soon and catch a train into the city."

Verbs would be taught in the context of complete sentences. There were no conjugations to learn. One learned from the sentences the difference between "I say," "he says," and "we, you, or they say."

MICHEL'S *"HANDLES"*

Michel explained to us that modals were important elements of mastering a language. He cleverly referred to them as *"handles"* and explained that "students learn how to 'grab *handles,*' meaning that these verbs are always followed by an infinitive or by two infinitives." They include verbs like "can," "must," "could," and "should." They are some of the most common words in the language. For example:

"I can do it," or "You must tell me," or 'I must go see it."

Once the modals are mastered in all tenses, one is able to communicate easily in the language.

As we mentioned earlier, Michel constantly emphasized the value of *a sharpened awareness of one's own language*. If you can't express something correctly in your own language, you will have a hard time expressing it in another language. In learning to speak another language Michel would help you gain *a sharpened awareness of your own language*, and he achieved this in a very subtle manner. He accomplished this by discreetly incorporating it into his teaching without making a huge issue of it so that the student would not feel uncomfortable in any way.

Michel's method, as we have said, was to introduce a new tense and reinforce it with examples until it was understood. The evidence of *understanding* was that the student was able to *generalize* it to other sentences. When one piece was mastered, Michel would move on to the next piece.

EXPLANATIONS AND *HEURISTICS*

How was the *Master Teacher* able to teach all that he did in three days and how were his students able to learn a language in such an easy, effortless and exciting way?

This is the ten million dollar question. The answer is found in the aspects of the method which we are covering.

> A major key to his magic lay in explanations and *heuristics* which, for the clever manner in which Michel incorporated them into his method, we have termed *"meaningful memory associations"*™.

In fact, Michel approved of our description of his customized use of explanations and *heuristics*. The explanations that Michel gave and the *heuristics* or *meaningful memory associations*™ that he created and used, were a critical and essential part of his method and also contributed to its efficacy

Heuristic is a technical term derived from the Greek word meaning "to discover" or "to find out." A *heuristic* is a teaching device that enables students to learn, discover, understand and solve problems on their own by experimenting and by evaluating possible answers or solutions, or by trial and error. *Heuristics* are rules of thumb which are useful *generalizations* for problem solving. Michel would use *heuristics* or *meaningful memory associations*™ (without using these terms) in a particular way —

he would use them as memory aides — incorporating them in just the right places within the structures of his method in order to enhance understanding.

> *Heuristics* transform meaningless labels into *meaningful memory associations*™.

As we have indicated, the usual approach to language learning is to learn a large number of terms and seemingly arbitrary rules and endless exceptions. The rules and exceptions don't make sense. They are arbitrary. There is no evident rhyme or reason to them. They just have to be memorized. The grammatical terminology consists largely of technical terms which are arbitrary labels that often don't make sense.

Explanations are critically important in learning. They provide the answer to the question "why?" as in "Why does it work?" or "Why is it this way and not some other way?" Explanations provide the reasons that allow students to make sense of things. Clear explanations produce the *understanding* that becomes *knowledge*. Without clear explanations, we are incapable of *understanding* and *knowing*. Without an answer to the "why" question, things appear arbitrary. We are told that things are simply the way that they are and that we have to accept them with no questions asked. And we are forced to remember an arbitrary fact that is not connected to anything else. Explanations connect things together.

> A clear explanation means that there is a reason for the way something is that makes sense, so clear explanations are indispensable in learning and in teaching.

Michel mastered the art of clear explanations. His approach was exactly the opposite of that of the grammarian. In fact, Michel's innovative mind shined through once again in the way in which he would explain seemingly complex notions with amazing clarity. In place of grammatical rules, Michel would provide clear explanations of practical concepts. Instead of memorizing arbitrary terminology and rules, Michel would provide his special brand of *heuristics* or *meaningful memory associations*™ that made sense and were easily remembered.

And the *Master Teacher* would always achieve clarity of explanation with great ease by creating a natural flow of words and meaning and *understanding*. He was a true master of clarity. Michel would explain things to his students so that they would make sense and so that they would not have to be memorized. Meaningless labels suddenly made sense and became meaningful in the minds of the students. With Michel, of course, there was no *trying to remember* anything. The student didn't have to do so.

To assist the student in remembering Michel provided two things. First was an explanation as to why something is the way it is. The explanation may have been historical or it may have related to a structure with which the student was already familiar. Now it made sense to the student because of the explanation Michel provided or because it was simply "like this." It simply "was that way," as he would say. The student understood it. The explanation was not arbitrary and it certainly didn't need to be memorized. The student's response would either be, "Oh, that makes sense," or "Of course, that is just like what I already know." Michel's ultimate goal with his use of *heuristics* was to create *understanding* in the minds of his students.

Thus, explanations were a critical aspect of teaching for Michel. *Understanding* occurs through proper explanations:

> Explanation is important for *understanding*. And *understanding* is never something that just happens. It is always the result of proper explanations. Explanations often make distinctions. Once the distinction is made, then what seemed confusing suddenly makes sense. Once students understand and know it, then they will be able to correct themselves.

If students didn't know something, they would often guess, and Michel would somehow always immediately detect that they were guessing. Even if the student guessed right, Michel would respond by saying, "It is right, but you guessed." Of course, at first, students would ask themselves "How did he know that I was guessing?" And in Michel's learning session, as we have already mentioned, guessing was wrong, even if the student guessed correctly. Michel would not accept correct guessing. It is also very important not to play it by ear because it sounds good. Michel explained this as follows:

> "Some students may think that they know it and that it should come out by itself. Whatever comes out by itself, even if it is correct, is still guessing.
> I don't allow guessing."

GOING INTO THE WOODS (*WOULDS*) WITH MICHEL

In addition to his explanations, Michel's clever use of *heuristics*, or as we prefer to say, his *meaningful memory associations*™ also served as learning aides. These are simple expressions or associations that the student easily remembers. Let us take a simple example. To explain the use of the conditional tense (which Michel never labeled as such, but which involves the helping verb "*would*"), Michel would tell his students that the conditional is a sign that "we are going into the '*woods*' (woulds)."

For example, in a Spanish lesson, Michel would tell his students to think of going "*into the woods*" by the river. "What is the feminine form of the *Rio* Grande?" he would ask. It is "*ría,*" which Michel refers to as the "*female river*" and which also conveniently happens to be the universal ending for the conditional tense in Spanish. Michel would say that "When you go into the woods (woulds), you will see the female river!" So whenever students hear *ría* at the end of a Spanish verb, they make the immediate association of going "into the woods," i.e., into use of the conditional verbs, or "woulds." Michel was always very clever and quiet effective each and every time in using his personally created *heuristics* or *meaningful memory associations*™.

Having gone through learning sessions with Michel for the purpose of modeling his method, and thus, having experienced his method first hand, we can say that one never forgets going into the "woods" (woulds). This ingenious way in which Michel renamed the conditional tense, literally engraved it into the minds of the students. By creating a *meaningful memory association*™ between what is known (going into the woods) and what is unknown (the conditional tense — the woulds), Michel ensures that the student never, ever forgets. It becomes an instantaneous and lasting connection.

By giving another name to the tense, in this case, the conditional, Michel took the concept out of the realm of expected difficulty of understanding into the realm of familiarity and comfort, so that it would become (no pun intended) part of the student's knowledge base. Students didn't have to memorize the conditional in order to use it correctly. They simply received an understanding of its use based on what was already familiar to them. And, as we have repeated Michel's personal mantram over and over again throughout this book,

> "What you *understand* and what you *know*, you will never forget."

MICHEL'S *"WINGS"*

Another example of Michel's use of *meaningful memory associations*™ or *heuristics* was his explanation of the imperfect tense. Most people don't even know when they are using the imperfect tense in English or in any language for that matter. As Michel rightfully remarked, "What in the world does the '*imperfect*' mean? Really, logically speaking, how can a verb be imperfect? Why is it called the imperfect tense?" The grammarian will be quick to add that the imperfect tense is the past tense of the verb "to be" followed by a gerund. Most people don't know or remember what a gerund means.

The standard explanation provided by grammarians usually makes no sense to the student. The students don't need to know what the imperfect tense is. All they need to know is how to use it correctly. So Michel, in order to make sense of it and to show his students how to use the imperfect tense correctly, ingeniously decided to name it *"the wing tense."* This immediately creates a *meaningful memory association*™ in the mind of the students. Again, this is another clever use of this heuristic tool which facilitates understanding without the need for memorization of conjugation. *The wing tense* (meaning the *w* from the verb was) — *w* followed by *ing* and (*w* from the verb were) — *w* followed by *ing*.

(*w* — *ing*)   was + *ing* equals the wing tense.
(*w* — *ing*)   were + *ing* equals the wing tense.

For example: I *w*ait*ing* to see him.
We *w*ere wait*ing* to see him.

Thus, in English, the imperfect tense or Michel's *w-ing* tense is always preceded by either the verb *was* or *were*. There is no "w" in the present tense. And when there is the "w" of the verb *was* or *were*, "You wing it," in the words of Michel. That is quite easy to recall. Michel made it easy, clever and fun all at the same time.

W—ing is a wing, and this association is so much easier to grasp than the word "*imperfect.*" Every time the students would hear Michel say the "wing tense," they immediately knew what tense he was using and they, too, understood how and when to use it correctly. In his classes, Michel never talked about the conditional, the pluperfect, the past subjunctive, etc. "They know how to use it," he explained. "That is what is important." What a phenomenal feat in the space of three days, when in our traditional system it takes years of study to learn all of the tenses in a given language! In fact, most students stuck in the *Mind Prison*™ end up dropping their foreign language courses before they even learn a fourth of the tenses unless they are completing a language requirement, in which case it represents double torture.

So instead of a list of seemingly ordered information and facts that makes no sense, Michel created a different kind of order. It was this innovative order which became the student's order. Moreover, it was a different structure than the grammarian's structure. It was a set of connected facts which

Michel would organize in a simplified way which made sense in the minds of the students. Michel would masterfully present the information so that the student was able to both use it and understand it with ease. And, most important, the student was able to do this immediately, on the spot.

Thus, Michel, the *Master Teacher*, was able to transform language learning from a process based on meaningless rote memorization of verb endings into a very exciting, effortless and immediately useful and inspiring learning experience!

These explanations and *heuristics* or *meaningful memory associations*™ were at the heart of Michel's method. They didn't happen by accident nor did they appear out of the blue. These ingenious elements required real creativity on Michel's part as well as the ability to create new patterns from scratch (As we will see in Chapter Nine, this talent reflects a behavioral trait inherent in Michel and in others with innovative minds.). Michel's explanations and *meaningful memory associations*™ also required letting go of the grammarian's traditional terminology.

In the traditional educational *dis-educational system*™, each generation of teachers is taught by the last. They are taught not to look at things from a new perspective, but are evaluated by their ability to repeat back the perspective of their teachers. As a result, there is little or no innovation in teaching. The blind follow the blind! Tragic but true. The same old models which were developed by the Greeks over two thousand years ago are still being used even though they don't work!

Part of the problem relating to a lack of creativity is due to a perceptual filter which we call the *"Change People Pattern"*™ (Chapter Nine). Individuals, in this case, traditional teachers who are uncomfortable with change and prefer to maintain the *status quo*, see the world through one type of the *Change People Pattern"*™ which we refer to as the *"Sameness People Pattern"*™. A teacher with this *pattern* takes in information from the world that is similar to what they already know and they often delete or ignore things that are different. As we will see in Chapter Nine, Michel's specific *Change People Pattern*™ was what we call the *"Difference People Pattern"*™. We will later explain how this *pattern* influenced his life, his teaching as well as the creation of the *Michel Thomas Method*.

Why did Michel's *meaningful memory associations*™ and explanations work so well? The answer to this question is connected to how the human mind works, in particular to memory. We have already discussed some of the research on memory. However, there is one piece that we have not mentioned thus far.

> Memory research reveals that the best way to remember something is to *associate* it with something that you already know.

Association has been called the mind's "glue." It holds things together in memory and is the basis of what are known as *"memory pegs"* used in many memory systems.

We have already mentioned that memory research reveals that there is a correlation between the time spent studying and the amount remembered. As we have also mentioned, the same research indicates that the method used to study is more important than the total time spent. With better methods students can recall more in less time. The best method for remembering more material in less time is to use associations as memory aids. This is exactly what Michel did as a vital part of his method. His carefully chosen associations allowed the student to remember easily and effortlessly without *trying*. Moreover, they are *meaningful memory associations*™ that make sense in the minds of students.

We also stressed that information is best remembered when it is organized and makes sense. Michel's carefully chosen explanations enabled the student to make sense of what he was presenting and to connect it up with what they already knew. In our modeling of Michel and his method we determined the following:

> This combination of clear explanations and powerful *meaningful memory associations*™, when coupled with a method that eliminates all *tension* and conscious interference with remembering, is the most effective memory process available.

Of course, the ability to interconnect all of these elements requires great creativity to craft the "right" explanations and to find the most memorable and *meaningful memory associations*™. Michel was truly a Master at both. The consistently remarkable results that he produced are testimony to this fact.

GENERALIZATION

A critical aspect of learning a language is the ability to *generalize* what you have learned.

> To *generalize* means to infer or to derive a general law or precept from particular instances.

Language has a structure and this structure is called grammar. It is regular in that it follows rules which have exceptions. And it is simply too time consuming to explicitly state all of the rules, just as it is too time consuming to provide explanations for everything. It is also unnecessary when learning a language because a student will be able to *generalize* from several examples. This is why choosing the right example is so very important. The evidence that the *generalization* has occurred is that the student will be able to express new content that fits the *generalization* correctly. The students are usually not even aware that they are *generalizing*. They just reason that if one thing is this way and another thing is also this way, then it follows that this must also be this way.

The *Master Teacher* creatively used *generalization* in his teaching even though he was not aware of the term *per se*. There were many things that he would not explain because he didn't need to explain them. Here is an example from French which Michel gave us:

> 'To see,' for instance is *voir, voir* because they will know from *Au Revoir*. So *voir* is 'to see.' So they know how to use *handles, je voudrais* (I would like), *je peux* (I can), *je vais* (I am going) etc. 'I can see.' is: *Je peux voir.* 'To see it' is: *Le voir.* I give no explanation. *Je vais voir. Je voudrais voir.* So I will say to them, this is *voir.* Then, 'to see it,' is *le voir.* There is no explanation. I am just telling them.

His use of *generalization* was effective each and every time. Once the students understood the new element, then Michel was able to *generalize* it to other examples. And the additional examples, too, were crystal clear in the student's mind.

Let's take another example. Next Michel would ask how to say: "I would like to see it": *Je voudrais le voir.* The process was quite easy and became automatic for the student, all this without Michel having to explain it. Then he might have said, "I am going to see it." *Je vais le voir.* Then, "I can see it." *Je peux le voir.* Once again, Michel would not give an explanation. He then might have asked: "How would you say: 'to see it'? *Le voir.* Then: 'I am going to see it.' *Je vais le voir.* 'I can see it.' *Je peux le voir.* 'I must see it.' *Je dois le voir.*" As if by magic, the phrase *le voir* was simply there with the student, understood, and it was not an *imprint*. Now, *le voir* was not an *imprint* in this case because Michel used it in different ways with *handles.*

Here is another example of how this *generalization* process works. The *Master Teacher* would ask: "What is 'to see'? V*oir.* What is 'to see it'? *Le voir.*" Again Michel was giving examples. He would ask the students how to say: "I would like to see it." And the students would know to respond with: *Je voudrais le voir.* Then when Michel would ask them how to say: "I am going to see it tonight." The student would answer: *Je vais le voir ce soir.* Likewise, "Are you going to see it? *Allez-vous le voir?*"

Now, the expression "to see it" became instantaneous in the mind of the students. They would immediately say *le voir.* Once the students knew perfectly how to make the distinction between *voir* and *le voir*, at any time then Michel would ask:

"What is 'to do'?" *Faire*. Since the students already knew this verb, Michel would make other clever associations such as, "It is very 'fair' to do it."

> Thus, Michel would creatively teach the students to build sentences in which he had incorporated the *meaningful memory associations*™.

The French verb *faire* (to do or to make) was associated with the fact that it is "fair" to do it.' And, students never forgot the association of *faire* and "fair."

Here is another clever *meaningful memory association*™ which Michel used. Take the French verb *venir* (to come). Michel made the association with veneer. He explained that: "Veneer doesn't *come* off on a table." And in asking the students how to say: "Do you want to come tonight?' they knew how to correctly respond with: *Voulez-vous venir ce soir*? Thus, the *meaningful memory association*™ of "veneer" (which doesn't come off on a table) and *venir (to come),* fits into the understanding of correct grammar which the students had already grasped.

Next, Michel would make a smooth transition to another *generalization* example. He might have asked the students how to say: "to make a reservation for me": Will you make a reservation for me?

Voulez-vous faire une réservation pour moi?

Within the first hour, even students who believed that they never had the ability to speak another language were able to say with confidence: "I would like to make a reservation" or "I would like to do it." Michel explained it as follows:

> Usually they would say immediately, *Je voudrais le faire*, but not always. Some may be stuck for a moment. They don't know how to say it. I say fine. So I say, 'What is 'to see'? They say: *voir*. OK. Then I say, 'What is 'to see it'?' and they

> say *le voir* and then they say 'Ah, the aha reaction.'

The light had gone on in their minds and the students knew how to correctly say the sentence having built upon their prior knowledge. The students were not spending time pondering over how to use correctly the newly introduced element. They knew how to use it without Michel having to go into a lengthy explanation.

Let us take another example. Michel would ask:

> So what is 'to do'? The students will say *faire*. Then I ask 'What is to do it?' and they will say *le faire*. And I didn't have to explain it. They will automatically say it and know it. I give no explanation. I don't say that in French when you have the infinitive, the pronoun is placed in front of the infinitive. No explanation. So 'I would like to do it.' is: *Je voudrais le faire*. They automatically know that 'I can't do it,' is: *Je ne peux pas le faire.* 'Will you prepare it for me?' They know that it is: *Voulez-vous le preparer pour moi*. They will automatically say it. 'I would like to have it.' *Je voudrais l'avoir*. That is automatic. And they can say it.

Michel was building upon reinforcement of *meaningful memory associations*™. There was a reinforcement of an expression, in this case, *le voir* and he gave the students different ways of using *le voir*. Once the student understood the concept, Michel was then able to introduce a new element into the sentence, adding another block to the foundation and the new construction. For example: *Je veux le voir* or *Je peux le voir* (I want to see him/it/ or I can see him/it.).

Michel would also use *generalizations* when he replaced a verb with another verb. Once the students understood the new construction, Michel could then add on the next element to it. He explained this to us as follows:

> And it is not a question here of not understanding. Once they automatically have it,

they are able to do it. It's automatic. It's not a thinking process at all. It is just there. It's just automatic. There is no explanation. It is not a thinking process at all, so it doesn't create *tension*... They are totally in the moment capturing that piece. The mind makes an immediate deduction. One doesn't have to think about it. It was this way and that's it.

Also, we would like to point out another important piece. It is that the students were grasping and assimilating that new element in what in our terminology we call "*the now.*" The students were focused on the present moment, not worrying about what they had done previously; and they are not anxious as to what to do next. They are totally in the moment focused on acquiring that new piece.

The *Master Teacher* explained that the above process became entirely natural for them, and if one had asked the students why they had done it that way, they would not have known. Michel explained the process like this:

It simply works this way. That's how it is. That's it. Once they know this, later I can explain to them: 'To see' is *voir*, 'to see it,' becomes *le voir*. Then I say *le voir* is also used in French to mean 'to see him.' I say to them that 'her' is *la*, so I ask them, 'How would you say 'to see her'?' And they automatically know that 'to see her' is *la voir*. They will say 'aha.' This creates excitement. Then they will automatically say when I ask, 'How do you say 'to see you'? They will say, *vous voir*. They will do it automatically in no time. 'I would like to see you.' *Je voudrais vous voir*. So I will add 'to understand' or 'to comprehend' is *comprendre*. And when I ask, 'How do you say 'to understand it'?' they will automatically say *le comprendre*. Then I say, 'I cannot understand it.' They will say: *Je ne peux pas le comprendre*. 'I cannot understand you,' is *Je ne peux pas vous comprendre*. That will be automatic.

Thus, Michel wouldn't have to explain anything. The students just knew it to be right and it became second nature to them. Michel carried out the whole *generalization* process in a smooth and effortless manner.

Why do *generalizations* work so well? We will explain. The mind has the ability to quickly detect regularity or patterns. Once the pattern is learned one can quickly generate many examples. This involves a combination of induction and deduction. Induction enables the student to *generalize* the basic pattern from a few well chosen examples. Once the pattern is discovered, then the student can use deductive reasoning to generate further examples. This short cuts the learning process tremendously. The student does not have to be taught all of the grammatical rules. Instead, the students simply need some well chosen examples; and they can generalize to other situations. They are usually not even aware of the explicit formulation of the grammatical rule. This is unnecessary.

All that is necessary is that they can generalize to other situations. It is critically important that the right examples be given from which to *generalize*. Otherwise, the student may form a wrong *generalization*. Michel was a master craftsman. His examples were carefully chosen to prevent ambiguity and to enable the student to make just the right *generalization* with complete clarity. The result again was *understanding*. This dramatically accelerates the learning process, and this is just one of the many reasons why we call Michel, the *Master Teacher*.

THE *MASTER TEACHER* AT WORK

Interestingly, the *Master Teacher* was able to accomplish what he did because he was never trained to be a teacher in general or to be a language teacher in particular. He approached teaching from the point of view of the learner. In fact, Michel taught himself to be a learner and a brilliant one at that. This was largely *in spite of,* and not *because of* good teachers. Michel was able to put himself in the position of the learner and was an example of what we call "*meta-cognition.*" This, too, was an incredible gift. In order to understand the perspective of the learner, he would ask two questions that are critical. These are:

1) How can I explain it so that it makes sense to me and so that I will *understand* it and know it?

2) What connection or association can I create that will help me to never forget it?

These are the questions of a learner. Michel would apply these questions to everything that he taught. This is why he was so remarkably effective in what he accomplished as a teacher.

Also, Michel didn't start with the assumption and excuse that the learner was to blame. He didn't make excuses to accuse students of being lazy or stupid. Instead, he would ask, "What is it about traditional methods that don't work?" In traditional teaching, what is not learner friendly? People are only lazy, frustrated or stupid when they are bored and when they don't understand the material. Real learning is exciting, very exciting. When you teach things so that students understand the subject matter, then they are able to do amazing things and to feel immense excitement for learning. When you provide them with powerful *meaningful memory associations*™ and *heuristics*, the students simply don't forget. And when they don't forget, they become even more excited and even develop confidence in themselves. This is exactly how Michel would teach his courses. He completely dissolved *"the complexity myth"* around language learning. Instead of triggering fear and dread, as in the traditional system, Michel would open the door to the excitement of learning by triggering that *innate drive for learning* found in all living beings.

Michel was truly a *Master Teacher* in every way. His innovative method required a creative and inquiring mind, and one that could make extraordinary distinctions and connections. One must be inquiring to go beyond the inherited modes of organizing and presenting material. And one must be creative enough to discover the simple patterns and *meaningful memory associations*™ that make learning easy. For Michel, this was part of the excitement of teaching:

> "To look, to seek, to find, to create, to make it simple and easy for the student to *understand* and to learn is part of the excitement of teaching."

This entails looking intelligently at something and seeing the simple pattern behind it. As the *Master Teacher,* and in his personal life, this is what Michel was able to do. He so brilliantly structured the learning experience in such a way that it:

1) Created excitement for learning
2) Enhanced the learning process and
3) Allowed his students to achieve *understanding* which leads to *knowledge*, lasting *knowledge*.

Michel was able to do this so successfully because of his remarkable ability to put himself in the position of the learner. He was literally able to walk in their shoes. Or we could say that he was able "to tune into their wave length." In our terminology, this is what we refer to as demonstrating "*an advanced rapport skill.*" Michel would not just listen to what the learner was saying. He would also listen to what was behind what the learner was saying. This is yet another secret to his Method which was revealed through the modeling process.

For example, he would ask, "How is it that what they are thinking is reflected in what they are saying?" This is the question he was able to interpret quite effortlessly. And, it was precisely what they were thinking and it was precisely what was in their minds that comprised the critical component. Michel would focus his attention on these significant components. Obviously, his war time experiences as an intelligence interrogator served him in good stead here in this context of observing and determining how and what was on the minds of his students. We refer to this ability to decipher the thinking of his students as "*calibration*," which we explain later in this chapter.

Early on in his life the *Master Teacher* developed great *calibration* skills which he ingeniously incorporated into his teaching method. This ability allowed him to monitor the students' progress on many levels. He was able to tune into the emotions and beliefs of his students and furthermore, to get on the same wave length. Michel was constantly quite aware of minute changes in physiology that enabled him to feel and to sense what the students were experiencing internally: "I am connected to my students... I know what is behind a gesture, a movement." Michel certainly understood that there was a close relationship between what they were thinking, i.e., their beliefs, emotions, skill base and previous experiences which, in turn, affected the way in which they interacted in a given environment.

TEACHER SELECTION AND TRAINING

> "....If they are not able to explain, then they are not capable of being a teacher."

Michel had native teachers who taught languages that he did not speak. Even the way in which he would go about selecting teachers to teach these courses was quite revelatory in itself. As Michel often stated, "It is rare to find a teacher who knows how to teach." He would lament the fact that often today, all that is required to teach at the college level is an advanced degree in the subject being taught. However, real teaching requires more than content knowledge.

Michel expanded upon this by saying: "The important thing is to establish the right vehicle for teaching, meaning that one needs to establish the proper vehicle for communication. Sometimes people don't know how to communicate with each other." For Michel, teaching meant positive interaction with his students. And the ability to communicate effectively is a critical component of positive interaction. In good teaching this is a component not to be overlooked or dismissed.

Let us discuss for a minute how Michel selected teachers to teach languages that were not part of his repertoire. In our follow-up book, we are writing about how to teach the method using Michel's personal strategies which he shared with us, as well how to assimilate and use other approaches to enhance the process further. The most important element for Michel in selecting them was that the teachers be "*teachable*" in order to learn his method. Of course, this ruled out practically anyone who had already had experience teaching a language. The reason is that they would have had to have learned Michel's method, and in order to do this, they would have had to have given up whatever method they were already using. Remember that he applied the same principle to accepting students: "If the students have to *unlearn*, I wouldn't take them." This is very difficult, and under stress they would revert back to their old ways.

With the Japanese language, Michel eliminated from the beginning as potential candidates, anyone with previous language teaching experiences. They could have taught another subject, but not languages. And he didn't want teachers who had been associated with other language schools because he would have had to unteach the patterns and the approach they were using. Next Michel would interview the candidates to see if he or she was suitable to learn how to teach his method. They had to be good communicators and had to have a good ability to explain things clearly. Before training them, Michel had the candidates listen to a few of his tapes so that they would have a feel for how his method worked.

Michel trained the teachers by having them teach him their own language. Let us take Japanese, for example. (Remember that with Japanese, Michel never took anyone who had taught Japanese before.) He would start by asking: "How would you say this in Japanese?" Then Michel would repeat it back to make sure that his pronunciation was correct. Michel described the process as follows:

> I am asking them something practical from the beginning. So this is 'What is it?' I repeat it for pronunciation and I ask another question. They will tell me and then I will put it together. Aha, this is what it means. Then they will say: 'In Japanese we don't say it that way.' Then they explain it to me. In that case, I will do it this way. Now I

understand how it is put together. The teacher may say we use a different word for it. 'Why?' I ask. They explain. Now it all gets into explanations which are understood. They explain it to me, the student, and it is understood. After half an hour or forty-five minutes, we have quite a number of sentences. And the teacher will say: 'You must know Japanese.' They don't believe me when I tell them no. They see something happening in front of them which I make them create. And after that, wait a moment, 'Look!' they say. 'You are doing it because you know it.' They thought I was fooling them. This is usually what happens with any of those languages.

In essence, what Michel was doing was teaching his teachers how to teach him using his method. In teaching them, they were observing and reacting to his responses as the student, and the excitement generated by the process brought joy to both teacher and student. His teachers, by the way, had to be completely bi-lingual, meaning demonstrating mastery of their own native language in addition to English, with a good, solid grammatical knowledge of both.

Through this process, Michel helped the teacher to create a structure. The teacher was trained to teach the way Michel learned. This was based on explanations and understanding. As Michel explained to us:

> If I don't fully understand, they explain it. Then I say, 'OK, can I say it this way?' And they say 'no,' so then they have to explain it to me. 'Why not?' I ask. So they have to explain it to me. All of this leads into explanations, and explanations lead into *understanding*. And once I *understand*, then I *know*. Once it becomes *knowledge* to me, then I will know how to use it. It is all based on explanations. They are key. If they are not able to explain, then they are not capable of being a teacher. If they just say 'Well, this is how it is.' or 'I don't know.' If they cannot explain, then it is thank you, no.

In this case, they were not going to be teaching for Michel. In teaching their language to Michel, the practice led the teachers into experiencing what occurred in the learning process. Michel excitedly explained to us: "I am the student. Maybe, I'm a better student. That is not the point. Yet, without writing anything down, I want them to explain it to me step by step. After awhile it becomes exciting to them because they [the teachers] see what is happening."

The beauty of his method is that you didn't have to wait to see the results. They are instantaneous. You also didn't have to wait until you knew any particular thing. The students knew at once because the fruits of learning were immediate and you could build upon these results with great ease.

Michel elaborated even further:

> Well, once I get them on the road, then, I can say how to go from there. And they are already into it with excitement because they can see what they have already achieved. So it is not just a learning process for them. 'Ah, I have to remember this or that.' They have learned already how to use creative thinking in proceeding and the reaction is excitement. If they don't have it, then they will be stuck and will not know how to go on from there… If they get stuck, that's it.

Michel personally found it exciting to see how these teachers progressed and to see how the processes worked. He said that the processes were effective with them because he didn't have to impose anything. Michel added, "They continue and in continuing they find ways to become creative and to use creative thinking. And I always help them with happy smiles."

Of course, Michel was the ideal student whose excitement was contagious. So here, in working with Japanese teachers, they would get more and more excited by what they saw as well. Finally they would reach the point where they were able to continue to develop the course on their own so that Michel did not have to go through the whole process with them. They had assimilated important aspects of his teaching which were to become creative and generative in the process of learning the method. First, they got the method going and then they were able to apply it on their own. Once they were on the way, they could not *derail.* If they *derailed,* then they were lost. Once on the way, they would be able to continue the journey. And as they continued, they could see excitement in their students. They realized that what they were doing really did work! You can imagine how very rewarding this was to the teachers. Good teaching is not only exciting for the student who is learning, it is also exciting for the teacher as well.

In short, this is how Michel would select and then teach his teachers the method. First and foremost, they had to be good communicators and they had to be able to explain things clearly. Moreover, they had to be creative and could not have any preconceptions about teaching. They had to start with a blank slate and have no bad habits. Creativity was the key in that the prospective teachers had to demonstrate a vital component of the method — ability to generate the appropriate *meaningful memory associations*™.

We would like to make the point Michel constantly emphasized:

> This method cannot be taught to just anyone, and not even to teachers simply because they are already teaching.

Just because someone is a teacher does not automatically mean that he or she will be able to use the method in their teaching. Regarding this, Michel always stated,

> "To me a teacher has to be a creative thinker. If they are not, they shouldn't teach. Why should I pick just anybody from the street? Not just anybody can be a good doctor."

That is precisely the problem we find in our current *dis-educational system*™. Of course, there are some very creative teachers out there who are doing a wonderful job with their students. Yet, for the most part, we have created generations of teachers, many of whom cannot engage in the critical thinking necessary to create clear explanations. Or else they lack the spark of creativity which is a vital element needed to generate the *meaningful memory associations*™ so critical to facilitating the students' memory process (See Chapter Nine, where we discuss the *Change People Pattern*™, the perceptual filter that is linked to creative thinking. It was a major key to Michel's ability to make distinctions and to create his method.). In recent years, some teachers have decided to leave the traditional school system to become "home-school teachers" specifically because their creativity was totally stifled in the *Mind Prison*™.

Students were delighted with the results they got in learning languages from Michel's teachers. The following was written by someone who had taken a course with one of his teachers:

> ... I am surprised not to be rolling around the floor begging to be released... You simply sit and absorb and the work is done by the teacher, who somehow manages to relax you enough to let it all melt into your brain... There is something so comforting about leaving the burden of learning...there is no fear of failure, and so I am absorbing more than I ever dreamed possible...

CHUNKING AND *SEQUENCING*

Chunking is a term in our work as trainers that we use to describe the process of breaking up the content of a training into smaller units or pieces. *Sequencing* is the term we use to describe the order in which the chunks or units or pieces are taught. Sequence is critically important and teaching has to occur linearly. One must learn to crawl before one can learn to walk, and one must learn to walk before one can learn to run. Similarly, in teaching one needs to work from the known to the unknown and from the simple to the complex. Both *chunking* and *sequencing* structure the learning process like building blocks. Each layer builds upon the previous layers. Concepts are presented and absorbed in the proper sequence. The learning process is thus structured in a logical progression, enabling the student to understand and retain the information easily and effortlessly.

Although he was not aware of these terms which we use in training, Michel was quite a master at *chunking* and *sequencing*. He rightfully described the process in his own manner:

> "I am the architect who designs the house, and it is up to you to decorate it."

Michel took three days to teach a language. Over a period of three days the student would learn all of the tenses, the entire grammar of a language and a practical and functional vocabulary. He would start with the present tense and then he would proceed on to the past tense, then to the future tense and then to the other tenses. Remember that Michel would teach all of the tenses (eighteen to twenty-two) in three days without ever labeling the tenses! *Chunking* played a major role in this.

In modeling Michel, it was quite obvious to us that *chunking* was a critical part of what he did. Here is where the element of *chunking* came into play in Michel's teaching his courses.

> *Chunking* is the process of breaking the language up into small, easily-digested pieces.

Everything in the language must be understood and used. Subject matter is not just "covered" as in many college language courses. The subject matter is understood and becomes *knowledge*. And time must be allotted to each piece. Each piece must come in the correct sequence and must take whatever time that it takes and no more.

> *Sequencing* is the process of ordering all of the pieces so that each piece can be assimilated before the next piece is presented.

In Michel's method, we have a continuous process of student responses and feedback with the language presented in small, easily-digested pieces. As these pieces are assimilated, they assume their place in the whole structure of the language. Thus, the student can at all times see the relationship of each piece to the whole. And because each piece is assimilated before the next one is presented, the student constantly builds upon a firm base of his or her own knowledge. Not only do students learn the language, but they experience strong feelings of achievement, and feel themselves learning, which produces self-motivation. This, in turn, accelerates further learning progress.

The pattern and sequence in which new information is presented and the method of assimilation through response and feedback are of critical importance in guiding students through their self-development of a hierarchy of language skills. It is this well defined *system* that assures learning and precludes the need for textbooks, learning by rote, homework, memorization and the other trappings traditionally used in teaching — especially in teaching languages. Not only was learning inevitable in the *Michel Thomas Method*, it was fun and enjoyable as well. Students were able to relax and to let the method do the work! His method never allowed students to be confronted with information which they were not prepared to absorb. This eliminated the confusion and frustration usually associated with learning a foreign language.

In summary, the *Master Teacher* was always aware of the student's level of comprehension and learning. He would always spoon-feed the student just the right amount of new information to move to the next level of complexity without complicating the existing understanding. Michel would build upon information that had become *understanding* so that any new concept was presented in a context that made sense, given the foundation upon which it was built. He would never overload the learner's mind. Furthermore, he would always be aware of how far he could go at any given point in time with new information, always maintaining a simplicity of presentation and building on material already presented and assimilated. Michel would not add more complexity to the sentence until he saw that the student had already integrated prior structure built on *understanding*.

MICHEL'S SECRET

People were amazed at how much material Michel was able to cover in such a short time. Just what was his secret? The secret of how he accomplished this feat is contained in the parts of his method which we have already discussed. In short, it begins with explanations, *meaningful memory associations*™ and *generalizations*. All of these are blended together to create a smooth flow of delivery and content. At all times Michel would be focused on the student *understanding* and knowing the language. As we have already seen, he did not use any of the traditional academic methods including lectures, textbooks, note taking, rote memorization, home work, mental reviewing and testing. This makes what Michel was able to accomplish even more astonishing!

How did Michel succeed in accomplishing so much in such a short time and without the use of traditional methods? Part of the answer is self-evident. Traditional methods don't work. They create *tension* and rely on short term memorization which is just as quickly forgotten. They are tedious, boring and time-consuming. There is much talk today about so-called accelerated learning. Michel had discovered the secrets of real accelerated learning, and he didn't use the techniques of so-called accelerated learning either (See Chapter Seven for more details.). As we have seen, Michel had his own magnificent method that actually did work — for engaging and captivating his students and for enhancing their leaning process to produce remarkable results every single time.

> Michel's method is intimately connected to the structure of the learning process itself.

Michel's process began by eliminating all *tension* from the beginning. Next the student began to learn at a rapid pace, which in itself, was exciting, stimulating and energizing. Once students realized how exciting learning could be, they didn't want to stop. Their attention was riveted. Also, Michel's method was interactive so that the students were constantly involved at every moment. There was no time to be bored or distracted.

The *Master Teacher* had divided the entire grammar of the language and a practical and functional vocabulary up into small, easily digestible pieces that the learner could master over three days. The pieces may have involved explanations, they may have contained *heuristics* or *meaningful memory associations*™ or they may have enabled the student to generalize. What was significant was that the pieces were progressive and built upon each other. Michel would begin with the familiar and then he would *"layer"* in the unfamiliar. Michel would not add a new piece until each previous piece had been assimilated by the learner. In this way the student was never presented with information out of sequence or with material that he or she did not already have a firm foundation with which to absorb the information. This process would continue until the course objectives were accomplished.

One aspect of Michel's success was in part due to his boldness. Most people would say it takes years to learn a language and would leave it at that. Often, many even say that what Michel accomplished was impossible. In their minds it can't be, therefore it isn't. Obviously, there must be some mistake or misunderstanding or trick. These people are victims of their own self-limiting beliefs. Fortunately for Michel, he had hugely empowering beliefs. In fact, it was his beliefs in accomplishing what others deemed impossible, which were certainly also a major factor in his having escaped the hands of death, and survived the tortuous years in work camps and concentration camps during the war. Moreover, it was this same set of empowering beliefs and convictions that spurred Michel on until his last breath in his dream of transforming the traditional educational system.

Michel had never been constrained by convention. He set out more than half a century ago to explore the learning process of the human mind. With each new student he would ask himself, "How can I explain this better?" He would ask himself how he could come up with better associations, which we named *meaningful memory associations*™. He would also ask himself how he could get the student to generalize what he was teaching more quickly. As he did this, the time that it took for him to teach a language began to decrease. Michel was never constrained by any beliefs as to how long it had to take to learn a language. He was not compensated by the hour. He was remunerated according to the learning session, and every session was an overwhelming success!

Thus, Michel's learning sessions evolved over a period of time. They were the result of years of refinement, and this did not occur by chance. His learning sessions were the result of trial and error. They were the result of Michel continually refining and improving upon his own process with his innovative thinking and brilliant mind.

> We believe that the lesson to learn here is that human beings are capable of incredible learning once the constraints to learning are removed, and once they are taught in the correct way.

Constraints come from the educational system, from teachers, from parents and from the students themselves. Michel had developed learning and teaching processes that removed these restrictions. The results seem amazing to those still under the constraints, to those still wearing the shackles of their disempowering beliefs generated by the *Mind Prison*™. For Michel, the refinement process continued until his passing. And he had no preconceived limitations of where it would end. In fact, he was well aware of what was yet to come.

LAYERING

In his learning sessions, the *Master Teacher* engaged in doing multiple things at once, a major factor that allowed him to do more in less time. Traditional learning is broken into lessons which must be presented in order. For example, we must finish one lesson before we begin another. This type of process is slow, tedious and frequently boring. Michel, of course, never gave a series of lessons. Instead, he was able to do many things at once. In teaching, the process of doing multiple things at once is called *layering*. This was not Michel's term.

THE *MICHEL THOMAS METHOD*: THE *MASTER TEACHER'S* MODEL

> *Layering* is based on the principle that it is faster and more efficient to do multiple things at the same time rather than one thing at a time.

As we have said, most teachers teach one thing and when that subject matter is "covered," they then move on to the next piece. This type of approach definitely slows down the learning process.

What does it mean to do multiple things simultaneously?

The answer to this question reveals yet another secret to successful teaching. *Layering* involves three things:

> 1) Pre-teaching
> 2) Teaching and
> 3) Post-teaching or reviewing.

First, pre-teaching is to introduce a concept that will be covered in depth later and then leaving it without filling it in with information. The student is "exposed" to the concept briefly in passing without elaboration or depth. The concept remains in the student's mind as something familiar yet incomplete.

Second, teaching is to round out the concept with explanations and associations and to begin to generalize and contextualize it. Third, post-teaching or reviewing is to come back to something that has already been learned and to use it in the process of learning something else. For example, Michel would introduce a word or concept in passing. It would be used implicitly and later he would come back to it. The student had already used it so that it was familiar to him/her. Michel would now make it explicit and then would fill it in. Now the student knew it. Still later, Michel would introduce something else and the word or concept would reappear somewhere in the sentence. For Michel this was a way of reinforcing it through use and in our terminology we know this to be a part of the *layering* process.

There is an important question which arises in the context of *layering*. Why doesn't everybody use *layering* in teaching? The reason why more teachers don't use *layering* is because their minds do not think that way. It happens to be a complex process.

> *Layering requires the ability to understand the whole as well as the parts of the whole.*

In order to *layer*, one must be constantly aware of the learning objectives involved and always focused on what one is trying to accomplish. One must start from the point of view of the whole and not be sidetracked by the parts. To *layer* successfully, the teacher always has to know what is coming up next and what has already been covered. Only then can you do multiple things at once. Most teachers can only focus on one thing at a time.

Some people cannot multi-task in the context of their everyday lives. The same applies to teachers. A teacher must be aware of how to pre-teach or in other words, be aware of how to introduce the next important concept in the context of the lesson in progress. Later on, once the concept has been used implicitly, the teacher must return to it and make it explicit. Once it is explicit and the student knows it, then it can be alluded to in the future. In teaching it is possible to do all three of these things at once. This is the essence of *layering*. And *layering* dramatically reduces the time in which one can learn a subject matter.

Also, in order to *layer* successfully as Michel did so elegantly, you have to be able to do what is called "*multi-tracking*." *Multi-tracking* is another important concept. It means that one has the ability to pay attention to multiple things at once. What it means is that one can perform multiple tasks simultaneously. Michel developed this wonderful ability as a child, an ability which helped him both to survive the hell that he endured in the slave labor and concentration camps, and later to become an amazing counter intelligence officer for the US Army. A great counter intelligence interrogator like Michel was able to focus on multiple things at once. A good liar learns to hide obvious signs. A skilled interrogator notices the less obvious signs of which the liar is not even aware.

In summary, Michel adroitly accomplished *layering* in the following manner. He would introduce a word or concept or explanation or association implicitly in passing. Later he would come back to it and then would fill it in so that it is explicit. Subsequently, he would use it in passing which would further reinforce it. At any point in the learning session, he might have been doing these three things and even more simultaneously. He might have been introducing a word or a concept implicitly, he might have been filling in a previous word or concept and making it explicit, and he might have been deepening the word or concept by reviewing or using it. This was one of the secrets of his success. This amazing ability to do three things at once in the context of translating one sentence is what made the method so fast and effective.

Also, he incorporated multiple levels of understanding. By using *layering*, one may cover the same subject multiple times, but each time one is reaching a deeper level of understanding. With some things it takes time to become familiar with them. Once you come back to the familiar, you are ready for further insight. In this way, one can reach deeper and deeper levels of understanding over time.

It had taken Michel fifty years to refine achievement levels from weeks to days. Over time, he had not only discovered the secret of *layering* without knowing it or calling it such, he had also become a master of *layering*. It is the key to doing more with less. There was no wasted effort in what Michel taught, and everything was intended to accomplish multiple outcomes simultaneously. Therein lies the beauty of his method.

BLOCK TEACHING

The *Master Teacher* was a staunch advocate of what is known as "*block teaching*." In most classrooms, one spends 45 to fifty minutes on one subject and then moves on to the next. In a day, one will have six, fifty minute periods with breaks in between. In contrast, *block teaching* divides a thirty-six to forty-two week school year into blocks. Each block may last from days to weeks. How long the block lasts depends on how long that it takes to learn the subject and the length of the block may vary. Sometimes it may be best to break up a block and then later continue with another short block on the same subject.

Also, within the block, the times vary. You may have a block with only a few days or one that lasts a few months. This is because the learning process is not based on the time of one day or two days or whatever. The beauty of *block teaching* is that you can spend whatever amount time you wish, leave off and continue from the point you left off without the need to start all over again. What we call *"the efficiency factor,"* inherent to *block teaching*, is unparalleled. *Block teaching* is far superior to and more effective than other alternatives. In fact, of this Michel specifically stated:

> "Block teaching is not only much more efficient, it is more dramatically efficient."

When asked what the advantage was of *block teaching* Michel adamantly stated, "You have one area, one subject where you can go into depth — where you are involved with it." By contrast, in the traditional classroom method, you have a whole series of short sessions by the time that you start and end each class. You end up breaking up a subject into many pieces. And then just when you get started, you stop the process, cut it off and go to another subject. You have a *mélange* of different teaching subjects, one after the other in short sessions. This is an inefficient process. Just when you get going you have to stop. It doesn't build momentum and is episodic. It can also create undue stress and often does so, as experienced in the *Mind Prison*™.

Also, traditional classroom teaching does not usually build excitement unless there is an amazingly creative and enthusiastic teacher who truly stimulates the students with a passion that is contagious. Those who have experienced this passion in a teacher know what we mean. The bottom line is that true learning is exciting. In true learning, no one wants to stop after fifty minutes to go onto something else. The passion to learn is so great that one wants to continue on and on to learn more. Why do six things poorly when you can do one thing really well! In fifty minutes one can make an *imprint* on the mind, however there is no time to grow the *imprint*.

> The key to learning is the process of continuous deepening or reinforcement.

In fifty minutes, one can just barely get into a specific subject matter and then it is time to move on. Also, whatever learning state is developed is broken or interrupted as one moves on to the next class. In a whole day, on the other hand, one can get into a learning state and deepen it as much as desired during the course of the day. Furthermore, in a whole day a great deal can be *layered* within the subject matter. Amazingly, Michel was able to *layer* in a whole language in just three days. Imagine in thirty days, one would be able to *layer* in a tremendous amount of material.

In short, the challenge with traditional teaching is that nothing is assimilated before one moves on to the next thing. In traditional teaching, one usually barely scratches the surface. One remains on a superficial level, whereas with Michel's method, one could create depth, depth of *understanding*. The key to learning and to deepening *understanding* into *knowledge* is to introduce a concept, and then to continuously reinforce it through practice, and to continue to deepen and apply it. This can be accomplished in a day. Therefore, it should be possible in six weeks to teach what is currently taught in several years.

The traditional *dis-educational system*™ thinks that the attention spans of most students are so short that it is necessary to continually change subjects. The belief is that a student can only focus and concentrate on one thing for fifty minutes or less. This is a sad commentary on the quality of today's teaching. On the contrary, Michel was able to hold a student's attention for days on end, even students who were diagnosed with ADD and ADHD, and who are the so-called problem kids of the traditional *Mind Prison*™. His students never wanted to leave. Michel's success is quite a contrast to the *dis-educational system's*™ mind-numbing solution of drugging children into vegetative states rather than awakening their *innate drive for learning*.

A good example of *block teaching* is the program that Michel prepared for Spanish-speaking students in a Los Angeles public school in the 1970's. Michel described it as follows:

> It so happens in the program which I used in that school for the whole year, that the first block was a six week block to teach English. I chose it that way because I felt it would take six weeks for the children to raise their level of Spanish from Barrio Spanish to correct Spanish. And also, I chose to teach them how to read and write in Spanish and to learn to read and write in English at the same time. So that was the first block. During these six weeks nothing else was taught.

Each day the class was divided in half. Half a day was devoted to listening to language tapes with Michel, and half a day was spent working with a teacher. Michel himself supplied tape recorders on loan so that each child had a head set and tape recorder. Michel added: "This way each child had their own privacy. Teachers were working with the students for half a day and then the students switched to the tapes, and vice versa. So every day they would switch between teachers and tapes."

In the first Spanish/English block, the students learned how to speak and write correct Spanish. At the same time they were also learning how to speak, read and write in correct English. The children began to read in English. Michel also had the students write short stories and discuss them in English. They even collected all of the stories together into a book. The students were so excited that they didn't even want to break for lunch. All of them came to class with their lunch from home. And Michel informed us that these were children whose only good meal of the day came from school.

After the first block, all the teaching was done in English because the children were now bilingual. They spoke with the press in English and people were amazed by their astounding progress. The second block was math. Again, it was divided between half a day with a teacher and half a day of a tape course which Michel designed. As Michel described it,

It may have taken two or three weeks. Again, it was a combination of tapes and practice with the teacher. It may have been less than half a day, I don't remember. The important thing was that it was *block teaching*. It was only math, and math taught in English. All the other subjects like social studies were done in blocks. The length of the block was determined by the subject.

Block teaching gives children an important edge in that they don't experience fatigue which, as we have discussed earlier, creates a major impediment to learning. Instead, students experience genuine pleasure and the joys of what real learning should be. What a stark contrast to the traditional *dis-educational system*™. With long, boring days of drudgery in the *Mind Prison*™, students quickly lose interest and often become agitated and disruptive. *Block teaching*, on the other hand, promotes great excitement in students and fires up that passion within to learn more and more.

When we asked Michel why he preferred *block teaching*, he immediately answered:

> Because it is highly advantageous to the children, because they don't get tired. On the contrary, they are excited. They feel the excitement of true learning. They are not subjected to the pain of drills and to what they "have to" do. They are exposed to enjoyment, to pleasure, to so much pleasure that they did not even want to break for lunch — their only lunch — so much pleasure that after six weeks of school when their own school library was closed, they would go to the public library to learn, not to be deprived of learning because learning is not imposed upon them. The doors to learning have been opened and not slammed by our educational system. They are not choked, but are happily breathing.

Whenever Michel described this experience with the children to us, his eyes would light up with joy:

Imagine that these young children were so excited about learning that they would go to the public library to read the encyclopedia after school! Those who interviewed them could not believe what they were hearing! Imagine that these same children did not even know what an encyclopedia was six weeks before! When asked why they went to the public library, the children declared with delight: 'Because we are learning!'

Michel did not excite them into learning. He said that he reawakened that *innate drive for learning*, that excitement for learning that had been dormant in the children. At least these children were blessed by Michel and will not, as he asserted, "die with their own immense potentials having been choked by our educational system."

Michel spoke more about what he believed to be the advantages of *block teaching*, as well as potential trouble spots if there are teachers who are clueless:

> The whole thing with *block teaching* is that it also has something to do with the teacher. Teachers who don't know how to teach will be lost with *block teaching* because they don't know what they are doing. If they don't know what they are doing, they are inviting trouble. I am talking about the excitement of learning which is caused by the excitement of teaching. If this is not being done or produced, then *block teaching* would only be an invitation to big trouble.

Michel elaborated on what he meant by "*big trouble*":

> Violence spreads among the bored inmates of an institution more and more. Once it is spreading, that means increasing violence against teachers. It's bad enough that teachers don't know how to teach, but this doesn't mean that they should be exposed to violence. And we are causing it. We are causing the violence and the increased spread

of violence, we, meaning society, parents and government, state educational systems, whatever.

Bored and unmotivated students in the *Mind Prison*™ have the potential to erupt into unruly behavior that can easily turn into violence. Correct *block teaching* may be one of the viable alternatives available to deal with the growing problem of school unrest. From Michel's perspective, the lesson is that if you don't have competent teachers who know what they are doing in the *block teaching* format, you are asking for problems. In Michel's words, "Since we already have these institutions where we have to serve time, let's turn them into institutions of learning."

He cited the perfect example with his other experience in the Los Angeles school system where he agreed to teach a group of militant and unruly students in Watts. The situation in this school had the potential for violence when he arrived because it had been just several days after a riot had erupted that had temporarily paralyzed the area. In fact, Michel recalled being told by the principal that he would be exposed to mental and physical abuse. There was a police patrol in case of additional violence and the doors of the classrooms had to remain wide open.

Michel was even told not to close the doors so that the students could run in and out. They had no idea whom they were coming up against in the likes of Michel Thomas. When the students started to run in and out, he told them: "If you want to be here, come in and participate. If you don't want to, Ok, go out." Well, of course, once Michel began to work his magic, the children wanted eagerly to participate in his class and everyone else in the school wanted to be part of the class as well. The excitement for learning that he created became so contagious that even the other teachers wanted to be part of the process. Tragically, this is just the opposite of what usually happens in the traditional educational system. We will come back to this story in more detail in Chapter Eleven.

In summary, the traditional fifty minute class period is based on a rote learning system. One memorizes isolated facts and moves quickly on to more isolated facts. One can parrot information, but one lacks the understanding that comes from seeing how the facts are interconnected. A pattern can only be extracted from multiple examples. In *block teaching*, one has the time to present the bigger picture as well as the interconnections. The result is a student who *understands*, who can *generalize*, and who can apply the material, as opposed to one who merely regurgitates information. And, of course, this creates "a high degree of excitement" in the students.

DRAMATIC DELIVERY

Delivery has to do with what the *Master Teacher* actually did during the teaching session. A language teaching session consisted of Michel doing two things. One was to demonstrate how to say something in the language and provide an explanation or *heuristic* or *generalization*, and second was to ask a student how one would say a particular thing in the language. Michel then would go to the translation and would then repeat the translation back to reinforce it.

During this time, Michel would always be calm and completely devoid of *tension*. He would always be observing the students to make sure that they were also free of any *tension*. If they were tense in any way, then Michel would determine the source of the *tension* and would take the necessary steps to remove it immediately. Michel and the students would be in comfortable arm chairs in a pleasant, relaxed surrounding with no distractions.

Any form of *tension* is the enemy of learning for two reasons as we have already discussed. First is that it blocks memory. Memory works best when it is free and spontaneous. Memory does not work well when it involves force and *trying*. The second reason that *tension* is the enemy of learning is because it drains energy. It requires energy to keep muscles contracted. The more energy that one uses, the more tired one becomes and the less focused as well.

Part of the dramatic delivery had to do with what we call Michel's *"endurance factor."* People were amazed that they were able to work with Michel for eight to ten hours or more a day and then come away energized rather than exhausted. This was due to three factors. The first factor was because Michel himself remained enthusiastic, calm and energized throughout the entire learning session. His *endurance* factor was unequaled and was most certainly a positive consequence of the time he had spent in concentration camps during World War II. In his learning sessions, never did Michel exhibit one bit of fatigue or anger so that his positive state and unrelenting energy would necessarily rub off on his students.

The second factor is that because the students were not tense and they were not expending energy. There was no *tension* either in Michel or in the room to create an energy drain with the result that the students remained energized. The third factor was that true learning itself is energizing and addictive. Michel constantly emphasized that learning is one of the most basic of all human drives. He explained in the following way:

> "I don't excite them —
> I just reawaken their innate desire to learn."

The important thing for him was to "open the doors wide open, the doors for learning." For Michel it was important not to go back to methods of teaching where "one slams the doors." If all learning did not create a high degree of excitement, Michel declared that it was due to improper teaching. He even suggested that when faced with improper teaching, the learners should walk away from it, "not from the subject, but from the teacher," because as Michel constantly reiterated:

> "All learning should reach and remain
> a very high degree of excitement."

With Michel, the students continually experienced success and the excitement of learning new things; and they experienced that very high degree of excitement to which he constantly referred. This excitement was both addictive and stimulating. There was none of the fatigue and boredom that accompanies traditional teaching. As we have pointed out, without *tension* one learns rapidly. Michel would constantly move on to something new so that the student remained continually engaged, and thus there was absolutely no time for boredom. He reminded us that the student was energized from the excitement of learning and was neither fatigued nor on overwhelm, as we often find in our traditional *dis-educational system*™.

The student found that success in learning was intrinsically motivating and therefore, did not require external rewards. In the end, these only hinder learning, for indeed learning is its own great reward. As we have previously mentioned, Michel emphasized that every successful interaction in the learning environment "generates important feelings of personal efficacy and self-worth." And he would use constant reinforcement to "stimulate the competence motive for each student."

In his learning sessions, the *Master Teacher* would ask the student how he or she would say a particular sentence in the target language; and the student was encouraged to think things out. Michel would give the student compound sentences to translate. "Thinking it out" meant translating the compound sentence one phrase at a time and thinking out the order of the verbs. Michel was able to determine whether or not the student was thinking it out because the student would translate the sentence in pieces in the order in which he or she thought it out.

The opposite of thinking it out is playing it by ear or sounding it out. For fifty years, Michel confirmed time and time again that the latter modes don't work. He insisted on knowing and not guessing. For Michel it was always wrong to guess even if you guessed right. You have to know what you are doing. Your answer has to be based on *understanding* which leads to *knowing*. Sometimes it may appear to the students that they are taking too long to think it through. If necessary, Michel would explain to them what he called the *"relativity of time."* What seemed long to the speaker was not long to the listener. The important thing was for the students to take their time to think it through and get it right.

The *Master Teacher* was always completely calm. He had the gift of intuitively tuning into the wave length of the student. While the student was translating, one had the impression that Michel was mentally transferring the correct translation to the mind of the student, one piece at a time. Not only would Michel get the student's message, the student would also get Michel's message as well. It helped the students in their thinking out loud.

All of this time Michel continued in his poised, unhurried manner. The students were encouraged to take their time and to avoid rushing. The students were to take all of the time that they needed to think it out. Michel would never seem rushed. It was up to the students to take all of the time that they needed.

In the context of Michel's calm delivery style, we would like to make mention of an important aspect of his teaching that, interestingly, reflected his own calm and poised manner. It has to do with the pace in which Michel would deliver his subject matter. He would create a certain rhythm of delivery which reinforced the *tension*-free ambiance of the learning session.

> Michel would literally generate a particular tempo of delivery in the manner in which he structured the learning session.

The tempo of Michel's delivery would generate a certain momentum in the flow which was passed on to the students. The students got pulled into this momentum which, in turn, would produce great excitement and a feeling of knowing and eager anticipation for what was to come next from Michel. The momentum would become so contagious that the students wanted to continue at that same pace without taking breaks. They didn't want to stop because they could see themselves actually accomplishing something on the spot. The students were enthralled and excited by their immediate progress. Each achievement along the way would build upon the previous one and this contributed to maintaining the tempo of the delivery as well.

It was as though Michel had been creating a special energy that led the students along with him all the way through the entire learning process from start to finish. Michel would at all times be cognizant of where the students were in their grasp of the subject matter, and he would never introduce new elements until the previous material was assimilated. This awareness on his part also contributed to creating a specific learning tempo which matched his own comportment.

> Michel would create a steady, deliberate flow of delivery by combining a poised physiology and gentle voice with his skillful structuring and *layering* of the subject matter.

The presentation of subject matter would always be just what was needed, never more, never less than what the students could handle at any given point in time. It was never too much and was always just right. All of this maintained a *tension*-free ambiance. Michel's calm manner and delivery style were often incorrectly perceived as patience and this erroneous interpretation of his demeanor really annoyed him.

In fact, many people often commented on how "patient" Michel was. This was from the students' perspective. Michel indeed had a different view of patience: "I am always calm, always, because as a teacher and in effective teaching there should be no room for anything else, especially not patience. I replace it with *understanding*. If I understand the learning process, there is no room for patience." When people commented on how patient Michel was, his answer was always: "To me patience is a form of impatience. I have to combat my own impatience in order to be patient." Michel expressed similar feelings about tolerance which he described as follows:

> Any form of tolerance to me is a form of intolerance. It means that I have to combat my own intolerance in order to be tolerant. No thank you. I am not tolerant because I don't believe in tolerance. There are other words one can use like acceptance, not tolerance. I don't have disappointment or disapproval. It seems that I feel strongly about words.

Yes, the *Master Teacher* certainly was a stickler with words. This was also evident in personal conversations with Michel and in his meticulous reading of this manuscript to make certain that every word, explanation and description of his method (in fact, every aspect of his life and work) captured its true essence as well as his mental processes behind the method. And in part, it was his ability to nuance the meaning of words which had added another dimension to his teaching of languages and to the creation of his method. There was never any doubt as to the meaning of what he was saying. Everything he said was deliberate, clear and perfectly positioned between what preceded and what was yet to come. We metaphorically liken this mental process to an assortment of beautifully set stones, carefully placed to form a stunning jeweled mosaic. After all, each learning session with Michel ended up being a *chef d'oeuvre* that could stand on its own.

Michel's attitude toward so-called impatience provided us with an interesting window into Michel's philosophy of life. Patience, tolerance, disappointment and disapproval were not issues for Michel. They were not at all issues because Michel did not experience impatience, intolerance, disappointment or disapproval in the context of the learning session (This perspective stems from his "*getting to know me*" period discussed in Chapter Nine.). Thus, there was nothing for him to overcome. No work was required on Michel's part because there was nothing to work on.

There was yet another reason that patience was a non-issue for Michel in teaching his students. He explained this quality as follows:

> "In teaching, I look for *understanding*. My job is to give *understanding*. If I don't get *understanding* back, then I missed something. This is not done as an expression of patience. To me there is no room for patience."

From Michel's point of view, if the student made a mistake, it was not the student's fault. We have already shown that Michel considered mistakes to be his problem and it was up to him to figure out why the student got it wrong in the first place and then to determine what to do about it.

The *Master Teacher* believed that teachers often get impatient because they blame the student for mistakes. Michel took complete responsibility for all mistakes, so there was no reason to be impatient in the first place. Michel did not experience impatience, but rather he experienced curiosity about how the student could make the mistake and curiosity about what he would do about it to create *understanding*. And Michel would never scold or blame the students if they were to make mistakes. In fact, these words were not even part of his vocabulary. In this situation he would always be the first to ask himself: "What did I do to have caused this?" This is a great example of what the new school calls *"meta-cognition,"* which we will discuss in Chapter Seven.

Curiously, Michel's reaction reminded us of his *getting to know me* period earlier in his life, at which time he sat in judgment of himself, always asking why he reacted the way in which he did in given situations. His way of thinking at that point in his life, helped him in terms of what he eventually did with his students in teaching years later (Chapter Nine). Just as he had asked himself why the student made a mistake in the first place, or why a particular thing happened during the course of a learning session, Michel would ask himself the same type of questions during his *getting to know me* period. "What did I do to cause this?" he would ask himself and this mode of thinking tied directly into his thinking system of his earlier years. We also think that it helped him to put himself in the shoes of the student, as we described in an earlier section of this chapter.

Michel's keen ability to separate from himself during his *getting to know me* period served to strengthen his ability to put himself in the position of the student, and to look at learning from the perspective of the student. And, as we mentioned earlier, this approach was obvious when he first began to create his teaching method, putting himself in the place of the learner. Also, the fact that he did not experience disappointment or disapproval probably goes back to the time of his *getting to know me* period in life as well.

Michel believed in what is known as *"collaborative learning."* He was never authoritarian and would never place himself on a pedestal. Michel considered the students to be on an equal level with him in a learning partnership. He would always remain calm and positive and was certainly never patronizing. Michel would never give an outward sign of either disappointment or disapproval because, as we have seen, he did not experience such emotions. At the same time Michel would not make extensive use of praise or encouragement. He felt that doing so was unnecessary because the positive reinforcement that the student experienced from continual success went far beyond any praise that he could have given the student. Thus, Michel preferred to remain neutral. Here again, we can see the *rapprochement* between Michel's discovery that learning is a powerful innate drive in all living creatures and his teaching style, in this case, the lack of praise in his teaching. Once the drive for learning is triggered, students don't need a great deal of encouragement. Learning becomes its own reward. In fact, learning is a life-long process which is far more motivating than any praise that Michel could have ever bestowed upon his students.

The *Master Teacher* would always maintain eye contact with his students and would always be calibrating the student for both *tension* and comprehension. There was none of the aversive control, scolding, raised voice and frowning that are so typical of the traditional *dis-education*™ of the *Mind Prison*™. Once again, this is because Michel would take complete responsibility for the student's learning and remembering. Therefore there was never any need to blame or threaten the student. Instead, Michel would maintain a pleasant smile and a calm but excited demeanor. He would never raise his voice or frown, and he would never reveal any sign of agitation because as he explained, he never experienced any of these negative states in the first place.

Occasionally, he would gently ask the student to think out what he was saying. Yet Michel would never give any indication of disapproval, and under no circumstances would he ever scold or blame the student for mistakes. For Michel, any scolding or blaming should rest on his shoulders and not on the student. Michel would simply ask what he had done to cause the problem and what he could do about it. Remember that the responsibility for learning would always lie with Michel and never with the student.

As we have indicated on several occasions, the *Master Teacher's* goal was to teach the students to think things out and, thus, to be able to correct their own mistakes. Michel wanted people to understand and to know so that they could think things out fully. Michel certainly did not want his students to be dependent on him because he wanted them to be able to use the language to converse on their own once the course was completed.

> Michel's real goal was to teach the students how to learn and to reawaken their love for learning.

In this way, once the learning sessions with Michel were completed, the students would be able to continue to develop their language skills on their own as well as continue to expand their vocabulary.

As we have seen, the *Master Teacher*'s method was based on explanations and on *meaningful memory associations*™ or *heuristics* which led to *understanding* and to the acquisition of *knowledge*. In short, Michel would explain everything. He would provide proper explanations to create *understanding* of everything. Explanations are conscious. They are designed to be fully understood. And, as Michel constantly reminded us, what is fully understood can be immediately applied. Thus, Michel provided explanations and then immediate exercises to reinforce the learning. This made the explanations take on additional meaning in a practical way. If for some reason the student did not understand, and, hence, was not able to immediately apply what Michel was teaching, then it was up to Michel to determine what created the misunderstanding and then figure out what to do about it.

GESTICULATION AND EXPRESSION

In his private sessions, (whether one-on-one or with a group) the *Master Teacher* would use gestures and facial expressions to reinforce vocabulary or a tense. "I use movements all the time in my teaching." he explained. "It's only when I record my course on tape, that I don't use movements." He may have associated a tense with a movement such as a push of his hand, as in the case of teaching the *pre*sent tense in Spanish, with the emphasis on the first syllable of *pre*sent to indicate the use of the present tense in speaking. The movement serves as what we refer to in *neuro-linguistics* as an "*anchor*" or reminder, in this case, to help remind the student of the tense. Sometimes students might have unconsciously started to use the gestures themselves. This served further to reinforce what they were saying. Over time Michel had come to realize that he associated "quite a lot of vocabulary with movements," and that it simply worked out that way.

GESTURE ANCHORS: A POWERFUL TOOLBOX

Thus, gestures used as *anchors* played a major part in Michel's teaching over the years, and in particularly unique ways, although for different reasons. *Gesture anchors* especially took center stage in the learning process with students like renowned French actor, the late Yves Montand, and the famous American comedienne, the late Lucille Ball, as we shall soon see. Michel's clever use of these gestures provided him with a variety of powerful learning tools. The *Master Teacher* recounted to us a time while on a set in Hollywood, there was a group of actors and actresses having a discussion together. There happened to be a French actress who spoke no English. Within the group speaking to her in French, were three of Michel's former students. It was quite obvious and amusing to Michel that they were his students because in speaking, they would use the same gestures he had taught them for certain verbs in his courses.

For example, *Je dois* in French means "I must." Every time someone would say *Je dois* the person would mimic the gesture he had learned from Michel, just as Michel had shown the person how to emphasize the meaning of "I must!" Another example, is the French verb *aller,* which means 'to go'; and to express this verb, Michel would make a gesture that signified going through an alley. For Michel's students, these and other gestures had become part of them; and his students never forgot these gestures, even years later. As one could well imagine, the whole scene on the Hollywood set turned out to be quite amusing and revelatory to Michel.

Lucille Ball was so intrigued by Michel's use of gestures that she would apparently use them all the time in speaking French. At one point she told Michel: "Don't say anything. Just move." Michel fondly recalled his memory of her using the gestures in conversation and that it was quite funny. For example, Ms. Ball would say, "*Allez le voir ce soir.*" (Go to see it (or him) tonight.) with gestures or "*Venez ce soir.*" (Come tonight.)

There is still another rather interesting example of Michel's use of gestures in teaching, which, although unrelated to what he did with Lucille Ball, is quite a striking example of Michel's virtuosity. This time he was teaching English to the well-known French actor, Yves Montand. It turned out that for Yves Montand, these movements were a critical part of his learning both languages, since, according to Michel, Montand did not know the grammar of the French language, his native tongue. With Montand, the gestures were not used for the vocabulary, but rather for the structure of the language itself, for all the tenses. In fact, Michel told us that Montand didn't even know the tenses in French. For example, Montand did not know what the basic present or future tenses were in his own language, so imagine having to teach him a foreign language to boot! It would seem to be a dauntless task for anyone but Michel. And, once again, he was more than ready for the challenge.

Michel would ask him what the future tense was, and he would respond, "*Je pars.*" (I am leaving.) For Montand, "*Je pars*" was the future tense. And when Michel would ask him what the future tense was for "I am leaving," Montand would say, "*Je pars demain.*" (I am leaving tomorrow.) For Montand, the present tense was equated with now, the past tense was equated with yesterday and the future tense was equated with tomorrow. These were the only three tenses that he would know how to describe, and nothing else. In Montand's mind, "I am leaving tomorrow," represented the future tense. The entire learning process with Michel was described in a French magazine in which Montand explained how he had learned correct French by learning how to speak English with Michel. The actor also strongly suggested that French children be taught French using movements because he felt that learning would be so wonderful that way.

While modeling Michel we asked him how he had gotten around this problem and how he had facilitated the learning process for Montand and he responded: "Well, by putting all the tenses, by associating all the tenses with a movement. Every tense had a movement. I created the movements for him." So Michel, with his innovative mind, had devised a whole series of gestures to correspond to specific verb tenses. For example, movement of his raised arm into the direction of the future became the future tense.

When Michel pointed his hand downward, that was a sign of the past tense. With the "woulds" or the conditional, Michel would point into the direction of going into the woods. The 'would have' or past conditional was expressed by another gesture known to all of Michel's students as *"the diving gesture."* Interestingly, even the so-called complex tenses, were each associated with a particular gesture or movement. Thus, Michel taught Yves Montand the entire grammar of the English language (and correct French grammar as well) by movements and gestures. Quite amazing to say the least!

Another rather remarkable attestation of Michel's brilliant flair came to life in the 1950's when he was asked to work with yet another Hollywood star, this time, Dorothy Dandridge. For those of us who do not recall who she was, Michel described her as "an actress and singer, a great talent who starred in some important films, notably, *Carmen Jones*, a film by Otto Preminger."

In any case, she was asked to star in a French film with another director who happened to be an American, even though she did not know a word of French! And she decided that she would accept the role under one condition: that condition would be that the company had to hire Michel Thomas to work with her. Of course, Michel got a phone call and accepted the offer. So Michel took off for the French Riviera to the location where the film was being shot. You would think, logically, that Michel would be teaching Ms. Dandridge how to speak French. No! There was no time for him to do so because of the filming schedule. The only option was for her to do the whole film in French without knowing any French, without having one single official lesson. Incredible!

So Michel coached her in how to act out each scene in French, word by word. He had to convey emotion and meaning to every word, every phrase, so that each day, Ms. Dandridge ended up interacting more with Michel than with the director. Needless to say, that sparked a minor crisis between Michel and the director, who began to perceive Michel as the one directing the leading actress in the film. Ms. Dandridge reacted by insisting that if they wanted to continue the film, this was how things had to be.

From a learning point of view, Michel also had to teach her how to match the appropriate gestures associated with certain emotions, and how to relax while speaking a language unknown to her. "So whatever she learned in French, it was always about how to express." Michel explained to us. He did such a great job that even the French press, who had been observing a part of the filming, was fooled. In fact, the French news media was apparently upset at Ms. Dandridge for not giving interviews in French. It wasn't that she was refusing to speak with them, but rather that she couldn't speak a word of French! Of course, no one believed her. The bottom line is that Michel was also able to add to his powerful toolbox, his ingenious system of developing a classification of gestures to fit every learning need. In passing we will note that Michel would also use facial expressions. As he said, "You can read things in my face."

MISUNDERSTANDING

The *Master Teacher* made some important distinctions in actually speaking the language. As we have already mentioned, Michel would teach his students to speak grammatically correctly. It is not just enough to be understood. It is important to speak correctly. To do this, you must be able to think out what you are saying and know when you have made a mistake and what to do to correct it.

Michel made a helpful distinction between "not being understood" and being "misunderstood." He pointed out that it is necessary to pay attention to the response of the other person in the conversation. If you say something that the person doesn't understand, he or she will look puzzled or will ask you to repeat it. Then you should think about what you said and make sure that you have properly thought out what you are saying to the person or persons with whom you are speaking.

The second response would be that they misunderstand what you are saying. The problem is that you often can't tell whether or not they misunderstand you. Michel felt that in some ways it was better to "not be understood" at all than to be misunderstood. In this way you then know that the other person doesn't understand you, and you can make the necessary corrections accordingly. People will indicate to you if they don't understand what you are saying, but you have no way of knowing in the moment whether you are misunderstood or not. What you said may have made sense to them. It just did not make the sense that you had probably intended.

This is a big problem in communication. During the modeling process, Michel used a tennis analogy in his personal explanation of misunderstanding. The latter has to do with words and not with structure and communication.

> When you say something to someone and get a blank stare, that look means that you have a net ball and you get another serve. If it is a ball that goes over the net, even slightly over the net, it will be picked up. Even if it is mispronounced, it will be picked up on the other side of the net.

So you watch out for the correct pronunciation. Even if the pronunciation is not totally correct, it may be close enough to be understood.

Guessing often leads to misunderstanding, so Michel would encourage his students never to guess on grammar. Even if you guess and get it right, it is an accident. If you can think out what you are going to say, however, then it is no accident and you can repeat it. Michel said that it may be alright occasionally to guess on vocabulary, but it is never okay to guess on grammar. As for guessing on vocabulary, Michel recommended it only once one had acquired a feel for the use of the language: "Once you know how to *swim*, I will encourage guessing of vocabulary."

CALIBRATION SKILLS

The *Master Teacher* was able to follow his students' progress on many levels because of one very important skill. In our terminology, we call it *"calibration."*

> *Calibration* refers to the ability to detect minute changes in physiology which correspond to specific shifts in a person's experience.

Michel had this ability to "*read*" or to *calibrate* his students. He was amazingly able to tune into the students' emotions, attitudes, beliefs and level of understanding. He had to be aware of minute changes in physiology to "*see*" what the person was experiencing. He knew that there was a close relationship between what the students were thinking, i.e., their beliefs, attitudes, emotions, skill base, and previous experiences which, in turn, affected the way in which they interacted in a given environment, and the way in which they took in information, interpreted it and assimilated it.

All of these components will necessarily affect the way in which students absorb new information based on mental and emotional structures already in place. Michel's *calibration* skills were truly remarkable. In observing him, one would think that he was actually reading the minds of his students. He was a master calibrator in that he would constantly and skillfully observe his students (and people in general), detecting minute changes which would go unnoticed by most people. Michel accomplished all of this in his typical casual and discreet manner.

Part of his ability to do this so well was based on his ability to put himself in someone else's place. As we mentioned earlier on, Michel had an uncanny ability "to walk in another person's shoes" or to look at things from the perspective of the person with whom he was interacting. He would ask himself how he would feel and think if he were to be the other person. We call this the ability to go to "second position."

This wonderful ability served him well as a counter intelligence agent and it served him equally well as a teacher. Michel would put himself in the position of the learner and would ask himself how he, as the learner, would respond to an explanation or *meaningful memory association*™. This allowed him to check out explanations and *heuristics* in advance, and to refine them before he actually delivered them. And when he would deliver them, his *calibration* skills would let him know immediately how successful these explanations and *heuristics* were with his students.

Michel would totally mesmerize his students with his natural charm and gentle, yet powerful presence. This, in turn, enabled him to connect with his students on a subtle level and to "tune in" even more closely to them, providing whatever help or guidance he would deem necessary at that point in time. Because of his highly-refined *calibration* skills, Michel would always be able to tell whether or not a student understood a given concept; and he would guide him or her accordingly to a complete *understanding.* He would make sure that he was aware of a student's prior language learning experiences as well.

In fact, he stated that the more language learning a person had experienced, the more time he had to spend in "undoing" any bad habits that they had developed. This meant changing beliefs and attitudes from the very start and removing any obstacles which may have gotten in the way of learning. It is important for teachers to be aware of the beliefs and attitudes of their students because they necessarily affect the way in which information is received and processed. When teachers ignore what we refer to as a student's (or any person's) given "*model of the world*" (i.e., their emotions, beliefs, attitudes, perceptual filters, values, etc.), they will not be able to calibrate whether or not the student has successfully transferred the information into practical working knowledge. Remarkably, Michel would be able to calibrate an entire class of students; and he had a clever way of getting everyone on board, as we will see in the next section.

GROUP DYNAMICS — *ESPRIT DE CLASSE*

In his language courses, the *Master Teacher* would usually work one-on-one or with a small group. However, he was just as comfortable and successful teaching a large group or a large class. The same dynamics worked with a large group or class as with one or two students. Whether Michel was working with two people or with a small group or a large group, his goal would always be the same. His goal for the group was for it to become one cohesive unit. This notion of a cohesive unit is what Michel referred to in the context of his teaching as "*esprit de classe."* Moreover, it also happens to be another of the key components of his method. Most people are familiar with the term *"esprit de corps."* Michel explained his distinctive expression, *esprit de classe,* to us as follows:

> "I leave that kind of *esprit* to the military or to ballet companies, where it belongs. I refer to *esprit de classe*, a confluence of dynamic energy easily recognizable by psychologists of all stripes as beneficial to a learning environment."

So what was Michel's formula for establishing *esprit de classe*? First, the critical component was eye contact between him and his students. With one student or with many students, Michel would always maintain continuous eye contact. He would be completely "with them" whether it be one student or fifty students. For Michel, it was eye contact which created *esprit de classe* among his students. Michel would do everything using eye contact. As Michel explained to us, "In teaching I am only concentrating on one thing. I am focused on the students' wave length."

Interestingly, students knew that they were not to raise their hand or to expect Michel to call on them by name. By Michel looking at them, the students knew that they were meant to respond. It was as though Michel had a special way of connecting with them so that he could understand and feel their emotions and thoughts. He would teach one student in the same manner that he would teach an entire group. They would become a unit — they literally became one. All the students!

In working with groups, the *Master Teacher's* aim was to have his students work together and become self-disciplining. He wanted to build *esprit de classe* and he would do so from the start by creating the perfect learning milieu in which to trigger the students' learning potentials.

Thus, we find that the elements we presented earlier in this chapter to describe the way in which Michel would create a favorable environment to release *tension* in his students, were also important factors in his creation of *esprit de classe* among his students. He would begin by rearranging the learning space. He wanted it to be clean and comfortable. For *esprit de classe* to take hold, students had to be in comfortable arm chairs rather than be sitting at desks. They had no need to write since note taking was not part of the learning session. Also, given the nature of his teaching, Michel would not need to write anything down, so no blackboard or flip charts were necessary.

In general, because his teaching was always based on eye contact, Michel would not have to ask a question of a particular student. Imagine! He would never have to call on someone by name. All he would have to do was simply to look at a student and that was enough. Michel described as follows:

> "You ask, you look at somebody and there is the response...and that does not interfere with the whole unit."

In the traditional system, by contrast, teachers call on students for answers, often by name. Students are taught to be competing with each other. They are competing for good grades and to prove to the teacher and to their fellow classmates that they know the answer. At times one will find the classroom to be a hand-raising competition to see who gets to give the correct answer.

> What we have in the traditional system is competitive learning rather than collaborative learning.

Competitive learning did not exist in Michel's learning sessions. Whether a student picked something up quickly or slowly wouldn't matter. Why? This was due to the *esprit de classe* that the *Master Teacher* so brilliantly created among his students. Therefore, because the class as a whole unit was experiencing the same thing, it would not matter that one student or a number of students were learning at different rates. At times one student might have understood a concept more quickly than another, and perhaps at another time, it would have been someone else.

It wouldn't matter because the group reacted and experienced everything as a cohesive unit, functioning with *esprit de classe*. Michel described the phenomenon of his *esprit de classe* in the following manner:

> It can be a large class of thirty or forty. The exciting thing for me in working with a large class or group of thirty or forty is how quickly that group becomes one unit. So whether it is a small group or a larger group or a very large group it does not matter to me. One thing with a group, they know and I make it clear from the beginning, never to raise their arms. If I have a question, I don't want to see any arms because the response will come on eye contact. In a whole large class, I am connected with everyone by eye contact. This means all of their eyes. All thirty or forty class participants are looking at my eyes. When I have a question, I will never call on somebody by name. Nobody will raise their arms or tell me that they know. They will simply respond on eye contact.

We cannot emphasize enough the importance that eye contact played in Michel's teaching. (And we have found that other successful teachers also make use of solid eye contact.) With that powerful *Michel look*, he was quickly able to get everyone on board. Whether it was one student or a whole class of forty students, the class would magically become one. We determined that on one level, what he was doing was creating a particular energy within the room which captivated the students on an unconscious level and kept them riveted to his entire being. In essence, what he would do was generate a particular energy flow in the room.

And by doing so, he would produce a feeling of unity, a connection among all of the students, which remained outside of their conscious awareness. The students were not necessarily aware of this energy flow. They just knew that it felt great, that it excited them and that is was wonderful to be learning in this way. In short, Michel would literally create a special energy in the room which transformed the individuals in the group into a unified whole.

A perfect example of Michel's *esprit de classe* in action occurred at a course that he taught for Air Canada in the Laurentian Mountains of Quebec in the late sixties. In a written report based on live observation of the course, the following remarks were made by the observer, Dr. David Abbey, the Coordinator of Research Studies for the Ontario Institute for Studies in Education:

> The motivation to learn was intense. One wished to learn, and to see one's colleague learn. In twenty years of formal schooling and seven years of post graduate work teaching, I have never before seen a group break into spontaneous applause when one of its members solved a difficult problem after obvious personal exertion.

Dr. Abbey went on to describe the tremendous sense of *esprit de classe* which developed among the participants in the group, all of whom were Air Canada executives who had come from different parts of the country to take Michel's course. These executives did not know each other beforehand. The "I" versus "they" quickly became a "we" versus "they" regarding outsiders, and Michel quickly became "*un de nous*" (one of us), as one participant described the class. Michel was not a "dictator," but rather a "helper." By the time the course was over, many of the participants had developed friendships with each other.

Sometimes in a classroom, for instance, with a whole group, there may be a few, maybe one, two or three students who didn't pay attention. These students thought that they would not have to respond. Michel gave the following description of them:

> I am always working with one of them and I expect everyone else to be with it [paying attention to the other student]. I don't ask them to do it but it happens because of the general eye contact. When I am working with one, I may notice someone in the corner who is looking away or may be looking down or up or doing something else. They are not maintaining eye contact, so I know that that person is not really paying attention to the

learning process. I may be in a situation of working out an individual problem which may also be interesting to everybody. All the others may not have this problem or some may. It doesn't matter.

At times the whole group would be following along with Michel except for one student who was having a problem. In that case, Michel would stop to help that one individual with the problem, and would solve it by working through the problem with the student, leading him or her into solving the problem. There is an interesting dynamic at work here. Very often the whole group would applaud the student who had been having the difficulty because the other students were totally with that person and were also going through it themselves. Once that student had solved the problem, it acted like a release for the entire class at the very moment the solution came to him. This is indeed *esprit de classe* in action!

And, by the way, no one would ever feel humiliated. Once someone understood something and had worked it out, everybody was mentally behind it. The whole class was participating. Also, because there were no grades, it was never a question of one student understanding it better than another or of a particular student bragging about his or her individual accomplishments over the other students. The lack of competition among the students meant greater cooperation and mutual support for each other in the learning process.

Once Michel had finished working with that one person, he would then address the student who he had noticed was not paying attention prior to that. Michel, of course had a strategy for dealing with this type of situation as well. He would use another problem very similar to the problem that had just been solved, and he would look at the person who was not listening along with the rest of the class. At that point, Michel may not have had eye contact with that person. He would keep looking at the person without saying anything. In fact, there might have been complete silence because Michel would be looking at the student who, in turn, was not making eye contact with him.

Michel said that this kind of scenario may occur in the beginning of a course, and not after. The reason is that there was very often a huge reaction from the class: "Hey, what's going on?" they might have said. Of course, such a reaction would get the attention of that one student who was not making eye contact. At that point, Michel would get eye contact and the whole class then knew the identity of the person who had not been listening. Now Michel would repeat the problem with this person and would have the student go through a similar situation to the one that had just occurred, the situation where he or she was not paying attention.

Here Michel would insist that the student really think out the problem and go through it, something which would not have been necessary had the student been paying attention in the first place. The answer would have come quickly and easily. However, because the student was not listening, he or she had to go through the entire same process again. Of course, Michel would lead the person into it and when the student finally got the right answer he would say:

> Why did it take you so long? *This is one time that I do ask them a question.* They respond: 'I don't know. I had a problem.' I say no! That is not the reason. I then say, 'you know, we went through the same problem just before and you chose not to pay attention. That's why. Because you did not listen.' That is usually enough. And I am talking about classes that are usually high school. At some point, a similar situation will happen with somebody else. This time, however, when I ask, Why did it take you so long, why did you have trouble? The student will immediately answer, 'I did not know it because I wasn't listening.' I am leading up to this.

Michel explained that this could happen twice in a given group, yet after that, there would be no one in the class who was not making eye contact with him. The entire group, the entire class, regardless of the number of students, would be listening to him and following what he was doing with them. There was a definite sense of oneness as the group became a cohesive 'one', a solid unit. As Michel described it, "The whole unit to me becomes one, whether I teach one individually or a whole, a class of forty or fifty, is always one. And to me this is exciting." Of course, it excited the students as well, all of them. Even in the context of a group, Michel succeeded at triggering their immense potential for learning and it would become contagious within the entire room.

MENTALLY REACHING

The *Master Teacher* had strong convictions about teaching to match his convictions on group behavior. As Michel very often reminded us:

> Teaching is not lecturing. There is a big difference between teaching a subject, whatever the subject, and giving a lecture or making a speech. A speech is not a teaching tool. One may learn something from a lecture or find out something from a speech.

For Michel, teaching meant something else which he described like this:

> "Teaching to me means *mentally reaching*."

For Michel, teaching meant mentally connecting with the learner and is what he called "*mentally reaching*" the student, whether there be one or one hundred, whether it be on an individual basis or on a large group basis. No matter what the size of the group, Michel's class was always a unit of one. Whether it was one individual or a whole class, the group was one unit. *Mentally reaching* also refers to reaching, to teaching everyone in the learning session based on eye contact. Michel described this to us as follows:

> "Teaching is *mentally reaching*. It is reaching everyone on eye contact, and that eye contact creates *esprit de classe* regardless of how many people there are."

With *esprit de classe* in teaching, no matter what you are teaching, whether a language or any subject, it is always addressed to the individual as part of the entire unit, the entire *esprit de classe*. Michel would always be working with one, with one piece of the whole, however, with this one piece belonging to the entire whole. In the traditional classroom, it is often just the contrary. The teacher is doing the opposite in that he or she is asking a question or is writing on the board rather than focusing on the students. Regarding this issue in the traditional system Michel stated, "The teacher is not paying focused attention on the students or else the teacher asks a question and all their hands go up. Here with me, my students know immediately never to raise their hands."

Michel insisted that in teaching a group, it was also important to stimulate questions of the group. It was also critical to not wait until one finished a section or a lecture to ask: "Do you have any questions?" or "What questions do you have?" He was adamant about the fact that in teaching each individual is part of the group. Questions are an important part of group teaching. He was the first to say, "Oh, that is a good question," because for Michel every question was a good question. Questions stimulate the thought process. Each question stimulates the thought process in a specific way.

Michel did, however, make a distinction regarding the issue of questions: "When I say each question is a good question, I don't mean those who are just there to provoke, like troublemakers [do]. There is no room for troublemakers. They cannot be part of the *esprit de classe*. To have troublemakers would detract from the *esprit de classe*. Otherwise questions are important."

Michel would never threaten his students and he was not a disciplinarian, even when he found himself in an unruly class of rebellious students in Watts. Threats are worthless. Congruent action speaks much louder than words. Michel wanted the students to become self-monitoring. The only discipline that he would use in a large class was to ask a student to leave the room for a short period of time if he or she had been disruptive (Such a thing had not happened since Watts.). Much more than most teachers, Michel knew exactly how to handle disruptive, difficult students, and even outright belligerent ones, as was the case he described to us in Watts. All students, even the rebellious ones, became excited and wanted to participate in Michel's class and to be in the same room with him.

How was this possible? This was possible because of the *Master Teacher's* magic keys. A huge key to Michel's success was that he made learning exciting, "immensely exciting." Another key to his success was that students were successful and it was obvious to them. In learning with Michel, the students were able to experience immediate success. Learning was exciting because it was what Michel called *"true learning"* and furthermore, the students remained engaged. As they succeeded, they would become even more excited. Their excitement became contagious.

Within the traditional system, the students were so used to being blamed for failure, that Michel's method was really surprising and even shocking in a good way to some of his students. Michel was responsible for their learning and they embraced this. If they forgot something, it would be Michel's fault and not their fault. It sometimes would take a short while for students to adjust to being free to learn without guilt or punishment, but once they had, they were able to relax more deeply and to learn at an ever accelerating rate. And, as they learned at an accelerated rate, they, in turn, became more and more excited with the learning process.

REMEDIATION AND METACOGNITION

"I 'un-confuse' them." — Michel Thomas

Another important key to Michel's method was the way in which he dealt with mistakes. In this section, we consider this facet of his method from the perspective of what is known as *"meta-cognition."* In learning another language, students may occasionally make mistakes. This is not unusual. The manner in which they are handled is critical. Students knew emphatically from the beginning that Michel, and not the student, was responsible for mistakes. Michel would not have to repeat this once he had explained it to his students. Michel believed that it was important never to repeat negative things. Instead, it was important to make something emphatic, to make it clear and that is all. If a student either did not remember a concept or if a student made a mistake, it was up to Michel to be aware of this and to know what to do about it. In fact, as we will see, the student was led to correct it himself, with Michel leading the way to self-correction.

The usual approach to education, which to Michel was a horror story, is "spare the rod and spoil the child." The students are taught that they will be punished for mistakes, and this puts them in a constant state of *tension* and anxiety where they are continuously on guard. In learning a language, the student is afraid to say anything for fear of pronouncing it or uttering it incorrectly. Michel deplored the fact that in a typical language classroom, one's mistakes are often pointed out to everyone else in the class. Not only are you wrong, but you should be humiliated and feel embarrassed about your mistakes in front of all of your classmates. This is truly horrible and totally pointless. Depending on the school, one may even be punished for mistakes. And, of course, we know that mistakes lead to poor grades and to failure in school and in life. You have to work harder and to be ever diligent. You are made to feel bad, and there is nothing you can do but *try* harder next time. Needless to say, all of this is totally antithetical to true learning and to the way in which Michel taught his classes.

Once again, Michel's ultimate goal in his complete course was to have students understand and to know the language, and to be able to speak it on their own. If they understand and know, then they will be able to think out what they are saying. If they made a mistake, then the ultimate goal was to be able to recognize the error and to correct it on their own. Once they were on their own, they would be able to continue to develop proficiency in the language.

This ability to be self-monitoring and self-correcting is part of what the new science of learning (which we will address in the next chapter) calls "*meta-cognition.*" *Meta-cognition* has been identified as a critical element of learning. It is an active learning process where students are taught to take control of their own learning. This involves knowing when something makes sense, monitoring their current level of *understanding* and knowing, and being able to recognize and to correct their own mistakes. This is precisely what Michel had been doing for more than fifty years! With Michel as their teacher, students didn't just learn a language. They learned how to take control over and to monitor their own learning. This invaluable ability dramatically impacted every area of their lives.

The best time to eliminate a mistake is before it ever happens. As we have said, Michel's method was based on clear explanations and on associations we termed *meaningful memory associations*™. These were all designed so that the student understood the language step by step, from the beginning to the very end of the course.

> The flawless interplay and *layering* of these *meaningful memory associations*™, all building blocks of *understanding*, were achieved with the ease and elegance of a beautifully constructed architectural wonder.

Students who understand and know will not make mistakes, or if they do, then they will recognize and correct their own errors. The entire process occurs flawlessly and effortlessly with an outcome of clarity and *understanding*. Michel stated this in the following manner:

> "It is not that complicated what I am doing. I eliminate confusion from the beginning so that it doesn't happen. Being on track is having *understanding* that leads to *knowledge*. This is always my objective. *Understanding* is the track to be on track towards *knowledge*, *knowledge* one will never lose. One can block it, but one can't lose it."

Michel's vast experience allowed him to do two things. First, Michel eliminated the confusion before it could occur. He gave clear and logical explanations. Often things in a language seem arbitrary and illogical. Michel was always providing an explanation that made sense as well as some *heuristic* or *meaningful memory association*™ to serve as a memory aid.

> This way, language was not a set of isolated, arbitrary facts to be memorized, but rather something that was logical and that made sense.

Second, Michel knew what to listen for at all times. For example, he would ask a student to translate a sentence. Michel would listen for any mistakes and for lack of understanding. If these occurred, he would immediately figure out why they happened and then what to do to correct the mistake. Michel would lead the students back to get it right at which point they would quickly have what Michel called the *"aha reaction."* The important thing was that the mistake would not be made again because the student had achieved *understanding*. And if they did make the mistake again, then they would recognize it and would immediately lead themselves into correcting it on their own. Amazingly, the students would always correct themselves.

So there are two important things about the way in which Michel would deal with mistakes. The first was that Michel realized that the pressure to "get it right" was a powerful source of *tension*, and, unfortunately, this is often what happens in the traditional system. By contrast, Michel would simply eliminate this *tension* at the beginning by informing the student that he was responsible for mistakes and not the student. If the student made a mistake, then it was Michel's responsibility to know what to do about it. This put the student at ease from the very beginning. The fact that Michel placed accountability on the shoulders of the teacher and not on the student represents a 180 degree turn-around and one which is completely at odds with contemporary education.

The second important thing about the way in which Michel would handle mistakes was equally remarkable. In one-on-one instruction, Michel would never point out mistakes to the student. Michel knew that pointing out mistakes when they happen causes the student to tense up and makes the student feel bad (or even worse, stupid) and self-conscious. It may even be embarrassing to the student, especially in a group situation.

Also, pointing out the mistake does not help the student to correct it. If the student had known the correct answer, then he would not have made the error in the first place. What would help the student to correct the mistake would be to figure out why the mistake was made in the first place and then to determine what to do about it. But the student could not yet do this. Only Michel could do this. This was why Michel emphasized from the beginning that mistakes were his problem and not the problem of the students. If a student made a mistake, it was because Michel had failed to present it in such a way that it made sense to the student. It would be up to Michel to figure out another way to explain the concept so that it would lead to *understanding*. Remember that all *knowledge* is based on *understanding*.

If the students realized that they had made a mistake, then they would usually correct their own mistake. Although he did not use the term, this is precisely the *meta-cognitive* ability that Michel wanted his students to develop. If they couldn't immediately correct their own mistake, then Michel would encourage them to think it out. Michel explained the process as follows:

> "If they just make a nonthinking mistake, I may ask them to repeat it, and in repeating it they will slow down and think it through. If not, then I will lead them into correcting their own mistake."

Students knew from the very beginning of the course never to apologize for mistakes or to blame themselves. If they became annoyed, then Michel would immediately take the student off of the hook by re-emphasizing that he had told them that mistakes were his problem and not theirs.

One common form of mistake is forgetting a word. If a student were to ask what a word was, Michel would either tell him or her directly, or else he would give the person a hint that allowed the student to figure it out on his or her own. Michel emphasized that he was teaching them the structure of the language along with an advanced, practical, working and functional vocabulary all along the way. It was not just a basic vocabulary. Michel stressed that "in teaching some basic vocabulary, they cannot do much with the whole structure and it will collapse the structure." The students did not need to continue to develop their vocabulary because Michel would give them enough vocabulary from the start. It was certainly alright to add vocabulary by reading and speaking, however, it was not necessary. The vocabulary which Michel would provide his students was more than enough to speak, to read and to write.

If a student were reading and didn't know a word, the normal tendency would be to look it up in a dictionary. This is a mistake. Michel explained that "in reading literature, for example, a writer has a lot of time to write and to use words which are not in common usage. Even in English, we may read words that we may never hear again. We will understand what the writer is saying from the context, but we will never use the word ourselves. So if a person who is a non-native English speaker looks up every word that they don't know, they will have no way of knowing if the word is used frequently or rarely."

The result is that the student may begin to use the word in English, when it is never or rarely used and is not part of common usage. When students reach the point where they can read newspapers, magazines and literature, they will naturally encounter words that they don't know. Here Michel would recommend to his students that they do not look up the words. In fact, there were only two instances where he would say to use the dictionary. The first was where there is a whole paragraph and there is a key word that is necessary to understand the whole paragraph. Otherwise, it is enough just to get the gist of the paragraph. The second instance was when there is a word or expression that reoccurs more than five or six times. By that time, you may have a pretty good idea of what it means, and you should look it up to make sure. The frequency of the word indicates that it is a word in common usage, and that it is not a word that will appear infrequently. Otherwise, Michel recommended not using the dictionary to look words up.

TEACHING OTHER SUBJECTS: GENERAL PARAMETERS

We have already discussed how one could teach a class using the *Master Teacher's* method from the perspective of both content and delivery (*generalizations*, *layering* and *sequencing*) as outlined earlier. Remember that any subject matter to be taught would be in an incentive based learning environment in which from the start, the teacher would present the objectives of the class as well as explain how the objectives would be met. No matter what the subject matter, the teachers would create a *tension* and anxiety-free learning session in which they take full responsibility for both the learning and for the remembering of the students. The teachers are to make this clear from the outset as part of the initial frames or ground rules which are presented to the learners.

As we have seen, these initial frames will immediately eliminate the sources of *tension* normally found in the traditional *Mind Prison*™. The physical aspect of the class would complement the *tension*-free mental structuring of the class. This would mean creating a relaxed atmosphere by including plants and ideally armchairs for the students in a room that has windows.

All physical and mental reminders of the traditional classroom would be removed. There would be no memorization by rote, no homework and no taking of notes. It goes without saying that there would be no textbooks and no tests, notions which are diametrically opposed to traditional courses where students are deluged with voluminous amounts of documents, papers and textbooks to memorize. Ideally, the teachers would create a learning structure that is based on presenting simple concepts or notions first, and then gradually building upon them.

Remembering, learning and *knowledge* are all based on *understanding*.

> Teaching, therefore, means making everything clearly understood and making everything understandable so that it can be immediately applied.

Clear explanations are essential to create *understanding*. The teachers should constantly gauge whether the students have achieved *understanding* of the content. Also, they should encourage questions and discussion.

Last and certainly not least, it is critical in teaching a particular subject matter, to demonstrate its relevancy to the students in relation to what we refer to in our terminology as their "*model of the world*" in today's society.

TEACHING HISTORY

In teaching history, teachers would incorporate all aspects of Michel's method described earlier in this chapter. When teaching a subject such as history it would be important to create a sense of relevancy for the students, helping them to understand how the subject they are learning is relevant to their present day lives. Just as Michel's language courses were interactive, so would history courses be taught interactively. A history course would be taught within a talking framework. The teacher would look at history not just as one nation's history because one does not live in isolation, but rather as the history of the world. Because everything is interconnected, history needs to be studied multi-dimensionally. On some level even something which occurred two thousand years ago will in some way affect what is happening today.

An example would be the fierce reaction to Mel Gibson's controversial film, *The Passion,* which chronicled Christ's crucifixion over two thousand years ago (Mel Gibson had been one of Michel's students.). The film triggered a firestorm of opposing views as to who was responsible for the death of Christ, and in some circles the film inspired a return to a more religion-based life. Just think how the life and works of this one man, Jesus, have touched the lives of millions all over the globe and it was his death which, as we all know, ultimately resulted in the establishment of a new religion at that time, Christianity. Even if one is not a Christian, one is impacted by it in some manner. The same may be said about Buddha, the Prophet Mohammad, Shiva, Moses and those others who, through Divine inspiration and by leading exemplary lives, founded their respective religions based on their beliefs about the nature of God and the Divine.

MICHEL'S *HORIZONTAL PERSPECTIVE*

The point is that even if an event occurred many years ago, on some level, upon closer examination, that event or events have in some manner large or small, left an imprint upon some aspect of life in our world today. Even if something may not be directly interconnected to another event, at least not on the surface, it doesn't matter because one needs to know what happened at the same time in other places. That is world history.

Michel pointed out that whether it is the modern history of today or history fifty years ago, or two thousand years ago, we are still all human beings. We are not any different now. Those were not different people living on the planet one thousand years ago, just people living under different circumstances and with different ways of life and different cultures. History should be seen in relation to everything else. In teaching history, we must look at what is going on in the entire world because any given event which has occurred is not just floating out there somewhere in time. This is what Michel referred to as a "*horizontal perspective.*" It means not only looking at the history but also at the thinking and at the culture of the time. This is a critical point because what happened before affects us now, and if we don't know and understand what happened, then we will not be able to learn from it. If we do not learn a lesson from history, then how will we know what actions to take now or know what might happen to us again and know what to do about it in the future.

For example, ask most students nowadays about World War II and more often than not one will get a blank stare. In their minds, the Hundred Years' War, World War I, World War II or whatever war are just all wars and no distinctions are made because they all occurred in the past, in a far distant past. So it is important to present the wars on a broad level. Why not look at the wars as part of a multi-leveled time line in which concurrent events can be discussed and understood. This is what Michel meant by looking at history from a *horizontal perspective* in which events and people are presented on a broad, wide level.

Traditionally, history is taught from a "*vertical perspective,*" meaning in a linear fashion with one event following or preceding another. History is traditionally studied with little or no regard to what was occurring simultaneously around the globe from different contexts of life.

> Looking at history from a *horizontal perspective* means wanting to know everything about what was happening concurrently at the time.

It implies gaining an understanding of how people lived, of what they believed in and insights into their entire culture.

Having a *horizontal perspective* always means looking at history all across the board, so to speak, rather than as "way back then" or "down there," totally disconnected from the present. As Michel explained it, "So I have a contact over there with what happened two hundred or two thousand years ago. In my mind, I know where it is and where we are. It is here not way back there." Seen in this light, we may consider this manner of viewing history as another type of what we named "*meaningful memory associations*"™ which, as we have discussed, Michel so adroitly used in teaching languages. It is another associated connection with past and present. One statement is made, the connection follows and that connection leads to more connections. It is another process of *layering* one thing over another.

In teaching history it is critical to have a talking framework from the beginning. Even the word "*framework*" implies a process of filling in. History is never limited to one nation's history because one simply does not live in isolation, even if there are some who would like to think so. History should not be a question of memorizing a date, or simply knowing that, for example, World War I occurred. Instead, history should be seen in relation to everything else. Moreover, history should be seen as a vibrant living thing which is never static and always changing.

In a certain sense, history is alive and will always be alive. That is the perspective from which it is to be taught. Michel gave an example of how to teach Biblical history. He suggested that we present the people in the Bible as still living as though one could talk to them now. It is important to understand them in the context in which they were living at their respective time. It is important to know what the world was like at that time, to know how one lived, how one used to live and what people's reactions were to living a certain way at that time. Teachers should encourage *meta-cognition*. For example, they could ask the students how they would have responded in a similar situation.

So what would a teacher do? A teacher could tell a story. In so doing the teacher would put history in context and would get the students to imagine how a person's behavior made sense under the circumstances in which he or she lived at the time. One could compare that person's life to the life of those around him or her and show how his or her behaviors could have been exemplary compared to what others were doing, or show how the behaviors could have been admonitory or reproachful in relation to others.

Michel gave the example of the patriarch, Abraham, from the Bible. Abraham was a very old man when he had his first son, Isaac, with his wife Sarah (He had already had Ishmael with their young, Egyptian maid.). Abraham and Sarah had waited an entire lifetime to give birth to their son and then he took his son to an altar to be sacrificed. From a historical point of view, the questions should be, "What did the act of sacrifice mean at that time? Was it a question of God testing him? Why would God ask him to sacrifice his son?" When you look at the story at face value, it is quite terrifying — the story of a father who sacrificed his son.

So in teaching this story, the teacher would ask the students about the context of life in which Abraham and Sarah were living. What really happened is that Abraham and Sarah lived at a time in the world when sacrifice was common practice. For hundreds of years, sacrifices were made to gods, all kinds of sacrifices in order to please the gods. However, the highest sacrifice one could have given God was the sacrifice of one's first begotten son. This was an accepted practice at that time in history.

Abraham knew that he had to offer the highest of sacrifices, which was his son. At the same time, as Michel told the story, Abraham began to question if he was trying to perform his religious duty by sacrificing his son. When it came time to do it, Abraham asked himself: "Why am I doing this, because I am supposed to do it?" It was at this point that the animal appeared on the scene. So Abraham began to think that the animal should be sacrificed in place of his son. He began to think that it was perhaps God who had sent him the animal. He continued to question the reason for his behavior. Was he sacrificing his son just because everyone else had done it? In his mind that was not right.

From a teaching perspective, this story about Abraham gives an overview and shows that in teaching history, it is important to present a wide perspective as a backdrop that facilitates understanding a particular context in which an event occurred. This is better than simply looking at a given event totally independent of other factors that might have influenced it in a particular way. Give a simple explanation of the facts of the period and then add on.

So with this little story, a teacher would be putting history in the context of the time period in question. A teacher would place a particular figure in the context of his or her time. It is important to get the students to imagine how a person's (or a group's) behavior made sense under the circumstances in which a particular event or action took place One could also show how the behavior or event in question was in advance of other behaviors later in history (For example, Abraham did not follow the established tradition and did not sacrifice his son; and eventually the practice of sacrifice ended for the most part.).

This entire learning session would be conducted interactively, with students asking questions and commenting on what the teacher is saying. The learners should be encouraged to disagree with opinions and to verbalize aloud their own points of view. And, of course, by interacting with students, the teacher would be able to gauge whether or not the students understood the concepts and ideas presented. If something is not understood, it is critical to create clarity immediately, on the spot, rather than build upon misconceptions. Always monitor for *understanding*. This is precisely how Michel "taught" history to his children.

According to Michel, in the past two and one half years prior to his passing, there was rarely a night where he and his son hadn't spent the entire evening discussing history, with Guri asking a plethora of questions, with Michel, of course, answering them. The manner in which Michel "*taught*" history to his children is the classic example of how history should be taught — within a framework of question and answer interaction.

Michel's children were certainly blessed to have as their father a great historical figure that also happened to have a huge knowledge of human history through the ages seen from his unique *horizontal perspective*.

Also, in making the history session interactive, a teacher could ask many questions to stimulate the thinking of their students. For example, one could ask the students what they would have done under the same circumstances if they had lived during a given time period. Or else ask them how they think a particular event affected another event at the same time or at a later time. Given the interconnected nature of all things, it would be important for teachers to ask students how the world looked at a given point in time. Who were other people living in other parts of the world during the same period? What were their customs and way of life?

The teacher would ask students what they knew about other countries and about how other people lived during that period of history. It is important to teach them about what was happening elsewhere at the time and to teach them about life in other countries during the same period. Once they have attained *understanding* and have a *knowledge* base from which to engage in lively discussion, then teachers could ask the students to make connections among different peoples and different countries. How were things the same? How were they different? Were different events related to each other, and if so, how?

In addition, history should also be taught in phases. Because it is seen from a *horizontal perspective*, it will be up to the teachers to decide what they are going to include in each phase. This will depend to a large degree upon their understanding of what they are planning to teach. The challenge in education, however, is to find enough creative teachers who are able to think in this way. This will require people who are not limited to linear thinking. We need teachers who can generate alternatives. There is no set rule for the lengths of the phases because that will be determined to a certain extent by the quality and length of the interchanges. In the course of the explanations and discussions that occur as part of the phases, it will become evident that some students have a more sophisticated understanding than others.

At the same time, there will be others who may have a misunderstanding of the events that occurred "*horizontally.*" This will require more explanations to achieve clarity. Briefly then, in order to teach effectively, the teacher needs to lay out the phases. The teacher also needs to have given some thought as to what level of *understanding* they want the students to have. This is important because the students' level of *understanding* is what will determine the shape of the discussion. The teacher should also be continuously monitoring the comments of the students in the discussion as a barometer of their level of understanding. Once the teacher sees that the students have reached a certain level of understanding which is appropriate, then the teacher is able to move on to the next phase.

Let us now review the process of teaching history. First, give the students some information as an overview so that they have something to discuss. Tell a story. Presenting information stimulates the thinking process. It also encourages questions, and depending on the level of understanding, the students' questions which may be far reaching in their scope. Teach students the meaning of history and about how things and all peoples are connected with each other. In this way, the students start making connections and thinking about how one thing could have impacted another thing, as opposed to saying thus and such happened in 1066 or whenever.

History is not a question of memorizing dates and facts.

> Instead, history is a process of finding out how and why
> things happened the way in which they did and how
> and why people reacted the way they did
> at any given point in time.

This approach teaches children how to think for themselves about events rather than merely rattle off the names and dates of events. These types of questions are important, again because of the interconnectedness of all things.

Michel gave the example of 732, the date that Charles Martel defeated the Moors during their invasion of France from Spain. If this had not occurred, the entire course of history would have been different. How many people know this? And how many people are aware of the interconnections between the scientifically and culturally advanced Moorish culture and the Renaissance? Michel often lamented the fact that so few people knew the answers to these questions because they had not been taught history for understanding.

The structure of a history lesson is similar to Michel's approach to language teaching in that one would start with simple bits of information, adding on step by step, creating a wonderfully colorful and imaginative picture of what life was like at a certain time. History is literally brought to life when using Michel's method, instead of it being a boring session of memorization of useless dates and facts which have no relevance to life today when presented in this manner. So what if a student is able to memorize dates of battles or of particular events, or reel off the names of historical figures? As we have said over and over, memorizing data for the purposes of regurgitating it in order to pass a test is a complete waste of time

First, one will not remember the memorized data four days later, if not sooner. Second, the memorized data does not represent *knowledge*. And third, none of it is based on *understanding*. In the context of history, memorizing dates, names and facts do not equate with the acquisition of *knowledge*. The important thing is to be able to understand how people, events, beliefs, cultures, etc. affected the world at a given period of time as well as to understand how these things are impacting us now. The emphasis will always be on making connections and on *understanding*.

When teaching a subject such as history, one may easily fall into the habit of lecturing, rattling off names, dates and events, etc. Teachers must make sure that they are not lecturing. Instead, teachers should ask the students to make interconnections based on what they already know and based on what has been presented as an initial framework. Engage the students in dialogues in which everyone participates. Make certain that no one is left out of the discussion. Make eye contact with each student and make certain that the students never raise their hands. The history session is not a competition to see who knows the most. It should be an experience in sharing information in dialogue and question and answer form. It should be a fun way to make interesting connections that lead to more questions and, in turn, to *understanding* which results in the acquisition of *knowledge*.

Make certain to ask questions and to give information that creates relevancy. For example, in speaking of the Italian Renaissance, teachers could ask their students to think about how the great Leonardo da Vinci's inventions and art impacts us in the modern world. What kind of man was he? How was he different from others around him? How do his views and inventions affect our thinking and our way of life today? What was happening in countries in the rest of Europe and in the world during the time of da Vinci? Have the students engage in an interesting and animated discussion, making new connections with every new insight and comment. If it hadn't been for Ron Howard's film, *The Da Vinci Code*, this Renaissance genius in all likelihood, would not have become a household word except as the artist behind *The Mona Lisa*. Even with the film, are students even aware of Leonardo's wide impact on anatomical drawings or even on modern conveniences of the day? Probably not. Bring alive the period during which Leonardo lived because it really is part of our lives now. Help the students to gain an *understanding* of the relationship between what happened then and with what is happening now.

Talk about the literature at the time, since literature is always a great reflection of the culture and thinking and of what was happening at any given period in history. Make the students aware of the lives and works of the authors who wrote at the time in history about which they are learning. Who was Shakespeare and how did his plays reflect the mores of his times? If studying the Middle Ages, talk about Chaucer or Dante and perhaps share *La Chanson de Roland* (*The Song of Roland*) or stories about some of the Knights of the Round Table. What do these stories reveal about the beliefs, the mindset and the societal structures in place during that time?

In the eighteenth century, the Age of Enlightenment in Europe was a fascinating time in so many ways. What was happening concurrently in Germany, France and England in the fields of literature, art, science and philosophy which led to new ways of thinking about the world and man's place in it? Who was John Locke, who was Voltaire, and who was Denis Diderot among others, and what were their contributions to our world? How many people realize that Diderot was the man who created what has come to be known as *The Encyclopedia*? What impact has this had on the world of education, particularly before the arrival of computers?

Introduce your students to the writers and to the philosophers of the time period under study to gain an appreciation of how their thoughts affected their world and how they continue to impact our present world in some way. And before the written word, *chansons* and stories passed in oral tradition from one generation to the next told much about life and about the mind-set prevalent at a particular point in history. Share them with your students by creating a participatory exchange.

All in all, history should be taught as a living entity with links to concurrent events and to past and to future events as well. Teachers should make history a living experience, creating life-like characters from those who lived before. Reawaken that drive for learning which is already within the students and you will be delighted to see just how the students will be truly excited about learning even more. That will open the doors to endless possibilities and will create joy in the process.

TEACHING MATHEMATICS AND SCIENCE

Mathematics and science are two subjects where the distinction between memorization and *understanding* are particularly critical.

> Research indicates that many students have difficulty with mathematics and science, because they have memorized formulas but do not understand the concepts behind them.

Beginning with basic arithmetic students are taught to memorize multiplication tables, but lack an *understanding* of what the operations of addition, subtraction, multiplication and division actually entail.

The easiest way to understand arithmetical operations is by working with objects like pickup sticks. A student is taught to multiply a number of piles of sticks with each pile containing an equal number of sticks. To do this they simply put all of the sticks in one pile and count up the total number of sticks in the combined pile. Once a student understands this operation, then they can always figure out how to multiply any two numbers. Memorizing multiplication tables is just a shortcut. Michel constantly emphasized the critical importance of *understanding* and being able to *figure things out* as opposed to memorizing. As mathematics gets more complex, memory becomes more and more taxed. By *understanding* the basics concepts, however, the student can always check their work and figure the answer out.

The situation becomes even more problematic when students are given verbal problems to solve such as: "Six students each have seven marbles. Four of the students give their marbles to a new student. How many marbles does the new student have?" Many students have memorized that 4 X 7 = 28, but they are unable to solve simple word problems because they don't understand the basic concepts behind addition, subtraction, multiplication and division. The situation becomes even more challenging when we move to higher mathematics such as calculus. Here *understanding* of concepts is even more critical. Many students can compute the right answer but have no *understanding* of what they are doing or why it is the right answer.

One university calculus professor would complain that in grading examinations he had to wade through pages and pages of tedious calculations in order to figure out where the student made the mistake that allowed them to get the right answer. In advanced mathematics classes teachers often see an "M curve" instead of the usual bell curve.

This is because there are some really bright students who understand and are able to figure things out and there are other really hard-working students who are able to compute and calculate until they get the right answer even though they don't understand why it is the right answer. This is a beautiful example of the difference between *understanding* mathematics and the rote process of memorization, calculation and trial and error.

The same thing that applies to mathematics also applies to teaching science. Students are able to memorize formulas and calculate answers, but they lack a basic *understanding* of the concepts behind them. They run into difficulty when they have to make complex applications of the formulas or use the formulas to solve problems. Students spend their study time memorizing formulas for an examination and then quickly forget what they have memorized. Once again it is easy to teach formulas. Real teaching for Michel, however, involves explaining why the formulas work. In science classes teachers will often derive the formulas in a non rigorous way using what are referred to as "hand waving arguments." The challenge is that this is only verifying the mathematics. If students don't understand the concepts, then the derivations are simply something else to memorize. As Michel constantly emphasized, "To teach is to explain."

Science education is in the sorry state that it is because the emphasis has been put in the wrong place. Instead of *understanding* concepts and theories, students are taught to memorize formulas and compute answers. Once more the challenge shows up in applications and problem solving. The deeper problem shows up in most students' lack of ability to do theoretical work. The growth edge of science is in new theories. This requires deep *understanding* of concepts. Students who have memorized formulas and who are computational experts will never be generative. They will be able to compute but not to develop and expand the theory.

Let us consider how Michel would approach teaching a subject like high school physics. In following Michel's method, the teacher would first break the course up into topics. Given the content nature of physics, one would spend some time on optics, on mechanics, on thermodynamics, on electricity and magnetism. These are the usual topics covered in high school physics. Let us focus on one of the topics — for example, mechanics. So how would one teach mechanics using Michel's method? All that we have said thus far about his method, of course, applies here as well. Teachers would incorporate the different aspects of his method including, *generalizations*, *layering*, establishing eye contact, etc.

Teachers should be creative enough to figure out how to present the topic of mechanics starting with Newton's laws of motion. The teacher would present, as with any subject matter to be taught, a basic overview with demonstrations so that the student could grasp basic concepts such as distance, time, velocity, acceleration and force. It is amazing how many students fail to understand these basic concepts. Most can understand velocity, but many never really understand acceleration and force. The teacher needs to have discussion to determine if the students really grasp the basic concepts. Once this has been accomplished, the teacher would continue to monitor for *understanding* within the framework of questions and answers.

Briefly, then, in teaching a subject such as mechanics, we have a presentation of concepts, theories, equations and laws. The different pieces developmentally lead to the laws governing motion. So teachers can tell the learners what people did experimentally and what people like Newton discovered, all of which led to the formulation of his laws of motion. Once students understand the laws the teacher would next explain how to apply them. The teacher can explain what the laws are and how to solve problems using the laws. Eventually, the teacher would explain how simple mechanics affects our current way of life and our standard of living. Again, the teacher would make connections between what life is like now compared to what life was like before Newton discovered his laws.

Also, it is recommended to engage in problem solving because it always stimulates questions. And questions from the students allow the teacher and the student to delve more deeply into the subject at hand. Some questions may not be immediately answered because of the time limits of a given class. In such a case, the teacher may suggest that it would be interesting to do some research and write a report which an interested student or students could share with the rest of the class.

If the subject were really interesting, the students would want to find out more. They would learn how to do their own research and then contribute it to the class. They would report to the group. The purpose of the research would not be to create competition or to single out a student as better than another. It would be a means to stimulate more discussion and to spark interest for more discussion and research. There would be no official papers to write and no official written reports assigned to the students. Of course, there may be students in the class who are better than others in a given subject. In this case, it is beneficial for those who know more to get the others actively involved as well. Establishing *esprit de classe* from the onset enhances this process. Participation of the entire class is the goal. In a way, the teaching becomes a participatory workshop of sorts. Again, like all of Michel's courses, the class should be an interactive learning session which is also an essential component of true teaching.

Obviously, subjects such as science and math are a little different than foreign languages or history in that they frequently rely on visual mediums where you have to write equations or work things out. Michel told us in that using his method, that it would be all right to use visual aids for the purposes of discussion in teaching science or math, and especially in science. It is important to use instruments and models as well. Laboratory equipment with which to conduct experiments is also a necessity.

And, of course, as with all teaching, the emphasis is placed on *understanding*. The problem in traditional science is that the teacher gives a test, asks the students to talk about Newton's Laws, for example, and then asks them to solve a problem as opposed to *understanding* what it is all about. This is another reason to encourage questions. Although no note taking is allowed, students can write down questions. They don't take notes on what is said, only on their questions.

Once again, in the teaching of science, in general, the teacher has to determine in advance what level of *understanding* they want the students to have about whatever the topic is that they are learning. To do this, teachers have to listen in and participate in generated discussion. By listening carefully to what the students are saying, from the students' ability to apply concepts and information in order to solve problems, the teachers will be able to determine the level of *understanding* among the students. And, if there are misunderstandings, then it is up to the teacher to determine why the students do not understand concepts. It is also up to the teacher to come up with explanations or to walk the students through issues so that they can figure out themselves if they have made a mistake. When the students know that they have made a mistake, then they will be able to self-correct and to figure out how to correct their own mistakes.

> In order for self-correction to work, it is important to present everything clearly, based on *understanding*.

However, with science in particular, it is all the more critical that teachers encourage their students to ask questions because there will always be someone who may not fully understand a given concept. Questions will provide elucidation and will help the students to reach *understanding*. So by asking questions, students will gain a fuller *understanding*. If there is the slightest question about *understanding* among the students, they will be confident and comfortable enough to ask for clarity. They will feel secure in knowing that it is perfectly wonderful to ask questions. Teachers must be able to monitor the students to make certain that every single student has achieved *understanding*. Answers such as, "I think I know it," or "I think I see what you mean," from students are not sufficient. Each student must fully and completely understand the concepts taught. Again, the responsibility for learning and for remembering is with the teacher.

Remember, too, that there are no textbooks. Also, the teacher should not read from a textbook or give a lecture. Often, in the traditional *Mind Prison*™, you will have teachers explain something and then say: "I will now read this to you." The teachers have to be able to explain everything to know how to teach. Real teaching is not about lecturing, reading from a textbook, or about telling students, "Do your homework and let me know tomorrow." Teachers must be able to create a meaningful exchange with their students. For this to occur, teachers should not stand behind a desk. They must be with the class, maintain eye contact with each student in the group, and create that sense of *esprit de classe*. Also, it goes without saying that there are no examinations and no grades, both of which create competition and *tension*.

LEARNING FROM THE *MASTER TEACHER*

It is often said that Michel was unique, and that no one else would be able to do what he did.

> The real truth is that Michel was unique and that other people are capable of doing what he did by closely following his method. It is important to point out that the method is certainly not for everyone, however.

What Michel accomplished requires both an in-depth command of the subject matter, a fertile and creative mind, as well as a particular set of perceptual filters through which he saw the world (Chapter Nine). Also, it is important to remember that Michel developed and refined his method by trial and error. It did not suddenly and miraculously one day come together.

This book is about Michel's method. So what can we learn from Michel and how can we use his method to design our own courses? What are the requirements and how do we proceed? Yes, Michel pointed the way. It will require, however, creativity and discovery on our part to follow in the direction that he indicated.

The keys to designing a course that follows Michel's method fall into two broad categories. The first is the design of the course. This involves the grouping and *sequencing* of the content. The second is the actual delivery of the content. Let us begin now with the course design.

Michel's method is based on *knowledge* and *understanding* and not on rote learning and cramming. In order to design a course based on Michel's method, it is first necessary to determine what are the structures and key concepts which you would like the student to understand and to know. It is also necessary to know how you will be able to tell if the student understands them or not. To gauge for *understanding* on the part of the students, the teachers can't just lecture because then they would not be able to determine the level of students' *understanding*.

Teachers need to find out what the students know up front and then determine whether it is right or wrong. If it is wrong, then the teachers have to make certain to clarify it, otherwise the misunderstanding or error will lead to more problems later on and much confusion. Therefore, teachers need to constantly monitor their students to make sure that they have achieved *understanding*. And, in order to gauge for *understanding* on the part of their students, teachers cannot lecture because this will not enable them to determine students' *understanding*. Instead, they will have to engage in some kind of interaction with the students.

As we have seen, Michel's method is completely interactive. There must be an ongoing dialogue between the teacher and the students. This may involve questions and answers, problem solving and discussion. These would reveal how well students understand and how well they can apply the concepts, principles and procedures. Of course, in the traditional *Mind Prison*™, teachers rely on standardized tests, multiple choice quizzes and the like for measuring their students' progress and abilities. These tests are not the solution for they do not measure *understanding*. Michel fully realized that tests merely measure one's ability to memorize and to recall facts and do not measure *understanding*.

Michel believed in the efficacy of *block teaching*, so the course needs to be continuous. In secondary school each course would be in a block. To design the course, it is first necessary to determine what content will be covered in the block. In general, one can cover a lot more in an intensive block than one would normally cover in a year of fifty minute classes. The course content must be distributed over the time allotted.

Once again, the course design must be based on what concepts, principles and processes the student will need in order to understand and to know the material. These need to be progressive and build upon each other. The first teaching sessions must begin with the known and then introduce new material. For each concept or principle that is introduced, there must be a clear explanation. There should be a set of *heuristics* or *meaningful memory associations*™ created for anything that the student has to remember.

There also needs to be some way in which to check the *understanding* of the students. The ideal way for this to occur would be through discussion and questions and answers, and not through traditional testing which simply measures one's ability to regurgitate information. Also, teachers would need to structure the class so that there are opportunities for the students to reveal their *understanding*. In this way, the teachers would be able to detect the misconceptions and correct them on the spot. Michel's method exemplified this *par excellence* because it was *dialogical*.

The key to course design, as we have already mentioned, is *layering*. This involves that the teacher, as Michel explained it, "plant a seed and then water and grow it." Such a process begins with an initial explanation followed by exercises to reinforce and deepen the explanation. All content moves through four stages.

1) First, it is pre-taught or introduced implicitly while something else is being taught.

2) Second, content is made explicit and thoroughly explained so that it makes sense.

3) Third, it is reinforced through use and practice.

4) Fourth, content may be reviewed periodically in use.

It is certainly not necessary to overdo content, or to constantly go over and over it. The content should be learned after stage two while stages three and four are just to confirm and deepen it. The powerful thing about *layering* is that all of these stages can occur at the same time. At any point, the teacher may be pre-teaching an idea while explaining another idea, while reinforcing previous ideas. In this way, a tremendous amount can be accomplished in a short period of time. This could not happen in the same way during fifty minute periods or with linear teaching.

There are several important elements a teacher needs to have in place before the learning session may begin. Once the key pieces of the content have been identified to provide the necessary *understanding* and *knowledge*, once the content has been ordered and sequenced for *understanding* and memory, and once the *evidence procedure* has been determined to confirm that *understanding* is occurring, then the actual execution of the learning session may begin.

Everything begins with the initial frames below:

INITIAL FRAMES

- Make yourself comfortable.
- Let go of any *tension* you may have.
- This course is about *understanding* and *knowledge*, not about memorization.
- Never *try* to remember.
- You don't forget what you know.
- You may block it, but you don't forget it.
- In this course, there is no need to take notes except for questions.
- There are no textbooks.
- There is no homework, but there may be research projects.
- There are no tests or examinations.
- The teacher is responsible for your remembering and *understanding*.
- If you don't remember or *understand*, it is the teacher's fault and not yours.
- The teacher will find out why you don't remember or *understand* and will know what to do about it
- Just sit back and experience the joy of learning.

The learning sessions are interactive or *dialogical* which means that they consist primarily of explanations followed by questions and answers and discussion. The discussion must be designed to reveal the level at which the student has gained *understanding*.

Teaching needs to begin with and to be built upon what the student already knows. All explanations must be in terms of the familiar, and everything must have a rationale and make sense. You begin with a total framework and then begin to fill in what is needed. Focus on what things mean and do not focus on facts. Meaning stimulates questions, and questions will lead to making interesting connections. Make the learning session a living experience. Bring it into the present. Make it a *"now"* experience.

As discussion occurs, the teacher must be monitoring the level of *understanding* of the participants. When the teacher realizes that a student does not understand something, then it is up to the teacher to determine the source of the mistake or lack of *understanding* and to lead the student to the correct understanding. Preferably, the teacher will do this without the student even realizing what is happening.

During the entire modeling process Michel would constantly remind us of the following:

> It is important to know that students never be publicly or privately corrected or told that they are wrong. There should never be any expression of disapproval. Never ever admonish or scold or punish a student for a failure to remember or understand. Failure to understand means failure of teaching. Failure to understand is a sign for the teacher to explain in an understandable way. Failure to understand means that the teacher should see to it that the explanation is fully understood by everybody.

Also, Michel insisted that there be no time pressure and that the student be encouraged to take the time to think things out.

And, of course, develop *esprit de classe* in the learning environments through maintaining eye contact. Remember that when a student is working out a problem, or if someone has a problem that has to be worked out individually, the whole class is with that person. This is how Michel described it:

> The whole class is participating and I am mentally with him [the student], once *esprit de*

classe has been established in the room. And often it will cause applause because they are with it, so it is never a question of feeling humiliated. Nobody is ever humiliated. When someone understands something and works it out, everybody is behind it. It is not a question of one student understanding it better than another student because there are no grades.

To study something means participative and collaborative learning. There is also the relativity of time. Students usually put pressure on themselves in thinking things out, believing that it is taking them a long time to solve a problem, when it really is not. In these cases, they often start blaming themselves and this is definitely not permitted at any time.

There are no textbooks and no homework. It should be noted that this is not to prevent students from studying and reading about those things in which they are interested outside of class. It is all right for students to study something which interests them or to do research which is shared later with the class and then to lead a discussion on the subject matter. Outside research is simply not a requirement. In fact, it is a great idea for students to participate in collaborative research projects together and report on the results.

The classroom should be fun, interactive, and exciting. The class may go on for six to eight hours or whatever. It should be an environment of heightened excitement, of great excitement. It is a learning session in which one doesn't watch the clock or wait anxiously for the bell to ring. In fact, just the opposite is true. Students will not want to stop for lunch and will not want to leave. Now that their *innate drive for learning* is being reawakened, they will be hungry for more learning. Because students are relaxed and focused, they will be able to learn easily and willingly. In such an ambiance, learning is a real high; and students will become addicted to it. The same applies to teaching because teaching in this way is also a real high, and teachers will become addicted as well. This is what Michel called "*true teaching*."

Often self-esteem is an issue in traditional education. Students are made to feel stupid and the *innate drive for learning* is stifled. This is the opposite of real learning. In real learning, the *innate drive for learning* is awakened and reinforced through continual successful interactions that generate critically important feelings of personal efficacy and self-worth. Constant reinforcement stimulates the competence motive for each student and self-esteem increases accordingly.

To accomplish all of this, teachers must know their subject matter very well, inside and out. And they must always keep in mind what it is they want students to understand and to know, as well as have a way to verify or know that the student understands and knows. Teachers must be creative and they must be able to make distinctions and see connections and patterns among diverse elements. That is a real challenge because many people simply delete elements of difference from their reality and see only similarities (In Chapter Nine we discuss the "*People Pattern*"™ linked to this trait.).

Just as Michel accomplished this so effortlessly, teachers also must be able to simplify that which is complicated and reduce complexity to simplicity. Moreover, teachers need to connect with their students rather than sit in front of a classroom lecturing facts that will merely be regurgitated in tests. They must be able to establish firm eye contact with each student and develop *esprit de classe* in the room. Teachers also should have refined *calibration* skills to be able to "read" their students and to know what they are experiencing.

Teachers absolutely need to reach their students, to *mentally reach* their students, otherwise they are not really teaching. They need to be able to give clear explanations that are understood by all of their students. Teachers also need to be masters of creating *heuristics* and *meaningful memory associations*™ to facilitate the students' memory. They need to banish impatience from their emotional range. In short, as teachers they need to take complete, yes, complete responsibility for the learning and for the remembering of all of their students. And then they must continue to interact with the students until this happens. When teachers do this, they, along with their students, will experience a high level of immense excitement that is unmatched to the point where it will become an addiction! And most important of all, teachers will have learned a better way to teach and will become examples of what is truly possible given the right mental attitude and the proper tools which Michel so generously provided, tools, which provide the perfect template for the future of learning.

Chapter Seven

THEORY AND PRACTICE: THE WAR BETWEEN THE TWO

Michel Thomas had developed and refined his method during a period of over sixty years of trial and error experimentation. His was a method which is based on what he discovered works best. From time to time, there have been several criticisms of Michel's method coming from the corridors of academia. One of these criticisms is that Michel's method was not scientific and that it was not based on sound pedagogical principles. In short, some critics have embraced the idea that his method did not meet the demands of theory. They also say that although Michel's method may produce results under certain circumstances, these results would seem to be idiosyncratic to Michel and were not reproducible in an academic environment. One academic critic even went so far as to call Michel's results a "menace to the lay public."

At the present time, there is a great deal of debate going on in contemporary education. Objective critics realize that there are many problems with the educational system as it now exists. The educational establishment understandably tries to justify itself and maintains that the critics are overstating the deficiencies and ignoring the benefits. The debate is further fueled by the demands of politicians for so-called accountability and the demand by employers who need graduates who can think critically and who have "marketable skills."

There is some consensus now emerging in education regarding how children and adults learn as well as how teachers should design and deliver their curricula. The challenge in education is similar to the challenge we face in many other areas of life in today's world. The challenge is simply this: How does one put theory into practice? Theory is great but how does one actually, as we say, "*operationalize*" it or put it into practice? This is the magic question to which many have been searching for an answer for a very long time.

On one side of the spectrum, there are theorists who present pedagogic theories about how to learn and how to teach. Their theories make sense within their academic framework. They are based on sound reasons and explain what needs to be done and why. These same theoreticians are constantly frustrated, however, because nobody seems to be able to put these theories into practice and to make them work in the real world of the classroom. The question always arises as to whether the failure is due to a poor implementation of a good idea or whether the idea itself is wrong and needs rethinking.

On the other end of the spectrum from the academic theorists are the real-world practitioners. These include the educators and teachers who are succeeding in the classroom by simply doing their job. Most of them are not concerned about implementing theory. They are simply interested in discovering what works and exploring how to make it work even better. The highly successful teachers are frequently well-known among their colleagues and within the circles in which they operate. Sometimes people try to reproduce what these remarkable practitioners do, and usually they are not able to get the same results. Consequently, they determine that the results are somehow idiosyncratic to that practitioner's personality and are not something that others can easily replicate. The truth of the matter is that "success leaves clues." The fact that these master practitioners have not been successfully modeled is a function of the methodology used to do so, and is not a function of the uniqueness of their skills. This whole study and the subject of this book is based on our professionally modeling Michel Thomas, the *Master Teacher*, and his method, using our proprietary *Advanced Behavioral Modeling*™ *Technology,* which determines *"how"* experts do what they do (Appendix A).

AN APPROACH TO RECONCILIATION

This chapter will examine the *Michel Thomas Method* in light of the contemporary scientific understanding of how people learn and how to teach them accordingly. When we study this scientific understanding carefully, we make a rather amazing discovery. It is that Michel's method agrees with the latest theories. Or perhaps we should really be saying that the latest theories agree with Michel's method. In any case, we make quite a remarkable discovery. The *Master Teacher's* results can be explained by modern theories of learning and teaching!

It must be emphasized again that Michel developed his method through trial and error. It was never Michel's intention to put learning and pedagogical theory into formal practice. Instead, he set out to probe the learning process of the human mind. From a practical standpoint, Michel was not interested in theory. Instead, he was interested in what worked. Michel was a master of "results" and of "doing." He was a master of achieving extraordinary results and of doing extraordinary things. The astounding discovery is that his "results" and his "doing" successfully embody modern learning theory. Moreover, Michel's method also goes beyond modern theory in critical areas providing new insights for future theories.

We have written this chapter for several reasons. First, is to show the critics that Michel's method is scientific, although Michel was not concerned about this aspect. The critics often say that his results were idiosyncratic to him and that they are not based on sound theory. Actually Michel's method, although not derived from theory, does, in fact, correspond with theory. This is an important point not to be overlooked. There is no longer any excuse to dismiss Michel's method as theoretically unsound.

> In fact, it turns out that the *Michel Thomas Method* is in the vanguard of modern educational theories.

What is so astonishing is that Michel had discovered from over fifty years of research what modern theoreticians are just now discovering decades later! This is no surprise to anyone who knew Michel, for he had always been an innovative thinker and a genius ahead of his time. When Michel read this chapter of our manuscript, he was gratified to see that the latest research in education was recommending precisely what he had discovered and put into practice so many years before. He felt that there was finally a long awaited glimmer of hope for the future.

The second reason for this discussion, and perhaps more important, is that Michel epitomized the *Master Teacher par excellence;* and his method is one of the best examples available of a practice that embodies the contemporary theory (Once again, remember that Michel never started with theory.). We are blessed to have had Michel among us, for what is truly exciting is that educators and theorists alike can finally learn from what Michel had accomplished so brilliantly for years.

As indicated earlier, the real challenge is how to put theory into action. Action requires creativity. Tragically in education, and in most other fields, this is sorely lacking; and it is a problem that is getting worse with each generation. Fortunately, the exciting thing for us is that Michel had created a successful method from which we can learn a great deal. And for Michel to share his closely guarded secrets with us as part of our modeling process was more than generous. It is difficult to move from theory to practice. In this case, we will move in the other direction. We will show, instead, that what Michel did can be explained by theory. Even more exciting is that by carefully studying the *Michel Thomas Method*, we will discover how to broaden and expand on the theory.

HOW PEOPLE LEARN

How People Learn: Brain, Mind, Experience and School - The Expanded Edition is the title of a book published in 2000 by the National Research Council which is organized by the National Academy of Sciences, the National Academy of Engineering and the Institute of Medicine. It was prepared by two committees of the Commission on Behavioral and Social Sciences and Education. The two committees are the Committee on Development in the Science of Learning with additional material from the Committee on Learning Research and Educational Practice. The book explores the critical issue of how to link research on the science of learning to actual practice in the classroom.

The above book begins by saying that "a new theory of learning is coming into focus that leads to very different approaches to the design of curriculum, teaching and assessment than those often found in school today." What is this new theory of learning? Where does it come from and how does it contrast with what is often found in school today?

The new theory of learning is coming from a convergence of research in seven areas. These are:

1) Cognitive psychology and its research into the nature of competent performance, the principles of knowledge organization and the mechanisms underlying problem solving.

2) Developmental research which has shown that young children understand a great deal more about basic principles of biology and physical causality than had previously been realized. In short children are able to engage in advanced reasoning at an early age.

3) Research on learning and transfer is revealing important principles as to how people can actually use what they have learned in new settings.

4) Social psychology, cognitive psychology and anthropology have all made clear different aspects of how cultural and social norms and expectations impact learning and the transfer of learning in very powerful ways.

5) Neuroscience is revealing how learning actually changes the physical structure and functional organization of the brain itself.

6) Cognitive and developmental psychologists in collaboration with educators are making new discoveries about the design and evaluation of learning environments.

7) Researchers are discovering new ways to learn from the "*wisdom of practice*" which comes from highly successful teachers who share their experience.

In passing, we will note that Michel's *wisdom of practice* is, in fact, what our book on his method is all about. Using our modeling process, we take this *wisdom of practice* to a deeper level and determine the "how" of Michel's expertise which we examined in the previous chapter. Of significance is that these seven areas of research just mentioned have resulted in new insights into learning and teaching which we will elaborate upon below.

In the generations of our parents and grandparents, there was an emphasis on the so-called three R's of reading, writing and arithmetic. Students were drilled in these basic literacy skills. They were taught within the confines of a rigid traditional system by authoritarian teachers who were not interested in developing critical thinking. In order to be successful, students had to memorize what the teacher wanted them to know and then to be able to regurgitate it back upon demand to the teacher in either oral or in written form.

During the nineteenth-century and into the twentieth, such skills would prepare one to be an obedient worker, a good, decent citizen and would help one to succeed in the work place. That was the way to become a so-called pillar of society. In schools one was taught to conform because making children behave in a similar manner is a way to control and manipulate the populace and to prevent them from thinking on their own, as we have seen in Chapter Four. Conformity breeds predictability and discourages individuality, which is more difficult to control. Also, society was focused on local issues and problems and wanted conformity.

The times have changed dramatically and are changing at a faster pace all the time. Today's work place requires an entirely different set of skills to compete and to survive in our global marketplace. Workers need to be able to think critically, to solve complex problems, to communicate clearly and persuasively and to adapt quickly to changing circumstances. The needs of society have also changed. The world is a far more complex place today than in years past, and the democratic process demands solutions to national and global issues. We are in dire need of an educated citizenry, as we point out in the chapter on "Education and Democracy" and elsewhere in this book.

Perhaps the most critical issue driving change is the accelerated growth of information and knowledge itself. It is neither possible nor necessary to know all that there is to know about a subject. Moreover, things — people, ideas, situations, conditions, circumstances, milieu, etc. — are rapidly and constantly changing. Also, as a child, one can no longer learn all the knowledge and skills needed for later success in life. Learning is a life-long process, and in order to succeed in this life-long process, one must master the principles of learning itself. This requires a major shift in our educational outcomes. As Nobel Prize winner Herbert Simon observed, "The meaning of 'knowing' has shifted from being able to remember and repeat information to being able to find and use information." This change also requires a shift in educational methods. Memorizing is out. Memorizing information is no longer a viable option in the context of life today. What is in, what is necessary is giving students the intellectual tools and learning strategies to enable them to think critically, to solve complex problems, and to ask the right questions to acquire the knowledge which they need to succeed in a fast-paced and rapidly changing world.

So what does this all mean for the new science of learning and how must education adjust its methods accordingly? The new science of learning is based on four key concepts which are interrelated and interconnected. These are:

1) Learning with understanding
2) The critical importance of pre-existing knowledge
3) *Meta-cognition*
4) Learning transfer.

Let us explore these in turn and see how they correspond to the *Michel Thomas Method*.

LEARNING WITH UNDERSTANDING

These days there is a major war raging in contemporary education. On one side, we find the old school that stresses memorizing facts and being able to repeat them on demand. One's ability to do so is traditionally determined by tests. Memorizing also forms the basis for much standardized testing. At the same time, many politicians are looking for a way to hold schools, teachers and students "accountable." In this pursuit, they have often settled on standardized tests that measure a student's ability to memorize and repeat back information as a test for the success of the educational process. Fortunately, modern researchers in education, if not the politicians, realize the short-sided nature of such an approach.

On the other side is the new school, which places its focus on understanding and not on the ability to memorize information. New school adherents point out that one can learn to memorize and to repeat back things that one has absolutely no understanding of at all. They also realize that information which is acquired through memorizing and cramming is usually quickly forgotten. Most important of all, however, they contend that understanding is essential for developing the ability to engage in critical thinking and the ability to solve problems. It is more complicated to develop assessments that measure critical thinking than assessments that simply measure the recall of facts. Educators of the new school insist that standardized testing must be changed to measure understanding, and that a new standard of accountability based on understanding must replace the old standard based on rote memory.

Thus, understanding is contrasted with memorizing and being tested on facts. In fact, the emphasis on memorizing and being tested on facts is often antithetical to understanding and to making sense of material. What is required is "usable knowledge" which is not a list of disconnected facts, and is, instead, knowledge that is connected to and organized around important concepts. Knowledge is critically important to learning, but the kind of knowledge needed is that which enables the learner to solve problems and make applications in other contexts. This is knowledge based on understanding and not on memorized, isolated facts which are readily and quickly forgotten. We are talking about knowledge that supports thinking about alternatives which are not available in memorized facts. Also, this is the kind of knowledge which can be easily transferred.

The National Research Council finds that one of the hallmarks of the new science of learning is its emphasis on learning with understanding. They point out that three things are essential to develop competence in an area of inquiry. These are:

1) A deep foundation of factual knowledge

2) A conceptual framework to understand facts

and ideas

3) A way of organizing the knowledge to facilitate retrieval and application.

Knowledge of a large number of disconnected facts is not sufficient to develop competence in a given area of inquiry. Competence requires, instead, that students learn with understanding. The National Research Council study concludes the following: "Deep understanding of subject matter transforms factual information into usable knowledge."

Part of the research underlying this conclusion is based on contrasting experts and novices. Research indicates that the experts don't necessarily have better overall memories than novices. Rather, what they have is an in-depth understanding of the organizing concepts of their area of expertise which enables them to see patterns and relationships that are not obvious to the novice. This conceptual understanding enables them to quickly determine what is relevant and what is irrelevant and then to organize the relevant facts and information in a meaningful way. Furthermore, they are able to quickly and fluently assess their knowledge to solve problems and to apply it in appropriate ways.

Thus, the job of education is to develop more formal understanding and, hence, expertise in students. This requires both the development of an information base and a conceptual framework to organize this information. We said that the four key concepts in the modern theory of learning were interconnected. Research shows that organizing information into a conceptual framework makes it easier to apply and transfer it to other contexts. In short, conceptual organization facilitates fluent recall, new applications and new learning.

Each of the four concepts in the new science of learning has important implications for teaching and curriculum design and assessment. In order to develop conceptual understanding, teachers must teach the key concepts of a particular subject matter in-depth. There must be an emphasis on depth rather than scope. There must be an emphasis on providing many examples in which the key concepts are applied as opposed to superficially covering all of the topics in a subject area. For this to occur, teachers must have an in-depth knowledge of the subject matter themselves. They must have an organized, conceptual understanding themselves of the entire subject area that they are going to teach. Teachers also need an understanding of the growth and development of their students' thinking about key concepts. Finally, assessment and statewide standardized tests must be designed to measure in-depth understanding and not just superficial surface knowledge.

It should be pointed out that many so-called educational institutions are still stuck in the old school. Many communities still have standardized tests to measure surface knowledge and not in-depth understanding. Many politicians are still vehement in championing standards of accountability based on the old standard of rote learning. The National Research Council's first recommendation is that educators and policy makers adopt their findings and implement their program. Their second recommendation is to get their message to anyone who influences educational practice. The war in contemporary education will go on until the issue is resolved with measurable success.

So where do Michel and his method fit into all of this? Most of Michel's critics have been of the old school. Fortunately, their time has passed; and what their *model of the world* is no longer considered valid by enlightened people in the world of education. These critics are still championing an increasingly indefensible position based on rote learning and surface knowledge. Michel had been creating his own "new school" for more than fifty years.

> Interestingly, what is new to the new school was definitely old hat to Michel.

So let us examine the relationship between Michel's method and the war in contemporary education. We will also touch upon what the new school can learn from Michel.

It should be noted in passing that whereas the first several recommendations of The National Research Council deal with spreading the word, with getting the word out, the last several recommendations are about how to expand research. These include doing research to combine the "expertise of researchers" and the *wisdom of practice,* and also to expand the study of classroom practice. The Council realizes that one of the best ways to advance the science of learning itself is to observe the learning that actually takes place in the classroom. This, of course, is exactly what Michel had been doing for more than fifty years. In addition, this is precisely what this book on Michel's method is all about. Moreover, it is exactly what Michel had been challenging schools to do for years — to come and observe the *Master Teacher* at work — to learn from him directly. Right up until the very end of his life, no one had taken him up on the challenge. Fortunately for the two of us, Michel blessed us with five years of personalized, one-on-one interaction with him and the experience of observing him doing what he did best. We literally had unlimited modeling of the *Master Teacher* and his method as well as endless conversations on a variety of subjects and priceless access to his life wisdom, to his expertise and to his *wisdom of practice.*

As we mentioned in the previous chapter, Michel based his method on two key concepts. The first concept is the critical importance of *knowledge* based on *understanding* and the second one has to do with never *trying to remember.* The major thesis upon which Michel's method was based is that "what you *understand* and *know* you will never forget" and what you merely memorize you will quickly forget. Michel's method went so far as to forbid all *trying to remember.* There was no memorizing by rote, no rehearsal, no mental homework and no reviewing. Remembering was in the teaching. You remember what you know. To say "I remember what I memorized," is meaningless because remembering is based on *knowledge*, and *knowledge* is based on *understanding*. Memory was the teacher's and not the learner's responsibility (Michel preferred to use the word "*remembering*" for memory.). This is a radical departure from all schools of education.

Michel stressed the critical importance of *knowledge* acquired through *understanding* and he had an in-depth knowledge of his subject matter. Michel taught foreign languages. These languages have a structure called grammar. Michel would organize his learning process around the key concepts relating to this grammar. He was able to detect patterns and relationships within the grammar which others had failed to see, and he had re-organized the patterns in such a way as to make them meaningful using *meaningful memory associations*™ and *heuristics*. It was his newly conceptualized patterns which helped the students achieve *understanding* of the subject matter. As we have seen, he would not use grammatical terminology and concepts. Instead, he would re-conceptualize the grammar into his own readily understood concepts. Michel would teach the key concepts of the language in-depth through the use of clear explanations followed by multiple examples and *generalizations* put into practice. The result was that his students were able to go out and apply their new language skills in real life situations.

In order to solve problems or to find new contexts to apply what we know, *understanding* is essential. The *Master Teacher's* method was first applied to language learning. To speak, read or write in a language, students must be able to use their knowledge of the language. It would be extremely difficult, if not impossible, to memorize thousands of isolated words and then try to fit them into a memorized grammar. Unfortunately, this is what much language training tries to do. Michel successfully accomplished it another way which was both exciting and effective. He insisted that you not memorize anything, but that you be able to think it out. This is a key concept. You could only think it out because it was based on *understanding*. If you memorized something, then you would quickly forget it when the memory faded; but if you were able to think it out now, you would always be able to think it out at any time.

Michel could always tell if a student was thinking it out by the response time and by the internal processing involved. Memorized answers are parroted back quickly whereas answers that are thought out go through steps to deliver. Michel would carefully watch for and would be very aware of these different responses at all times.

Michel did not say that memory was not important (*Trying to remember* is a different concept.). What he did say was that there is a better way than rote learning. Michel would take responsibility for his students' remembering (memory in the new school). He created what we call powerful *meaningful memory associations*™ and *heuristics* as memory aides for the student

(It is important to mention that memory is different from memorizing.). He would rely upon association which acts as the mind's glue to "lock in" key concepts. These associations reflected an in-depth knowledge rather than surface knowledge and allowed the students to generate other alternatives on their own once the course was over.

Michel's concept of *block teaching* was also ahead of the times. He realized early on the importance of in-depth knowledge rather than surface knowledge. The effective way to achieve in-depth knowledge was by devoting specific blocks of time to a particular subject rather than by changing subjects every fifty minutes. In this way, one could delve deeply into any given subject, focusing on what was relevant and useful information that could be transferred and applied to other contexts.

So what can the new science of learning learn from Michel's *wisdom of practice*? Michel had spent fifty years exploring the learning process of the human mind, and he had made many powerful discoveries. Two of his discoveries are particularly relevant to the subject at hand. The first has to do with how to create *understanding*.

> What Michel adds to the new science is an acute awareness of the critical importance of clear explanations and *meaningful memory associations*™
> as a basis for *understanding*.

Also, Michel did not just passively accept traditional grammatical concepts. Far from it. What he did was to re-conceptualize the entire grammar from scratch! Often the problem in *understanding* has to do with "un-thought out" or outmoded concepts that need to be replaced.

A second major discovery of Michel has to do with the connection between *tension* and remembering (memory in the new school). The recall and utilization of *understanding* and *knowledge* works best when there is no *tension*, and Michel would see to it that there was no *tension*. As we have seen, Michel would always eliminate any form of *tension* whatsoever in his students. Michel had discovered that efforts to *try to remember* were actually counterproductive because they created *tension* which, in turn, blocks memory. It is the *trying to remember* that Michel rejected because any attempt to remember creates *tension* (This does not mean not to remember.). Here we find an interesting dynamic regarding remembering.

By relieving the student of the responsibility for remembering, Michel was able to remove and eliminate entirely all sources of *tension*, which itself interfered with the learning process. At the same time, by the use of powerful *meaningful memory associations*™, he was able to aid and bolster remembering (memory in the new school). This one/two combination enabled him to teach a student the entire grammar of the language with all tenses, including the subjunctive and a complete practical and functional vocabulary in just three days. Time and time again, Michel would achieve what many in the old school considered to be impossible. Yet, he continued to accomplish feats of magical learning for six decades! This was quite remarkable, and his hundreds of thousands of successes provide the overwhelming evidence for the power of what we have termed his *"memory mechanisms"*™.

THE CRITICAL IMPORTANCE OF PRE-EXISTING KNOWLEDGE

The second interconnected concept in the new science of learning is the importance of pre-existing knowledge. The new science of learning has verified that people construct new knowledge and understanding based on their current knowledge and beliefs. In other words, we try to understand new information in terms of what we already know. We evaluate everything in terms of our current understanding and try to connect it to what we already know. We all bring to any new experience pre-existing beliefs, values, skills, concepts and knowledge that determine what we pay attention to and how we organize and interpret the information. And this, in turn, affects our ability to remember, reason, solve problems and acquire new knowledge.

In all of this, there is both an upside and a downside. First, the upside is that we don't start with a blank slate but, instead, with many preconceived ideas. Meanwhile, the downside is twofold. First is the fact that these preconceived ideas may be wrong or incomplete. Second is the fact that even though we may know better, we may revert to these old misconceptions under pressure or in contexts outside of the classroom. The new science of learning focuses on ways to utilize the upside and prevent the downside.

Given that new knowledge is based on current knowledge, teachers must pay careful attention to the students' current understanding and knowledge. Students often have false beliefs and misunderstand or only partially understand concepts. They will try to make sense, but in so doing, they may make the wrong sense.

Therefore, teachers need to do two things. First teachers need to know what base of understanding students have initially so that they can build upon it. They need to constantly monitor the students to check for understanding. They also should know the filters through which students will be processing what they are learning. And teachers need to start with the current knowledge, beliefs and understanding and build upon all of it. In order to accomplish this, the teacher must actively draw out the student's thinking by creating classroom tasks which would reveal it. The teacher has to have some way to have the students reveal what their thinking and understanding is. Standardized tests are not the answer since they do not measure understanding.

Second, the teachers need to constantly monitor the students for misunderstandings, misinterpretations and mistakes. These must be corrected as soon as possible, preferably on the spot. To monitor for misunderstanding, the teacher must have some way of assessing understanding. This is either done through discussion or through tests that measure understanding. These are not quizzes that require rote memorization, but are assessments which provide the students opportunities to revise and improve their thinking. These also help teachers identify problems for remediation. In addition, any standardized tests, as we indicated in the last section, must measure in-depth understanding and not just superficial surface knowledge.

As the National Research Council puts it,

The roles for assessment must be expanded beyond the traditional concept of testing. The use of frequent formative assessments helps make student's thinking visible to themselves, their peers and their teacher. This provides feedback that can guide modification and refinement in thinking. Given the goal of learning with understanding, assessment must tap understanding rather than merely the ability to repeat facts or perform isolated skills.

The way in which assessment is done can have a strong impact on students' achievement. If students are chastised or punished for mistakes, then they will quickly start to avoid risk taking. This is exactly the opposite of what needs to be encouraged. Teachers must encourage their students to take risks and give them the opportunity to make mistakes so that they can obtain feedback and revise their ideas. Therefore, assessment and the norms of the school (whether the norms mean competency-based learning which encourages creativity and risk taking, or whether they mean performance-based learning which discourages risk taking and provides negative reinforcement for mistakes) need to be designed to encourage students to ask questions and to reveal their preconceptions so that both the student and the teacher can monitor their progress toward understanding.

In summary, "learning is enhanced when teachers pay attention to the knowledge and beliefs that learners bring to a learning task, use this knowledge as a starting point for new instruction, and monitor students' changing conceptions as instruction proceeds." This is sometimes referred to as an "*inquiry-based approach.*"

So how does the Master Teacher's Method relate to this and what can the new science of learning gain from a study of the wisdom of Michel's practice? Michel had developed powerful ways of dealing with the upside and the downside of learning. He realized that it is much harder to *unlearn* than to learn. Bad habits are not easily broken, and misconceptions are not easily corrected. Because it is more difficult to erase bad habits, Michel would not usually accept students who already had a partial knowledge of the language which they wanted to learn from him, although he had occasionally taken students with some previous knowledge of the target language. Students such as these very often begin with many misconceptions. That is why he preferred to teach students who had no prior knowledge of the language or some school knowledge which, according to Michel, was the equivalent of no knowledge.

In fifteen or twenty minutes with students, Michel would determine where they were in the target language. If they made a lot of mistakes and if they were using the language incorrectly, then they had bad habits which needed to be undone. It was critical to erase the mistakes and bad habits, otherwise Michel would have been building upon misunderstanding and the incorrect use of the language. That would have created immense problems. The biggest challenge he encountered was with students who had learned a language at some language school. In these cases, Michel would have had too much to erase because such students had acquired bad habits and very often had used the language incorrectly. With these students, the tapes would do wonders. As we discussed in Chapter Six, Michel preferred to start with a *tabula rasa*, otherwise there would just be too much to erase. Also, it would have taken so much longer to erase bad habits than to start teaching the language from scratch.

> In short, it is always harder to *unlearn* than to learn.

Michel's method was inquiry-based. It began with the students' initial *understanding*. As Michel would frequently remind us, "If you already know how to speak one language, then you can learn another." This is an interesting point. Language students begin with the ability to speak their own language which they may or may not do grammatically. So the students bring their own understanding or misunderstanding of the grammar of their own language to the table. They also bring the vocabulary of their own language. With the Romance languages, there will be many cognates or words that are similar in the native language to words in the target language. So the student already begins with some recognizable vocabulary. This provides a foundation of familiarity which puts the student at ease.

Michel would begin his learning sessions with simple sentences and simple grammar that incorporated some of the vocabulary that the student already knew. He would elegantly present new pieces bit by bit, and in so doing, he would add complexity a little at a time. Everything flowed well with elements fitting together in a readily usable and understandable way. Michel would also add explanations so that the language made sense to the student. Once it made sense, the student was able to think it out. Michel would ask the student how to say something in the target language and then would listen for the response. If the response was correct and was based on *understanding* and not based on parroting or guessing, then Michel would be able to move on.

Michel would constantly ask his students to translate sentences. Doing so enabled him to have continuous feedback on their *understanding* and recall. Any misunderstanding showed up immediately as a mistake. As we have emphasized, Michel would use clear explanations and *meaningful memory associations*™ to create the right *understanding* from the start. By starting with a blank slate and by writing on it correctly, there was nothing to correct (It is important to note once again, that in the context of Michel's method, mistakes, albeit rare, referred to remembering structure, and not vocabulary.).

If mistakes occurred, which they occasionally did, then they happened for one of two reasons. Either the students failed to understand or they failed to remember. If they failed to understand, then the explanation was not clear to them. If they failed to remember, then they needed a *meaningful memory association*™ to assist their recall. Michel had a unique way of dealing with the mistakes that occasionally happened. He would always make certain that students achieved *understanding* and when rare mistakes were made, Michel handled them gracefully and smoothly, effortlessly leading the students back to a point of previous *understanding* so that the new *understanding* would be reinforced.

In essence, if the students didn't remember something, Michel would lead them back to remembering. He never directly corrected mistakes because 1) that doesn't work, and 2) that doesn't help the students to get it right. The only thing that works is self-correcting. Michel had discovered that correcting students directly or pointing out mistakes often made them feel bad or even embarrassed. Furthermore, it created *tension*, and then students often became fixated on avoiding mistakes, which would set them back even more.

So Michel approached this issue in another manner. As we have said over and over, Michel would take full responsibility for all mistakes, lack of understanding and memory lapses. In this way, students didn't have to focus on learning. They could just sit back and "receive." As Michel describes it, "I am offering and the students are accepting." He would handle the mistake indirectly. Michel would immediately lead the students back to what they already knew correctly and would provide re-enforcing explanations and *meaningful memory associations*™ so that the students were able to recognize and correct their own mistakes. He would lead the students back to what they knew, or more precisely, to what Michel knew that they knew. He would lead them back to something which he knew they had already assimilated. Michel said that giving one example to the students was just enough for them to catch on. In any case, with good teaching, the probability of making mistakes is greatly minimized.

The challenge with a teacher pointing out and correcting mistakes directly is that doing so does not guarantee that the student will not repeat the mistake in the future.

> However, if the students can recognize when they make a mistake and can think it through, then they will not make the mistake in the future, or at least will have the chances of repeating it greatly diminished.

This was the beauty of Michel's approach. From a certain perspective, it was actually an ancient approach implemented in a new way. The Greek philosopher Socrates was famous for leading a student through a series of questions to a new insight. Similarly, Michel would lead his students to new insights in which they were able to detect and correct their previous mistakes. Fortunately for the students, mistakes in Michel's world of teaching were more the exception than the rule.

In summary, what can the new science of learning take from Michel with respect to pre-existing knowledge? First, is to take an inquiry-based approach. Remember that Michel did not lecture. He would continually engage the learner during the entire learning session. Second, start with what the student already knows. Third, scan continuously for any indications of misunderstanding and any guessing. And fourth, and perhaps most important, always lead the students to correct their own mistakes. This element of leading the students to correct their own mistakes steers us directly to the third of the four key concepts in the new science of learning. As the *Master Teacher*, Michel mastered all of these elements with elegance, grace and effortless ease. Proponents of the new science of learning would do well do learn from his expertise and *wisdom of practice*.

META-COGNITION

The new science of learning emphasizes the importance of helping learners take control of their own learning. People must learn to recognize when they understand something and when they don't. If they don't understand something, then it is essential that they recognize the need for more information. Students need to be aware of their own learning process. They must address issues such as:

1) What are their learning goals?

2) How can they monitor their progress in achieving them?

3) What strategies might they use to determine if they understand something?

4) What kind of evidence do they need to believe particular claims?

5) How can they develop their own theories and test them effectively?

These active learning strategies are part of an area called *"meta-cognition"* which refers to people's abilities to predict their own performance with various tasks and to modify their current levels of mastery and understanding. This involves knowing when something makes sense, monitoring one's current levels of understanding, testing assumptions and reflecting on what works and what needs to be changed.

Research indicates that experts often differ from novices in their *meta-cognitive* abilities. Experts are able to monitor their own understanding and identify gaps and inconsistencies. They also are able to create analogies that will further their understanding. These *meta-cognitive* skills often take the form of an internal dialogue or internal conversation. These traits are aspects of what is called *"adaptive int*elligence."

Some students develop *meta-cognitive* skills on their own, but most students need to be taught *meta-cognition*. It is important for teachers to integrate the teaching of *meta-cognitive* skills into all of the subject matter that they are teaching. This may often be accomplished by teaching the students to pay attention to and utilize their internal dialogue to ask questions and propose solutions.

Also, the students need to be taught to recognize when they understand or partially understand a concept versus when they are confused. Once again, classroom norms are critically important. Students must be encouraged to be able to recognize when confusion sets in. They must also be encouraged to ask any questions rather than being afraid to do so, for fear of appearing to be stupid or slow. Also, as we have stressed earlier, learning with understanding is harder to accomplish than mere memorizing. It also takes more time. Curricula must be designed to support learning for understanding and the development of *meta-cognitive* skills. This requires avoiding the mile wide, inch deep surface approach and focusing, instead, on an in-depth approach. Moreover, tests and assessments must stress understanding and *meta-cognition* and not simply the memorization of surface knowledge.

In our current *dis-educational system*™, teachers themselves are often not taught *meta-cognitive* skills during their training in institutions of education. Teachers need both to be taught *meta-cognitive* skills themselves and also be taught how to teach *meta-cognitive* skills to their students. This is a critical area that is, unfortunately, often overlooked in teacher colleges as well as in classes on education.

So, once again, does Michel's method include the development of *meta-cognitive* skills? And what can the new science of learning discover from the wisdom of Michel's practical methods? Again, so far ahead of the times, Michel's method stresses the development of *meta-cognitive* skills although he did not label it as such. As we have seen in the Method Chapter, he called it *"thinking it out."*

The *Master Teacher's* method is based on the learners being able to know when they make mistakes and on their being able to correct their own mistakes. The students know how to correct their own mistakes because they can think it out. Guessing, even if correct, was not accepted by Michel. Michel's goal was to make the language student self-sufficient. At the end of the learning session, they needed to be able to speak, read and write the new language on their own. They needed to recognize when they make translation mistakes and to be able to think out how to correct the mistake themselves. Michel's whole method was designed to ensure that this self-correcting happens smoothly each and every time.

> For the *Master Teacher*, it was important that the students not just know. It was important that they *"know"* what they know.

What can the new science of learning learn from Michel's approach to meta-cognition? For one thing, Michel provided a basic understanding through his use of explanations and what we named *meaningful memory associations*™. This served as a basis for the learners to think things out, and Michel insisted that they always understand each of his explanations. If they did not, then they needed to ask for clarification. Michel would masterfully teach his students how to think things out. He would constantly monitor the students to make sure that the learners were not guessing or sounding it out by ear, and that they were thinking out what they were saying step by step. He would teach the learners to do this by starting with simple sentences and then building in complexity, keeping it crystal clear in the minds of the students all along. Also, the learner was able to fall back on Michel's carefully worded, crystal clear explanations and the *meaningful memory associations*™ as a basis for their thinking it through.

> Michel did not explicitly teach *meta-cognition* as part of his method, but his whole method was designed to implicitly install this valuable and essential skill.

There is more. Michel also made another wonderful contribution to the science of *meta-cognition*. His own life is a textbook example of a child who developed and refined his *meta-cognitive* abilities from an early age. As a child he was able to engage in the process of self-reflection on his own internal process, and remarkably, he did this on a conscious level. He even gave the process a name: *getting to know me*. One of the discoveries of the new science of learning is that children often possess greater intellectual abilities than they have previously been given credit for having.

Michel was a case in point. He was certainly considered a precocious child. At an early age Michel realized that adults had forgotten their childhood, and he was determined not to do so. He made a conscious effort as a young child to remember his life from the beginning in great detail so that he would not forget who he was, as did the adults around him. Later on, Michel also developed another *meta-cognitive* skill. Every evening he would review the day in detail, as he would sit in judgment of himself.

For further details see Chapter Nine, where we discuss Michel's *getting to know me* period and show its connection to his method and to his perceptual filters and *model of the world*. In his evening review, if he had discovered that he would have preferred to have responded in another fashion to some event or situation of the day, then he would create a similar situation in his life where he could respond accordingly as he knew he should have done initially. Michel's *meta-cognitive* abilities served him in good stead during his entire life and probably account for many of the things that he had accomplished so successfully both in the context of his teaching and in his amazing life.

TRANSFER PROBLEM

All new learning builds on a transfer from previous experience. A major function of education is to prepare students to flexibly apply their knowledge to new problems and new situations. How well the students can do this provides educators valuable feedback to assist them in evaluating and improving the educational system. The ultimate goal is to achieve adaptive learning.

> The ultimate goal is to move learning beyond the classroom into the myriad contexts of life where it can make a measurable and valuable difference for both the individual and society.

How do you transfer new learning into the world? How do you extend what is learned in one context into other contexts? How do you use knowledge to solve problems? How do you discover new areas of application? In learning a language, how do you move beyond the classroom to be able to actually use the language to speak, read and write in the outside world? This is the universal problem with which education has struggled from the beginning. No one is born with the innate ability to function competently as an adult in society. It is the purpose of education to develop this competence. The value of education is determined by its ability to affect the quality of life. For education to be useful, it must extend beyond the classroom. This is what the issue of transfer is all about. Now the question we face is what can be done by teachers and educational systems to facilitate transfer.

Tragically, the usual solution to the transfer problem, which has been championed by what we are calling the *"old school,"* has been based on a false premise and a false method. The false premise was the fact that the key to transfer was memorizing as much information, often meaningless, as possible. This leads to cramming and the concomitant results of slow memorization and rapid forgetting. The false premise has been coupled with the false method of testing which determines the students' ability to remember surface knowledge consisting of isolated facts and information. As we have said, this tests memory and surface knowledge and not understanding.

The underlying conflict is between "breadth and depth." The underlying conflict is between "wide and shallow" and "deep and narrow" and between surface knowledge and deep understanding. The new science of learning favors the latter because it is the only approach that will adequately allow problem solving and transfer to new applications. The new science of learning believes that it is better to broadly educate people than to just train them to perform particular skills.

Research has shown that certain factors reliably influence the transfer of learning. Some of the most important factors are:

1) The initial degree of mastery of the subject which requires the necessary time to develop in-depth understanding. Also, it is necessary to clear up any misconceptions that may lead to further misunderstanding.

2) The depth of understanding of the subject as opposed to the memorization of facts and procedures.

3) The use of deliberate practice with feedback as opposed to simply reading and rereading a text.

4) An active *meta-cognition* by the learner to evaluate their strategies and level of understanding.

5) The teaching of knowledge in multiple contexts so that students can begin to generalize.

6) The teaching of students to extract underlying themes and principles and to know when and where and how to apply them.

7) Competence motivation which embraces challenges as opposed to performance motivation which is often more focused on

avoiding errors than on learning. It is also important that teaching be at an appropriate level of difficulty. If things are too easy they become boring, yet if they are too difficult they become frustrating.

There is a distinction between what is called *"near transfer"* and *"far transfer"* learning. *Near transfer* learning involves the ability to repeat procedures. This works as long as procedures remain constant. *Far transfer* learning involves the ability to perform well as procedures continue to change. To do this requires an understanding of process and not just the memorization of procedures. As we explain in our own trainings, in teaching, one or more of five things can be emphasized. These are concepts, principles, processes, procedures and facts. The old school focuses on memorizing facts and procedures. This produces technicians who need to be constantly retrained as procedures change. The new school focuses on concepts, principles and process. An in-depth understanding of these enables the learner to anticipate change and develop new procedures when necessary and appropriate.

Research indicates that the major key to understanding and to the transfer of learning is to have an organized and coherent knowledge base. These are interconnected schemata of concepts and regularities (principles) built up by observing similarities and differences across a variety of contexts. This is called pattern recognition. Once these concepts and regularities are in place, analogical reasoning can be used to induce general schemata for the organized conceptual base which can be applied to subsequent problems. This also facilitates memory retrieval, since it is easier to remember a general rule than a list of specific instances.

Research on the performance of experts versus novices reveals that experts have an ability to retrieve relevant knowledge that is relatively effortless (fluent) if not automatic. This is important because effortless processing places fewer demands on conscious awareness (which, as we indicated in the Method Chapter, is limited to seven plus or minus two chunks of awareness according to scientific research). Over the years, in our modeling of experts with different areas of expertise, we have found that by automating certain aspects of a task, the expert has more conscious awareness to focus on other aspects of the task.

One of the challenges that have faced educators is to develop assessment methods to measure transfer. Assessment methods that focus exclusively on the remembering of facts and procedures have been demonstrated to not adequately measure transfer and use. People may have good memories but poor or no understanding and, consequentially, poor or no transfer. Therefore, the key is to have memory plus transfer. This is facilitated by teaching students at a level of abstraction that transcends the specificity of particular concepts and examples.

What are the implications of the understanding of learning transfer by the new science of learning for educational practice? As we have said, all of the four keys to learning are interrelated and interconnected. Transfer begins with learning with understanding from the get-go. Pre-existing knowledge is critical for two reasons. First, is that previous experience serves as the basis for future *generalizations*. Teachers need to activate this knowledge in order to build upon students' strengths. Second, is that if there are any misunderstandings and misconceptions in pre-existing knowledge that are not identified, then they will lead to transfer problems later on down the road. Teachers must strive to make the students' thinking visible and to find ways to help students re-conceptualize faulty ideas. *Meta-cognition* is critical in helping students to begin to identify their own confusions and misunderstandings, so that they can be rectified before they lead to future errors. Teachers must connect everyday knowledge to subjects taught in school and apply what is taught in school to everyday situations. That is the essence of transfer.

So, what does the Master Teacher have to teach the new science of learning about transfer? Michel was a master of transfer. He was able to teach a student the complete grammar of a foreign language with all of the tenses and a practical and functional vocabulary in a matter of days. The evidence of the transfer was that the student was able to effortlessly speak, read and write in the target language by taking Michel's course. What were the keys to Michel's transfer mastery? They are as follows:

1) The first key was the elimination of all *tension* and performance anxiety which interferes with transfer, by taking the complete responsibility for learning, remembering and mistakes away from the students and taking it on himself.

2) The second key was his use of critical explanations and *meaningful memory associations*™ to give the student an organized and coherent in-depth understanding of the language.

3) The third key was his *meta-cognitive* teaching of the student to think it out.

4) The fourth key was his use of *block teaching* to provide the necessary time to teach in-depth.

5) The fifth key was Michel's utilization of deliberate practice and constant reinforcement with feedback to stimulate the competence motivation of each student.

6) The sixth key was Michel's method of remediation which trained the students to detect and correct their own mistakes.

7) The seventh was his excellent use of *generalization* strategies to enable the learners to transfer to new contexts.

Michel was without a doubt a master of all the above and he would skillfully combine all of these elements to facilitate the rapid acquisition and transfer of knowledge.

> With this overview of the connection between the new science of learning and Michel's method, we can see that there are no grounds for saying that Michel's approaches were not based on sound pedagogical principles.

Michel's academic critics are wrong on two counts. First, Michel was way ahead of most of them when it came to incorporating the new science of learning. In fact, he had been making similar discoveries and successfully incorporating them into his method for more than fifty years, during which time the norms of the old school were solidly etched in stone within the *Mind Prison™*. Second, the evidence that Michel's method worked is overwhelming. He had personally trained over ten thousand students and his tape courses have reached hundreds of thousands of students worldwide. In short, the evidence for the efficacy of the *Michel Thomas Method* is overwhelming.

Before leaving this chapter, there are several more areas that need to be touched upon which reveal, once again, Michel's genius in creating his ground-breaking method.

ACCELERATED LEARNING

Accelerated learning is a movement in education that began with the Bulgarian teacher Georgi Lozanov. He called his method *"suggestology"* and *"suggestopedia."* It involved a variety of techniques including positive suggestions, relaxation, active-passive balance, playing Baroque music and breathing in a certain way. Interestingly enough, Lozanov applied his method to language learning and he made spectacular claims that no one else has ever been able to reproduce. Lozanov's method was further popularized in a book by Ostrander and Schroeder called *"Super-Learning."* Also, many universities and the US and Canadian Governments were intrigued by Lozanov's claims. The Canadian Public School System conducted a massive experiment using Lozanov's methods and failed to produce any of the claimed results. At this point one can only wonder if the whole thing was not cold war propaganda by the Russians.

Today there are many people who still claim to do accelerated learning in one form or another. There have been several associations of accelerated learning practitioners. The first was the Society of Accelerated Learning and Teaching (SALT). The current association is called the International Alliance for Learning (IAL). It holds yearly conferences and is just instituting three levels of Accelerated Learning Certifications.

At present, accelerated learning comprises an assortment of techniques drawn from a variety of sources. This is undoubtedly part of the impetus for standardization. What people usually call *"accelerated learning"* involves some form of experiential learning. It is frequently based on the assumption that all necessary knowledge lies within the group and that it is up to the teacher to facilitate the interaction of the group to discover its own resources.

One popular area of application for accelerated learning, following Lozanov himself, has been foreign language learning. Many of the methods are taken from Lozanov with some additions. Techniques include the name game, physical learning, videos, the radio play, visualization, parallel reading, mental movies, memory maps, and active and passive concerts. This is quite a smorgasbord of techniques that don't always work. What is interesting is that the results of one study claimed to reduce three years of beginning French learning to three months and to produce fluency within six months. What a curious way to think of "accelerated"! Michel did in three days what the study took three months to achieve. Obviously, there are different ideas about the meaning of "accelerated" alive in the world today.

What we find interesting is that their approach is so different from Michel's approach. If anyone in the world could make a legitimate claim to do accelerated learning, it was certainly Michel Thomas. He was able to accomplish in a week what most high school and college language departments fail to accomplish in several years. If this isn't accelerated learning, then we don't know what is.

The people who do so-called accelerated learning indeed have a lot to learn from the *Master Teacher,* who had been practicing actual accelerated learning for decades! Unlike those who practice so-called accelerated learning Michel never used gimmicks such as multi-media and fun and games, nor did he use name games, parallel reading and radio plays. He never played music nor did he make positive suggestions, but rather he used positive reinforcement. Michel did not adopt a rhythm of active and passive activities, nor did he tell people to relax. He did not create a participant-centered learning environment because he viewed himself as a teacher and not a facilitator (With Michel's method, the student actively responds.). In short, Michel used none of the techniques of so-called accelerated learning; and he was able to produce more accelerated results than any accelerated learning practitioner has ever been able to. This fact alone should call the entire field of accelerated learning into question.

Michel's method in many ways is the opposite of so called accelerated learning. Michel's method is teacher-centered as opposed to participant-centered. Michel would take complete responsibility for the learning. He assumed responsibility for all remembering and also for all mistakes. Instead of focusing on relaxation, Michel focused on the elimination of all *tension*. For him the words "relax" and "relaxation" did not apply to his learning sessions. As we explained in Chapter Six, from Michel's perspective, eliminating *tension* from his students was very different from relaxing them. He began with his initial frames which were designed to remove all *tension* and performance anxiety from the student from the start.

Michel's method concentrated on a combination of in-depth understanding and deliberate practice as opposed to fun and games and caring and sharing. He would engage in continuous interaction with the student and would elegantly orchestrate the whole process. The learner actively responded and Michel would build competence through continuous feedback and positive reinforcement. And, of course, Michel generated great excitement and energy; yet it was an innate energy which derived from the basic human drive to learn and not from some superficial excitement generated by silly games and social interaction. Michel developed *meta-cognitive* awareness of the learning process which enabled the learner to function on his or her own without any need for group interaction or group reinforcement.

In summary, much can be learned from the study of the *Master Teacher* as well as from other teachers who have mastered their teaching skills and who are highly successful over a long period of time. Michel was a Master Teacher in every sense of the word and merits special recognition as such. For years he had been able to produce real and lasting accelerated learning. Michel's magnificent accomplishments in learning which represented real accelerated learning should at least encourage those who claim to do accelerated learning to reexamine their methods and to rethink the learning process.

TAPE LEARNING

A major battle is taking shape within the worldwide training community that has implications for learning in education. On one side of the spectrum are traditional trainers who train to a live audience. These trainers develop a course which they deliver to a live audience whether in person or by satellite hookup. On the other side of the spectrum are training design specialists who design courses that are taught by computer or by audio or video tape. Computer and audio and video training have several advantages.

One advantage is that they can be done anywhere at any time. Second, is that they can be self-paced. What this means is that each participant can proceed at his or her own rate rather than at a group rate which may be too slow for the gifted learner and too fast for the slow learner. A third advantage is that it is often less costly since there is no need to transport people to a room for a training. With computer assisted instruction and the use of audio and video tapes, participants can learn at their leisure in different parts of the world. All that is needed is a computer or a VCR or a tape or CD player. Each side in this battle has its advocates and critics.

Most people are divided into two different worlds on this issue. They have a foot in either one world or the other. Michel lived in both worlds. He had developed a powerful method for live instruction of an individual or a large class and he had also created a highly effective tape course which has sold over a million copies world-wide. His tape course, as we have mentioned, is innovative in several ways. Michel even held a US Patent on the tape learning method. The critical element of the process is that the students must push the pause button and give the response themselves before they hear the answer on the tape. When they do this, they become an active participant in the language course. So Michel's audio courses have the advantages that we mentioned above. They are self-paced and can be used by anyone any place in the world at any time.

Unfortunately, tapes have gained a bad reputation as learning tools. This is partly due to their inadequate use in high school and college language laboratories and to the poor quality of tapes currently available on the market.

THEORY AND PRACTICE
THE WAR BETWEEN THE TWO

Michel was quick to point out that most commercially available language tape courses are a fraud. He believed that they do not deliver what they promise and that they are dangerous for two reasons. First, they take the consumer's money under false pretenses and second, even worse, they end up installing inaccurate beliefs in the learner. Unfortunately, yet understandably, the public is not in a position to evaluate the different claims of the competing tape courses. What happens is that students try the tape course and quickly discover that it does not work. This leads them to one of two equally problematic conclusions.

The first conclusion is that there is something wrong with them. They immediately buy into the myth of not having a gift or an ear for languages (Chapter Five). Since they do not have a knack for language learning, they reach the erroneous conclusion that there is no reason or need to pursue other language instruction. They reason incorrectly that the tapes must work or otherwise they would not remain on the market. Since the tapes must work for most people, then the problem must surely lie with them. This false belief is even worse than the fact that they have been exploited — "ripped off." The other equally fallacious conclusion is that tape language courses simply don't work. Just because one course doesn't work, they quickly generalize that none work. According to Michel, all of this contributes to fraud on the part of those who create these ineffective language tapes for the unknowing consumer.

The real truth is twofold. The first truth is that there is no such thing as a gift or ear for languages. If you learned to speak your own language, then you can learn to speak a foreign language. In short, the problem does not lie in the abilities of the learner. The second truth is that most commercially available language tape courses are frauds and simply don't work. Amidst the fraudulent claims, Michel's course was the welcome exception.

According to Michel, one of the biggest frauds going is the so-called *US Foreign Service Course*. This situation particularly infuriated him whenever he would speak about it. He said that the course is public domain paid for by American taxpayers. Because it is public domain, anybody can record it on tape and several companies have done so over the years. Michel told us that if you complain to the State Department, they respond by saying that it is public domain and that they are not selling it. What angered Michel was the fact that the State Department knows, of course, that the course does not work, but it is difficult for them to admit that they have developed an ineffective course. Michel believed that although they are not committing fraud, they are nevertheless contributing to it. Anyway, in the world of commercial language tape courses, it is a case of "buyers beware."

Michel suggested to a business executive working in the publishing industry who needed to learn a foreign language quickly, that he take his course. Michel explained that the language courses which they were selling were making fraudulent claims, and that this executive should compare Michel's courses to the ones which they were selling. Much to Michel's delight, the gentleman took him up on the challenge. He tried the various tape courses including Michel's and came to the satisfied conclusion that Michel was indeed right. While the other courses didn't work, Michel's courses came through with flying colors.

Furthermore, the gentleman in question believed that he was incapable of ever learning a foreign language. Michel proved him wrong. To his great amazement and delight, the gentleman discovered what he could actually accomplish by taking Michel's course, i.e., that he could indeed learn another language with great ease. In fact, he was so thrilled and excited about learning in this way that he decided to take Michel's one-on-one course in Spanish later on. And soon after the course, this executive was interviewed in both Spanish and English. In spite of all of this, the publishing company that employs him continues to market all of those courses that simply don't work. Michel thought that it might be a good idea for some consumer reporter to investigate the fraudulent language tape market rather than sit idly by and allow the charade to continue to the detriment of all.

CONCLUSION

Michel was truly the *Master Teacher* in every sense of the word. The proof is in the pudding, as they say. He consistently produced amazing results. Critics use the pejorative word "claims" to refer to his results. The correct word is "*evidence.*" The quantity and veracity of the testimonials to the success of Michel's method are overwhelming. No objective or impartial observer can deny the legitimacy of the evidence for the success of his method. Since this approach on the part of critics simply does not hold up, they have been forced to result to another subterfuge. They said that Michel's method contradicts sound pedagogical principles. The real truth of the matter is that it is the methods of the critics which are not based on sound pedagogical principles.

As this chapter has shown, Michel was a master of both practice and theory. The time has come for his critics to discard their skepticism, their jealousy, their envy, their egos and their academic pride and to transform their criticisms into a genuine desire to learn from the *Master Teacher* himself — Michel Thomas, who was able to accomplish what they cannot, and has been doing so for decades. When this happens, a new excitement about learning will sweep across the globe, a new light will shine upon the earth, and no one will ever again have any excuse for not being multi-lingual and for not being able to communicate with their fellow men and women. Perhaps that "Tower of Babel" will finally be eliminated as we begin to understand and to connect with our sisters and brothers everywhere. Perhaps thought control will give way to *freedom of mind*. Furthermore, there will be a new dawn for education as old and inadequate methods fall away to be replaced by methods that are far easier, effortless, exciting and effective, while freeing minds one person at a time.

Chapter Eight

PRACTICAL APPLICATIONS OF THE *MICHEL THOMAS METHOD*

Given the existence of this revolutionary gift of learning to humankind, known as the *Michel Thomas Method,* what can students, parents, teachers, educators and politicians do to change what we refer to as the *dis-educational system*™? Also, what can be done to bring down the walls of the *Mind Prisons*™ and to erect a new edifice, one which honors f*reedom of mind* and that will serve the needs of education throughout the twenty-first century and beyond?

As we have discussed in prior chapters, children are born with an *innate drive for learning* which is usually ignored or shut off by parents who are either unaware or too busy to make time for their children. This *innate drive for learning* is then further suppressed and, more often than not, finished off by the *Mind Prison*™. Michel believed this to be perhaps the greatest tragedy of all. We are in a dire situation indeed. So what can be done? In this chapter we will have the courage to tell it like it is in the real world of the *Mind Prison*™ and to make some practical suggestions for how things can and must change.

THE SYSTEM

The whole problem with the *dis-educational system*™ often begins at the level of school boards which usually consist of staunch moralists with dichotomized thinking. All they want to do is to perpetuate their personal *model of the world* and to impose it on parents and children. Most school boards are quite *sameness* in orientation which means that they have a difficult time dealing with change. They would rather maintain the *status quo* than to introduce something that is revolutionary. School boards are like judges who make certain that the sentencing of the children remains a constant and is not threatened by anything innovative which may rock their boat. They intend to maintain their control at the helm. This is, in essence, where many of the problems begin.

The school boards do not make decisions based on pedagogical reasons, but rather on the need to meet political and social agendas. These people see the world through black and white lenses with no possibility of gray entering into the picture. For those who live in a rigid world of right versus wrong, anything that does not fit their mold is unacceptable. In their minds, their values work for them; and, therefore, they believe that these same criteria must work for everyone else. Because of their immutable beliefs, effecting change to the *dis-educational system*™ is a major challenge.

No major change has yet to occur and the tragedy is two-fold. First, no real change can occur when the decision makers refuse to accept or even consider other points of view which will provide real solutions. Second, Michel had the method, the wisdom and the on-going track record which has the potential, in his words, to "change the world" of education and, thus, the world itself. Now is the time to adopt the "better mousetrap."

> We would like to emphasize that real change will not occur within a system until all parts and all levels of a given system are changed.

To remedy any given part of the system merely serves as a band-aid solution that does not create meaningful and lasting change to the whole. So let us describe briefly the different parts of the whole which make up the system in question. The current *dis-educational system*™ is a compromise between competing interests on all sides.

First, there are politicians who have to balance different constituencies and special interests. They need to allocate enough money for schools in order to appease the voters, but they cannot allocate any more than need be to maintain relative calm among their constituents. Political leaders would also like the school system to produce citizens who think just like they do, and who share the same beliefs and opinions about what should be done because obviously, like-minded constituents will keep them and their party in power. They prefer to have people who conform rather than those who dissent and disagree, and they also prefer to have people who are easily convinced to join their side.

Then there are business people who want a system that will provide educated and competent employees who are ready and able to enter the work force. The corporate world seeks employees who are self-motivated, productive and industrious because their bottom line is to increase profits. At one end of the spectrum we find the trades people, and at the other end are the professional people. In the past, the educational system would often force students to choose between one and the other. In today's world one should be prepared for both. Unfortunately, now there is no choice.

Then we have parents who would like an educational system which will ideally prepare their children to make a good living that will provide a comfortable lifestyle. Parents look to an educational system which will help their children to establish a respectable profession of some sort in order to ensure them a prosperous and productive life in a highly competitive world. In general, most parents do not know what is necessary to produce this particular outcome. They are usually not in a position to know about the innovations in education, nor do they know how to stimulate their children to learn or how to evaluate or assess their local school system. Parents are aware, however, of standardized tests. They know that how well students perform on these tests is often used as a barometer to measure the effectiveness of a given school system.

The situation has become so ludicrously competitive that in some areas passing certain tests has become a pre-requisite to enter pre-school. And around the country there are now coaches who promise to prepare these pre-school children to pass these tests. Of course, in this highly competitive world, parents will do anything to make sure that their kids get into the right schools no matter what their ages. This obviously puts tremendous pressure on these little children to do well and turns them into competitive monsters very early on.

Then there are the more recent trends in the United States to send high school students to summer school classes and to special summer camps designed to help them pass the SATs to get into college. More often than not, parents are not necessarily aware of what these standardized tests are measuring. Many of these tests still measure rote memory rather than understanding. Even though there is now an essay question which has been added to the SAT exam, if the overall level of students is not very high, then the results are relative and don't really measure true understanding or great critical thinking. Also, one would need to have rather high standards for the essay question responses that measure students' ability to think and to engage in problem solving.

Meanwhile, politicians are looking for ways to hold the school system accountable and often turn to what is most easily measurable, which, of course, is rote memory. As we have seen, such an approach is measuring the wrong thing. These tests based on memorization definitely don't reflect one's ability to think critically and to solve problems, let alone one's ability to think at all.

Then there are school administrators who would like a system that is easy to manage. They want funding from the politicians, and they fully realize that they have to measure up to whatever standards of accountability are currently in vogue. For ease of administration, they want a standardized curriculum in which their teachers are all teaching the same thing in the same way. That certainly facilitates things for them all across the board. Conformity is their best friend. Meanwhile, school administrators judge teachers by their ability to prepare their students to score high on the various standardized tests. This merely creates a vicious circle in which students are forced to pass from one teacher to another who has helped them move on to becoming nonthinking citizens of the future.

With all of these factions and viewpoints surrounding them, teachers are caught in the middle. Of course, teachers want to make a living. Everyone knows that for the most part, teachers are terribly underpaid for the great responsibility that they are meant to take on. In addition, they are forced to take courses in education which quagmire them in what the traditional schools of education think is the best way to teach. They are expected to follow the standardized curriculum and to be accountable for their students' standardized test scores.

In short, teachers are overworked, underpaid and are under a lot of pressure to conform and to produce impossible results given the circumstances. Teachers also have to deal with the students who are often bored and rebellious, and as we have seen more and more in our society, with students whose violent actions can be deadly. Moreover, nowadays teachers are dealing with more and more disrespect from students who claim that the word "*respect*" means nothing to them. Teachers' hands are tied to prevent them from taking disciplinary action for fear of lawsuits. Often in their frustration, teachers blame the student, the student's parents and the school system. Certainly there is enough blame to go around in this vicious circle that leads nowhere. The blame game must stop now, not in two years or in ten years.

And last are the students who are largely the unfortunate victims in this unhealthy quagmire. They are required by law to serve time in the *Mind Prison*™ where they are frequently bored and/or disinterested and would rather be somewhere else engaging in what they consider to be some pleasurable activity other than learning. Very often, their *innate drive for learning* has been stifled or at least diminished by the system. The result is to condemn them to "a life of vegetation" characterized in today's world by TV watching and video game playing to the point of addiction.

There is a bright spot, however, in that there are some students who are smart enough to observe the world and to realize that many adults are lying to them. Many also realize that the great myth passed on for generations is simply not true. This is the myth according to which there is a direct correlation between good grades in school and future success in life. Young people look around and see uneducated people, many of whom can't think on their own and who nevertheless end up wealthy and successful while many educated people are just squeaking by to make ends meet, or else they are often unsuccessful in finding jobs to fit their expertise.

Furthermore, they may even be aware of the research by Daniel Goldman and others who maintain that success in life is more highly correlated with emotional intelligence or EQ than with intellectual intelligence or IQ. So why spend years being tortured by the drudgery and tedium of the *Mind Prison*™? Students may even wonder why they are not taught emotional skills which have been proven to have a greater correlation with success in life than what they are being taught in school. In addition, students are forced to serve their time in the *Mind Prison*™, slaving away with homework, reports and tests and all of the other *tension* and anxiety-producing aspects of the traditional system. So it is not at all surprising that students who are bored and stressed out and who realize that they have been misled by the adults around them, sometimes resort to violence, which is the physical expression of their rebellion. They are rebelling against a system that forces them to "serve time" in a bad institution. They are rebelling against imprisonment which is both mental and physical. With good teaching, there is no room for violence.

So what can be done? The first thing is to face the truth, a truth which is two-fold in nature. One is that the present system does not work and two is to know that there actually is a better way. People may agree that the current system has problems, but they don't always know what to do about it. What we must do about it is to replace the present ineffective system with one that has been proven to work, with one that has an astonishing on-going track record of successes. Of course, we are referring to Michel's method, which provides the perfect blueprint for us to follow.

Where does one begin with the process of revamping the current *dis-educational system*™? Although we will make a few points here, in our follow-up book we discuss specific ways in which to do this. The place to begin is with a pilot program for a model school. Creating a model school would demonstrate on all levels what can be achieved by the use of Michel's methods. It would have a carefully designed curriculum utilizing experts in a variety of subjects. The teachers would participate in an on-going teacher training program. The model school would have facilities to teach students from nursery school right through high school. In order to ensure the success of the model school, there would be a competent and knowledgeable support staff that would be an integral part of the operation of the school and the appropriate and necessary facilities to support the staff would be provided. At *The CLWF Institute for Global Leadership*, we have a viable and workable template for changing the system that synthesizes a variety of elite models for training and learning.

Parents and community leaders should put pressure on educators and politicians to begin to introduce Michel's methods into their local school system. Such an approach would demonstrate to students and teachers what is possible to achieve in record setting time. Students will become quickly excited about their potential for learning. They will experience achievement levels that they never thought possible to attain. Once this is accomplished, it is necessary to nurture and expand this excitement so that students realize that their learning potential is not limited to foreign language learning.

Be committed to the cause! Be persistent and don't give up! What is important is to get the ball rolling and to keep it rolling faster and faster, keeping the momentum going. The challenge we face with change is to know how to keep people and systems from reverting back to the way that they always were beforehand. Therefore, it will be necessary to burn bridges so that there is no retreat, no going back to the *status quo*. Once you discover that there is a better way, it must be incorporated and integrated into the system so that it becomes permanent, and not just a fleeting fancy or some temporary trend that momentarily gets attention.

TEACHERS

Teachers are usually well-meaning people who care about their students. They probably went into teaching because they genuinely wanted to help children to learn. Unfortunately, they quickly discovered that teaching was frequently hard work and that they were forced more often than not to be disciplinarians rather than educators. And now with violent incidents arising within schools, teachers find themselves in an even more delicate position. Tragically, teachers are forced to teach a standardized curriculum with little or no opportunity to be creative.

Furthermore, they are often held accountable for getting their students to memorize facts for tests. When students fail, the teachers take the blame. In short, the teachers are held accountable for things over which they don't directly have control. From the perspective of teachers, students should learn discipline at home, not in the classroom. If the students' *innate drive for learning* were reawakened, discipline would not even enter into the picture. Remember that discipline and scolding a student simply did not exist in Michel's teaching. There is no room for discipline with good teaching. Also, it would seem that students' ability to memorize is largely determined by either the student's aptitude or by the amount of time and energy that the student dedicates to memorizing. Obviously, the teacher does not have direct control over either of these factors.

Within our current *dis-educational system*™, what does it take to enter the teaching profession? To be a teacher, one is required to take courses in education; and it is up to the person to pass the mandatory courses to be certified. Once certified, there are so-called in-service training and continuing education courses to take. Although these are commendable, they present a big problem. Why? It is because the system simply does not work. Educators will argue that the teachers are to blame and that they are doing a poor job of implementing a great system. So blaming and finger pointing continue to be the rule rather than the exception and don't solve the problem of proper teacher training.

What can a teacher do? One solution is to start by understanding the method. Next, select an area of a given subject to which one can apply the method. We suggest that one choose a subject which one understands and which one enjoys teaching. Inform your students that you are putting the responsibility for their learning on your shoulders. We recommend that teachers encourage discussion within a framework of questions and answers. Teachers should give clear explanations. Facts and opinions are healthy elements of the discussion. Encourage students to express their opinions, remembering that they may not necessarily agree with the opinions of their teachers. This helps them to develop critical thinking. It is critical to avoid lecturing and to really connect with the students. Teachers should use eye contact, and should never ask students to raise their hands. Hand-raising simply creates an atmosphere of competition which often triggers *tension* and anxiety. Moreover, competition interferes with learning. Instead, create that sense of *esprit de classe* in which everyone in the class is participating and where there is a feeling of group unity.

Next, craft clever explanations that make sense to the students. Use discussions to determine the student's level of understanding of the concepts that have been presented. Don't be afraid to look at the subject from a new perspective. Look for patterns and relationships that have previously gone unnoticed. Look for analogies to things that the students already know. If the students can't remember things, then the teacher needs to go back to clear explanations. If a concept is not explained clearly from the start, and if the students don't understand, then it is up to the teacher to explain the concept again, using clear examples until understanding is achieved. In addition, if there is a lack of understanding on the part of the students, then the teacher needs to be creative and to come up with powerful *meaningful memory associations*™. Use visualization or mnemonics to complement the above.

As a teacher, there are three critically important things to do:

1) First is to teach for understanding. This requires clear explanations and what we have named good *"memory mechanisms"*™.

2) Second is to teach the students how to learn. It is important to teach *meta-cognitive* skills. These will serve the students well for the rest of their lives in a variety of circumstances and situations.

3) Third is to install or reawaken in the students a love of learning, to reawaken their *innate drive for learning* so that their tremendous potentials are not lost forever.

Also, it is critical to give the students a genuine feeling and sense of accomplishment that will carry over into all aspects of their lives. Building a sense of self-esteem and a sense of personal responsibility for one's actions is an essential part of the process as well. Remember too, that every student is a good student if one has a good teacher. Just imagine the possibilities if one were to have a great teacher, a really great teacher!

THE BENEFITS OF COOPERATION AND COORDINATION

It is so easy to point the finger of blame at others, yet teachers and parents need to work together if there is going to be success on all levels of the system. Michel was very clear about the responsibility of education as it applies to the delegation of authority to the teacher and the responsibility of parents in this arrangement. Historically, in primitive life, the parents assumed the responsibility for the caring and training of their young. In so-called primitive societies in certain parts of the world, this is still the case. With the increasing complexity of socialized living and the growth in cultural requirements, specialization in function and vocation emerged. One function to arise required formalizing the teaching of the child. Specialists such as nursemaids, governesses, tutors and teachers were hired to perform this function. This involved a delegation of duties but not a delegation of responsibility on the part of the parent. If the specialists did not perform in the manner which had been arranged and decided upon, the only alternative to the parent was to find another specialist. Thus, the field of education continued to emerge.

Two difficulties arose as this system began to take hold. The first was that the parents were specialists in other fields and ignorant of the field of education. The second was that the parents were often anxious to pass the buck onto others. The system also had advantages when the parents and educators decided to cooperate with each other. First it is necessary to look upon the child as a learner from birth, from the moment the infant takes its first breath. At this point, the parent needs to shepherd the child through this initial stage. Allow the child to naturally breathe in the excitement of learning early on. The excitement for learning does not have to be created, for it is already there within each of us. The parents must also begin to teach the child how to learn. In turn, the educator needs to continue this process.

> The emphasis needs to be on teaching the child how to learn and not just on content mastery.

And certainly avoid interfering with the child making a multitude of discoveries and with the child's innate creative abilities.

The parent and the educator must work together. The teacher is delegated to teach a specific subject matter to the child, while the parent is responsible for teaching basic values which the child must learn if he is to live and function as a social being in the outside world. In reality, the duties of both parents and teachers overlap in the last area. And, it is of mutual advantage that the method of teaching be somewhat the same in both situations. Although the teacher passes each student on to another teacher at the end of every school year and inherits each student from another teacher, the method of teaching is made easier by having students whose behavior is appropriate to the school environment. The parent, on the other hand, must carry the same student to maturity. This responsibility is made easier by a good school environment.

Each of our lives is usually influenced by a number of individuals. There may be parents whose character flaws and weaknesses have an undue, unhealthy influence on their children. In such cases, these negative parental influences may be counteracted and softened by a great teacher who compensates by providing a positive influence on the children. Also, the reverse applies as well, where weaknesses or flaws in teachers which may also unduly influence their students can be counterbalanced by a great parent. Tragically, there are children in our world with both parents and teachers who influence them in a negative manner. They often end up falling through the cracks. Ideally, parents and teachers must work together as much as possible to produce the best results for children. Criticism directed in both directions between the home and school needs to give way to coordination and cooperation for meaningful and successful outcomes.

PARENTS

The parents' responsibility begins at home, a concept which some parents seem to have forgotten in our society. Unfortunately, it seems that the only requirement for parenthood is a biological one. Tragically, many parents have children that they didn't necessarily want or that they soon discover they don't want for whatever reason. Of course, in all of this, it is the children who all too often suffer the consequences. Serious parenting takes time. In our present day society of conspicuous consumption, most parents are too busy making a living or pursuing a career to spend the necessary time with their children to help them become responsible citizens of the future. They use television and video games as a method of child-sitting and look forward to the time when they can send the children off to school to get them out of the house. Obviously, this does not apply to all parents, although the number is a tragically high one.

> What a parent should do is what we call "*parent-centered teaching*™."

The parent needs to spend quality time with the child and to answer the child's questions. It is critically important for the parent to keep alive the sense of curiosity and the innate drive to learn. On one hand, this is accomplished by doing three things and, on the other hand, by not doing three things. The three things which parents should do are:

1) To answer the questions that the child has whenever they come up.

2) To create situations in which the child is exposed to new experiences that will lead him or her to explore and to ask further questions.

3) If they don't know the answer, then they should say so. Then they should find the answer and share it with the child or, if appropriate, tell the child to ask their teacher.

As for the first thing, children should be free to ask questions and be encouraged to do so. They must be told that there is no such thing as a bad question. All questions are good. Such a mind-set encourages more questions and triggers the thinking process.

As for the second thing that parents should do, that is, to create situations in which the child is exposed to new experiences, this is more challenging because not all parents are capable of being creative. This requires a fertile mind and not every parent can generate new patterns. Parents should encourage their children to make discoveries starting in the context of their everyday life.

Third, it is really important that parents be able to say, "I don't know the answer," to their children. Very often parents are reluctant to admit that they don't know something for fear that their children will think that they are ignorant. Remember that it is impossible for a parent to "know it all." Ideally, a parent would respond by saying to the child, "Let's find out together," or "Maybe you should ask your teacher." With certain subjects, the teacher often does know more than the parents; and it is perfectly fine to refer the child back to the teacher. It is really a bad idea to give children answers that you know to be incorrect for the sake of not appearing ignorant and clueless.

The three things that parents are not to do are:

1) To ignore their children's questions.

2) To do anything to make the children believe that their questions are not important, since doing so may trigger feelings of shame or inadequacy that may also carry into other contexts of life.

3) To make up an answer when they don't know or give an answer which they know to be incorrect.

If parents can carry out these six requirements (the three things to do and the three things not to do), then they will have kept the spark of learning alive.

Now the dilemma occurs. Parents are required by law to deliver their children into the hands of the *Mind Prison™* which may undo all that they have worked so hard to achieve. The parent is faced with several alternatives. One is to home school children which may or may not be legal in your community. This was the path which Michel had chosen for his own children yet he was quite outspoken about the fact that home schooling should only be done by parents who are competent to do so. Another alternative is to assist your child in surviving the *Mind Prison™*. To do this, the parent must teach the child *meta-*

cognitive skills and how to learn and work with them each day to develop visualizations and mnemonics that will help them memorize anything which they will have to learn by rote. Our *Learning How to Learn Technology*™ and *Program* incorporates these skills (www.TheCLWF.org). Make the time spent engaging in these activities fun and challenging.

Also, the parents should answer the children's questions that the *dis-educational system*™ either ignores or does not have time to answer. Most important, parents should focus on creating *understanding* that leads to real *knowledge*. They need to be able to explain clearly what the system fails to explain. Parents need to be able to monitor their children to make certain that they have achieved understanding. They will have to set the time aside to do so. What often occurs is that parents are preoccupied with their own personal or professional issues or are too busy at work and come home too tired so that they don't spend quality time with their children.

Parents need to interact with their children in a positive manner without putting pressure on them. A *tension*-free learning environment at home will encourage children to discover and to question. We stress how important it is for parents to share the joys of their children's own learning and not compete with them. Competition with parents will simply discourage the children. Let the children learn to experience the excitement of learning on their own. Instead, we encourage parents to reexperience the joy of learning yourselves and begin to share it with your children as you experience their joy. When children experience the joy of learning as their *innate drive for learning* is triggered, they begin to have an incredible feeling of self-confidence and self-assurance. Now they know that they can learn and furthermore, that they can feel great excitement in learning and in discovering new things. This will carry over into school and into life in general.

Unfortunately many parents do not have the time or the creativity and ability to pursue the learning of their children. So they are sadly left with consigning their children to the *Mind Prison*™. If parents are going to do this, then they need to put political pressure on politicians and educators to change the *dis-educational system*™ into one that incorporates the *Michel Thomas Method*. In doing this, they will have to fight to overcome the entrenched interests of the old school of education. This will not be easy. Like any other worthwhile political endeavor, it will require constant pressure and perseverance.

Parents are in a difficult position. The educational system is large, complex and diverse. Schools today are more like factories holding mass numbers of students. Advancements made in education are neither systematic nor universal. While there are areas and locations where progressive methods are being adapted, there are also areas and locations where education has not changed in the last fifty years or more. Moreover, in each local area, the advancements made may be difficult to identify among other areas of curriculum and instruction that lag so far behind.

Parents must encourage educators and politicians to bring about change as we described in the first section. Don't just buy into the system. Change it. Take action now! Don't condemn and consign your children to the same, terrible *Mind Prison*™ that you were forced to endure for years. Insist on a better way for your children. Realize that it is not money that will change the system. Putting money into the system is like "changing deck chairs on the sinking Titanic," to quote Michel. Don't let educators and politicians tell you that it can't be done. It can be done. Stand up against the institutions that have absconded with your children's minds. Engage your local school boards. Shake the dust from antiquated beliefs among those who prefer to maintain the *status quo*. Insist that the systems and the teachers change their methods. There is a better way and you have to fight for it. Standing by and waiting for others to get involved, will only ensure that the present system stays *"in the stagecoach era,"* to use Michel's metaphor. *Standing or sitting idly by* will not produce change, only a perpetuation of nonthinking children who become followers rather than leaders. It will certainly and rapidly lead to loss of *freedom of mind* with all of its undesirable repercussions of which we are all too aware.

STUDENTS

It is tragic that children are largely victims of the *dis-educational system*™. They are born with an innate curiosity and a passionate drive to learn. This curiosity and learning drive are usually quickly stifled by two things. First, is that when children ask questions, the adults around them either ignore them, tell them to shut up, or tell them that their questions are stupid and irrelevant. Children quickly get the message that their interest in knowing about things is unimportant as well as aggravating to adults, and that they should stop asking questions which only provoke exasperation, irritation or anger rather than the much desired answers. Their healthy curiosity should be encouraged instead of stifled.

Even worse, children may become emotionally crippled as they are led to believe that they are stupid, dumb and ignorant. That in itself kills critical thinking of any kind. They begin to believe that it is not appropriate to ask questions about the things in which they are interested. Or else children may discover that certain subjects such as sports and the news are legitimate topics for discussion because these topics are talked about in most circles. The issue here is that memorization of sports trivia and the like does not lead to thinking. The capability to rattle off sports trivia or any trivia for that matter may impress game show devotees, but does not reflect thinking skills or problem solving ability.

What often happens is that children end up memorizing countless statistics because they think that this is an acceptable outlet for learning. And they also believe that memorizing these statistics will impress their parents and friends. In any case, curiosity and the *innate drive for learning* take a huge hit and are reduced to being worthless attributes rather than qualities to encourage. Are parents being nasty and mean? Not really. The truth of the matter is that parents are usually well-meaning, but are either ignorant or too busy to interact with their children in meaningful ways. Some may be too busy trying to support their family financially to be part of their family.

In our present culture, parents are usually too busy to find time to answer their children's questions. Often, parents believe that children are incapable of the understanding required to understand the answer to their questions. Other parents may think that it is healthier for children to figure things out on their own than to be told. In either case, these parents assume that it is better to ignore the question for now, believing that the child will find the answer when he or she is old enough to understand. Research shows that children are far more sophisticated in their understanding than they are given credit for in our society.

Even if the child has any spark of curiosity remaining, the *dis-educational system*™ is quick to extinguish it. Children are by nature active and gregarious. In the *Mind Prison*™ they are like inmates who are told to sit still, to shut-up and to pay attention or to take their medication for hyperactivity. This is punishment. Real torture! The teacher delivers a prepared curriculum designed by some so-called educator in which each year they are to teach certain content. It is the teacher's responsibility to deliver that content and then for students to be tested on the material. As we said earlier, teachers are being held accountable for their students' test scores. Given this situation, the teacher wants well-behaved (obedient) students who will work hard to get good grades. There is barely enough time to cover the required material and little or no time for extraneous matters.

Students naturally have questions and opinions. If they are not relevant to the curriculum, then the students are told that either the question is irrelevant or unimportant and that there is no time for it, or else that they will have to wait until the material is covered in some future year. How preposterous is this! The system is designed for the so-called average student. Meanwhile, the gifted student is quickly bored and the slow student is gradually left behind. Furthermore, the testing process measures memory and not understanding. So children are conditioned to believe that success in life comes from memorizing and from being able to regurgitate all sorts of irrelevant or meaningless information in the context of living, which they don't need to understand anyway.

So what is a child to do? As Michel would always say,

"Students are victims of a conspiracy between their parents and the law. They are forced to serve time in institutions called schools."

Even worse, unlike the inmates of prisons, they have no advocates or representatives. It is a tragic situation to say the least. A few unique children survive the *Mind Prison*™ with their drive for learning intact. The number is indeed too little. And they survive in spite of and not because of the system.

If you are a student and find yourself trapped in the *Mind Prison*™, then what can you do? Michel was rather pessimistic on this subject. About all that you can do, given the present system, is find something that interests you and then pursue it with a passion. Make sure that it is not something that negatively impacts the health and well-being of another. The internet is becoming a great source of information and will increase in this role in the future. The issue here, however, is to be able to distinguish quality from nonsense on the web. Without the ability to think critically, many students are incapable of making such a distinction. This is already a major challenge which needs to be addressed by those who are capable of understanding and who still care to make a difference. Many students and adults as well, believe that because something is on an internet site, that somehow it must be correct information about a given subject and even expert information. This couldn't be farther from the truth. There are also libraries at our disposal which contain books that can be a great source of information and inspiration. Nowadays, with the internet, it is all too easy to simply do research on line, rather than go to the library. And the rise of online research has given way to increased and often rampant plagiarism on the part of students. Plagiarism is not only dishonest, it also eliminates the need to think independently or to solve problems.

The big quandary today is that students are so overloaded with homework and other assignments, that they don't have the time to study and research the things in which they are interested. And any spare time is spent in front of the "idiot box" or playing video games to the point of addiction. The children are left with the tragic choice of ignoring the requirements of the *dis-educational system*™ in order to have the time to pursue their passion, or else they may figure out how to work the system in order to get by in the easiest way possible. Neither option is the answer.

As a child or student, one of the greatest skills that you can master is to learn how to learn and to develop a *meta-cognitive* awareness of the learning process. We have spent many years researching how people learn and have modeled successful learning strategies about which we will continue to write in the future. Because of our personal concern for the children of the world, who are our future, many years ago we created and began teaching our *Learning How to Learn Technology*™. As we continually emphasize, *learning how to learn* is the single most important thing you can do.

> By learning how to learn, you can learn in spite of and not because of the system.

The system is focused on content and amazingly spends no time teaching students how to learn the content. If you must play the memorization game, then there are tricks like what we call "*memory mechanisms*"™ that will help you. As we have mentioned elsewhere in this book, the secrets to rote memorization lie in visual associations and mnemonics. The key to memorization does not lie in memory at all. We have found in our own research on learning that the key lies in the ability to convert what you want to remember into a picture or a mnemonic. Then remembering what is memorized is easy. Children who do well in rote memorization usually don't have good memories. What they have are good memorization strategies. No one teaches kids how to memorize. Even worse, some educators think that these systems are cheating. This is a tragic reminder to what extent that the old school will go to preserve its legacy. In our follow-up book, we carry this discussion to the next level and present more ways to integrate the changes on a systemic level.

Learning is a powerful innate drive. If it has been stifled in you, then begin to reawaken it. Once you have re-discovered the joy of learning, you will come out of the experience totally confident in yourself, and you will carry this confidence into all aspects of your life. You will discover many new things about yourself and your environment. You will feel a sense of great excitement within which will motivate you to learn more and more. And the more you learn the more excited you will become. Your excitement will even be contagious. This experience will demonstrate all that you are capable of achieving and will light the way to a new you!

The time has come for you to remove the shackles that enslave your minds. The time has come to help your children and yourselves escape the confines of the *Mind Prison*™. The time has come to carry forth Michel's dream! We invite you to join us in our campaign to "*Free Minds Now*"!

May you carry Michel's light within you as a beacon to guide you throughout this mission and throughout your entire life!

Chapter Nine

MICHEL THOMAS: A UNIQUE PROFILE THE DIFFERENCE THAT MADE THE DIFFERENCE

"In reading this chapter, I learned so much about myself that I didn't even know."

— Michel Thomas

Those who experienced the joy of meeting Michel Thomas usually found themselves mesmerized by a man who captured their attention from the moment his intense gaze met their eyes. Who was Michel Thomas? What was it about the *Master Teacher* that was so intriguing and seemed to magnetically attract people from all walks of life to know more? What enabled him to create his phenomenal method?

As behavioral modelers and experts in human typologies, we wanted to find answers to these questions. Most of all, we wanted to find out what set Michel apart from others as such a remarkable expert in learning and teaching. In order to answer these questions, we had to model the *Master Teacher's* teaching method. In order to determine what is was about Michel that distinguished him from others and enabled him to create his method, we also had to identify the key components of the behavioral profile which made Michel the genius teacher and man that he was.

This is why it was important to include a chapter about Michel's typological profile in a book about his method and philosophy of education. The revelations in this chapter were new to Michel, and he was quite delighted to learn how his "profile" had impacted his creation of a teaching method that represents the future of learning. He quickly "got it" and wanted to learn more. What was it about Michel Thomas that distinguished him from other educators? As modelers, we ask "*How is it possible*?" So, how is it possible that Michel was able to single-handedly create his revolutionary method?

In this light, we thought it would be helpful to guide the reader to a deeper understanding of his unique personality by presenting facets of this behavioral profile from the perspective of our work in behavioral modeling and of our research and work in human typological analysis and values theory. First, let us make it clear that Michel, the powerful presence of a man, was both a complimentary and inseparable part of Michel the brilliant educator. The two went hand and hand, and if it were not for a particular combination of behavioral and personality traits, combined with a series of extraordinary life challenges and situations, perhaps he would not have created his amazing method. Or would he have? Did Michel the man, his personality create his mission and his destiny, or was it his mission and his destiny, that made Michel the personality who created the amazing method that truly towers over others in the teaching world? We will leave it up to the reader to reach his or her own conclusions. However, here we will provide the behavioral answers to the question: Who was Michel Thomas?

Before we give a brief overview of the particular traits which made Michel Thomas the extraordinary human being and educator that he was, it would be helpful to describe the various typological models to which we will be referring in our discussion. Our work in human typological analysis refers to the study of human types. Every one of us has what we call a personal *"model of the world"* which is comprised of our particular mind-set, our emotional make-up, our perceptual filters or *People Patterns*™, our values, beliefs, attitudes and all those personality elements that make us who we are. Our *model of the world* refers to the fact that each of us sees the world through our own set of different filters which reflect the various typologies that comprise our behavioral profile. Our internal *model of the world* serves as a guideline for action in our daily interactions with those around us in the different contexts of our lives.

In order to understand Michel's *model of the world*, we will be examining a certain set of typologies about which we have written and have been teaching for years. We will consider those which had been most significant in the context of Michel's life and in particular, how the elements of his typological profile impacted his teaching and the creation of the *Michel Thomas Method*. One set of typologies is what we call "*People Patterns*"™ (For more information about the nine *People*

Patterns™, visit www.peoplepatterns.com). From the perspective of our behavioral modeling, these patterns are simply one part of the whole picture. Any profile is a sum of all parts fitting together in a particular configuration. And in the case of Michel, it is a configuration which contributed to making him the unique and multi-faceted person he was — the brilliant teacher, the creative genius, the dignified gentleman, the courageous fighter and the man with the remarkable mission among other things.

So what is this set of patterns of human behavior which we have named "*People Patterns*"™? Although as human beings, each one of us is unique, we do, nevertheless, behave in set ways or *People Patterns*™. Every individual has his or her own set of *People Patterns*™, and yet we share different patterns in our set with others. In our work, we refer to these patterns as "*perceptual filters.*" *People Patterns*™ represent the different *perceptual filters* through which we take in information about the world around us, through which we evaluate that information, through which we experience time, through which we are motivated and through which we take action, among other things. Just think of these patterns or "perceptual filters" as a lens that magnifies or brings certain aspects of our environment into sharp focus, while diminishing or distorting other aspects or causing them to disappear. Our distinct perceptual filters through which we look at the world, i.e., our distinct *People Patterns*™ refine and customize our experiences throughout life.

What made Michel unique and each one of us, for that matter, is our particular combination of *People Patterns*™ and other elements that make up our personal *model of the world*. We have identified the particular *People Patterns*™ which have most impacted Michel's life and teaching. They are the following:

1) The *Change People Pattern*™

2) The *Evaluation People Pattern*™

3) The *Motivation People Pattern*™

4) The *Information People Pattern*™

THE *CHANGE PEOPLE PATTERN* ™

The *Change People Pattern*™ reveals first and foremost how an individual will be able to deal with change or not deal with it in the context of life. It also reveals the manner in which a person handles and reacts to new experiences and situations. It tells us how an individual associates elements of his present experiences to his past experiences. Moreover, the *Change People Pattern*™ reveals a great deal about a person's lifestyle. Later in this chapter we will identify Michel's *Change People Pattern*™ and show just how it influenced him throughout his life, including how it influenced the creation of his method.

The *Change People Pattern*™ reflects the four different ways in which individuals perceive the world around them using one of these four specific perceptual filters to take in the thousands of sensory stimuli which bombard us on a daily basis. From the perspective of the *Change People Pattern*™, in any life situation or experience, an individual will focus his attention on one of four elements. The one he or she chooses, thus, determines the specific *Change People Pattern*™. These four elements are as follows:

1) Similarity
2) Similarity and then some difference
3) Difference
4) Difference and then some similarity.

SAMENESS

People who focus their attention on similarity are called *sameness* people. They will always notice similarities in a given situation or experience. People who filter the world around them through *sameness* filters have great difficulty tolerating change in their lives, no matter what the context. They prefer to live in a *status quo* world that breeds the comfort of familiarity. *Sameness* people represent approximately five to ten percent of the modern industrialized world, and this proportion increases in developing countries and in rural areas. Now, as far as Michel Thomas was concerned, he was definitely not a *sameness* person, for he certainly did not choose to view the world through *sameness* colored lenses. By the way, *sameness* people are most likely to disregard Michel and his method. They will also be the people who will not appreciate this book because they like the system just the way it is.

QUALIFIED SAMENESS

People who filter the world through this *pattern* first see similarities in a situation and then obvious differences. They are called *qualified sameness* people and they represent the majority of society. Although people with this pattern are basically *sameness* in orientation, they occasionally need a bit of variety injected into their lives from time to time. The additional elements of diversity provide just enough spice to avoid a monotonous lifestyle. In some way, *qualified sameness* people lead lives which are more balanced than those of their *sameness* counterparts, who are much more one sided. *Qualified sameness* people comprise about fifty-five percent of the modern world. Michel most assuredly did not fit into the *qualified sameness* mold.

QUALIFIED DIFFERENCE

In a given situation or experience, people who focus their attention first on difference and then on similarity are called *qualified difference* people. These individuals first notice differences and once they have observed the differences, they will notice obvious similarities. *Qualified difference* people like change, but it does not have to be radical or earth shattering change to provide satisfaction. This category to some degree represents the flip side of qualified sameness, except that the accent is placed upon difference in the former group and sameness in the latter group. *Qualified difference* people represent approximately twenty-five percent of the modern world's population. And, by the way, Michel Thomas was not a *qualified difference* person.

DIFFERENCE

As the word implies, *difference* people wear a totally unique set of lenses through which they view the world. Unlike *qualified difference* people, pure *difference* people thrive on constant change and variety. They are bored by anything that is ordinary or routine in life and detest continuity. Moreover, they are masters of making distinctions of all kinds and tend to be quite creative in extraordinary ways. Like the *sameness* person, the *difference* person deletes or ignores part of reality. Where the *sameness* person reduces reality to similarity or *sameness*, the *difference* person reduces reality to elements of *difference*. Things that are totally obvious and visible to a *difference* person will usually be totally ignored or go unnoticed by a *sameness* person. Who do you think will walk into a room and will not only notice, but will also adjust a crooked frame hanging on the wall? Why a true *difference* person, of course.

Difference people comprise approximately five to ten percent of the population and are more likely to be highly educated and from industrialized countries and urban centers. In short, difference people are truly a unique breed in every way — by the way they think, by the way in which they react to situations, by their wonderful ingenuity and creativity, by the way in which they stand out among the crowd, and by their very manner of being. It is literally a totally unique and different mind-set which sets them apart from most of the world.

> In every sense of the word, Michel Thomas embodied a true *difference* person, reflective of all the above traits, in his own very singular and consummate manner.

Before we begin to discuss the manner in which the *Difference People Pattern*™ had manifested in Michel's life and had impacted his experiences, we must make an important distinction. We are, after all, talking about the *difference* filter, so why should it be surprising that there are distinctions to be made within the world of *difference*! Of course, *difference* needs variety and we find that there are two types of *difference* people:

1) Polarity responders

2) Mismatchers.

Which type was Michel, and how did this nuance his *Difference People Pattern*™? We shall soon see. We call the first type of *difference* person a *polarity responder*. This is the kind of person who will always do the opposite of what you tell him or her to do. Those who are parents can easily relate to this type of behavior when their children are going through a *polarity responder* phase of development. You may tell the child to do something and he or she will react to the contrary by engaging in a behavior that is the exact opposite of what you asked. Over time parents have learned to use so-called reverse psychology in dealing with such behaviors. There are some, however, who maintain this dubious trait throughout their entire lives. They are often perceived as major annoyances by the rest of the world.

The second type of *difference* person is called a *mismatcher* or *counter-exampler*. The *mismatchers* among us are those who are constantly pointing out exceptions to everything. They are masters of providing counter examples and will be the first to figure out why something won't work or can't work. *Mismatchers* have a favorite expression: "Yes, but..."

Mismatchers are the troubleshooters of the world and the more evolved ones provide a useful and essential service to society. The more evolved *mismatchers* are those who instinctively know when and where to provide the counter examples, and often end up making useful and relevant suggestions for positive change. Moreover, the so-called good *mismatchers* of the world are experts at making very refined distinctions about their environment and their experiences, distinctions which often remain invisible or imperceptible to the eyes of most other people. Their unique perspective frequently leads to highly innovative outcomes and ingenious creations.

MICHEL THE GOOD *MISMATCHER*

Such was the case with Michel. The skilled *mismatcher* with the eyes of a hawk and a heightened awareness of all his senses, Michel had time and time again in his remarkable life, viewed and experienced the world through the lens of his exceptionally refined *difference* filter. In fact, we can say that it was probably his command and refinement of the *difference* filter which played a role in his very survival countless times during World War II, for Michel was able to "see" and discern things in his surroundings that others could not. His ability to engage in *meta-cognition* allowed him to see things from an entirely different perspective than the majority of the rest of the world. His *difference* filter enabled him to take in information from the world around him from the perspective of a *difference* person, one that was certainly unlike the view of most of the people with whom he interacted.

In fact, it is this *difference* pattern, the basis of his unique view of the world, which enabled him to find "exceptions" — different means of escape from concentration camps and challenging situations, different ways of observing people and things around him, different ways of reacting to situations and to people, counter examples of his own sort which when chosen wisely, meant life rather than death, "exceptions" which may have saved his life more than once during the war.

It was also his highly evolved *difference* filter which triggered the creation and eventual refinement of Michel's unique teaching method and which also inspired him to probe the learning process of the human mind. We can see this *Difference People Pattern*™ develop early on, from his childhood and teen years, right through his time in the French Resistance, his living hell in the concentration camps to his work in counter intelligence for the US Army, through the initial creation of his first language school in Beverly Hills, through his fifty plus years as a great pioneer and innovator in education right up until his last days, continuing to work his magic and to apply his creative genius with his students.

MICHEL THOMAS: A TRUE *DIFFERENCE* PERSON

Remarkable as it may seem to most people, Michel wore his very special lens of *difference* filter as an infant. He quite vividly described to us the manner in which he viewed his world through the eyes of a baby from his crib. It was obvious to us that he was already experiencing and interacting with his environment from a *Difference People Pattern*™ perspective even at such an early age. Even more remarkable, was that Michel remembered these events with great detail, which in itself is quite revelatory regarding his *model of the world* as we shall discuss later in this chapter.

Perhaps the most striking example of his *Difference People Pattern*™ was from his childhood, when he was already making a distinction between himself and the adults around him. What he did at that time was to have a tremendous impact on his entire life. He was just a child of five or six years old living in Poland. What occurred one day is that the young Michel began to notice that when adults spoke to him, they would change their tonality and engage in "baby talk." The fact that a young child would even make such a distinction is exceptional. He asked himself: "Why do adults behave the way that they do, because they were children once, so why do they talk that way to children?" His "two mothers," whom he adored, and they him, certainly did not speak to him in "baby talk," so why did other adults he wondered? Such behavior made no sense to him. Michel came to the conclusion that these adults must have forgotten their own childhood, otherwise they would not behave in such a manner. This thought was repulsive to Michel. It may have been several hours or several days after this initial realization that Michel began thinking about the whole incident again. For a child, days seem so long, that it could have been later that same day that Michel came back to his thoughts on this incident again.

He told us that this time it hit him harder and explained why:

> "If they grew up and forgot their childhood, then I will grow up, become an adult and I will forget my own childhood. I will have forgotten. That was very disturbing to me, that my whole life, who and what I am now, will be completely forgotten. I will be one of those adults and I could not let that happen."

So Michel decided that he had to do something about it. He began to ponder how he was going to handle it and what he was going to do about it. It is quite amazing that five year old Michel could come to his own conclusions as to why adults behaved the way that they did, and decided to make a change within himself so that he would not lose his sense of identity, his sense of who he was. He wanted to make sure not to forget his life up until that point. He promised himself that he would remember as much as he could, that he would retrieve as much as possible from before that moment so that he would not end up like the other adults.

How far back could he go? Michel decided that he would go back to the crib, where throughout his entire life, he could see himself in that crib, experiencing sensations of taste, touch, and smell and seeing what was happening around him. Michel's description was as vivid as the Proustian *tilleul* and *madeleine* episode, a synesthesia in which sensory impressions recreate an entire world abounding in a plethora of rich details. Several months before his passing, he once again related this story to us, retaining the same vivid memory of that child; and he was immediately able to relive the sights, sounds and feelings of that child as though he were still there. It was obvious that on some level that child was still a part of Michel.

Whenever Michel would describe this "child" to us, it was always quite evident that he still was so very grateful to that child for having made those observations and for deciding to change the way he would look at his own life:

> "I know that I owe a lot to that child. Because of that child, I am who I am."

GETTING TO KNOW ME

This entire incident marked a turning point in Michel's life and sparked the creation of his own system of self-analysis and self-criticism, which he called his "*getting to know* me" period Just as he had asked the question, "Why?" as a child, he continued to do so during his *getting to know me* period. This *getting to know me period* was quite important in his life, and without realizing it at the time, it had prepared him as he explained, "in many ways, maybe in every way, how to survive." It was a time to ask questions and to make distinctions about his own behavior that only a *difference* person could make.

The real purpose of his *getting to know me* period was to find out about himself. "Who am I?" Michel asked. And with his *Difference People Pattern™* he began to put himself into all kinds of different situations in order to see how he would react. "In order to 'get to know me,' I had to be alone with myself, but exposed to all different situations in the world, starting with life on the road." He ended up hitch-hiking (a new and *different* means of travel at that time) around Europe, North Africa and the Middle East because he knew that he would be meeting different kinds of people. And his *getting to know me process* would reveal how he would react to these different people and different cultures.

As a *difference* person, Michel was not happy with the *status quo* or with routine. He literally experienced life on a daily basis as change. As he made more distinctions about himself, he would continue to make additional changes in his behavior until he was happy with the result. Michel's ability to sit in judgment of himself and to go to a position of *meta-cognition*, allowed him to understand the essence of who he was and then to make the changes he wanted in order to grow and evolve to higher levels.

So time after time, Michel would experience different situations and then would analyze his reaction. *Getting to know me* meant asking questions like: "How am I going to handle it?" "How am I reacting?" and "How did I react?" And then he would sit in judgment of himself that night. He would ask himself: "Now what did I do today, and how did I handle that, and why? What did I like about it, and what did I not like about it?" Interestingly, whenever Michel did not like his reaction in a given situation, it meant that he would have to put himself into a similar situation to see how he was going to react the second time around. He wanted to make sure not to react in a way that he didn't like. While working with us, in describing this time in his life, Michel told us that he had recently come to the conclusion that a main reason for his *getting to know me* period was to create a role model for the father that he did not have.

Michel had strong maternal influence from the love of his mother and aunt, whom he adored, and yet, as he says: "I had to create my own role model in myself because I did not have a paternal role model." And Michel was quite demanding. He explained that his early role models had come out of mythology, first Greek and Roman, and then Norse mythology whose heroes stood up for "what is right." This is significant because "fairness" and "justice" are major issues for Michel, as is fighting for a just cause in "the name of what is right," both of which are characteristics of his particular personality type.

Although in this book we will not go into depth into another typology which we have been teaching, writing about and using for years, we will mention in passing that Michel's personality type was that of an *Enneagram* Eight, one which we refer to as a "*Venge.*"

> The energy from this type is what propelled Michel on his life-long mission to correct what he perceived to be the injustices of the current educational system as well as the social injustices in the world.

And beware if you are to do or say something to a *Venge* which is perceived as an injustice or unfairness towards him or her, or towards others for that matter, "for hell hath no fury like a *Venge* scorned," i.e., the origin of the term "*Venge*," short for vengeance. Given such a mind-set, it was no surprise to us that Michel created his *Twelfth Commandment: Thou shalt not stand or sit idly by* (Chapter Five). A *Venge* has no tolerance for injustices or for those who sit back and allow the injustices to occur. This type will often go out of the way to make his opinion known and will often do so in a rather obvious manner, as would Michel in expressing his disgust of the wrongs in our society.

Another characteristic of the *Venge* type is the marked sense of invincibility, which, in the case of Michel, was certainly a factor in his miraculous escapes during the war. Michel told us that he was aware of this invincibility even as a child, an awareness that was largely based on his remarkably quick reflexes. "What made me feel invincible were my quick reflexes. Up to my teen-age years, I was always ready to fight." Curiously, Michel did not remember feeling that sense of invincibility as an adult during the war. However, his *Venge* mind-set and quick reflexes came to the rescue once again when he was hit by a stretch limousine in Manhattan in 2003. It was his extraordinarily quick reflexes that literally saved his life. His mantram, "I don't give up," had certainly stood him in good stead throughout his life.

His *Venge* sense of invincibility is probably also tied into the fact that he managed to overcome rickets, the very serious disease that he suffered from during his childhood. When he realized that his mother was upset at seeing him unable to walk, this young Michel immediately wanted to show her that he could indeed walk and started to walk around the table. Not only did Michel overcome rickets with the help of great doctors, helpful nutritional supplements and the immense love of his "two mothers," he never had to wear leg braces to straighten his legs, as did other victims of the disease. Of this latter feat, Michel spoke quite proudly. Even more astounding is the fact that his legs straightened out and he ended up becoming a rather good athlete in his time. This is key into the mind-over-matter, "I can do anything," mind-set of the *Venge*. In many ways, Michel was always going into a position of *meta-cognition* and changing his behavior, accordingly, to fit his *Venge* stance of "I am stronger, I am better than, I can overcome anything."

Another facet of the *Venge* in Michel was the socially outgoing individual whose appeal shined through whenever he felt comfortable and able to trust those in his company. His life experiences during the war had taught him to be wary of others. However, once he was realized that a person was genuine with no hidden agenda, his interactions with people were quite warm and he would touch so many. Michel could charm just about anyone. In fact, throughout his life he was quite a ladies' man and his reputation lives on beyond his passing.

Last, and certainly not least, Michel's concern and caring for the underdog is another characteristic of the *Venge* personality type. There are many times during his life that this trait shines through and we will simply mention one incident which occurred at the age of seventeen of which he was particularly proud. This story is a classic example of Michel following his own *Twelfth Commandment. Thou shalt not stand or sit idly by.* At that time, Michel, as the good *Venge* that he was, had come to the aid of a young man who had a birth defect in one leg and who happened to be the cousin of his friend, Karl Heinz. That day there was a celebration for young people in the park and Michel noticed that there was a group of people watching something. He went to see what was going on and noticed that a big bully was provoking this young man.

In any case, by the age of seventeen, Michel already believed that he was invincible because of his strength and reflexes: "I was the fastest, why, because I had convinced myself that no one could get me, that I was invincible, that I could fight someone bigger and stronger and that it didn't matter to me because of my reflexes." He saw the bully draw a line, daring the disabled boy to cross the line so that he could beat him up. Well, that type of provocation is the last thing one would want to do when face to face with a *Venge*. When Michel saw the utter humiliation of this underdog, a situation which he perceived to be a great "injustice," he immediately stepped in front of the bully and drew another line.

Of course, the bully dared to ask Michel to choose the place where he would like to be lying on the ground. Needless to say, the *Venge* usually wins out. Michel chose the exact place where the bully would be lying on the ground, pointing it out to him; and that is exactly where the bully ended up. The point of this little anecdote is that Michel would always come to the defense of those treated unjustly. For almost six decades he continued to fight for the underdog in his mission to revamp the educational system which he perceived as the perpetration of a major injustice against all humanity. As we have already indicated in other chapters, Michel believed that it is a system that keeps our children and all learners in shackles of ignorance so that they can continue living as underdogs while the elite maintain control. He truly believed that it was his mission to rescue students from the misery and injustice of a "criminal institution," the terrible educational system in which they are forced to wear learning "straitjackets."

Michel was also drawn to injustices towards animals. They sensed this and were drawn to him. We also noticed how pets were drawn to Michel because they could see a caring person with an authentic love of all life, humans and animals alike. He felt that animals should have a voice as well, again, as a *Venge*, seeing them at a disadvantage and wanting to right the wrongs of those who mistreated animals.

Before completing the discussion of the *Difference People Pattern*™ in Michel, we would like to comment on another aspect of Michel's period of self-judgment, this time in regards to its connection to the *Michel Thomas Method*. There is a particular element in his Method of which we have made mention on numerous occasions throughout this book because of its critical connection to *understanding*. It is the element of self-correction. Although mistakes were rare in Michel's classes, when they did happen, it was up to Michel to first determine why the mistake had been made in the first place and then figure out what to do about it. Although students could usually correct their own mistakes once they realized that they had made them, in the rare instances when they did not, Michel would lead them into the process of correcting their own mistakes.

Whenever they *derailed,* as he would say, Michel would always lead them back to get them on track again. The purpose of doing so was to get them to a point of *understanding* by getting them back on track to learning. There is a major connection here between the younger Michel and the *Master Teacher*. Earlier in life, when Michel sought understanding of his actions during his *getting to know me* period by getting back on track to what he perceived to be the "right" way to behave, he applied the same principle of self-correction with his students years later. He also wanted them to reach understanding of their actions, in their case, having committed a mental error and then getting back on track to correct the mistake.

There is another connection between the self-correction element of his Method and his practice of self-analysis during his *getting to know me* period. The thought processes in both cases are so similar. During his *getting to know me* period he would carefully analyze in detail what he had done previously that was not right in his mind. He did so to achieve understanding of his actions, so that he could correct what he had perceived to be wrong and not repeat the behavior.

Similarly, Michel had taught his students to be able to detect and then to correct their own mistakes so that they would not make them again. If they did make errors a second time, it was quite rare, just as it was rare for Michel to repeat an error of judgment he had self-corrected. In any case, in both instances, it was a question of looking at oneself and making the appropriate adjustments to get back on track. In one case it was a matter of making mistakes in language structures, and in the other case it was a matter of what was perceived to be wrong choices in life, both of which had to be self-correcting. Thus, as a young man and later as the great innovator in education, Michel ingeniously exhibited his mastery of *meta-cognition* which, in turn, he would teach his students by means of the concepts in his method.

In addition to the connection between the self-correction element and Michel's *getting to know me* period, there is also a definite link between this period and the *Difference People Pattern™* component of his *model of the world*. As we explained, Michel would always sit in judgment of himself during this time in his life. When he would go back the next day and put himself in a similar situation, he would resume the self-correction mode. If he didn't like his response again, he would return until he did, always aware, however, of not falling back into the same judgment. What Michel was doing in essence, was trying to *change* his feelings, his reactions and his judgments. A *sameness* person could not conceive of purposefully changing any aspect of his or her life. Whether it was something he had said to someone, or something he had done which he didn't like, then he would have to go back and *change* it, as he said, "in words, action, everything." Michel never considered himself to be too critical of himself because to him, to be critical was really important. This mind-set allowed him to learn more and more about himself and his choices in life. Furthermore, it allowed him to grow and evolve to higher levels of self-awareness. In so doing, he tried to make sure that he didn't miss a piece about *getting to know me*.

There are many more examples of Michel's *difference* orientation early in life, too many to mention here. However, there are two particular situations which merit acknowledgment here because Michel took pride in recalling them to us on several occasions, and also because these incidents also shed light on Michel's extraordinary *calibration* ability, a talent which he has used throughout his entire life, including in his teaching, as we discussed in Chapter Six.

The first incident is when he was a young student in Germany which he described to us as follows:

MICHEL THOMAS: A UNIQUE PROFILE
THE DIFFERENCE THAT MADE THE DIFFERENCE

> "I discovered again, as a child, that I don't like to do anything out of habit, like going to school."

This is an iteration that can only be uttered by a *difference* person. A friend asked him at the time which way he was going to go to school. Michel replied that he didn't know. His friend couldn't believe Michel's answer: "I don't' know which way I will go today or tomorrow. I don't want to know." What a great line! Like the great *difference* person that he was, Michel found it inconceivable to take the same way to school every time, much to the dismay of his friend, who was probably a *sameness* person. Michel could not understand his friend's perspective, nor could his friend understand Michel's point of view. These reactions occur rather often when a *difference* person interacts with a *sameness* person.

There was another incident in Michel's life which is revelatory in relation to the *Difference People Pattern*™. It deals with another situation during Michel's very fruitful *getting to know me* period, which is connected to another facet of who Michel was. Another thing he decided to do during his *getting to know me* period was to dismiss everything and anything that one would usually have to respect. Michel was breaking away from the norm as he began to change his own beliefs. He came to the conclusion that respect had to be deserved, and that one could not simply be told to respect something, no matter whether it was a person or a thing. Michel applied his new belief one night during his travels in France, near Toulon. Around midnight he was walking down a narrow, one way street in a slum neighborhood.

There was a wall on one side and little buildings with narrow stairs on the other. He happened to notice a huge pile of trash surrounded by very large rats. His immediate reaction was an expected one of repulsion and he began to walk away. Then, suddenly, he stopped himself and said: "What are you doing? Why did you react that way? What do you know about rats, only what others have taught you about them? Do you discriminate against rats? No! No! No! Now you have to find out. Go back." What a perfect example of Michel's *meta-cognition* ability! He created his own strategies to understand himself and developed his own self-tests for validation. Michel told us that rats had gotten an "unfair" reputation. Here again, is an example of the *Venge* mind-set of defending the underdog. As we shall see, upon Michel's return to the rat-infested alley, he intended to right the wrong in his behavior towards the rats, which, in his mind, are traditionally wrongly perceived as ugly and intolerable.

Michel so enjoyed telling us this story, which, by the way, still meant a great deal to him in terms of his *getting to know me* period particularly with respect to how it had enlightened him. He returned to the mound of trash on that one way street to sit in judgment once again and to see how he felt about rats. Of course, the moment he got there, all the rats quickly disappeared. Michel decided to sit on the stairs beside the mound of trash and wait for them to return. The whole thing turned out to be very interesting and a great example of how the mind of a *difference* person takes in information about the world. The rats had disappeared into one wall which had holes, and Michel noticed that all the rats had their own holes.

Here Michel once again, began making distinctions. He found it really fascinating to discover the different ways the rats behaved: how they came out and how the different rats reacted to and observed what was going on around them. He made even more distinctions. Michel pointed out that there were some that were afraid, others a bit more daring who walked out and then ran away again. He described how during this whole time he did not budge and gradually the daring rats would come out followed by more and more other rats until they would again approach the mound of trash. Within an hour or so, the rats had surrounded him and the trash and Michel was able to observe them closely the entire night as he kept watch: "I found them absolutely fascinating...in observing their behavior and in observing the differences in their behaviors...the leaders and those who were led, and their action and their reactions. They turned out to be highly intelligent."

Here was Michel, once again, exposing himself to yet another lesson, making subtle distinctions. And by means of his astute *calibration*, he was learning about a species he really knew nothing about, seeing *differences* in their behavior that others would have ignored. At the same time, he developed even more insights into his beliefs and character. Michel basically prepared his own learning itinerary, went into the situation, experienced it, and then made judgments about himself in order to change his behavior accordingly.

Already at this time, we see Michel's sharp *calibration* or observation skills at work, which he would later put to good use as the *Master Teacher*. He explained to us how this incident with the rats affected his notion of respect for things in life in general. Michel would apply the insights he acquired from the rat incident regarding "respect," to his opinion of traditional education. He quickly realized that the *dis-educational system*™ in no way deserved his respect on any level, only disdain.

The ability to calibrate well is largely based on one's ability to make highly refined distinctions, a task that is much easier for *difference* people since their view of the world is based on detecting *difference*. Michel was a master of detecting *difference*. He was a master of making highly refined distinctions, a talent which had served him well throughout his life. Obviously, these skills came in very handy while he worked in counter intelligence for the US Army. In fact, he had the reputation of being one of the best interrogators around. He would succeed time and time again to get information out of people which others could not. Part of his success came from his superb *calibration* skills which were due to his *difference* orientation.

As a highly gifted *difference* person, Michel was not content to conduct a simple interrogation. His method was a two-phased process. As he had explained to us, the first phase was the easy one in which he seemed to carry on an almost casual conversation with the prisoner. This part would be a piece of cake perhaps to the person being questioned or to the outside observer. There was far more to come, for the second phase of the interrogation marked a drastic change in tone and procedure. It was during this phase that Michel would turn the screws very tightly and get information that otherwise would have remained unknown. Being such a pure *difference* person, Michel would notice the slightest movement or gesture or the slightest voice change while the person was speaking. He observed all reactions, perceiving *differences* and making distinctions that would be clues to information. No wonder why

Michel's reputation as a top notch interrogator had followed him throughout his life.

> Michel's refined *calibration* skills enabled him to form great insights into human nature, a kind of intuitive wisdom which helped in his eventual discovery of the critical keys to understanding the learning process of the human mind.

His time as a student at the University of Bordeaux is reminiscent in this regard. While there, he was earning money to attend classes by taking photographs of children playing in the park. Michel would go to the park to take photographs of only children, and children in action, playing and so forth. He would not take photographs of their parents or of adults, for that matter. After developing the shots, Michel would then visit the parents, showing them pictures of their children in action, on horses, on the carousel, etc.

What is of significance here is a detail that would go unnoticed by most people. It is that Michel took pictures only of children because he realized that the adults would probably not have liked their own pictures and would be more reticent to buy any of them. And he needed the money to attend school so he knew that he could not rely on adults to buy pictures of themselves. That in itself reveals a great insight into human nature on Michel's part early on as a young college student.

There were so many examples of the *Difference People Pattern*™ manifesting throughout Michel's life, that they would be too numerous to mention here. There is one more, however, which we will note in passing because it deals with Michel's creative mind and, in particular, the development of specific teaching instruments before he created the *Michel Thomas Method.* In 1946, after World War II, Germany was divided into different zones: the American zone, the British zone and the Russian zone. During that time, the Nazi government had taken all of the top scientists and evacuated them into Weimar. However, that area was to be taken over by the Russians. The result was that the Nazis immediately decided to evacuate all German scientists from what was to be the Russian occupied area, to a city named Heidenheim, near Ulm.

Meanwhile, some of the German scientists were sent to the United States to work on a missile program called "*Operation Paper Clip.*" At the time, Michel was with the US Army and had the opportunity to talk with a number of these scientists. He and his colleagues were told to overlook party membership because the scientists would only be sent to the United States for a limited period of time. Michel and his colleagues were instructed to get as much information as they could out of them because they would eventually be sent back to Germany. "That was wrong information," Michel told us. "They remained in the United States."

The other scientists who were not involved in the missile program remained in Heidenheim, a detail which quite intrigued Michel. So he talked to Headquarters about working with these scientists. After all, here there were so many top scientists who, for years, had been paid to work and do research for the Nazis. Michel thought it would be a great idea to tap into the minds of these brilliant scientists rather than just let them sit idly by and let their research fall by the wayside. When Michel asked Headquarters about using them, their answer was that these scientists were already in "*Operation Paper Clip,*" so that they would not be using them. Once again, Michel, with his *difference* filters, realized that here was a creative opportunity not to be missed, one in which he could organize a group of these scientists for research purposes.

Even though Headquarters was not going to use them, Michel got official permission to carry out his idea of getting this group of brilliant scientists together to help him develop instruments for teaching physics. He and the German scientists ended up building teaching models for physics, and this turned out to be a very successful operation which was used internationally. The point of this story is that Michel was, already in his own innovative fashion, finding new ways to teach, in this case physics, and developing creative and practical instruments or models to facilitate the learning process.

Michel's *Difference People Pattern™* would continue to manifest in his teaching right to the very end. Although we have discussed them in the context of his method, we will simply make brief mention of a few of the examples now. First, as we have seen, each time Michel taught a course, he would have very specific objectives in mind (to teach the entire structure and grammar of the target language, including all tenses, etc.) which he would tell the students up front. Michel, being a *difference* person, would not have been comfortable doing it the same way each and every time. This is how he unconsciously expressed his *difference* orientation to us with respect to teaching his courses and with respect to his life:

> "I have objectives, but the road to reaching those objectives I never know in any course... That is also probably something which is part of my life."

So although the objective remained the same, the means by which he achieved his objectives every time he would teach his class were different. This is because Michel, as a *difference* person, did not like to repeat himself, just as he did not like taking the same route to school every day as a youngster. This was another aspect of his teaching which seemed to elude his critics, a fact which always annoyed Michel.

As we mentioned in the Method Chapter, there have been certain critics who have said that Michel always started teaching his courses by explaining cognates, or that he always started with the same verb or with the same sentence to translate. This couldn't be farther from the truth. These critics picked on one particular point and then generalized it into a routine part of the method. This would really infuriate Michel and with good reason. Could it be that these critics are *sameness* in orientation and instinctively look for similarities? As such, they would seek out how what he did was always the same. In essence, Michel's approach was that of a *difference* person, preferring to vary what he did each time. The two types have difficulty understanding the mind-set of the other because they literally see things from two diametrically opposed perspectives, one from similarity and the other from difference.

Within the context of his teaching, Michel was not a creature of habit, but rather a creature of change. He relished knowing that things would be different each time around. His method was not about always starting a course the same way with a particular thing. In fact, he was proud of the fact that he always found ways to change.

> What Michel would do, was create a workable framework from the beginning that led to accomplishing his objectives; and the manner in which he would do so was different every time.

There was also another element of *difference* in that Michel realized that each student was different, and he would interact with each one accordingly. He viewed every student as unique as well as each group as different and unique as well.

Michel's creativity shined through, as we have seen in the discussion of his method, in his ability to make distinctions about grammar that no one else had before him. Being a *difference* person, making distinctions was second nature to Michel. For example, as we discussed in Chapter Six, over the years he had come up with some remarkably clever ways to teach verb tenses. By making distinctions, by seeing that certain endings are the same, while others are different, he cleverly devised his own system which put similar ending in one box and the exceptions in another box. "Why is this ending that's different in the same category as the others? It doesn't belong there." Only one who was a *difference* person would think that way, and one who had an understanding of how the parts fit into the whole.

Grammarians, who tend to be *sameness* people, want everything in a certain, structured order. Michel was different. What he was doing was creating his own structure with built-in flexibility for *difference*. This was part of his genius. He could not conceive of continuing to use an ineffective model just because it has been around since the Greeks and had been used for over two thousand years. Michel jokingly remarked that, "It doesn't matter that other languages don't fit the ancient model. It sounds like Greek to me!"

Let us compare now, for example, how verbs are conjugated in the traditional way versus the way in which Michel cleverly created his own more simple and far more elegant model of verb conjugation:

I	We
You (informal)	You (plural or formal)
He, she, it	They

The above is a structured order, which in traditional language schools, must always be followed to a tee.

Let us take the verb "to speak," in French (*parler*). It is normally conjugated in the following way:

Je parle	*Nous parlons*
Tu parles	*Vous parlez*
Il parle, Elle parle	*Ils parlent, Elles parlent*

This conjugation method above is confusing to the student because it seems complicated. The student is thinking to himself, "How am I going to memorize this?"

First, as we have seen, Michel would not ask his students to memorize the verbs as in traditional language learning. Michel realized that mere memorization of a given conjugation was a complete waste of time because it did not create *understanding* which leads to *knowledge*. And, memorization creates undue cognitive and physical stress.

Second, the traditional format of verb conjugation makes no sense. Why is it that third person plural, *ils parlent* and *elles parlent*, are placed with *nous* and *vous* when the endings of *ils parlent* and *elles parlent* are pronounced the same way as the first, second and third person singular forms? That makes no sense. So Michel decided to place all the verb forms that sounded the same on the same side in what he referred to as the "*short box*." There was definitely "method" (no pun intended) to what traditionalists may perceive to be madness on the part of Michel. He was a master simplifier.

He explained that all the verb forms are quite easy to understand and sound the same. The only exceptions are the endings for *nous* and *vous*, which he placed in what he referred to as the "*long box*." Where the traditional approach to teaching verb conjugation complicates learning, Michel would simplify the subject matter and in so doing, facilitated learning through understanding. Michel's long and short boxes have nothing to do with the number of verb forms in the corresponding list. Instead they refer to the endings involved. Here is Michel's long box:

> *Nous parlons*
> *Vous parlez*

Nous and *vous* endings are the exceptions as far as pronunciation is concerned and they go in the long box. Again, as Michel explained, nothing fits into the long box except *nous* and *vous*. Everything else fits into Michel's short box. Below is Michel's short box:

> *Je parle*
> *Tu parles*
> *Il parle, Elle parle*
> *Ils parlent, Elles parlent*

Endings for these forms are all pronounced the same way so Michel put them in the short box. And if it is not an "*er*" verb, you don't sound the consonant.

This small change in verb conjugation turned out to be monumental in that it allowed the students to understand what they were learning. It was logical to teach verb conjugation in precisely this way because Michel's *heuristics* simplified the process and made sense in the minds of the students. Also, this teaching trick unconsciously facilitated learning by building the students' confidence in their ability to easily conjugate a verb, something which had always been out of reach for most people. They now had command of readily available and usable *knowledge* that could be applied in different contexts, rather than meaningless information that is quickly forgotten.

Thus, instead of a list of seemingly ordered information or facts which made no sense in the students' minds, Michel created a different kind of order, his own unique order. So what was normally painstaking and tiresome verb conjugation became usable information rather than useless rote memorization of verb endings, as is done in traditional language teaching.

In modeling experts in many different fields (whether in sports, manufacturing, education, sales, public speaking, etc.) we have found that experts always have a specific way of organizing information in their heads. Although the particular method may vary with each individual, based on his or her personal typologies and *model of the world*, each one is quite adept, given the individual's inner model, to make associations. In addition, each is able to organize these connections in a way that not only makes sense to him/her, but that also facilitates the transfer of this knowledge base to different contexts. This skill is what enables them to come up with different strategies to deal with change and with new information.

Moreover, as we have mentioned many times, a significant part of Michel's method was his ingenious creation of *meaningful memory associations*™. In essence, they are associative distinctions that no one else had made before him. We simply cannot overemphasize this fact. One of the master keys to his method was his ability to generate these *meaningful memory associations*™.

We know that Michel would use these distinctions to teach the grammar, and he would successfully teach the grammar without using grammar books. As we have seen in Chapter Six, Michel did not look at the grammar from the point of view of a traditional grammarian. Instead, he looked at the actual use, found a pattern that the grammarian did not see, and then came up with *meaningful memory associations*™. He made sure that these mechanisms made sense to his students and connected in some way to their personal experience or *model of the world*. By doing this, he triggered a positive feeling within them; and they would never forget.

Michel would look at words to see what patterns existed, would make distinctions among the patterns, would simplify the patterns and then would find a way to communicate the patterns and distinctions to his students. He did so systemically and effortlessly. Again, he would view everything through his *difference* filters. Michel brilliantly connected patterns which he organized in a simplified version that made sense in the minds of the students. Michel would masterfully present the information so that the students were able to use and to understand the information immediately. His mind moved from complexity to simplicity. Michel constantly simplified all things and in so doing, demystified them.

> His ability to do so from a *difference* perspective makes his accomplishments all the more amazing, in that he was able to communicate differences in a target language by reducing them to categories of *sameness*.

Doing this unknowingly allowed him, in effect, to reach the more prevalent *sameness* and *qualified sameness* people. Of course, the rare *difference* students would have immediately resonated with his clever, innovative mind and *model of the world*.

There happens to be a majority of people in the world who are *sameness* or *qualified sameness* in orientation, and are not capable of dealing with complexity. Nor are they capable of making distinctions. And this is part of the challenge, to find more teachers who are capable of seeing *difference* and of making distinctions. Here, we are making a distinction between teachers and teachers as creators.

MICHEL THOMAS CREATOR AND TEACHER

Michel was both a creator and a teacher. He created an entire method of teaching, and he taught the method he created as well. In order to create in this way, it helps to be a *difference* person who has a creative mind. As Michel pointed out: "Unfortunately, people who are teaching don't even look and see what is there…and they don't always have to get the students to memorize each single verb, but they do." Most teachers do this because they do not look at things in the creative and innovative manner in which Michel would.

The challenge we face is that most teachers do not think in the way that Michel thought. And it is more than a question of being a *difference* person or not. It's about the ability to create something new which isn't there already and of seeing things literally in a new light. Michel would often remind us that this creativity is a big part of the excitement of teaching, just as is simplifying and making things understandable for the students.

In the *Mind Prison*™ just the opposite is happening. Michel summarized it well:

> "So far, if you look at the textbooks, you see that everything is the same, nobody, no academician, will point it out. What does it take to intelligently look at something differently?"

Michel's words are obviously those of one who sees the world through *difference* filters.

The answer to this question is one of education's biggest challenges. The reality is that not every teacher out there is going to be able to think in the way that Michel did. Not every teacher will have the ability to create and to see things and to see patterns to generate new possibilities. This means that the part of Michel's method which requires active creativity on the part of the teacher may not be easily assimilated into the teaching of all people. We also modeled creativity several years ago and we found that innovative thinking reflects a cluster of specific elements which work synergistically, and which are not found in everyone. What teachers can incorporate from his method, however, can only be a huge improvement over what they are already doing.

It would be remiss of us not to mention in the context of our discussion of the *Difference People Pattern*™, how Michel, the master of making distinctions, came up with the three major keys to learning all verbs. Leave it to the creative *difference* person and particularly to a great *mismatcher* to figure out why things don't work, and to devise an alternative that not only works, but one that facilitates and simplifies the entire learning process. It is important to realize that by the sheer creation of his unorthodox method, by rejecting much of the traditional educational system, Michel expressed his *difference* genius in grand style for the benefit of all who have the wisdom to appreciate his unique gift and contribution to education.

THE *EVALUATION PEOPLE PATTERN*™

The Evaluation People Pattern™ deals with one of the more basic human activities, that of making decisions and judgments. The *Evaluation People Pattern*™ reveals how a person makes his or her decisions and judgments in life. There are two ways in which this happens. Some people will base their decisions on internal criteria, while others will base their decisions on external criteria. The criteria that one uses to make these judgments and decisions are called their *referential filters*. Those who use external criteria when making decisions have what we call an *External Evaluation People Pattern*™. On the other hand, individuals who use internal criteria to make decisions have *Internal Evaluation People Pattern*™.

However, some people who have an *External Evaluation* orientation and base their decisions and actions on what others think, may also combine it with some sort of internal verification. In such a case, we say that they have an *External Evaluation People Pattern*™ with an internal check. On the other hand, with individuals who make decisions and choices based on what they know is right inside themselves, and then check to see how their decision affects others, we say that they have an *Internal Evaluation People Pattern*™ with an external check. That external check may also come in the form of data or information that is used to make a decision.

THE *EXTERNAL EVALUATION PEOPLE PATTERN*™

People with an *External Evaluation People Pattern*™ base their choices and decisions, not on "inner knowing," but rather on people, ideas and events which are outside of them. For example, they know that they have done a good job based on what others tell them or because of some type of feedback such as data or statistics. Their sense of who they are is largely based on what others say and think about them. For those with an *External Pattern*, the external referent may also be a system, such as a political party, movement or philosophical system, or it may be a significant other. As far as Michel was concerned, he was the complete opposite, as we shall now see.

THE *INTERNAL EVALUATION PEOPLE PATTERN*™

Individuals with an *Internal Evaluation People Pattern*™ base their decisions and their choice of action on what they know instinctively to be the right decision or choice for them. When faced with a choice or decision to make, the person with an *Internal Evaluation Pattern* goes within and evaluates the options based on his or her internal experience. Often, this may take the form of an "inner knowing" of what to do. Those with an *Internal Evaluation People Pattern*™ have an internal barometer to evaluate all that they do. Most *Internal Evaluation* People will say that they simply know inside that they are making the right choice or that they are doing a good job. People in this latter group decide things for themselves without relying on the opinions of others.

MICHEL: HIS OWN ULTIMATE DECISION MAKER

Such was the case of Michel, who had a sense of "inner knowing" about his choices and decisions in life. Michel was his own judge of things and certainly did not look to others for approval. A perfect example of Michel's *Internal Evaluation People Pattern*™ appeared early on in his life, during his *getting to know me* period which we discussed earlier in this chapter. What he did, in effect, was to create a rather sophisticated *Internal Evaluation* System for himself at an early age, with its own internal check, with no need to seek approval outside of himself. Michel created his own internal barometer that would make evaluations of all aspects of his being. And whenever his *Internal Evaluation* did not meet with his approval, he would modify his behavior accordingly.

It was Michel's decision to find out about who he was, and it was Michel who stood in judgment of himself in order to grow and evolve to another level. He certainly did not rely on the opinion of others to decide whether or not to change his behaviors. He didn't have the need to ask other people what they thought about what he did or said. On the contrary, Michel realized that he alone could make decisions about himself. After all, how could another person tell him how he was to behave?

In fact, we have found that Michel had one of the strongest *Internal Evaluation People Patterns™* we have come across to date. His *Internal Evaluation People Pattern™* reflects his *Venge* mind-set and was the basis of his "*Eleventh Commandment*": *Thou shalt not follow the multitude to commit evil.* He had amazing, unbending self-confidence and probably knew more about himself than others do about other people, not to mention about themselves. Nor had he ever relied on the opinion of others to boost his self-esteem. He simply didn't need to do so. And his intense *Internal Evaluation People Pattern™* was most likely another factor which had contributed to his being able to survive and maintain hope during the war, even under the direst of circumstances that he had to endure.

THE *MOTIVATION PEOPLE PATTERN* ™

The *Motivation People Pattern™* reveals how a person is motivated. There are two ways in which people are motivated. When people are motivated to do something because they want to attain a personal goal or outcome or to obtain something, we call this type of individual a *move toward* person. They are motivated by carrots and the key is to determine what the right carrots are. On the other hand, when people are motivated to do something in order to avoid some situation or a particular thing, we call this kind of individual a *move away from* person. A *move away from* person only responds when he or she is threatened by sticks, and it is important to know what sticks to use. People will *move toward* or *away from* things, specific situations or circumstances, jobs or other people.

The whole concept of attraction/aversion has been part of the human condition for centuries and understanding of its dynamics greatly facilitates communication. We are focusing on the trigger behind the motive, rather than on the direction in which it is going. So it is important to focus on the source of the attraction or repulsion, rather than on the consequences of the action. About forty percent of the population is *move toward*, forty percent of the population is *move away from* and about twenty percent are both.

MOVE TOWARD PATTERN

Move toward people will move toward things that they desire. These individuals will *move toward* things and situations that appeal to them and which provide enjoyment or happiness. The more intense the enjoyment or pleasure, the stronger the *move toward* behavior will be. *Move toward* people focus on what they want rather than what they don't want. They are the ones who will concentrate on the positive side of a given situation. *Move toward* people abhor sticks or punishment. They, instead, live in a world of incentive based behavior.

MOVE AWAY FROM PATTERN

Move away from people will be motivated by sticks rather than by carrots. They will *move away from* things or situations that are unpleasant or, repulsive to them. *Move away from* people don't want to know what they want, but rather what they don't want. They are always the first to see drawbacks in a situation and often ignore positive aspects of situations. They will *move away from* things that they want to avoid. People who move away from cannot compute the notion of incentives in their mind. They react to sticks, that is, threats or punishments.

THE *MASTER TEACHER* AND HIS INCENTIVE BASED LEARNING

In his teaching, the *Master Teacher* would use a *move toward* strategy with his students even though he was not aware of this or the other *People Patterns*™. His *move toward* orientation was why his entire method used incentive based learning. Because he embodied the *Move Toward Motivation People Pattern*™, he would always emphasize all the positive outcomes to be achieved. When Michel would teach, he managed to create a *tension*-free atmosphere in which the students thrived. He would offer carrots rather than sticks. Moreover, as we have pointed out many times, Michel would specifically state from the start of a learning session, that there would be no blame placed on the students for mistakes or for not understanding.

Blaming is characteristic of *move away from* people. Of course, the responsibility for learning and for remembering was on his shoulders as the teacher and not on the students. There was absolutely no punishment whatsoever in the context of his learning sessions with his students. *Move toward* people cannot conceive punishing others or themselves, for that matter. Punishment and threats are used by individuals with a *Move Away from People Pattern*™. Because Michel was *move toward* in orientation, he believed that scolding or punishment for incorrect responses served no purpose except to create *tension* in the students.

Michel instinctively came to the conclusion that providing incentives to the students was the best way to enhance their understanding of the subject matter. And in our own work we have seen that incentive based learning makes a huge difference in reinforcing associations in the mind of the students. He certainly did not need to threaten them. As a *move toward* person, doing so was inconceivable to Michel and would have been an insane approach in his mind, given his *Motivation People Pattern*™.

Michel would work with his students at another level. He would essentially reawaken their *innate drive for learning* by opening the doors to learning within the students, doors which in his words "have been slammed shut by the system." He believed that learning was itself an inherent drive, a truly powerful drive, so once he triggered this *innate drive for learning* in his students, he did not have to motivate them. In a sense, the *innate drive for learning* is itself *move toward* in its essence.

Michel would never use *move away from* strategies because he was there to create great self-confidence in his students by getting immediate results, a feat which he accomplished each and every time. Because he would achieve results so quickly, he had no need to get them motivated. *Move away from* strategies create *tension*, which is the exact opposite of what Michel desired in his courses. He would not spend his time, warning them that they had to work hard to do well or to memorize.

Instead, he would focus on achieving the objectives he presented at the very beginning of the course. In fact, from the start he would tell his students what they could expect to achieve, rather than focus on any negative feelings such as anxiety or guilt or self-imposed *tension*. Also, his creation of *esprit de classe* among his students in a group setting reflects the *move toward* orientation. From beginning to end, Michel would use *move toward* strategies which, in turn, were reinforced by his own physiology and by the atmosphere or energy he created in the room, whether it was with one student or fifty students. Michel was so effective in his teaching that he even succeeded in reaching *move away from* students with his *move toward* method.

THE *INFORMATION PEOPLE PATTERN*™

The *Information People Pattern*™ consists of two parts:
1) The Perceptual Source People Pattern™ and
2) The Chunk Size People Pattern™.

The first, the *Perceptual Source People Pattern*™, has to do with how we take in information from the world around us and how we represent it to ourselves internally. It reveals how we create an internal representation of this external world. The important distinction determines the source of the information that comes to us, whether it comes through our five senses or from somewhere else. The second, the *Chunk Size People Pattern*™, deals with the amount of information which we communicate with the source of that information. It reveals how we break down information into units of communication.

THE *PERCEPTUAL SOURCE PEOPLE PATTERN*™

The *Perceptual Source People Pattern*™ reveals the two ways in which we take in information, either through the senses or from elsewhere. We call information that comes through our five senses of sight, touch, hearing, taste and smell, *tangible* information because we can actually determine the source and identify it. On the other hand, we call information that comes from somewhere else *intangible* because it does not correspond with any direct sensory input. One may think that it may come from several of the senses, or else that it is intuition based. We often refer to the latter type of information as coming from a *"sixth sense."*

Tangibles pay attention to what they can see, hear, touch, taste and smell, and they also want concrete data and information. They are the empiricists of the world. Meanwhile, those who get their information from non-sensory means are called *intangibles*. *Intangibles* are great intuitors and look for the relationships, possibilities and connections in situations. Although, they accept the senses, they believe that they can know things just as well or better by other means. *Intangibles* are the visionaries of the world.

MICHEL: THE BALANCED ONE

Michel was the great intuitor and yet, he had, at the same time, unusually keen sensory awareness. This balanced combination of both *tangible* and *intangible* sources allowed him to take in a wealth of information about the world that was powerful in its consequences. It is this unique combination of the *Perceptual Source People Pattern*™ which certainly gave Michel the upper hand on more than one occasion during his many escapes from death in WW II. He had developed quite a sophisticated inner sensory system that allowed him to take in information through his five senses with great ease and variability. In fact, it is quite remarkable that during his *getting to know me* period, Michel was able to go back to the time when he was in the crib, and he could remember in great detail the sensory information he was taking in: the sights, smells, tastes, sounds and kinesthetic qualities he experienced around him.

For example, on several occasions Michel described to us a time as an infant in the crib, when a nursemaid had been sewing in the same room. He vividly remembered seeing the sewing machine with all of its mechanical parts and the huge, black dog sitting there alongside. At one point, he made sounds so that the nursemaid would give him a bobbin to play with for awhile. She did so and Michel vividly recalled the smell of the oily residue, which he could still taste in his mouth when he was telling us about the incident. In addition, he described the shiny pieces he saw on the sewing machine as well as the sound of metal coming together. Almost ninety years later Michel was able to relive the entire scene with great sensory details, experiencing it with both his *tangible* and *intangible* filters. Needless to say, he refined his sensory perceptions as he grew older; and his talents in this area certainly served him well when he needed them during the war.

Just imagine combining this gift of *tangible* awareness with the ability to take in information on an *intangible* or intuitive level which he neither consciously depended upon nor distorted. That is what Michel was able to do. Imagine the sensory data he was absorbing on that dreadful day in Lyon, France when he came face to face with the Gestapo "butcher" himself, Klaus Barbie. Michel had recounted to us many times how while walking up the stairs to go to a meeting with Jewish refugees for recruitment into the Resistance, he twice heard a voice within warning him not to proceed because the Gestapo was there. At the time, Michel chose not to listen to and not to accept the voices in his head, and ended up being caught and interrogated by Barbie, who eventually released him. As we saw in Chapter Three, it was a chilling incident which had Michel within seconds and inches of being ruthlessly shot and killed. It was no coincidence that he was spared and released, while all the other captives in the room had their lights extinguished forever.

Michel's balanced *Perceptual Source People Pattern*™ was an asset to his teaching as well. It enabled him to calibrate or carefully observe his students. He would not only use his five senses in his interactions with them, he would also skillfully intuit many things. For example, he would be able to intuitively "*see*" who may have been having a problem with something, and would proceed to correct the situation. Michel would instinctively know when the students had reached the point where *understanding* had become *knowledge* in their minds, and then he could move on. He would not have to wait for a student to say anything about being ready to proceed.

From his *intangible* awareness, Michel would know exactly what to do each and every time. Besides, Michel somehow would let his students know that they were succeeding at the task before them, i.e., the task of learning a foreign language. And his gift of acuity did not end in teaching. His balanced *Perceptual Source People Pattern*™ went far beyond his teaching to manifest in all contexts of his life. He was certainly both a visionary and an empiricist, and was one or the other whenever contextually appropriate.

THE *CHUNK SIZE PEOPLE PATTERN*™

The *Chunk Size Information People Pattern*™ deals with the amount of information we give and the specificity of that information. The amount of information that is presented in a given situation or interaction is what we call the information quantity. The amount and depth of information is so important in any communication. The quality of the information has to do with the scope and depth of the information. Depth is measured by the amount of detail that is presented, while scope is determined by how many aspects are included.

Those who give a lot of information and who go to great lengths to do so have what we call a *Specific* People *Pattern*™. They prefer depth and prefer to communicate the details and specifics. We call this "*chunking down.*" Those who prefer the overview or the big picture communication are called *global.* They prefer scope to depth and "*chunk up.*" When *global chunkers* are presented with more information than they can handle, or if presented with too much detail, they will often feel as though they are on overwhelm. On the other hand, if they are *specific* and are not getting the depth of information they require, they will become easily distracted or simply get bored with the interaction.

THE SCOPE AND DEPTH OF MICHEL THOMAS, THE *MASTER TEACHER*

Although Michel was basically a *specific* person who mastered the art of in-depth communication, he also had the keen ability to chunk up and to present the big picture when necessary in the context of a given interaction. He would be able to look at any situation as a whole, and then would be able to arrange the details or pieces in such a way as to make sense of the whole. Michel would be able to both see "the forest for the trees" when necessary, as well as see "the trees for the forest." He quite effortlessly would utilize this ability as a master interrogator during the war, and would continue to elegantly use it in the context of his teaching and in his everyday life as well. Once again, Michel was balanced in terms of the *Chunk Size People Pattern*™ in that he was able to provide both scope and depth as needed in any situation or context.

> This ability to incorporate scope and depth is so critical to teaching because one needs to be able to present information when needed in the appropriate amount or quantity, and it needs to be presented just when needed.

The latter is what we call *"the timeliness of the information."* Michel, in his courses, would know exactly what to present at any given point in time. He instinctively would know when too much was too much, and when he would have to add more depth. The depth of information he would present in his interactions with his students was always "just right." For example, in teaching the grammar, he would begin with simple sentences. As he perceived the students' *understanding*, he would gradually add on complexity.

As we have seen in the chapter on the *Mind Prison*™, what we call our *dis-educational system*™ is based on memorizing details and on rewarding students who can remember them. With half of the students of the world from the *global* group, and who are not interested in detail anyway, they will forget it all. This is not a reflection of their innate ability to learn. With Michel, it would not matter whether he had a *specific* or *global* student. It would not matter in that his students learned the material anyway because he was presenting it a way that works for both types of people, that is, global and specific alike. He would begin the course by presenting his overall objectives. And when he would begin to teach the structure of the target language, he would often start with the big picture. Then he would make sure that everyone got it, at which point he would begin to get into more and more detail. With his method, Michel had created a particular rhythm for the flow of information so that it was captured by everyone.

> Michel was able to move back and forth with great ease from *global* to *specific* and vice versa when called for in the context of his teaching.

This is the essence of explanation. You have to be able to start with the big picture and then move to the details. In proper teaching, you need to begin with a brief overview for the *global* students and then move on to details, and then back to *global*. In this way, the *global chunker* is comfortable when you lay out the forest for the trees, while the *specific* person will be ready for the change. Michel would accomplish this quite flawlessly, no matter what language he was teaching. As such, he would create a smooth flow of information in a manner which would reach all of his students.

When students are having difficulty or if they are lost, either they don't know where they are, or else they don't know where they are going. Michel instinctively (his *intangible* filter) would know where they were, why they were lost and would take full responsibility for whatever it was that they were doing incorrectly. Remember that if they make a mistake, he would know exactly why they made the mistake and was able to lead them back so that they understood why the mistake was made in the first place.

What Michel was doing was "*chunking up*," so that the students would know where they were and how they got there initially. In this context he was again creating another type of flow of information which brought the student back to an earlier point so that *understanding* and then *knowledge* were achieved. He was also able at all times to monitor the chunk size of the information he was giving. Without even being aware of the *Chunk Size People Pattern*™, Michel had mastered its application in his teaching.

THE *DECISION PEOPLE PATTERN*™

The *Decision People Pattern*™ deals with how people make decisions. Most people think that they make decisions based on logical reasons. If you were to ask them, "Why do you do what you do?" the most frequent answer will be, "Because it makes sense." Most people do not make decisions based on sense. They simply think that they do. It is just that "making sense" has become an acceptable practice and, in a certain respect, has become an institutionalized given. In fact, less than five percent of the population makes decisions based on sense. The reality of the situation is actually quite different. People actually make decisions based on one of four reasons which are:

1) It looks right.
2) It sounds right.
3) It feels right.
4) It makes sense.

Looks right: A person with a *looks right* decision making strategy is literally creating a visual representation in his or her mind of the alternatives and then comparing those pictures to the internal picture of the ideal choice. When the two pictures match, they experience an internal sensation that translates in their minds to making sense. This confirms the decision to be the right one.

Sounds right: A person with a *sounds right* decision-making strategy is making an internal or external auditory representation of what each alternative sounds like and is comparing this to the ideal sound in his or her mind. Again, when there is a match, the *sounds right* person experiences an internal sensation that translates into "making sense". This is a confirmation that it is the right decision.

Feels right: The *feels right* person compares an ideal internal representation of what feels right inside to the feeling associated with each of the alternatives before him or her. When the two feelings match, then the *feels right* person translates that sensation into "making sense." And the "makes sense" feeling confirms that it is indeed the right decision.

Makes sense: The *makes sense* person comes at this in a way that is different from the others. Instead of dealing with experience by means of internal pictures, sounds and feelings, the *makes sense* person sidesteps them by dealing in words and symbols. In making decisions, the *makes sense* person translates the experience into words, focusing on the linguistic aspect rather than on the direct sensory experience of pictures, sounds or feelings. This type of person creates a checklist of ideal criteria which is then compared to the alternatives available to him or her.

MAKING SENSE OF MICHEL

In the context of his teaching, Michel did not use the *looks right* strategy, or the *sounds right* strategy, or the *feels right* strategy. In teaching languages, Michel would use the *makes sense Decision People Pattern*™. In fact, in stating his objectives from the very beginning, he would tell his students that their learning was going to be based on *understanding* which leads to *knowledge*. *Understanding*, of course, lies within the realm of making sense.

Given the way Michel taught his courses, students could not use a *looks right* strategy in learning a language. Initially, they did not see what they were learning since Michel did not write anything down for them. There was never a blackboard and there was no note taking. Without seeing any written words until they had acquired "a solid and comprehensive knowledge of the entire structure and grammar, including all tenses," the students would not have had the pictorial elements in their minds to compare, for example, an incorrect spelling of a word to the correct spelling. It was not until the fourth day of the course that they could see actual words, when Michel would introduce the students to reading. At that point, the *looks right* students could use their own pattern to verify correctness.

As for the *sounds right* decision pattern, Michel would insist from the very beginning that the students were not to sound anything out or to guess. Even if they sounded something out, and they guessed correctly, it was still guessing for Michel, therefore, it was unacceptable.

> Throughout his learning process, students were to base their progress on *understanding* each piece that Michel presented, and not on the way something may have sounded to them in their heads.

This is a critical point.

The *feels right* pattern was also anathema to Michel's method, since for him it was always a question of thinking out each bit of information that he would give his students rather than focusing on "feeling" that something was correct. He would keep them thoroughly occupied during the learning session. They were so captivated by their learning that even *feels right* students forgot to think about engaging in activity. There is one context in which Michel used a *feels right* decision strategy. It was very, very rare and appeared only in a few decisions regarding his interrogations of suspects. In these limited cases, Michel explained to us that he did not try to reason anything out.

In his teaching, Michel, from the very beginning of the course right to the very end, would insist on acquiring a solid comprehension of the language. Comprehension implies *understanding* and making sense. This was achieved by Michel explaining every piece so that the students reached an *understanding* of the material which, in turn, became *knowledge* that they would never forget. They were told to think out everything so that what they were saying made sense to them. It was not a question of it *looking right*, *sounding right* or *feeling right*.

In his school days, Michel used a *make sense* strategy in his own learning. He always had to understand every situation, every problem and every person with whom he came in contact. *Make sense* people such as Michel, are really good at abstract reasoning. Like Michel, they love coming up with solutions to problems. Like Michel, they are also great analyzers and are superb at researching, examining, unraveling and discovering. Michel was a master of all of these mental operations and more.

3

> These combined abilities allowed Michel to quickly determine relevancy of information to the final outcome of *understanding*.

Therefore, he was able to delete anything that was arbitrary, inefficient or irrelevant. This was one of the ways in which he had been able throughout the years, to refine and streamline his method and reduce his teaching from twelve weeks to five days.

Remember that Michel never wanted to be a language teacher or any teacher for that matter. What led him to teaching was his professor who stated that "no one knew anything about the learning process of the human mind." That was the spark which triggered Michel's innate desire to understand. So Michel was driven to uncover those secrets, to figure out from top to bottom the ins and outs and of how we think, and in particular, to "probe the learning process of the human mind."

Michel had always had a need to understand things, and this remained with him until his passing. He had always had the need to analyze everything from top to bottom in order to reach satisfactory answers and conclusions. His *getting to know me* period was a case in point. Remember that this was the period in which he would sit in judgment of himself, analyzing his every thought, word and deed and would then make the necessary judgments in his behavior that made sense to him. He needed to understand every aspect of who he was. In fact, he needed to acquire a solid and comprehensive *knowledge*, with the emphasis on *knowledge*, of who he was during his *getting to know me* period. And it was Michel's *Make Sense Decision People Pattern*™, his ability to combine and use every mental operation humanly possible, which contributed in a huge way to the development of his unsurpassed method.

You will find an in-depth presentation and analysis of all nine People *Pattern*s™ in our book, *People Pattern™ Power: The Nine Keys to Business Success*.

Chapter Ten

MICHEL'S MODEL SCHOOLS: DREAM OR REALITY

"Here again could be established a bastion of Basic Freedom to which all the intellectual world would flock and form a vast army to stem the flood of thought controlling vandals no matter from what quarter of the globe they threatened."
— *Michel Thomas*

Michel's burning desire to "probe the learning process of the human mind" did not end with the creation of his learning center in the United States which, with his passing, no longer exists. On the contrary, his dream of beaming the rays of enlightenment around the globe became a battle cry for change, positioning Michel on different occasions against the traditional bastions of education, unscrupulous executives and recalcitrant royals. The precarious state of the world and the need to change it remained an *idée fixe* in Michel's mind. He had dreams of creating a model school. He also envisioned a *supra-national university,* where the best achievers from their respective fields from around the globe would instruct an international student body of the highest caliber. His *supra-national university* was to be the way to secure "*Freedom of Mind*" for the citizens of our world:

> In time to come if, through the unwisdom of leaders and the apathy of people, the world is plunged into a calamitous period of darkness as has happened before, this [Michel's] university might conceivably be the last bastion of Freedom from which man can find hope, courage and inspiration to resist and fight back. It is suggested, therefore, that the greatest care be given...so that the single proposition — Freedom of Mind — upon which this institution is founded, will be made as safe and secure as possible.

Michel specifically asked us to include this chapter in our book about his method in order to further his message about changing the world. He also wanted the public to be aware of the different paths he had taken over the years to establish his own intellectual "Bastion of Freedom." This was to replace the "criminal institutions" known as traditional schools, and it would have been a central meeting point for the great minds of the world.

Early on, a long time friend of Michel's named Jules Stein, who happened to be one of the more powerful moguls in Hollywood at the time (the founder of MCA which eventually became Universal Studios), saw the uniqueness and market potential of Michel's method. So Mr. Stein proposed a partnership to create a series of national language schools which were to open all across the United States.

Unlike most people who would have loved to go into business with Mr. Stein, Michel turned down the offer. Michel was not yet ready to commit to the concept of the model school because there was still so much more research and empirical knowledge to gain before his dream could become a feasible and successful reality.

However, Michel continued to make discoveries about the learning process as he refined his method with more and more insights into the workings of the mind. He figured that it was time to make a move in the direction of creating his university. His vision was to start with a school for only graduate students from all fields (diplomatic corps, politics, business, etc.) and then to expand it to a *supra-national university* with professors from all over the world. This university was to have its own sovereign status independent of any nation. Michel had envisioned it to be a university state like the Vatican without any national dependency or control, including no government control. It was to be a sovereignty with its own post office and stamps as well.

Michel's university was to be a place where all academic research in each field would be conducted by the world's most competent people as part of an international center. It was also to be a place which would establish a sense of brotherhood among all people everywhere. Michel thought of this university as a place where "what is achieved is for the world, and not in the world." In 1959, Michel conferred with Robert Hutchins, a former President of the University of Chicago, a former President of the Ford Foundation and who, at the time, was President of the Fund for the Republic and Chairman of the Encyclopedia Britannica. Both he and the Fund were intrigued by Michel's idea to create a model school. It seems that the Fund for the Republic had attempted to realize such an idea in 1957 with no success because "the attempt was partial and inadequate". They were interested in pursuing the idea once again under the umbrella of an international university.

In a letter to Michel, Dr. Hutchins expressed his full support of Michel's idea:

> Long reflection on the state of the intellectual world has led me to the conclusion that the trouble with it is that there is no leadership in it. There is no concentration of intellectuals dedicated to the task of leadership anywhere in the world. There is no intellectual beacon or lighthouse to be seen. It would not take much to create one, and one should be created before it is too late. A group of ten or a dozen of the most intelligent men in the world who came together in a single place, strategically located, to work together on the identification and solution of the great problems of the second half of the twentieth century, could have an overwhelming influence on the thought and the events of our time. The reason for this, of course, is that the world is waiting for leadership that such men could supply.

After several meetings with Dr. Hutchins, Michel knew that he was "the most suitable person to assist in creating a comprehensive academic blueprint" for his *supra-national university*.

Dr. Hutchins quickly put together a group of international notables. He contacted the Fund's own group which included such notables as Nobel Prize winning scientists Niels Bohr and Isador Rabi among others, and the Princeton group which included such great minds as Paul Tillich, Jesse Oppenheimer, Jacques Maritain, Walter Lippman and others who all "came to the same conclusion." The answer as to why no "existing intellectual institution can do what he (Hutchins) says has to be done...is that the universities of the world have accepted such enormous obligations by way of vocational certification, scientific research, and the accommodation and entertainment of student in vast numbers that they are completely swamped by these activities." The project was to be done with Dr. Hutchins in charge of the entire university from an academic perspective. Everything was set up, ready to go. All that was needed was the appropriate site for the university.

MICHEL'S DREAM TEAM

Michel continued to maintain a straight course on his mission of changing the world. His prior disappointment brought him to a new level of awareness. Now he had to find new paths, new contacts and also significant financial backing to create his university. Michel was well on his way to building his own "dream team" with Dr. Hutchins responsible for the academic side, and soon another person to handle financing would join them. Michel would turn to a close personal friend, Joseph Hirshhorn, a wealthy American industrialist who had amassed a fortune in uranium mining. Mr. Hirshhorn was an astute businessman who could see the value and potential of such an undertaking and was enthusiastically willing to take care of the financial side of the project. In fact, Mr. Hirshhorn told Michel that "it was only money." Michel's friend had already spoken to Rothschild about the project. Mr. Hirshhorn's only concern was finding the appropriate site whose location could rival the prestigious nature of the school.

It so happened that around this time, in the late fifties, a member of the world's "elite" had come to Michel to learn French. That person was American actress, Grace Kelly. She was to marry Prince Rainier of the prestigious Grimaldi family, which had sovereignty over the Principality of Monaco. The future Princess and Michel developed a good friendship as a result of their learning partnership, and their warm relationship continued after her marriage to the Prince, enduring until her untimely death.

So Michel was quite comfortable in initially proposing to Princess Grace an ideal site for "establishing a seat of learning in Monaco." She quickly embraced the idea, which she saw as a way to transform Monaco's reputation as a gambling oasis and tax haven into a reputable place of learning. Princess Grace was very excited about Michel's vision and she immediately got her husband on board. The proposal intrigued the Prince, who then invited Michel to their chalet in Gstaad, Switzerland to have a nice place to discuss further the plan for the university.

With the enthusiastic endorsement of his wife, Prince Rainier welcomed Michel's idea; and he immediately asked: "Where do we find the land?" Each time the Prince selected a site, he realized that the lack of land was the issue. "We don't have enough land." he said. He explained that Monaco was a tiny municipality with no extra land on which to build a school of such proportion. The Prince was totally taken by surprise when Michel responded: "I don't want your land. We want your water — your territorial water in the sea. I want to create an island in the Mediterranean!" The Prince certainly did not expect Michel to say that he wanted rights to territorial waters to create an island. The idea of reclaiming land would change the entire geography of Monaco.

Why the need for another university? In his proposal to Prince Rainier, Michel gave his answers:

> We need an INTERNATIONAL university. All universities tend to be excessively nationalistic. This is natural and unavoidable... The whole place tends to reflect the customs, traits, characteristics — political, social and economic — of the country...and it quickly becomes rigid, hidebound and reactionary.

All the great universities of the world are nationalistic: Oxford is British, the Sorbonne is French, Harvard is American, etc. Michel's vision of a *supra-national university* was, in his mind, a solution to the critical need. He explained his thoughts as follows:

> ...the dire need is for a seat of learning that CANNOT be or become nationalistic, but must, by

its conception and from its very inception, be INTERNATIONAL and not subject to the forces and elements that make for nationalism...

Those elements would include a country and its people, history, traditions, etc. What Michel foresaw was the need to seek and to promote internationalism and not nationalism in a university.

Now, why would Michel have chosen to build the school in Monaco? Michel felt that Monaco was the ideal site for his international university because it reflected "none of the elements that make for nationalism and all of the elements that make for internationalism." In addition, Monaco was ideally suited geographically because "it was on the Mediterranean, the so-called cradle of European civilization." Monaco was also close to sites of ancient cultures such as Greece, Egypt and Rome which had given birth to new ways of thinking and to new forms of art and philosophy, among other things. And, of course, Monaco was known for its cultivation of music and the fine arts.

Michel informed the Prince that he wanted to create an island which would be an independent sovereignty in the middle of the Mediterranean and which would not be under the jurisdiction of Monaco, even though it was to be connected to Monaco by a bridge. Although Michel's idea of reclaiming territorial waters and creating an island seemed a bit far-fetched to Prince Rainier, it continued to intrigue him. The university was to have its own research center, so that everything would be centralized in one location. This was a new concept for the time. The Prince asked for a specific plan, so Michel returned to the States, confident that his meeting with Rainier had gone very well. He eagerly and arduously began working on getting things into motion. Michel got another member of the "dream team" on board, the highly reputable architectural firm of Victor Gruen Associates, which was very excited to be involved in the project. They came up with preliminary concepts and detailed drawings for what was to be the International University for the Principality of Monaco.

In a letter to Michel, Victor Gruen wrote: "It is highly gratifying to have a part in the architecture of an institution which promises to make major contributions to world peace and understanding." Mr. Gruen was well aware of the privilege of his involvement in this amazing project, which would have had wonderful repercussions around the globe. In his architectural study for the school Mr. Gruen wrote: "The concept of this university is that of an educational center, open to all nations and serving as an international meeting place. The exceptional beauty of this general location gives impetus to the creation of this exciting project, unique in the world of education."

Meanwhile, Dr. Hutchins, Mr. Hirshhorn and Victor Gruen were in complete agreement regarding the project and the way in which it was to be realized. Michel was ready to have his "dream team" meet the Prince to expedite matters. That meeting never happened. Nevertheless, things appeared to be proceeding in the right direction. The cost of the project exceeded fifty million dollars at that time, although Joseph Hirschorn seemed undaunted in face of such numbers. Experts located an area in which an island large enough to house an entire university of the scale of Michel's dream university could be built.

At first Michel had a hard time acquiring hydrographic maps, but he eventually got them in Cannes. Surveys of the ocean floor were carried out, and with the hydrographic map plans in hand, plans could go forth for the site of the university. A statement of Mr. Hirschorn's guarantee of financial backing was presented. Everything seemed to be right on track. Now it was time for the Prince to respond and after a rather long hold up, he responded to Michel's proposal: "I must ask you to excuse the delay in answering your letter, due to the fact that I have been giving your project my most earnest attention. There are several points that remain obscure and which must be considered before going any farther."

The Prince wanted to know how Michel was planning to recruit students and how Mr. Hirschorn was planning to raise the fifty million dollars. Michel was taken totally unaware by a revelation that would put an abrupt and painful end to the project. According to the Prince, "the site of the proposed island would interfere with the new plans for reclaiming land from the sea and for embellishing the water-front; these plans are in process of realization." The big shock, however, was the following disclosure on the part of Prince Rainier: "...do you realize that, by tradition, education in the Principality is largely under the control of the Catholic Church, Monaco, being a Catholic country?" Unfortunately, such a revelation immediately slammed shut the door on the entire project.

This one statement clearly meant that the Prince wanted the university to be under the jurisdiction of Monaco, an idea which totally defeated the purpose of Michel's *supra-national university*. Needless to say, these revelations devastated Michel. His "dream team" had been ready to go: Hutchins — Hirschorn — Victor Gruen and Associates. As Michel explained to us, "It couldn't have been more ready." Everything, all the plans were there waiting to be realized; and then this last statement unraveled and undermined the entire project for all practical purposes. As Michel would later lament, the project had ended before it even began. After months and months of putting the project together, his vision and hope of creating an international university had literally floated out to sea. Michel had never been one to compromise in either his personal or professional life, and he was certainly not going to do so this time.

Curiously, five years later in 1963, Michel discovered in a Louella Parsons column in the Los Angeles *Herald-Examiner* that revealed the following information:

> The visit of Princess Grace and Prince Rainier is not entirely to be with her family and to attend civic and social affairs. The Prince has a real estate deal up his royal sleeve which is novel to say the least. Monaco, like many countries, is hurting for land. And Rainier is sponsoring a project which calls for an artificial island adjoining his principality to be built up as a lavish resort area. Tourist trade is one of the biggest sources of income for Monaco.

What a royal reversal indeed. This is exactly the plan Michel had proposed to the Prince. In fact, it was the same site which Rainier had turned down for the *supra-national university*. Shortly thereafter, the French press lauded the genius of Prince Rainier for coming up with such a brilliant idea. How the truth can be so easily veiled...

Upon his return to the south of France, Michel became painfully aware of the real intention of the Prince. At the Monte Carlo casino, Michel saw a mock up of the proposed casino and hotel which was to be built on land reclaimed from the sea. It sounded all too familiar. Michel had been taken, and he was totally demoralized. In spite of this turn of events, he would maintain his friendship with Princess Grace, who, according to Michel, was embarrassed by the whole incident. In 1979, shortly before the untimely passing of the Princess, the PR man for Prince Rainier asked Michel if he would write a proposal to establish an international language center which was to be under the Prince' sponsorship.

This international language school in the Principality of Monaco was to "serve, primarily, the personnel of multinational corporations and professional organizations scheduled for work assignments abroad." In a letter to the Prince, Michel expressed his feelings about the project:

> The international language school for multinational corporations and professional organizations is 'an idea whose time has come.' I am honored that you wish to be a part of it and that the Principality of Monaco will host this prestigious language center. I am determined with your help and support to make it a reality within the coming year.

With the death of Princess Grace, Michel did not pursue the project and it never came to fruition. That was not the end of Michel's determination, however. Afterwards, he attempted on several occasions to buy a Greek island, to no avail, however.

THE QUEST CONTINUED

"No school can be better than its teachers. But teachers themselves can become better if the school provides the teacher with proper assistance."
— Michel Thomas

Back in California, Michel would pursue his quest to create a "school to serve as an international/national ideal of what a school should be" and nothing less than that. The model school and the university were, from the very beginning, two separate and distinct entities in Michel's mind. It continued to be a driving force within him, a veritable passion, because in the depths of his very soul, Michel knew, even then, that he couldn't give up. He would so eloquently express why:

> "...the spirit of man is under the severest strain in all history, and... The inclination is to give up, surrender, to the master nearest at hand, the voice that is loudest, and the pressure that is most imminent."

In spite of the prior projects crumbling under his very eyes, Michel could not yield or surrender and be overpowered by the recent turn of events. He knew that he had an important mission to accomplish — to enlighten the world using a new and exceptionally effective method of teaching. Michel was fully aware at every level of his being that a superior educational system would lead the way to real freedom — to *freedom of mind*. His model school was to serve as the shining example for the entire world to emulate.

So Michel created the non-profit, *"Foundation for Better Learning,"* as a means to stimulate interest and obtain funding to establish a pilot school. Michel described it as an "independent Demonstration School, from the Nursery through high school, which will bring together under one roof the most successful and proven teaching techniques and curricular procedures." Any part of the school could be taken and adopted by any school and could also be observed by anyone. The goal was to provide a necessary general education, and not a trade specific education, for those who wanted to pursue a college degree or a profession from the start. The student body was to represent a cross section of children all across the board with different aptitudes and from a variety of social backgrounds.

This school was to be open to children from all socio-economic backgrounds, and was not to be an elitist school open only to children from affluent families. What Michel envisioned was a program in which average children, by the time they would graduate high school, would have at least the equivalent of a Bachelor of Arts degree. His school was to provide an accelerated program where students could have their B.A. before entering the traditional university. Also, the school was to include teacher training with a whole center devoted to teaching teachers how to teach. Although Michel conceived this idea fifty years ago, it is still applicable today, and even more so. Once again, Michel proved himself to be years ahead of his time. One person who was instrumental in the planning of the project from the very beginning was Mrs. Katherine Mann.

This Demonstration School was to become the National Center of Learning for Elementary and Secondary Education and serve as a brilliant showcase for the entire world to see. Michel's plan was extraordinarily well thought out. He was well aware of what improvement in teaching techniques and in curricula was needed to effect real changes in education. This model school provided the blueprint for doing so. The Demonstration School was to be set up to provide a faculty of first-rate teachers for every grade level using affordable programs which any public school could adopt. A Teachers' Assistance Program was to include the following:

1) A staff of experts specializing in a given field who would help the teachers prepare their curricula. A supplementary program of sophisticated audio-visual aids would be included in addition to educational assistants to take on administrative tasks that would get in the way of teachers' focusing on their real task — creative and effective teaching.

2) A guidance department would concentrate on achieving better and greater understanding between students and their parents, and between teachers and students.

3) Members of the community at large including industrialists, scientists, writers, doctors, artists, lawyers and the like…would participate on particular assignments where "they are better qualified than any available teacher."

4) A program which would regroup students around three kinds of activities: large group instruction, small group instruction and individual study. This would give students more opportunities to grow and to explore new concepts. The role of the teacher is to "create a relaxed atmosphere; to assure the student that his questions will be respected and understood."

5) A teacher internship program similar to those used for medical school interns would allow apprentice teachers to observe and work with master teachers.

6) A program of ongoing teacher workshops which would give the faculty an opportunity to further create and refine their own approaches, since most teachers simply do not have the time to "keep abreast of the accelerated developments in their own or general fields of knowledge."

Such an enterprising and phenomenal project began to spark the great interest and enthusiasm of a number of far-sighted and gifted individuals. Amidst this flurry of excitement, Michel would keep a cautious eye on things, for the memory of the prior attempts to create other model schools remained etched in his mind. Meanwhile, the list of exceptionally bright and forward thinking supporters who shared Michel's desire to revamp the educational system began joining forces with him. Dr. Goodled, the Dean of the Graduate School of Education at UCLA was the person with whom Michel worked for over a year and a half developing the plan and blueprint for the Demonstration School. They wanted to set up a model school in order to give a superior general education to random students with a goal to be repeatable in any community.

For this endeavor, Michel got full support from the Ford Foundation which was happy with the team of Michel, Mrs. Mann and Dr. Goodled. The Foundation wanted community backing so Michel and his associates got together twelve corporations which were represented on the Board. Michel wanted a national model school. Parents wanted a better local school and the Ford Foundation wanted a university as a sponsor. They choose the UCLA School of Education. For two years, Michel worked with Dean Goodled and his assistant to set it all up. All that was needed was a signature from the head of UCLA. Then, as circumstances would have it, the Dean received a rather large grant and left UCLA.

Ford then requested another sponsor. Mr. Ed Meede of the Ford Foundation recommended that Michel meet Marvin Adelson of the Systems Development Corporation, Education Division (a parallel corporation to the Rand Corporation) where Michel and his foundation would try to get this think tank company to take on what UCLA had let fall through the cracks. (The funding process had to follow a particular bureaucratic procedure, going first to an established university, then to the Ford Foundation which would, in turn, provide the funds to the school.) In time, Dr. Adelson turned out to be one of the more vocal and active supporters of Michel in this endeavor.

According to Michel, Marvin Adelson, is a brilliant scientist and original thinker in his own right, and like Michel, he believed that the educational system needed a major overhaul. In fact, he too, was interested in accelerated learning models. Michel said that when Marvin Adelson first heard about his method, Adelson had the same skeptical reaction as many others. How can that be? He figured that if Michel's method were so great, that it would have been greeted with open arms in the corridors of academia. His mind quickly changed once he had experienced Michel's tapes, and Michel told us that Adelson became a great supporter after that.

There was great irony in what was to transpire next in a bizarre twist of events. After working 18 months with Marvin Adelson at SDC to get the proposal and detailed blueprint together, Michel was delighted to learn that the Ford Foundation was very pleased and had given their approval for total funding of his school. All that was needed from the Ford Foundation was the signature of the President of SDC. At that time, a group of politicians contacted the President of SDC and asked him to set up a separate school that would be totally under the control of SDC. The result was that the President refused to sign off on the Ford Grant to fund Michel's school. Even worse, the

President of SDC told Michel: "I am free to take all of your thoughts. They are not protected. I am free to use whatever I want." Imagine blatantly telling Michel that his ideas were public domain and that he would steal his ideas and do anything he wanted with them. "It affected me deeply." said Michel of the entire episode. Was it just another case in which, in Michel's prior words, "the better mousetrap doesn't work" due to forces working against it?

Thus, after four years and two sponsors with funds from the venerable Ford Foundation, nothing happened. Absolutely nothing. "I was totally disillusioned by the whole thing." Michel sadly recounted. According to Michel, Marvin Adelson, a top executive at SDC, felt the same way, so much so that he resigned his position as a result of the actions of the President of the corporation and joined Michel's Foundation. Michel said that Adelson was eventually offered an important professorship in the Architecture and Urban Studies Department at UCLA where he spent over twenty years. Michel, of course, was both grateful to and respectful of Mr. Adelson for standing up for his personal conviction in the face of unethical actions.

It seemed that each time Michel was on the verge of signing a deal to bring his vision of a model school into a feasible and tangible reality, the floor would crumble rather unexpectedly under his feet. Even with the support of so many creative and innovative thinkers in their respective fields, educational institutions, nevertheless, rejected Michel's ideas for the model school. Each time some flimsy excuse or pretext would be presented which stonewalled further action in the execution of the project.

Were these successive rejections a sign that Michel was totally off track with his brilliant plan, or was it simply that all of the elements to realize the dream were not yet in place, or was it that he was just too far ahead of the times? We believe it to be the latter. We also believe that the time has now come. When we initially wrote this book, fourteen years after this last incident, Michel had begun to speak publicly in interviews about what he considered to be the external aspects of his method. Moreover, he had graciously, willingly and enthusiastically revealed to us his method in its full glory. We knew that the time had come for the educational establishment worldwide to recognize his genius. Perhaps the recent and ongoing events of the last few years which have cast a dark cloud over the nations of the world will somehow awaken the pundits at large and the reluctant members of the academic community to a new way of "seeing" and understanding what needs to be done in order to ensure the safe, healthy and prosperous continuity of life as we know it. We can only pray that the wisdom be forthcoming to them sooner rather than later.

Chapter Eleven

MICHEL THOMAS' TEACHING TRIUMPHS: THE RULE RATHER THAN THE EXCEPTION

Over the course of his almost sixty years of teaching, a myriad of students of all ages from different walks of life have had the privilege of experiencing Michel's magic firsthand by learning a foreign language from the *Master Teacher* himself, either in a one-on-one setting, or as part of a group. Each and every time, with no exception, the students have reacted in a glowing manner, expressing immense gratitude to this warm and charming gentleman whose passion for learning took hold of them as well, and literally transformed the very core of their being.

During their time with Michel, his students developed a new sense of inner tranquility about their ability to communicate in another language. Yes, Michel would reawaken their *innate drive for learning,* freeing minds one person at a time. In so doing, he would reveal the true joys which we are meant to experience as living beings on every level. He would make learning totally effortless, effective, easy and exciting. As we have seen in Chapter Six, Michel literally would lighten the mind/body interaction by eliminating all *tension*. During this time, he would be planting seeds of understanding and assurance which blossomed into trees of knowledge and self-confidence. He would transform the fear of language learning into a permanent resource of excellent communication skills, so necessary in an interconnected world that is shrinking more each day. Furthermore, Michel would imbue his students, and all those who crossed his path for that matter, with a new perspective on the fragility and preciousness of life. He instilled within everyone, a joy for life in a world where he believed there were dark forces at work, ready to extinguish at any moment, the light within each of us — each individual light that he saw as our only hope for the future.

There are so many amazing stories, too numerous to tell in the pages of this book. We will highlight, however, some additional experiences and anecdotes not previously mentioned in earlier chapters; and we will touch upon earlier ones already referenced, related by individuals and groups which spanned Michel's five plus decades of enlightening minds with his teaching brilliance.

First, however, a book on Michel's method would not be complete without mentioning the ongoing accolades which followed Michel like his shadow, as a supportive companion throughout his illustrious years of teaching. Needless to say, Michel's prowess and success stories have intrigued many and, consequently, have made their way onto the scene of the international press. Among the noteworthy publications in which stories or mentions of Michel have appeared are the following: *Business Life*, USA *Today, The* LA *Times, Daily News Business, Forbes, The* New York *Post, The Daily News,* Manhattan *Inc., Gannett Westchester Newspapers, The Robb Report* (a magazine for connoisseurs), *Avenue Magazine, In Style Magazine, People Magazine*, United *Teacher - Los Angeles (*a publication of the Teachers Union), *The Big Valley* (The San Fernando Valley Magazine), *Diversion* (a leisure magazine for physicians), *The International Herald Tribune, The Guardian* (Great Britain), *The* London *Times* (Great Britain), *The Conde Nast Traveller* (British edition), *The Financial Times* (Great Britain), *The Daily Telegraph* (Great Britain), *Business Life Magazine of British Airways, Manager Magazin* (Germany), *Der Spiegel (Germany), The* Calgary *Herald* (Canada), *The* Lethbridge *Herald* (Canada) and *The* San Juan *Star* (Puerto Rico). At the end of this chapter we have included endorsements from the press of Michel and his method.

The laurels do not end in the above publications. In 1982, *La Société d'Encouragement au Progrès* under the guidance of the *Académie Française* had Raoul Aglion, *Ministre Plénipotentiare*, present Michel Thomas with the Gold Medal for outstanding achievement in education and teaching and as a fighter for freedom:

> ... His unorthodox method has gained admiration from scholars as well as businessmen and artists, and his system has gained recognition all over the world. Thus for Michel Thomas' service to his country and Allied Forces in the time of war, and for his great contribution in the field of

foreign language studies, the *Société d'Encouragement au Progrès* is bestowing upon him its highest award.

This is quite a distinguished honor in itself, and yet there are still many more triumphs with students from around the globe.

SUCCESS AGAINST ALL ODDS

Celebrities and dignitaries alike entered Michel's magical world of learning, from the hills of Hollywood, to the boardrooms of major corporations around the globe to the palace of Monaco. And even more appreciable is the fact that Michel had spread his wisdom in places of less public renown, where his impact was so much more significant in the grand scheme of things: at inner city schools in which underprivileged children were blessed by both Michel, the caring man of conviction, and Michel, the revolutionary teacher. Practically every single course Michel had ever taught over the years has been received with great enthusiasm, gratitude and often surprise at the extraordinary results.

INNER CITY MIRACLE

We previously mentioned one outstanding example of Michel's success when we discussed the experimental class which he conducted at the George Washington Carver Junior High School for ten days in Los Angeles in April of 1969. Whenever Michel talked to us about his success with the youngsters at this school, his eyes would light up. As Michel related to us, he was assigned to teach French to a group of twenty-four recalcitrant eighth grade students who were described as "below average in basic skills development including work habits, listening skills and reading skills and who had generally poor standard English skills." They were also described as having average intelligence.

Many of the students also had disciplinary problems and lacked the self-discipline necessary for the learning process to take hold. As though the situation were not challenging enough as it presented itself, there was so much more that lay ahead.

Just before Michel's arrival, the school had been shut down due to sit-ins and a riot which ended up destroying much of the school. According to the Principal at the time, Andrew Anderson, these events then triggered a walk out "due to the unreasonable working conditions at the school. The protests seemed to rally around the fact that our children were getting a substandard, irrelevant education."

Given this scenario as a backdrop, it was all the more quite a daring move in itself to walk into such a hostile environment, let alone teach these so-called militant, inner city youngsters as they were described. In a letter Principal Anderson stated that they wanted to see "whether Mr. Thomas could take an irrelevant subject, French, and make it relevant, for one of the criticisms of the militant community is that what we teach is irrelevant to black youth." Of course, the more the challenge, the more at ease Michel, the *Venge* personality type, found himself to prove others wrong. So he took them up on it. "Just give me a class on Monday morning." he said. Even to the end, Michel's battle cry continued to be: "I am always ready to be challenged." This was again the reaction of a *Venge* personality type.

Much of the school had been smashed to bits and usable classrooms were doubling as storage rooms for typewriters and other equipment. "It was wild." said Michel. In fact, J. Michael Fay, the Instructional Coordinator at the time, described the situation as follows: "There was hostility, uproar, restlessness, lack of attention and the usual ruckus — in a school which had recently undergone an explosive riot." Michel found himself in a storage room *cum* classroom which was far from typical, and that was fine with him nevertheless. There was no desk for the instructor [Michel] and he never used a desk as a pulpit or prop anyway.

In any case, Michel immediately addressed the issue of relevancy by asking the students if they knew where French was spoken. One of them responded by saying: "Yes. French is spoken in London." Michel asked: "Why in London?" and the student replied, "Because London is in Paris." Michel made no attempt to correct the student and went on to explain that French was an important language in certain parts of Africa. By reacting in this way, Michel immediately accomplished two things. First he established the way in which learning French would be relevant to these students. This might motivate them to learn, now that they could see the connection to their own lives. Second, Michel told us that this approach gave the students an immediate experience of having accomplished something.

At first, the atmosphere remained rather wild and helter-skelter, with students popping in and out of the classroom all the time. Of course, Michel handled the situation by getting the students involved from the start. He informed those who kept walking in that they had to sit and participate, and when they realized that they were not getting support from the other students, they left. That penetrating *Michel look* probably took over and with that critical eye contact with each student, relative order was established out of seeming chaos. Once again, Michel was well on his way to establishing a sense of *esprit de classe* within the group, although not yet entirely. To the amazement of all, during the rest of the week, more and more students wanted to visit "that class" and teachers wanted to participate by observing the *Master Teacher* at work.

Michel, the incredible calibrator and *difference* person that he was, immediately noticed in the first few hours that there appeared to be three distinctive types of students. Knowing this, he dealt with each of them accordingly. The first were the timid or shy ones who wanted to blend into the woodwork or hide behind other students. It was this first group upon which Michel focused his attention early on and quite successfully for that matter. This immediately attracted the attention of more and more of the second group which consisted of the indifferent students who were not participating or else were fidgety.

To no surprise of ours, Michel managed to pull them into the unifying energy of the class by the end of the first day. The third group included the students who were outright hostile and rebellious to the point of antagonism. Any verbal exchange with these students could have meant trouble, so the street-smart and worldly Michel, wisely ignored them for a while. Consequently, by the end of the day, students in the third group were fewer in number. It is significant to note that Michel, true to his method, did not resort to any punishment or scolding of the students, not even with those in the third group.

In spite of this rather unusual and somewhat belligerent situation, Michel characteristically held his ground and eventually succeeded in winning over the youngsters. At the end of the first day, with his usual air of confidence, Michel, informed the class about his observations, that some students were there to learn, and that others simply couldn't care less about learning. From his perspective of a *Venge*, for whom fairness is an issue, Michel also told them that "it is unfair that those who want to learn should be disturbed and bothered by those who do not." He told the class that those who did not want to learn did not have to stay. Moreover, the students who did not want to learn did not have to come back to continue the next morning. "Those who don't want to learn can leave right now." Michel told them.

Those who wanted to stay and learn were asked to raise their hands, and every single hand went up and no one walked out. "I will not ask you again," Michel said. "I will know anyone who doesn't want to stay and I will throw you out!" At one point after the second day, Michel instituted only one sanction: a ten minute time out for disruptive behavior.

Having now laid out the ground rules, Michel could focus on real teaching. Over time, the result was an overwhelming success. The students expressed a genuine desire to stay in class and during a recess when Michel was in the faculty room talking to other teachers, a student knocked on the door to say: "Please, Mr. Thomas. We are waiting." Even though disruptions had dropped off considerably, Michel noticed that some of the students still had a hard time focusing and paying attention to him and to the other students. This time he used another trick from his magic box, and created a kind of question and answer game in which he would ask why the students did not know what the other student had said in French. The typical response would be, "I don't know." Eventually Michel got the entire class to admit that it was because they had not been paying attention. From that point on, Michel had a hard time picking out the students who were not listening.

Another interesting anecdote relates to Michel's walking out. At one point, on the third day he decided to walk out of the class as a result of very minor noise interference. This was not meant to be a disciplinary move on his part. "I am leaving." he said, and went to the teacher's lounge. Fifteen minutes had gone by and still no sign of the students. Michel began to wonder if he had made a mistake this time, and then a delegation of several students sent by the class arrived at the teacher's lounge to inform him that by unanimous decision, the whole class had voted to beg him to come back to teach. They finally convinced him to go back under certain conditions and he did. In fact, they also begged the principal to convince him not to go. What a coup! When Michel returned to the room, it was totally transformed. He recalled to us that after that point you could hear a pin drop. There was one thing that still bothered him, however. It was the sound of the students chewing bubble gum and even that ceased once he told them, "No bubble gum."

Once again, the brilliant Master Teacher taught his students a lesson — this time a lesson on the importance of taking responsibility for one's behavior and of thinking about one's fellow students. Michel not only taught French to a group of students who were considered by all unlikely to succeed, he also instilled within them a sense of pride and accomplishment as well as a sense of self-discipline and self-confidence. We know all too well the significance of developing self-confidence, particularly in young people, who can be so influenced by their peers, for better or for worse. Rather impressive results for Michel, to say the least, considering the rather adverse conditions in which he began the entire process.

The Instructional Coordinator, J. Michael Fay, noticed some "startling changes" as a result of Michel's method which he listed in a personal letter to Michel:

1) The students as a group became highly motivated to learn what was considered an irrelevant subject to them.

2) The students achieved some degree of success in speaking French, and none seemed frustrated by your approach.

3) Attendance was remarkable as was interest on the part of students not in your class.

4) Teachers of these students remarked that students who were not responding in their class were highly motivated in yours.

5) Attention span of these students amazed me, especially with the all day session.

6) Students unanimously expressed a desire to continue the class after its scheduled conclusion.

Was this overwhelming success a result of Michel's charisma or a result of his method? Mr. Anderson, the school principal expressed his belief that it was the latter. He was so convinced by Michel's success and brilliance that he later wrote to the Ford Foundation to request support for teaching Michel's method to the faculty of his school. He described the behavioral outcomes of Michel's teaching as follows:

1) Attendance has been perfect since the second day.

2) Mr. Thomas has had the complete attention of the group and can use the threat of elimination from the class for ten minutes as punishment.

3) A score of teachers who have had these children in their classes have come in to observe, and have found it hard to believe that they are the same children.

4) Though their English is non-standard, their French accent is superb.

5) Though the class was scheduled for just one week, the students have on their own unanimously voted to have Mr. Thomas return for a second week, which we arranged due to their high motivation.

6) The reputation of this class has spread throughout the school, and other pupils, though skeptical, want very much to be a part of it.

7) Teachers have indicated they wish to have Mr. Thomas share his techniques.

The above results are all the more astonishing given the milieu in which Michel was asked to perform his magic.

Meanwhile, the students in the class made their own insightful comments. They were as follows:

"He understands us." — "He is patient."— "He knows how to teach."

"He didn't yell at us." — "He makes us feel good when we do something right."

These are very revelatory comments in themselves, let alone coming from a group of what were initially uncontrollable and militant students with seemingly no desire to learn. Certainly teachers from the traditional educational system would do well to take heed of Michel's comportment and teaching method. J. Michael Fay wrote the following to Michel: "I would state without reservation that you brought about a positive change in this group of students, and I would agree with the student who said you really know how to teach... Furthermore, we appreciate the amount of time you spent at Carver and how you showed us what can be done."

Yes, Michel indeed showed what could be done and more. They asked him to stay on longer and help with other courses. This experience at the George Washington Carver Junior High School serves as a shining example of Michel's teaching genius. His method belongs in a category of its own, where nothing else even comes close. Yes, he also gave the African-American leaders what they wanted — relevancy of an irrelevant subject and much more than they could have ever dreamed possible. Everyone loved Michel so much that he stayed on for an additional five days, and then five more days because his teaching spilled over into other subjects.

Michel completely transformed these students. And he did so by using his incomparable method. Here at an inner city school in Watts, he found himself face to face with some students who absolutely did not even want to learn. Yet, as he always pointed out, even people who don't want to learn have the *innate drive for learning*. He knew that all he needed to do was to reawaken it. In keeping with his learning process, individual progress of the students occurred with support from the group. Michel established an *esprit de classe* in what he described as probably one of the most hostile environments any teacher would have to endure.

Michel once again took complete responsibility for learning and remembering. He used all the classic pieces of his method, i.e., no note taking, no mental homework of any kind, etc. In spite of the aggressive nature of the students, Michel did not resort to *move away from* strategies of punishment, but rather turned to his usual *move toward* approach of incentive based learning. He masterfully created a threat-free and a *tension*-free environment. He sought *understanding* from his students and never memorization. And the list goes on.

Of course, Michel with his usual calm and gentle manner, succeeded once again in reawakening their *innate drive for learning*; and in so doing, he triggered a joy for living in the children as well, by helping to transform these irresponsible, undisciplined, unruly, disrespectful, unteachable rebels into responsible, self-disciplined, respectful, teachable youngsters who wanted to learn even more. He taught them the importance of taking personal responsibility for one's actions and of respecting oneself as well as others. The students learned how to control their desires for immediate gratification that disregarded the needs and desires of their fellow students. Last but certainly not least, he instilled within them the hope for a better life and a brighter future.

ANOTHER L.A. MIRACLE

As we discussed in the Method Chapter, another remarkable success story was Michel's teaching a fourth grade class of thirty-four Spanish-speaking children at a school in Los Angeles. With the administrative support of the school's principal and the help of a bilingual aide, Michel once again achieved the almost impossible. He succeeded in teaching these children how to speak, read and write English in a block of six weeks, a prime example of his concept of *block teaching*.

MICHEL'S VIEW OF BILINGUAL EDUCATION

The experience at the above school touched upon an issue which had always annoyed Michel — that of bilingual education. However, we will emphasize first that Michel found himself in yet another unusual environment in which he came through with flying colors once again. Before his arrival, the principal, Mrs. Kasza, had already implemented a series of State, Federal and local school district programs to deal with the special educational needs of the students. Among these was a program to teach English-speaking teachers the Spanish language so that they could teach and interact more easily in the context of a bilingual environment. From the very onset, Principal Kasza had given Michel her whole-hearted support. In the Curriculum Product Review she stated: "No one program has generated as much enthusiasm as Thomas. By word of mouth, the news of his…intensive learning program traveled fast... We have a crisis in our schools right now, and the need for bilingual education is great."

Alyce Burns, a gifted teacher who participated in Michel's program had this to say: "…The successful learning experience prompted us to ask what such strategies could accomplish in our classrooms. If we, as adults, with many years' collections of faulty attitudes and preconceptions about learning could learn to speak Spanish in a ten day group course, what could happen to young, eager learners?"

Precisely. Imagine what could occur in our educational system around the globe if students and teachers were able to rekindle that *innate desire for learning*? Why is it that so few educators have come to this very same realization?

Michel managed to perform a wonderful miracle with these Hispanic children. In just a matter of a few weeks these children were able to read in both Spanish and in English, and read the encyclopedia at the public library! The tragedy of the story is that because of the requirement for bilingual education at that time in the United States, Michel was unable to get into the school district, despite his dramatic demonstration of how his method actually got results. In spite of rave reviews from the Principal of the school and great support from other school officials, parents and students, Michel could never realize his great desire.

His disillusionment from this last rebuff finally took a toll on Michel:

> After my experience with the children, and the endorsements and the articles I had written, I

really expected to have calls from the educational department and from the school system. I still believed in a better mousetrap. It was the last time that I believed in it. After that I gave up on it.

This was truly a sad commentary on the terrible state of the system overall. This episode marked a heartbreaking turning point for Michel. He would never again try in the United States to change the system after this episode. Now, more than thirty years later, change in the system has yet to occur.

The reason that the doors closed shut for Michel in the States just then was because of a certain agenda that had begun to make its mark in education. Bilingual education was a strong political issue at one time and is obviously still an issue today because not only was it introduced as a long-awaited panacea, it was also imposed by Federal law. What this meant was that children should be taught in their own native language, including all the undocumented aliens. Michel expressed his frustration and his thoughts about bilingualism as follows: "Every aspect of bilingual education is an expression of insanity. It doesn't work. It didn't work. It wouldn't work and it couldn't work at any time."

He continued to explain to us that the insanity of bilingualism began by making it federal law in America. The issue was initially ignited in California, when a Chinese family in San Francisco sued the school district because they felt that their child, who didn't know English, could not get a proper education. The parents felt that their child should be taught in their native tongue. Michel was against bilingual education then, and he was still against it just months before his passing, when he sadly declared to us:

> What that means is that if children don't know English or enough English to be taught in school, they should be taught in their own language. Where are we? As if we didn't already have enough problems in our educational system, we have to have this!

Michel described how bilingual education had invited and created a series of organizations with vested interests. A new political agenda had taken shape at that time. However, according to Michel, there was one man in Silicon Valley who had the courage to speak out and to stand up against bilingual education. He exemplified Michel's belief in the power of the individual. That one man succeeded in arousing enough interest to pass new legislation that would abolish bilingual education. It greatly saddened Michel to think that the traditional system still provided no solutions: "They still don't know what they are going to do, but at least they don't have to have bilingual education." The question still remains as to what we can do now. The answer is to adopt Michel's approach. We address the concept of bilingual education in our follow-up book.

In any case, no change has yet to occur and the tragedy is two-fold. First, no real change can occur when the decision makers refuse to accept or even consider other points of view which will provide real solutions. Second, Michel had the method, the wisdom and the ongoing track record which has the potential to change our educational system and, thus, the world itself. Now is the time to adopt the "better mousetrap."

THE SAN JUAN INTERNATIONAL CONFERENCE

Michel's successes were not limited to America. In fact, Michel proved the brilliance and effectiveness of his method, this time, with the use of his tapes during the Seventh Annual International Bilingual Bicultural Education Conference in San Juan, Puerto Rico in 1978. Prior to the opening of the Conference, Michel conducted workshops for two groups of volunteer students over a period of two weeks. One group was to learn English and the other Spanish. During this time, staff members of the Department of Education of Puerto Rico, which had requested and arranged the live demonstration, were in attendance to observe Michel's learning process. As usual, the results were staggering. By the time the learning sessions were to be over, Michel had promised two outcomes for the learner:

1) Within one week participants would be able to communicate in a second language using the most commonly used verb tenses in speaking, reading and writing.

2) Within two weeks participants would know and be able to use the entire structure of the target language in speaking, reading and writing, and would have acquired a solid foundation in the language that permits continued growth in fluency and vocabulary.

Michel also promised to meet three overall objectives:

1) To demonstrate in a live, learning situation that language proficiency can be acquired in a matter of days.

2) To demonstrate that rapid and effective language acquisition is primarily a function of the instructional methods used.

3) To show that a method exists where rapid language acquisition is possible, and that the effectiveness of this method can be demonstrated in a very short time and immediately assessed.

Amidst an atmosphere of skeptical observers, Michel fulfilled his promises by meeting all of the above objectives and literally took their breath away. Much to the dismay of the doubters, Michel proved them all wrong when he showed them all how it could be done — how everyone at the Conference would be able to speak to his students in the target language. The students, of course, were elated with the results. The proof was there for all to witness at the Conference. At one table were Conference attendees who began speaking English with the one group of students who did not know a single word of English before the Conference.

One week later, this same group was able to communicate comfortably in English. The other group, students who did not know a word of Spanish just one week before the Conference, was able to speak Spanish with other people at the Conference. Imagine two groups of students with no prior knowledge of the target language in question, and who had been personally selected by the Puerto Rican Government, not by Michel, to participate in the language course. All came through with glorious results, excited, thrilled and motivated to learn more as they realized the significance of their accomplishment.

These were indeed dramatic results brought to light and proven in the context of an international conference. What more could one ask as proof of the remarkable merits of Michel's method? Michel assumed that given such a dazzling outcome, that something on a larger scale might have come through. Perhaps he could bring his method into the school system, but to his dismay, nothing ever happened. "Did it lead to something? No! And I was very disillusioned." he exclaimed to us with sheer disgust and disappointment. Once again, some of the more hopeful prospects and promises to help Michel to build a school simply vanished into thin air, never to be seen or heard from again.

AIR CANADA

We have already made reference to Michel's teaching courses to Air Canada employees in Chapter Six, in the context of establishing *esprit de classe*, so we will briefly mention it here as yet another example of the *Master Teacher*'s artistry at work. Remember that Air Canada, which is part of the Canadian Government, had asked Michel to set up and teach French courses to their executives. They sent as an observer, Dr. David S. Abbey, the Coordinator of Research and Studies from the Ontario Institute for Studies in Education to attend and also to write an evaluation. Dr. Abbey said the following about Michel's course in a written report: "What is striking to note are the changes in the attitudes of the students at the start of the course to the end."

On the first night, when Michel began to lay out his initial frames about his learning process, the reaction was one of skepticism. For example, he told the students that if they made a mistake, it was his problem, not theirs. Michel's remark triggered a roar of laughter in the class and looks of incredulity. A chosen observer remarked that "by the fifth day participants were inquiring actively into the learning sequences — the strategy being used by one another and by Thomas." Quite a turnaround!

Michel was described as "a dynamic, dedicated teacher. He is also a master at handling individual learning problems." Also, as mentioned in an earlier chapter, a beautiful air of *esprit de classe* permeated the entire room. As a result, "the motivation to learn was intense. One wished to learn, and to see one's colleagues learn." Interestingly, the sense of *esprit de classe* had taken such intense hold of the group that the students at first did not even want the outside observer to come into the room. He was finally accepted by the others, "...because he really digs his method…"

The outside observer had results which were just as astounding as those of the students in the group, and he made this observation of the group: "By Friday evening it appeared that most (say 75%) of the group felt a sense of wonder and pleasure at being able to translate French poetry, technical material and journals." Once again, Michel successfully created a nurturing sense of *esprit de classe* among a group of students who did not know each other initially. By the end of the first week, they had developed into a cohesive unit, fostering an *esprit de joie* which they brought back to their respective locations throughout Canada. They even maintained friendships long after the course had ended.

PRIVATES AND OFFICERS SIDE BY SIDE

One of the more fascinating aspects of Michel's method was his ability to break down barriers among students and to create an *esprit de classe*. In the case we are describing here, he single-handedly managed to break down imposed hierarchal barriers created in the military. In 1973, the Department of the Army at the well-known Presidio in Monterey, California called on Michel to teach a class of soldiers French using his tapes in the first phase, and then to learn with several of Michel's teachers for the second phase. Michel had taught the teachers to give the course because the Army insisted on keeping Michel away from the class. They did not want his presence to affect the outcome.

On the first day Michel arrived, he almost immediately left when he noticed that there were no armchairs in the room where the course was to be given. He then informed them, "No armchairs, no course!" So the Army ended up renting armchairs, flowers, and pictures for the wall. At least the rentals made it a comfortable room. As we have discussed in the Method Chapter, Michel was quite particular about the setting and ambiance of the room. That wasn't enough for Michel. Even with the rented furniture and accessories, somehow things were still not right. Why? It was because the soldiers were still wearing their uniforms during the learning sessions.

Michel had to go speak to the administration and get permission from the managers of the Monterey School to allow civilian dress in the class. "They will not be taught in uniforms!" Michel insisted. The initial response was that such a request was impossible to grant, after all, "This is the Army. This is absolutely impossible," to which Michel retorted: "If you cannot do it, then I will not have the course!" Remember he was not actually teaching it. Needless to say, Michel won the argument hands down in the end. He insisted that every student come in civilian clothes. After all, how could he create a *tension*-free atmosphere with uniforms that served as a constant reminder to the soldiers of their respective positions within the army hierarchy? Michel was so proud of the fact that here together were a captain, a colonel and a sergeant mingled in with privates.

The interesting phenomenon about this group was that both officers and privates alike were sitting side by side listening to Michel's tapes at that time and learning French. The entire room was enveloped by a feeling of oneness, that which is created by the *esprit de classe*. In this room there was no chain of command visible on any level. All the participants were equals, with no distinction based on rank or position, at least not in this room. Whenever Michel would recall how well the young private and the colonel worked together, it brought a smile to his face. It was obvious that every student was in the "moment," learning with great excitement, feeling energized and confident, ready to learn more. All of this transpired without Michel in the room because he was not allowed to teach. The whole course was conducted without Michel, using only his tapes.

As usual, the course was a complete and utter success. Unfortunately, once the class was over, the results were classified and were never released after that. Michel told us that his friend, Marvin Adelson, had tried to get the results and was told that they were indeed classified. However, the memory of the colonel seated next to the young private was forever engraved in Michel's mind. It just goes to show you how Michel had worked wonders even with the US Army. Michel's *esprit de classe* again magically transformed a group of separate and hierarchal individuals of distinct parts into the oneness of a unified whole. Imagine, too, eliminating the official uniform code, always *de rigueur* in the military; and at the Presidio to boot. All the students after only one week of French were already unanimously ebullient in their reaction to their accomplishments. Bravo Michel!

SAN FERNANDO VALLEY STATE COLLEGE

Success shined its spotlight on Michel again after teaching French to a group at the San Fernando Valley State College (which is now California State University, Northridge). The students, none of whom had had any formal instruction in French, included three faculty members, fifteen undergraduates and two individuals who had nothing to do with the college. It goes without saying that the outcome was amazing. One of the students in the course, Howard A. Fleming, Professor of History and Associate Dean, School of Letters and Sciences wrote soon afterwards: "The results were astonishing to me, for frankly I had been highly skeptical of the claims made by Mr. Thomas. In terms of vocabulary and oral and written proficiency, I would rate the results as about the equivalent of the first year of college French... To say the least, I remain enthusiastic about Mr. Thomas' highly unusual course."

Yet another skeptic who turned into a Michel Thomas believer was added to the ever growing list of supporters and admirers.

MICHEL'S METHOD FINDS A HOME IN CANADIAN HOUSES OF LEARNING

Michel taught his courses with his usual panache at three major universities in Alberta: The University of Calgary, the

University of Alberta and the University of Lethbridge. The Canadian government paid for about half the cost under its bilingual program. The reactions of the students were incredible. Hayden Roberts, a Professor at the University of Alberta said: "It has helped me an enormous amount. I feel really quite confident for an upcoming trip to France." A librarian who took one of the courses said: "And it doesn't seem to be as exhausting as you expect it to be. I feel that I'm learning quite fast." Even students who initially were not motivated "became motivated due to the excitement of learning," explained Michel. Rob Karthaus, a senior officer in charge of bilingual education at the post-secondary level, said in an interview: "His course so far seems to have had more success, in fact, than the federal government has had with its immersion program for civil servants."

Michel, by the way, did not like to use the word "immersion" because it has been so "abused." An official with the Department of Advanced Education said of Michel's courses: "extremely impressive." It is also impressive that a bilingual country such as Canada rejected traditional teaching methods and happily embraced Michel's unorthodox method into their own places of learning — into their universities. In spite of the tremendous publicity generated by the success of his course on the university level, nothing came of Michel's accomplishments. "In the big picture, it shows what I have tried to do all these years and how it always led to nothing," Michel declared to us with a look of great frustration and sadness.

THE UNIVERSITY OF PITTSBURGH

Michel found the President of the University of Pittsburgh, Wesley Posvar, to be a great advocate of his method. At one time they offered a series of four day seminars in German, French and Spanish which were taught on campus. Mr. Posvar wrote the following about Michel's teaching in a letter to the Chancellor at UCLA: "This experience is exciting, effective and captivating, and relies not only on his personal talent, but a remarkable architecture of special sequences...which make learning and comprehension far easier than any other method I have encountered... In two weeks, one can accomplish conversational and simple reading proficiency, equivalent to well beyond one year and up to two years of regular college class attendance."

And at the University of Pittsburgh, there was not a large enough student body to sustain the classes over time. Hopes for integration of Michel's method into the university fell to the wayside. The language department also intervened and denigrated Michel's method in the university paper, thus, revealing their total ignorance of it. A certain faculty member came to the conclusion that the results Michel obtained with his students are 1) impossible, 2) unprovable and 3) a menace to the lay public. Imagine! We would rather say that Michel's method is, instead, a menace to our current *dis-educational system*™. Of course, the faculty letter infuriated Michel. He, therefore, refuted their fallacious arguments one by one in a vitriolic letter that was determined to be "entirely too long and unmanageable for our [the paper's] format" to publish.

SUCCESS IN LOS ANGELES SCHOOL DISTRICTS

In the 1960's Michel had achieved such amazing results in all of the Los Angeles schools in which he taught his courses, that his successes caught the attention of the Office of the Los Angeles Superintendent of Schools. Vincent Bello, a Consultant for Inter-group Relations at that time, had the opportunity to attend some of Michel's workshops and personally witnessed the phenomenal results. Of this experience he writes: "...the motivation, and the feeling for the culture — Mexican American and Chicano — on the part of the teachers was the most impressive experience in education that I have ever experienced. The most amazing thing was that this was all accomplished within six days or Phase I." This consultant was so impressed, that in a letter to the Department of Education for California in Sacramento, he formally requested the following: "State Department approval regarding Article 3.3 be granted" to the Michel Thomas Language Institute.

This was quite a powerful endorsement of Michel and his method. Approval meant college approval and college credits for teachers who took Michel's courses. Mr. Bello went on to say: "If districts ascertain that the learning of a language is their solution (or one of them) to relating to minority and ethnically different students, then I can think of no more complete process for learning the language and beginning the acquisition of cultural feeling and understanding, and eventually, acceptance."

Of interest, is the fact that Mr. Bello received an immediate and positive response from the Department of Education within two days. In it, they confirmed that Michel's courses met the necessary criteria and the guidelines outlined. And the State granted:

> ...the approval of the Department for use of the Institute's courses to meet the requirements of Section13344 when 1) the language studied by a teacher or other member of school staff is one used by a substantial number of students and their families in that attendance area and 2) such language training is a part of the school district's program plan for in service work under provisions of Section 13344.

Frederic R. Gunsky wrote on behalf of the State that it was "a pleasure to learn of this exemplary approach to teaching language and culture, and to assist in encouraging its use by school personnel." As a result of this prestigious endorsement, Michel's courses were then approved by some colleges in California. Still nothing came of this either.

HUGHES AIRCRAFT COMPANY

Thanks to Katherine Mann, a friend of Michel's, the Hughes Aircraft Company in California had the privilege of going through his French language course with the usual exciting results. This was an interesting success story because it also included cultural training. The Educational Relations Administrator for the company, M. W. Welds, expressed in a letter to Mrs. Mann their indebtedness to her for having acquainted them "with Michel Thomas and his unusual competency in language teaching." At that time, in the late sixties, many employees of the company were to be living abroad and needed to learn French.

Mr. Welds explained in his letter that "his method of totally involving his students in the French culture and language...offers dramatic contrast to the usual classroom learning with its limited retention due to the diluting effect of living in an English speaking environment while learning French...comparing cost versus effectiveness it appears that the Thomas basic course of French language instruction is superior..." They were so very pleased with his "outstanding" results and were thrilled by the sense of self-confidence instilled in their employees as a result of taking Michel's course: "...a confident employee is likely to be a happier employee and this helps the company achieve its project goals." This was quite a powerful endorsement of the *Master Teacher*.

THE RAND CORPORATION

A very successful experiment in intensive French was conducted by the Rand Corporation which again produced amazing outcomes. The Rand Corporation selected a student at random, one with no prior knowledge of the French language to take Michel's course over a weekend. They wanted to see what could be achieved. After just two days with Michel, the student demonstrated her newly acquired skills which were described in a letter from the Rand Corporation to him as follows:

1) an accurate and unhesitating knowledge of all tense forms, including the subjunctive of all the regular French verbs

2) a similar knowledge of a number of the more important irregular verbs

3) a knowledge of compound sentence structure...

4) an appreciation of several important idiomatic phrases

5) a plausible accent naturally tinged by her background in Spanish

The evaluation was outstanding. In the same letter, Michel was described as "an extremely competent and persuasive teacher of conversational French" and the writer recommended that "promulgation of [Michel's] techniques together with a further evaluation of them is very much in order." As a result of this successful experiment, an acquaintance of Michel's, Dr. Stephen S. Friedman, attempted to get the government to pursue the experiment. Much to Michel's dismay, there was no positive outcome.

"FIRST BILINGUAL STAFF WEST OF THE BRONX"

The above headline appeared in *Action*, a publication of the California Teachers Association (known as CTA), to describe an unusual two week intensive course given by Michel to its staff. The program was arranged by the Los Angeles Urban Project, a jointly sponsored program of NEA (National Education Association), CTA and United Teachers Los Angeles (UTLA). The purpose of the Urban Project was "to help teachers and staff make a difference in multi-cultural urban environments." Its director, J. Michael Fay, along with several members of the local association, decided to send staff members through a Spanish language program which would enable them to use Spanish "in the field." This is the same J. Michael Fay who had met Michel while he was Instructional Coordinator at the George Washington Carver High School in Watts. This was the same school where Michel had taught that memorable French course to the group of what he described as "militant youngsters."

Michel shined brilliantly again, teaching his crash course in Spanish with the Urban Project and the staff was thrilled with the results. "Michel is a genius. Not only have we learned how to speak Spanish in such a short time, but we have been learning the customs, ways of making the students and parents feel welcome." Another said: "It makes it easier for all of us to relate to one another." As we have already mentioned, Michel believed that teachers should be bicultural and bilingual so that they can communicate with parents and get a better understanding of the culture in question. This doesn't mean that the teachers should teach the children in their native language. Everyone who had taken the course reacted with great enthusiasm. They expressed much gratitude towards Michel for having transformed their lives, and in so doing, the lives of the children and parents with whom they could now communicate in a meaningful way.

Of course, the Spanish-speaking community was absolutely delighted with the program. One elementary school teacher among many others commented on Michel's work by saying: "I hope that educators all over the country are planning to study what Michel is doing. Heaven knows it is much needed and has been for a long while." Enthusiastic, raving endorsements for Michel's work appeared in publications of the Teachers Unions: *NEA Reporter*, *United Teacher* and *Action*. The latter wrote: "Training for the UTLA staffers won strong endorsement and support from CTA and NEA as a positive step toward better serving the members and students and parents the members are working with." It is about time that educators around the world pay attention to Michel's achievements which spanned five decades.

MODERN LANGUAGE ASSOCIATION

When UCLA decided not to participate in the experimental language project using Michel's method, Richard I. Broad, Director of Special Projects for the renowned Modern Language Association showed their support at that time in the following letter to Dean Herbert Morris of the University of California: "... I would also point out that such an experiment, if UCLA were willing to undertake it, would be of great benefit to colleagues elsewhere, even if UCLA itself decided not to repeat the experiment or follow up on it in any other way." He explained that Michel's approach to overcoming anxiety and to presenting the grammatical structure was "illuminating and effective." And he went on to say that "... I am not so naive as to believe that Michel has found a magic 'cure' for language learners. I do believe, however, that some new ideas deserve a test, and that the best tests are those administered by experienced professionals."

UCLA did not know anything whatsoever about Michel's method and chose to reject it outright. Their comment was that Michel could never achieve success in a university such as theirs. These were meaningless words. That does not say much about the willingness of our higher institutions of learning to improve the quality of their teaching. Was it jealousy, protectiveness or simply ignorance or a combination of these?

Over the years, Michel had encountered opposition by some academicians to using his method because they were unable to accept a paradigm that did not fit into their learning model. Change is difficult for those who wear *sameness* filters in the current *dis-educational system*™.

UNIVERSITY OF SOUTHERN CALIFORNIA

The University of Southern California conducted a test program for French using Michel's method, and the evaluations were, as usual, quite supportive and enthusiastic. According to the Acting Chairman of the Department of French at that time, the evaluations were based on "the students' remarkable comprehension of essential concepts of language and...their surprising control of the entire body of French grammar. Needless to say, I consider the accomplishment especially startling, knowing that it was achieved after only three weeks of work with Mr. Thomas." Michel was described as "an extraordinary teacher. To produce results such as these, even with a relatively small group, is an achievement of major proportions."

THE BEVERLY HILLS SCHOOL SYSTEM

In the early 1970's the Beverly Hills School System wanted to show what could be done using Michel's method. Michel agreed to teach a class for five days to show what could be achieved, with the goal of getting his method into the school system. In spite of an overwhelming enthusiastic response from the students, the language teachers wrote an article besmirching the whole process. Once again, Michel responded to correct the mendacious claims being made, at which time the third side made up of educators at UCLA came to his defense in the front pages of the Beverly Hills Newspaper. Marvin Adelson, then a professor at UCLA's School of Architecture and Urban Planning, commented as follows:

> I cannot help feeling that Mr. Jacquard's (high school teacher) statement is intended to discredit the Michel Thomas method in ADVANCE, so as to

AVOID the possibility of an empirical comparison... Now that Mr. Jacquard has publicly cast the gauntlet in the student's face, I trust that Beverly Hills...will arrange for a carefully conducted and evaluated experiment by a neutral and competent outside agency. For this is a matter that affects much more than the teaching of French, and much more than Beverly Hills.

Another supporter of Michel, Garth Sorenson, Ph. D., and Chairman of UCLA's Educational Counseling, Graduate School of Education at the time, commented as follows: "Mr. Thomas, by methods he can describe and that most other teachers could learn, reduces anxiety, frustration and fear — the strong emotions that interfere with learning. He motivates students to work long and hard, and with great concentration in teaching in such a way that they experience an immediate, realistic and continuing sense of accomplishment."

The argument raged on as Stephen Sheldon also from the Graduate School of Education at UCLA wrote in the article: "There are implicit in Mr. Jacquard's statements, assumptions about the nature of education and learning which are shared by many teachers and many college professors... These are that the acquisition of skill, knowledge, understanding have to be hard and painful, and that the student must face the difficulties which are inherent in becoming educated." He goes on to say: "For some reason we have come to accept the educative process as one being conducted in a punitive, threatening, disciplined environment. This tradition is fortunately changing and Mr. Thomas' method is an outstanding example of what education can be." Here is another time when Michel had generously opened his method up to everyone, and where once again, it led to a dead-end.

UCLA

UCLA finds its way into another chapter of the saga in the early 90's. At that time, Marvin Adelson, Michel's staunch supporter of his Demonstration School decades earlier (Chapter Ten) had asked Dean Herbert Morris of the Division of

Humanities at the time if he would be interested in improving the quality of foreign language instruction at the university. Indeed he was, and Dean Morris soon met with some language teachers at UCLA "who were skeptical, doubtful and somewhat resistant to the claim that someone can learn a language in two weeks." At first Dean Morris joined the side of the skeptics and then had a change of heart:

> I was skeptical even though I had received numerous testimonials from distinguished scholars and others about Thomas' remarkable program... My experience entirely confirmed — and this was after only two days of work together — the most enthusiastic endorsements of what he could achieve. Perhaps most important, along with having acquired considerable knowledge of the Spanish language, was the pleasure involved in learning and my eagerness to continue learning.

Michel related how remarkably, some nine months later, without having additional exposure to Spanish because of professional responsibilities, Dean Morris took a Spanish Language Placement Examination (at the suggestion of the Chair of the Spanish Department at UCLA) and missed by only one question, testing out of the full year Spanish requirement. Several years later in an interview with the Wharton Business School, Dean Morris summarized his experience: "Motivation was intense" and he felt "a real excitement in learning..." and "Michel Thomas is so charismatic, he seemed to take the language, crack it open, and put it together in a logical progression."

The enthusiasm was contagious. As Michel explained to us, he, along with Marvin Adelson and Dean Morris, proposed a test program at UCLA during the summer which would prepare students for a placement and proficiency exam. In a memo to Dean Morris, Mr. Adelson expressed his views concerning the feasibility and validity of instituting Michel's method at UCLA:

> In my own mind, his approach does not compete with, or reflect upon the adequacy of what UCLA is now doing or expects to do, but

rather is a way of possibly augmenting and supporting it. At a time when the reinstituted language requirement will burden the university's language-teaching resources, the challenge of how best to provide the basics to a constituency of questionable readiness no doubt deserves to be looked at in a strategic sense.

According to Michel, for a period of several years, Dean Morris tried to get UCLA to adopt Michel's method. The response was always the same — no one could possibly teach a foreign language in two weeks. Thus, in spite of their enthusiastic efforts to persuade the language department of the need for language teaching reform, using a remarkable and innovative method, their attempts were in vain. Much to the dismay of all involved, certain academic circles again turned their haughty noses down on Michel, without even trying out his method. In essence, these academics clearly rebuffed Michel without really knowing anything about him or his method.

Michel was quite frustrated by a letter to Dean Morris from the Chair of the French Department at UCLA at that time, which stated the reasons for the committee's rejection of the program:

> After examining the material you forwarded to us, very frankly we feel that the Michel Thomas Method, though obviously successful in very specific contexts (notably as described in the brochures and testimony you forwarded to us), nevertheless, would not be able to achieve the results for a university language program such as ours... Our direct method, *designed* by our own faculty, well-known and implemented in many universities nationwide, achieves far more than strictly basic communicative skills for the simple everyday use... It would seem an unwise investment of time and energy on our part and a potentially serious disturbance of the existing sequence in our program to engage in an experimentation as you suggested.

What unmitigated insolence! Michel was stunned in disbelief by this letter and the sadness in his eyes when he showed this letter to us said it all. Imagine rejecting outright and turning away from a proven and highly effective pedagogical innovation. Michel believed that traditional teachers didn't like the fact that he would take the responsibility for learning away from the students. He also thought that they did not appreciate the concept of no homework assignments or any of the other modalities he espoused. Could it possibly be that the teachers were afraid to admit that bad teaching was really the reason for students' failures? Remember that Michel believed "there was no such thing as bad students, just bad teachers." Did the teachers fear that the existing language program would pale in comparison to Michel's method and would have to be abolished? Was it fear of job losses or was it outright stupidity? One will never know or perhaps, like Michel, we do know.

By the way, the committee's final conclusion was: "Our skepticism concerning the Michel Thomas Method is strong enough and well-grounded enough for us to conclude that our participation in an experiment with this method would not be a wise investment of time and energy, nor would it serve the best interest of our language instruction." As Michel frequently reminded the two of us, "This is where we are at!" It is a pretty sad state of affairs when our institutions of higher learning are so mired in their own bureaucratic ways and blinded by their own self-importance, that the doors to real learning "are tightly slammed shut" by the existing system.

TEACHING FEMALE INMATES

One of the more unusual backdrops for Michel's language teaching sessions was in a female prison in California in the 1970's before he moved to New York. He was asked by the Police Probation Department to teach French to a group of young women and teenage inmates. Some of the women were imprisoned because of gang related crimes and violence, with differing degrees of severity, although Michel was not made aware of the specific crimes committed. The course was to be given for training purposes, as a way for the Police Department to have a teaching tool for difficult inmates. The course was to show the Police how to talk to these young women, how to deal with them in a learning situation and how to handle them in general. Michel agreed to teach the course knowing the full purpose behind it. So Michel taught the women French for five days in the actual prison.

To Michel it didn't matter that these women were inmates. His goal remained the same: "to free the mind and to open up that *innate drive for learning* that is within all of us." Michel, as usual, worked his magic, transforming the prison walls into windows of enlightenment for those girls and women. Michel inspired these less than appreciated women so much that they actually began to write poetry for him, and he told us that the women were, in fact, quite gifted and had written some incredible poems. Michel represented a breath of fresh air to these female inmates. He opened them to a new appreciation of themselves as he enabled them to tap into creative potentials that had remained previously dormant. The girls and the women were so grateful to their wonderful teacher that many of them remained in touch with Michel many years after getting out of prison.

What a wonderful testimonial to the *Master Teacher* who proved, once again, that he was able to *mentally reach* anyone, even students whom society may consider to be unteachable and unreachable, and who are tragically abandoned by a system that has no room for them. The lesson here is that every single living being is capable of learning, even when the future appears grim. Everyone can learn, no matter how forlorn, no matter how dire or dreadful the circumstances in which people may find themselves. Anyone's *innate drive for learning* may be reawakened by proper teaching. After that, everything is possible! Michel certainly proved this and more.

TRAIN TEACHING

Michel can work his magic anywhere in the globe, in any setting, at any time — even on a train. Imagine the wonderful opportunity to simply hop on a train to learn a language from Michel.

In February 2004, Michel was asked to teach a "train course" for the European Parliament which had invited a group of journalists on a trip from London to Brussels and back, accompanied by a photographer from *The Financial Times*. The whole "wagon" was filled with members of the press who listened to Michel speak about the importance of communication and of learning languages given the existence of the European Union. What a way to go!

The response was so wonderful that soon afterwards a group of nine of these journalists went to London to learn Spanish from Michel over a two day weekend. At the end of the weekend course, the participants all stood up and applauded Michel, saying that although it was hard at first to believe that he could actually teach them to speak a foreign language over a weekend, they were totally convinced and excited after having experienced Michel and his method first-hand. The group also said that what they had experienced in a period of two days with Michel would have taken five years in a traditional school. Yet another powerful endorsement for the *Master Teacher*.

ENDORSEMENTS FROM THE PRESS

Michel Thomas proudly gave us the following quotes from the press, from his students and from other teachers who had experienced his teaching firsthand. He asked us to include these testimonials in this chapter of our book.

The New York *Post*: "His program is so successful that the New York Chamber of Commerce and Industry has officially endorsed it, and businesses are among his most avid clients."

Diversion: "The Rolls-Royce of language schools... The roster of graduates reads like the Who's Who of Hollywood or a survey of the Fortune 500... This revolutionary learning method has received accolades from the academic community... Michel Thomas guaranteed the impossible and delivered."

The Daily Telegraph: "Michel's rules contradict all that you learned in school. Number one is: no memorizing or rote learning closely followed by no taking notes..."

The Los Angeles *Times*: "In an hour or so the startled student finds himself rattling off long sentences with aplomb — if not the *patois* of the concierge at *Le Bristol*. And what's even more fun, he's silently congratulating himself on his brilliance and enjoying every second of it."

People Magazine: "Michel and his staff have turned out at least 10,000 mostly satisfied students." and "His academic credentials are beyond dispute."

The Robb Report: "The soft-spoken Thomas is indeed a convincing promoter of his courses. But if he were not, his corps of stellar alumni would speak glowingly in his stead."

Executive Magazine: "His methods are untraditional. There are no textbooks, there is no memorization, no exercises, but there are results."

Forbes: "The teaching sessions are impressive. Thomas must literally remember just about everything he has mentioned..." Also: "... Michel starts immediately with simple phrases... He builds communication outward from there, always drawing upon what he has already explained, like a sculptor packing successive layers of clay around an armature."

Manhattan *Inc.*: "His teaching methods, though unorthodox, are acknowledged by all to be highly effective. There are even those who call him a genius."

The Sunday Times: "The very notion that anyone can achieve a degree of mastery of a foreign language in a few days in the classroom has to be impossible. Yet with language teacher Michel Thomas — and his method — practically anyone can achieve verbal proficiency in three days... It sounds impossible, laughable even, but Thomas not only insists it is perfectly possible, he has been proving it for years."

The Daily News: "Everything is presented in easily digestible steps."

The Big Valley: "You are taught grammar, but all the methodology is different... That's the whole trick. He teaches you grammar without even knowing it."

National Educational Reporter (NEA Reporter) says: "After just 20 contact hours, staff members obtained a comprehensive grasp of Spanish usage and grammar. After two weeks they were holding informal, everyday conversations in Spanish and also had been ingrained with the difference in cultural nuances."

WHAT STUDENTS AND TEACHERS SAY...

Michel also shared the following endorsements with us to include in this chapter:

Woody Allen, New York filmmaker, said in *The Sunday Times*: "Learning with Michel: it's like a kid who loves baseball and who knows every ball player, every batting average, every statistic about the game. They've learned all of it effortlessly. It's the same with Michel. You learn a language effortlessly. It is amazing."

Emma Thompson, actress, told *The Guardian*: "Michel not only taught me Spanish, he opened my eyes to the possibilities of a different kind of learning... It's very impressive to get a working knowledge of a language in a few days. Michel is a very extraordinary man."

François Truffaut, French filmmaker, wrote to Michel (he had arrived in Los Angeles two days before the Watergate hearing started): "At first, I learned from you the word 'impeachment' and four weeks later, I was able to have a meeting in English at the Warner Bros Headquarters. Thank you, Michel." Elsewhere Truffaut wrote from Bel Air: "For the first time tonight I understood some...sentences in Watergate Hearing on TV... I was very happy about that and I know that I couldn't have done it without you."

Raquel Welsh, actress, wrote in a letter to Michel: "You certainly do have a unique talent of making everything flow. The lessons seem natural and logical and enlightening, all at the same time. You have discovered a way to make the learning process something that a person can embrace instead of dread."

Ann-Margret, actress, told *People Magazine*: "If you don't remember something, he puts the blame on himself. You relax and soak it up like a sponge."

Dr. Herbert Morris, UCLA Dean of Humanities and Professor of Philosophy and Law, and great advocate of Michel's teaching, told *USA Today*: "I had the sense of having somehow or other cracked the language open and having gotten to its very essence. And in the most direct, simple and organized way, leading you into the heart of the language." In an interview with the Wharton Business School, Dr Morris said: "Michel Thomas has an unbelievable ability to analyze and put together the language which allows you to enter gradually into the language."

Dr. Michael Fay, Director of Joint Projects UTLA, CTA and NEA, said: "The learning process is exciting. The staff was amazed at the rapidity of their learning. Your Method developed their self-confidence in using the language... We are still enormously impressed with the results of your program...our education system is in need of an effective and rapid learning approach..."

Peter Blackman, Vice Chancellor UCLA (student of French and Spanish) said: "in past attempts to learn French...there was a lot of blockage associated with *trying to remember* words or phrases...but not with Michel Thomas. This method is intellectual and provides an easy path to learning — the structure is quite fluid and accessible."

Garth Sorenson, Professor of Education, Graduate School of Education, UCLA commented: "He motivates his students to work long and hard...by teaching in such a way that they experience an immediate, realistic and continuing sense of accomplishment." Elsewhere he writes: "An important element of Mr. Thomas' program is that it induces learning without fatigue and...makes the learning process both enjoyable and more efficient..."

David Diet, Director of AT&T France told USA today: "What he did was present a whole arena of the basics of the French language in three days."

Robbie Justice, travel writer, *The Los Angeles Times* wrote: "I'm tucked away in a comfortable black chair with my feet on an ottoman. I'm sipping coffee; I can smoke if I wish. There are no textbooks, blackboards, pencils or paper."

Karen S. Brethower, Vice President, Chase Manhattan Bank, wrote in a memo to the Development Council of the Conference Board: "Some of you have heard me expound on the wonders of a particular language training we are using at Chase. I am formalizing my support of it by introducing you to Michel Thomas and Michel Thomas to you. His training provides fluency in a 10 day intensive course in western languages. It has been effective for us with very high level executives and with mid-level managers who will be moving into a foreign country. If you are in the market for language training, I strongly invite you to try it out." Elsewhere she wrote: "The promises are not excessive. It really is the best language program I've ever seen."

Dr. Rose Hayden, President of the National Council of Foreign Languages and International Studies said in the magazine, *Manhattan Inc.*: "He has the ability to put the learner at ease, to make the learner comfortable with grammatical principles without hammering you on the head. It provides a foundation that drilling doesn't."

Hughes Aircraft Co.: "Mr. Thomas' French language instruction was entirely different in class concept, technique and results...comparing cost vs. effectiveness, it appears that the Thomas course of French language instruction is superior."

California Teachers Association said: "Not only have we (teachers) learned to speak Spanish in such a short time, we have been learning the customs, ways of making the students and parents feel welcome." CTA *Action* wrote: "Training for UTLA staffers won strong endorsement and support from CTA and NEA as a positive step toward better serving the members and students and parents the members are working with."

United Teacher: "Thomas has completely rearranged the usual approach to and content order of the structure of the Spanish language. He presents to the student small crystal-clear doses of the language."

National Education Association Publication, Washington, D.C.: "At Carver Junior High School in Watts (California), we gave Michel Thomas a storage room filled with a group of basically illiterate children. After two weeks, they were proficient in French."

Office of the Los Angeles County Superintendent of Schools wrote: "I attended some of his workshops and saw for myself the incredible results of his Language Institute... If districts ascertain that the learning of a language is their solution (or one of them) to relating to minority and ethnically different students, then I can think of no more complete process for learning the language and beginning the acquisition of cultural feeling and understanding, and eventually, acceptance."

San Antonio Texas School District Evaluation (1979): "The success students experience continually throughout the First Phase is reflected in the Second (and third) Phase through their reading and writing. The program is very effective for teaching a language in the least amount of time, in the most effective and successful way possible for the greatest gains."

Jeff Arch, screenwriter, *Sleepless in Seattle,* wrote: "If what you are looking for is a quick and painless way to gain confidence with a foreign language, then this is it. Instead of a bunch of stock phrases to memorize, Michel Thomas gives you an intuitive understanding of how each language works — and he does it in a civilized, kind, patient and completely innovative and refreshing manner. I am totally amazed at how much I've been able to absorb — and retain — in such an incredibly short time. I could've learned math if somebody had taught it this way!"

Walter Curley, US Ambassador to France, in *The New York Post*: "Michel is such an amazing teacher. I've already told President Mitterrand about him."

Joseph Verner Reed, Undersecretary General, United Nations wrote in a letter to Michel: "I saw the article in the November issue of *Avenue* and it brought back many happy memories of my close association with you prior to my assignment to the fabled Kingdom of Morocco. Your sustained efforts and interests encouraged me, and has given me strength through the years. I shall always be mindful and grateful of your counsel."

Wesley Posvar, President of the University of Pittsburgh told *Manager Magazin* (Germany): "The pupils are stimulated to think and to combine in a type of intellectual acrobatics. The student learns to his astonishment the unexpected ability to learn quickly... The course is so fascinating that one is disappointed every time the lunch break begins."

Sharon P. Smith, Dean of the Business School, Fordham University writes in a letter to Michel: "I have just returned from the first European and American Traders Conference which was held in Paris... Thanks to your brilliant system of teaching language and your generosity in sharing it with me, I was truly prepared not only to benefit from the conference, but to add value to it."

Joan Sherman, Business Consultant in Monaco told *Business Life Magazine*: "He makes it so simple... Michel kept reminding me not to memorize, which is hard to do. But once I let go of that, I found weeks...months later, things were popping out of my mouth that I was not actually memorizing."

Donald Beldock, Chairman of Fundamental Properties, Inc. of New York told *The Herald Tribune*: "He [Michel] deals with those anxieties that seem to prevent most Americans [from] speaking another language. I manage business effectively in French. In Italian, I can carry on a conversation with some ease."

Rob Karthaus, Canadian Senior Officer in charge of bilingualism at the post-secondary level told *The Lethbridge Herald* (Canada): "Michel Thomas' unorthodox approach to teaching French in Alberta's three universities has been 'extremely' impressive."

William Sadler, former administrative Vice-President of Air Canada, responsible for promotion of French language competency, told *The Calgary Herald*: "The Thomas system gives you tremendous confidence, and you want to learn the language. His system is designed to stimulate a person... There isn't a better method in existence."

Janis Kelly, a medical journalist in NY: "...after two solid weeks with Michel, I was in Stockholm covering the AIDS meeting and was perfectly able to talk to delegates in French. The method is so simple and logical it organizes your brain; you can reach for words and find them."

Warren Keegan, Professor of Business at Pace University: "I'd say he has created an algorithm which gets you into a language probably in the way you learn it as a child."

OTHER TEACHERS

"... I have learned not only the language, but some very important ideas of teaching itself. And I hope to employ them in my classroom."

"The THOMAS process is unique. And it works, according to his students because of the way he teaches learning."

Chapter Twelve

CONCLUSION

There is still so much that we could say about Michel Thomas, the *Master Teacher*, the wonderful man, his amazing accomplishments and his brilliant teaching method. However, the time has come to get his message out to the world. The time has come to take action now. If we are to have our final word here, it is to appeal to the citizens of the world to rise up and contribute to building a solid educational edifice which the *Master Teacher* staunchly believed will free the minds of our children by rekindling the joy of learning and will the world from the shroud of what he considered impending disaster.

First, however, we would like to express our heartfelt gratitude on all levels to our dear friend, Michel Thomas, for sharing with us the inner secrets of exceptional method. As we have seen, its origin was delicately intertwined with all that Michel embodied throughout his life — a true champion of freedom — intellectual, physical, emotional and spiritual freedom — an inspirational educator and a larger-than-life legend of the educational world for future generations. He had so inspired both of us in our own life-long, mutual quest to enlighten our world with the wisdom, with the educational foundations and with the knowledge and dignity necessary to assure our passage through the ever complex twenty-first century and beyond.

The journey for the inhabitants of our planet in the months and years ahead may not always prove to be an easy one, particularly if the tides of darkness continue to wash the shores of our lands unchecked. Learning "straitjackets" will tighten their grip and thought control will continue to prevail in the most insidious ways. Thankfully, however, the personal journey of Michel Thomas has already proven to be both invaluable and enriching to all of us in combating the shadow of ignorance. Michel's amazing life was filled with a series of unusually challenging events which allowed him to accomplish extraordinary tasks meant for him alone. Each of these well-documented accomplishments represented but one small step in what turned out to be a long, arduous and, at times, exceedingly painful journey leading to his desired destination. Without a doubt, the *Master Teacher*'s greatest achievement, and one which had only partially realized his dream of changing the world, was the development and refinement of the *Michel Thomas Method*.

Our purpose in writing this book about Michel's method was many-fold. The first was to kindle the brilliant light of Michel's genius and to shine it brightly for all to see. The second was to help Michel on a personal level, while he was still with us, and now posthumously, by encouraging like-minded, enlightened people everywhere to come forth and pay tribute to Michel by championing reform to an educational system that "chokes learning" and promotes conformity rather than individuality.

Although Michel had *mentally reached* and transformed over ten thousand students through his one-on-one and group teaching, and over one million additional learners through his tapes, these numbers represent just a tiny bucket of sand on the beach. Thus, the third purpose of this book was to reach the millions of people who have not yet heard about Michel and his outstanding breakthrough in learning, as well as those who still don't get it.

Once we got to know Michel and began modeling him and his method, we knew that the time had come to take a momentous step forward in spreading the word about his teaching accomplishments to all corners of the globe, for it had been far too long in coming. With all the respect and admiration the *Master Teacher* received in life, there is so much more awaiting him, even now after his passing, as the world at large becomes aware of his personal and professional achievements. We are delighted to be already writing our follow-up book to *The Future of Learning,* sharing more of Michel's insights and refinements to the method. We intend to continue sharing his wisdom on all levels of the current *dis-educational system*™ and beyond.

In order for our many-fold goal to be realized at this time, it was important to showcase Michel's method. Yet for us, as well as for Michel, this is simply the means to an end. Once we developed the model, we had to show how his philosophy of life and his vision for the world are so intertwined. They are all parts of the same whole. It would not be fair to Michel's memory nor would it be possible to discuss his method without explaining how his *model of the world* as well as his life experiences had triggered and kindled his driving, burning passion to educate all people "properly," in the noblest sense of the word, in order to empower them against any form of mental tyranny or mind control. Michel's teaching method is a proven and viable answer to changing the system in a way that really works. The time has come for the academics and educational powers that be, to acknowledge the inherent weaknesses and failures of the current *dis-educational system*™. The time has come to take action and to remedy the situation before it is too late.

We must begin by reaching the countless millions whose *innate drive for learning* remains dormant in *Mind Prisons*™ around the world. Until Michel's message is disseminated all around the globe, until more of the masses can experience the joy and excitement of true learning, until more educators open their eyes and welcome Michel's method with open arms, his desire to effect meaningful, lasting change will not occur. As we often iterate, for real change to occur, we must change the system on every level. For real and lasting change to occur, we need a complete revamping of the entire educational system. Otherwise, Michel's vision of changing the world — by making a monumental difference in the quality, strength and effectiveness of our educational institutions — will not be realized. This task is even more challenging than ever, given the quickly changing, intricate nature of the diverse conditions and *milieus* in which we live.

In order to deal with these complex global problems, we need future generations of leaders, not followers. We need leaders who think independently and who are unwilling to play the power game to control the masses. For this to occur, we must educate our children so that they do not become mindless idiots who willingly absorb the babble of data and useless information that bombards them on a daily basis in the media and on the internet, and without questioning the quality or the validity of the information. The complex global challenges we face today and their increasingly interconnected nature demand minds that can synthesize, problem solve, think, create and innovate on their own. The time has come to take action, and this can only be done by eliminating the learning "straitjackets."

Michel had provided the solutions to our educational dilemma, and it is time that decision makers come forward and listen to what he had to say. If we do not act quickly, in a number of years we will be relying on adults whose only claim to fame will have been their participation in that senseless and ridiculous genre of so-called reality shows which bury the viewers' minds into an even deeper level of ignorance. We need discerning leaders who seek the truth. We need capable leaders who will welcome and support a diversity of thinkers with the expertise and competency to deal with the particular challenge in question. At the same time, we must foster innovative minds that can create new paradigms and change approaches and behaviors that are no longer useful or relevant in today's world. For one, this means eliminating what Michel called "*criminal institutions*" that "choke learning" and replacing them with schools that awaken the *innate drive for learning* by using Michel's method.

It is our hope that this book will bring Michel Thomas posthumously the profound recognition around the globe that he so merited in life, for having created his learning masterpiece which will continue to inspire and motivate people everywhere for years to come. His life-long desire and almost consuming passion of challenging the entire existing educational system, was a huge responsibility, and one from which Michel Thomas had not shirked one bit in spite of a series of disappointing setbacks along the way.

On the contrary, Michel's destination was set long ago, with a starting point and no end point because the huge responsibility of educating humankind and of eliminating ignorance is an ongoing process that continues with each generation, until the time that all minds are set free. Education should be a dynamic process that changes with the times, so that we are able to deal with new challenges and contexts in the appropriate manner.

Michel's mission was not completed, for there are still some rather large steps remaining in order for his dream to be realized on a grand scale. Part of that dream is to make millions of people aware of the efficacy, adaptability and user-friendly nature of his method. Everyone, parents and their children, teachers and their assistants, school boards and every level of the educational establishment must be made aware of Michel's huge breakthrough in learning. Perhaps then, the complementary part of Michel's dream may be realized — one that incorporates all that Michel believed, with all that he represented and all that he had developed as the *Master Teacher* with his teaching method.

Our wish is that the corridors of academia, which heretofore have been closed to Michel Thomas, the *Master Teacher*, and to his method, now begin to echo Michel's name with the respect that he so deserved in life. Our wish is that students everywhere clamor to learn, inspired by Michel's groundbreaking ways, and that parents far and wide, rebel against the traditional system and demand that their children be released from the restraints imposed by the *Mind Prison*™. Our wish is that we reach those who don't get it, so that they quickly join the ranks of those who do get it.

> Our wish is that now *Michel Thomas* will become synonymous with the man who helped change the world — by opening the doors of all educational institutions to his innovative teaching — by opening the doors to learning within each of us — doors which have been tragically "slammed shut by the system."

We also hope that somewhere, a special group of like-minded, forward-thinking individuals from all walks of life will come forth to join the two of us in realizing Michel's dream of changing the world by building a new educational system. His vision will serve as a stellar blueprint for the future of learning.

Let us hope that Michel's message will reach those who understand what is at stake — our very *freedom of mind*. If we do not take heed of Michel's message about nonaction, we will continue to be "led" by those who are deliberately enslaving our minds so that the masses continue to follow so-called leaders who use technology to brainwash our nonthinking minds. We have had enough of the stupidity and the conformity of public opinion. We have had enough of the technologically sophisticated distractions designed to entertain us and to keep us from discovering the truth. May others who get it have the passion and the capability to take action now, not in two years, not in ten years, now! The time is upon us to carry forth Michel's legacy and to implement his ideas before it is too late, without a second to waste, as he so often reminded us, to ensure the healthy survival of humanity. The time has come to begin *freeing minds one person at a time.*

In this light, let us bear in mind Michel's own thoughts on this subject:

> ...we are dedicated to this single proposition. To do all in our power to free and to keep free the Mind of Man, and wage eternal war against any means that ends to chain, control, or dominate it — believing that whenever the Mind of Man is held in a leash by any single thought or creed or philosophy, the light is out and mankind is plunged in darkness.

APPENDIX A

ADVANCED BEHAVIORAL MODELING™ TECHNOLOGY

This book came about as a result of our modeling Michel Thomas and his revolutionary teaching method. Michel was an expert at what he did. In fact, he is one of the most extraordinary experts with whom we have worked over the years; and we have modeled many wonderful experts in a variety of fields including business, professional and Olympic sports, manufacturing, education and more.

Just what is *Advanced Behavioral Modeling™ Technology*? It is the process of capturing, encoding, replicating and transferring expertise from one individual to another in any given field. Over the years, we have refined the process to what it is now, a unique, synthetic approach to capturing and transferring expertise. Within the context of our modeling experts in a wide range of different professions and abilities, we have created a process that is a unique synthesis of highly effective techniques combined with our research and work in a wide variety of human typologies. This synthesis allows us to understand and to utilize the diverse facets of human behavior in a multitude of contexts. *Advanced Behavioral Modeling™ Technology* is a sophisticated approach to capturing expertise because it operates at a process level and distinguishes the characteristics that are actually causally connected to expert performance. Also, we create our models based on what superior performers actually do, rather than on someone's theory about what works.

In *Advanced Behavioral Modeling™*, no one typology suffices in understanding human behavior and personality. This is why we have synthesized different typologies and have made multi-level interconnections among the various typologies. The result is a balanced model that incorporates the mental, physical, emotional and spiritual components involved. We then synthesize these aspects into an even more powerful form that takes into account contextuality. Our approach is based on systems theory and the understanding that performance is improved by optimizing the interactions of the different parts, and not by building new parts and putting them together.

In our work as typologists, we focus on human difference. We know that every human being has what we call a unique *"model of the world."* And in working with experts, we determine the diverse yet interconnected components of their particular *model of the world.* As we have stated, *Advanced Behavioral Modeling*™ is the process of capturing, encoding, replicating and transferring expertise. We work with experts (like Michel Thomas) who are able to perform a task or manifest an ability or talent at an exceptionally high skill level. *Advanced Behavioral Modeling*™ *Technology* addresses the following question: "How is it possible that one person can achieve such amazing and extraordinary results while other people can only produce average or mediocre results at best?" In the case of Michel Thomas, how is it possible that he was able to achieve overwhelming success every time he taught a language course while other language teachers cannot? Michel was an extraordinary and singular expert who, with his brilliant, *difference* mind, among many other characteristics, created an equally extraordinary "expert" process by which he could demonstrate his own expertise.

We have found that some experts know what they do to achieve their results, but they simply don't know how they do it. They cannot answer the question, "How is it possible?" because they are working out of what we refer to as *"unconscious competency."* As *Advanced Behavioral Modelers*™, we decode the diverse components of experts' *"unconscious competency."* Thus, in addressing the question, "How is it possible?" the answer is that the experts may know the *"what"* of their particular task, yet they do not know the *"how"* of what they do.

Most people have found themselves in a situation in which they know what they would like to do, are spurred by great motivation to do so, and they are still not able to do what they would like. The reason is that they don't know how to mentally organize themselves to accomplish the task or goal, or else there is some sort of mental block preventing them from doing so. In such cases, for example, in our working with Olympic athletes and Olympic coaches, with top executives and with other superior performers, we not only capture what these experts do, we also help them to eliminate these performance blocks.

As a result of modeling experts, we design trainings that are model-based. We model an expert or experts in a given field and then design a training to transfer the expert skills to other suitably selected individuals. Every individual cannot become an expert in a given field just because he or she has gone through a training. Can a person off the street take a two week course and suddenly perform brain surgery? Of course not!

The same applies to transferring any expertise which is captured by modeling experts. The model is readily transferable to those individuals who share certain aspects of the expert's *model of the world*. In the case of modeling Michel and his extraordinary method, what we have done is to present a model for learning which can be replicated in many areas. In the context of teaching, we have pointed out on several occasions in *The Future of Learning*, that not all teachers will be able to replicate Michel's method because they lack the creativity and the ability to make refined distinctions. Furthermore, being able to replicate Michel also requires certain perceptual filters. It is not enough to know what to do or how to do it. One must actually be able to do it. At times this may require behavioral changes, and we focus on this process in our model-based trainings in order to achieve the desired outcomes. However, any teacher will be able to apply some of the general components of the method which deal with the delivery of the material and the creation of a specific learning environment.

Advanced Behavioral Modeling™ Technology can have three major by-products. First, it can reduce training times and increase skill levels over conventional trainings. Second it can help to design the man-machine interface of equipment. We call this *psycho-ergonometrics*. This is the science of designing human machine interfaces that actually work. Third, it can help in personnel selection. We know that pre-selection is always more important than training. We live in a society that believes you can train anyone to do anything. This is simply not true. It is important to select the right people and to train them properly. The key to selecting the right people is to choose people who have the same talent and innate abilities as those who are already successful at a given job or at performing a particular task.

This is where *Advanced Behavioral Modeling™ Technology*

is of great help. Traditional methods of hiring rely on education and job experience, both of which do not suffice in determining future success. These methods do not take into account behavioral factors which can only be determined by modeling the successful people or experts. For example, *Advanced Behavioral Modeling™ Technology* is a sophisticated approach that can identify competencies that are directly related to superior job performance. It is not enough to identify the skills needed for high performance. One especially needs to know whether people are capable of performing the skills needed.

We are grateful to Michel for understanding the importance of capturing his method. Michel Thomas, the *Master Teacher*, was certainly the leader among experts in the field of learning, and in so many other ways, a leader who provided exquisite paradigms for the future of learning.

APPENDIX B

MICHEL'S LANGUAGE COURSES

Over the years, Michel designed several language courses. The first was his complete course which he had perfected during his fifty years of teaching. In it, one spent three days with the *Master Teacher* and two days with one or more of Michel's instructors. This course was usually taught one-on-one, but it was also taught to a small group or with special arrangements to a large group. In the three days with Michel, students were taught French, Spanish, Italian or German.

In this short time frame of just three days, the students acquired a solid, comprehensive knowledge of the entire structure and grammar of the language, and a practical and functional vocabulary enabling them to read, write and converse in all tenses of the language. The student learned the mechanics and tools of the language and how to use them. This occurred without the need to memorize by rote, take notes or complete homework. Having acquired the comprehensive knowledge of the target language, and able to use the language in speaking, reading and writing in just three days with Michel, the learner was ready to go into the phase of using the language.

This phase was spent with Michel's instructors (who were all specially trained native speakers) in the practice of speaking reading, and engaging in general discussion in the target language. In this phase, learners applied the mechanics and tools which they previously acquired from Michel. The *Master Teacher* described it as follows:

> The language begins to flow. They thrill at the astonishing fact that they can actually speak, read and even write in the language! They quickly develop the confidence to tackle speaking, reading and writing situations because they have the knowledge and tools to do so. If they make occasional mistakes they always know why, and self-correction is easy because of their foundation.

In this phase with Michel's native teachers, the emphasis was on contemporary reading and not on authors of the classic period. For example, in French the student would read Antoine de Saint-Exupéry, with his charming *Little Prince*, Jean Cocteau, with some of his plays about the human condition, and Jacques Prévert with some of his emotion-laden poetry. Michel explained the process as follows: "Usually one starts reading and this leads to a discussion of what you read in the target language." This was done with another teacher for two days. After the course, the learner was encouraged to continue to read and converse in the language. After just five days the student was "in the language" and did not need further instruction from Michel or his teachers. In five days the learner was taught, as Michel would say, "*how to swim*." How fast he *swam* was up to the individual learner.

Michel's innovative mind spurred him to develop courses in languages other than the ones that he spoke. This may seem to be an almost impossible task. Not for Michel. For example, he did not speak Japanese or Chinese; and yet he created courses in these languages and others, which were taught by instructors who were personally trained by Michel in the use of his method. His instructors first took one of Michel's tape courses to familiarize themselves with the method, and then they taught Michel their native language. In the process of teaching him the course, they ended up developing the course that they would be teaching to others using Michel's method.

Finally, we have the CD courses for French, Spanish, German and Italian which are commercially available to the general public. Michel developed a special method for the tape or CD courses which is protected by a United States Patent. In the method, Michel taught a language to two students, one of whom was male and the other female. Neither student was purposefully selected in that they were chosen at random. One was an American and the other was British for each language taught. The student interacting with the tape course becomes, in essence, the third member of the class. It is virtual group learning at its best! For example, Michel will ask one of the two students on the tape how to say something in the language. The student interacting with the tapes will pause the tape at this point and answer before starting the tape again, and will then listen to what the student says (Method Chapter).

Until 2004, only the initial audio courses for acquiring a practical and functional use of the language were available. These courses consist of eight tapes or CD's and are available for English speakers to learn French, Spanish, Italian and German. Since 2004 a two CD Language Booster and a five CD Advanced Program have been added. Recently further tapes have become available which use an interpretation of the *Michel Thomas Method*. However, they are neither designed nor recorded by Michel. They include courses for English speakers to learn Chinese, Russian and Arabic with other languages to come.

DIFFERENCES IN THE METHOD BETWEEN TAPES AND PERSONAL TEACHING

According to Michel, there was little difference in the method between teaching live and by audio CD's or tapes because it is he who is doing the teaching. The introductory eight tape or CD audio set presently on the market quickly gives the student a practical and functional use of the language. Even though it is not an in-depth course, one can immediately go and use the language. Both methods, audio and in person, work because it is Michel who is doing the teaching. It works on audio because in interacting with the tape or CD, the learner must respond to each question. He or she uses the pause button to stop the tape or CD and answers before the response comes on the tape. Afterwards, the student will release the pause button to hear the response from one of the students on the tape. If one of the students on the tape gives an incorrect answer, Michel does not point out the error and directly correct the student.

As in his live courses, Michel did not point out errors or directly correct his students. It would have been quite easy for him to erase the mistakes made by the students on tape and have everything be perfect, and he intentionally did not do this. Michel believed that it would be unrealistic to have perfect tapes with no mistakes. Everything is not perfect, so that if a student makes a mistake, Michel would lead the person to correct his or her own mistake. We explained this process of self-correction in the Method Chapter of this book, and in Chapter Seven, we discuss how it corresponds to what the new school calls "*meta-cognition.*"

Besides, according to Michel, that is exciting to the learner. Why? Because if the learner by tape happens to give the correct response, and the student on the tape gives an incorrect response, it will allow the listener to realize that even the students on the tape can make mistakes. They are not perfect either, and this realization serves to boost the confidence of the student who is learning by interacting with the tapes. They realize that the students on the tape were not chosen because they had a prior knowledge of the language. It is exciting for the learners by tape because when they hear an incorrect response, they are observing what is going on. Their initial reaction may be to wonder what is happening.

The doubt only occurs the first time because by the time it happens again, they already know that the students on the tape are not perfect. The learner by tape realizes that the students on the tape are at his/her level, not above. Also, when the student on the tape makes a mistake, the learner who is listening will hear how to correct his/her own mistakes. The learner may begin to wonder why the student on the tape made the mistake, and this helps the listener as well in correcting his/her own mistakes, step by step while listening. On the other hand, if the student learning by tape makes a mistake, he/she will immediately hear one of the students on the tape answer correctly and the listener will then correct himself or herself accordingly.

It is also possible that the person on the tape may give an incorrect answer and the learner by tape may give the correct answer. The first time that happens, the listener is thinking: "Now what is going on here? Maybe they are right and maybe I am wrong." Then later the student interacting realizes that his or her response was correct after all. And this creates excitement because the student learning by tape realizes that the others are not perfect, and that he/she is sometimes even better than the students on the tape. Whether on tape or one on one, Michel never said that students were wrong. He went along with them and led them back, right into it, so that they were able to correct their own mistakes in a similar situation. He would go exactly to the same problem as before so that the student could correct it and say "Now I know." The method on tape allows students to monitor their own progress and to correct their own mistakes, and this boosts their self-confidence. This enables them to carry the process forth later on their own. This entire process is so unique that Michel held a US Patent on it.

All of the above scenarios create great excitement in the learner. So not only did Michel's one-on-one teaching create great excitement in the learner, so do his audio tapes. "My tapes are a very exciting experience for everybody who takes them," boasted Michel.

In this book we describe a rather dramatic example, among many others, of his success with teaching on tapes which came at an International Bi-Lingual Bi-Cultural Education Conference in San Juan, Puerto Rico in 1978. Here two groups, one learning English and the other Spanish, were able to converse with each other and with others at the Conference in the respective language which they learned only a week before the conference began by using Michel's tapes.

One of the few differences between the way that Michel taught on the audio tapes and the way that he taught in live courses is that there are no visual cues on the audio tapes. Michel was careful not to give any visual cues to the students on the audio tapes: "I will not shake my head. I will not use my hand or my eyes. Absolutely nothing visual because any visual help, the slightest sign, would handicap the learner by tape." In his live courses Michel used gestures quite a bit as well as facial expressions which we discussed in detail in Chapter Six.

APPENDIX C
PHOTOGRAPHS AND DOCUMENTS

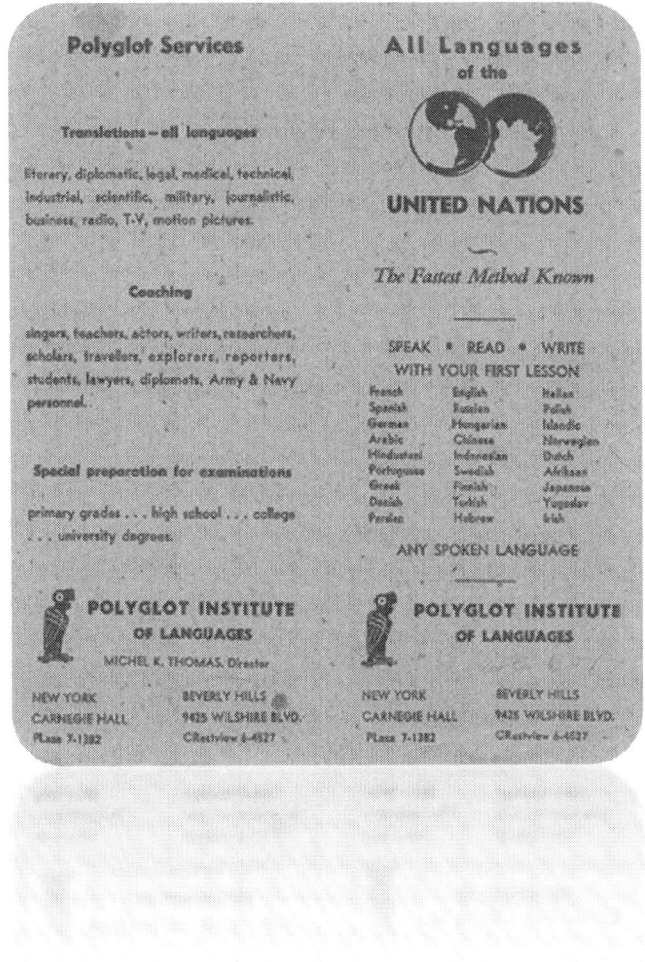

The brochure from the *Polyglot Institute* which Michel created in Beverly Hills, California in 1947.

Michel, circa 1944,
in front of the French General's vehicle.

Michel in New York, early 1990's.

Michel with Marilyne (above) and Wyatt (below).

APPENDICES

In these photos Michel is discussing the manuscript of this book with the authors.

Michel Thomas with French Ambassador Jean Louis Levitte on May 25, 2004, when he was awarded the Silver Star, presented to him by Senator Robert Dole and Senator John Warner at the World War II Memorial in Washington, D.C.

"It is with great pride that I stand here with you today, and with our fellow comrades in that worthy battle to defend both freedom, and the sanctity of human life. In just a few days, this Memorial is to be dedicated. A Memorial that you, Senator Dole, sacrificed to make a reality. I think that of no greater honor than to have my contribution to our common struggle recognized by you here today, and by Senator Warner, and by the Ambassador of France, Monsieur Levitte. I am deeply moved and humbled by this gesture from each of you, and immensely honored to receive this recognition from the United States of America. Thank you."

Michel Thomas, Silver Star Recipient
Nominated 1944, Awarded May 25, 2004

ABOUT THE AUTHORS

Marilyne Woodsmall, Ph.M., and Wyatt Woodsmall, Ph.D., are renowned behavioral modelers, international trainers, and experts in human typological research. For twenty plus years they have successfully synthesized their expertise and research in the areas of performance enhancement, learning and creativity, leadership, management science, Neuro-Linguistic Programming, and cultural change.

Known as the *"experts on experts"* ™, Wyatt Woodsmall and Marilyne Woodsmall are the President and Vice-President, respectively, of *Advanced Behavioral Modeling*™, Inc., a consulting and training firm committed to increasing the performance and productivity of organizations and individuals through the use of advanced behavioral science and learning technologies. They are also the co-creators of *Advanced Behavioral Modeling*™ *Technology* which is a behavioral science change technology for capturing, explicating, replicating and transferring expertise. The theory and structure of the modeling process is a synthesis of many technologies which they have explored and utilized over the years.

In addition, Marilyne Woodsmall and Wyatt Woodsmall are experts in human typologies. They are the President and Vice President, respectively, of the International Research Institute for Human Typological Studies, which specializes in research on human difference. Their emphasis is on the connection between human differences and performance, as well as on the shaping of cultures to create high performance organizations and global cooperation. Their goal is also to increase awareness of and generate solutions to global issues affecting the survival of our planet.

The Woodsmalls have pioneered the development and application of behavioral modeling technology in numerous fields. They have developed models to increase and maintain high performance levels in high stress situations, in both the private and corporate sectors as well as in athletic competition. Their work has resulted in the development of behavioral models and the design of model-based training programs that dramatically increased performance, reduced training time and slashed costs.

Some of their modeling projects have included top sales people, supervisors for telemarketers, negotiators, assembly line workers, entrepreneurs who created high growth start-ups and elite athletes, as well as other experts and superior performers. They have also developed models for the U.S Olympic Diving Team to help them prepare for the two Olympics in the nineties. They have also modeled the top diving coaches and developed a coaching model applicable to both athletics and business.

Marilyne Woodsmall and Wyatt Woodsmall also design and implement organizational and culture shaping projects that strengthen the productivity of people and technology. Their focus has been on integrating socio-technical values models to enhance productivity in an increasingly complex world in which the interconnectedness of people and technology demand highly innovative approaches to deal with change.

As highly respected international trainers, they jointly and individually conduct trainings on all five continents. Some of the training programs include entrepreneurship, creativity, learning, leadership, management development, values, culture-shaping, advanced interpersonal communication, stress management, time management, negotiations, coaching, *People Patterns*™, parenting, performance enhancement for children, and Trainer's Trainings (including 37 nineteen day Neuro-Linguistic Programming Trainer's Trainings in twelve countries). In the context of their Trainer's Trainings, their focus is on training design, platform skills and on teaching how people learn.

In the late eighties, the Woodsmalls created *Learning how to Learn Technology*™ which focuses on how people learn. They have also developed *Learning How to Learn Programs* for adults and children. All of their trainings and workshops are part of *The CLWF Institute for Global Leadership* (www.theclwf.org), whose mission is to develop enlightened global leaders capable of critical thinking and problem solving skills, using new educational models, expert wisdom, and innovative technologies from different fields.

For more information about their trainings, books, CDs and other products, visit:

www.peoplepatterns.com

www.newmindsforthefuture.com

www.themichelthomasmethod.com

www.theexpertsonexperts.com

www.mindbraintechnologies.com

www.thechildrenoflightandwisdomfoundation.org

INDEX

80/20 rule, 166-167
Abbey, Dr. David S., 225, 391
Abraham, 240, 241
accelerated learning, 194, 289-291, 373
acquisition of *knowledge*, 61, 79, 86, 89-90, 98, 105, 114, 126, 146, 214, 244-245
adaptive learning, 284
ADD, 201
Adelson, Marvin, 373-374, 394, 401- 403
ADHD, 201,
Advanced Behavioral Modeling™, 1, 262, 421-424, 437
Age of Enlightenment, 245
aha reaction, 123, 132-133, 181, 233
Air Canada, 225, 391, 414
Allen, Woody, 34, 82, 409
ambiance, 105, 107, 209-210, 257, 393
anchors, 96, 215
Anderson, Andrew, 380, 384
Ann-Margret, 34, 410
annoyance, 137-140
anthropology, 265
Arch, Jeff, 412
arithmetic, 56, 246, 266
assessment, 264, 268-270, 275-276, 281, 287
associations, 104-105, 107, 113-114, 177, 180, 195, 197, 315, 342, 349
attention, 66, 86, 114- 117, 127, 168, 194, 198, 201, 218, 225-227, 229, 274-276, 281, 313, 317, 381-382, 384
authoritarian teacher, 114
authoritarian teaching, 108
Ball, Lucille, 34, 215-216
Barbie, Klaus, 11, 26-28, 32, 352
Barry (Michel's Landseer Newfoundland dog), 32
Beatty, Warren, 34
being "misunderstood," 218
Beldock, Donald, 414
Bello, Vincent, 396-397
Bergen, Candice, 34
Beverly Hills School System, 401
bilingual education, 85, 386-389, 395
blackboards, 107, 411
Blackman, Peter, 410
blame, 64, 67, 69-70, 119, 137, 184, 211-213, 234, 301, 303, 348, 410
block teaching, 96, 199-206, 253, 273, 288, 386
blocking, 85, 127-129
Bohr, Niels, 363
breakthrough, 106, 416, 419
Brethower, Karen S., 411
Broad, Richard I., 400
Brosnan, Pierce, 34
Burns, Alyce, 387
business people, 17, 299
calculus (teaching), 247
calibration, 96, 185, 219-221, 258, 332, 334-336,

California Teachers Association (CTA), 399-400, 410, 412
Cannon, Dyan, 34
Cardinal Bevilaqua, 34
Cardinal O'Connor, 34
Change People Pattern™, 176, 191, 319-320
change the world, 9, 13, 17, 20, 23, 35-37, 298, 419
Chaucer, 245
children, 6, 11, 17-18, 20, 44-45, 47, 56, 62-76, 83-84, 86, 89, 91-92, 119, 138, 153, 157, 201-205, 216, 241-243, 261, 265-266, 283, 297, 299, 303, 307-316, 323, 325, 330, 336, 370, 379-380, 384, 386-388, 399, 412, 415, 417- 419, 438-439
Chunk Size People Pattern™, 350, 353-355
chunking, 96, 191-192, 353, 355
chunks, 95, 145, 168, 191, 286
cognates, 15, 95, 146-149, 277, 338
cognitive psychology, 265
collaborative learning, 109, 212, 223, 257
comfortable arm chairs, 107, 206, 223
competence, 208, 258, 268-269, 284-285, 288, 291
competitive learning, 223
concentration, 86, 116
confidence, 91, 97-98, 121, 138, 180, 184, 315, 341, 412, 414, 425, 428
conjugations, 131, 159-160, 163-165, 169
Connelly, Governer John, 34
Connelly, Nellie, 34
content, 94-96, 102, 121, 145-146, 178, 186, 191, 194, 235-236, 248, 252-255, 306, 313, 315, 412
Coppola, Sophia, 34
correct guessing, 117, 173
Counter Intelligence Corps (CIC), 30
course objectives, 96, 99, 101, 195
cramming, 80, 112-113, 115-117, 122, 126, 135, 164, 252, 268, 284
criminal institution, 20, 56, 62, 330
criminal institutions, 38-39, 48, 362, 418
critical thinking, 3, 13, 47, 51, 53, 56, 58, 75, 127, 135, 190, 266, 268, 300, 304, 312, 439
critics, 3, 13-15, 93, 95, 261, 263, 270, 288, 292, 295, 338
Curley, Ambassador Walter, 413
Dachau, 30
Dandridge, Dorothy, 217, 218
Dante, 245
da Vinci, Leonardo, 245
Day, Doris, 34
Decision People Pattern™, 355, 357
delivery, 95, 194, 206, 209-

442

210, 235, 252
democracy, 37, 39-40, 43-45, 49-50, 52-53, 57-58, 69, 91, 135
desks, 107, 223
dialogical, 96, 255
Diderot, Denis, 246
Diet, David, 411
difference, (perceptual filter), 176, 258, 314, 320-324, 326-327, 332- 335, 337-339, 342-344, 349, 381, 422
Difference People Pattern™ 177, 322-325, 327, 331-333, 336-337, 344
dis-educational system™, 1, 6, 16, 20, 39, 46, 61-62, 68, 81, 83, 100-101, 108, 116-117, 135, 143, 161, 168-169, 176, 190, 201, 203, 208, 281, 297-298, 302, 304, 310, 312-314, 335, 354, 396, 401, 416-417
Dole, Senator Robert, 436
Dutchess of York, 34
Dylan, Bob, 34
ear for languages, 82-83, 293
educated citizenry, 33, 37, 266
education, 1, 2, 6, 14, 18, 33, 37, 39-41, 44-45, 50, 53, 55-58, 62, 65, 69, 76, 79, 83, 85, 91, 98, 122, 126, 135, 165-167, 213, 231, 233, 242, 246, 248, 257, 261, 263, 264, 266-271, 281-282, 284, 289, 292, 295-300, 304, 306, 311, 317, 324, 332, 335, 342, 344, 361, 367, 370-372, 378, 380, 388, 396, 402, 418, 421, 424
Education and Democracy, 37, 39-40, 53, 58, 266
Educators, 68, 78, 93, 111, 146, 148, 262, 264-265, 268, 270, 284, 287, 297, 303-304, 306, 310-311, 315, 317, 387, 400-401, 417
effort to remember, 122-123, 134
Eleventh Commandment, 74, 347
emotional intelligence, 301
esprit de classe, 96, 221-226, 228-229, 250-251, 256- 258, 304, 350, 381, 385, 391-394
Evaluation People Pattern™, 74, 319, 345-347
excitement, 13, 20, 64, 75, 77, 83, 85-86, 90-91, 100, 107-108, 114, 116-119, 137, 140-143, 182, 184-185, 188-190, 200, 203-209, 230, 257-258, 291, 295, 303, 306, 310, 315-316, 343, 372, 393, 395, 403, 417, 428-429
Experts on Experts™, 1, 437
explanations, 93, 96, 98, 125-126, 132, 159, 167, 170-173, 176-178, 188, 191, 194-195, 197, 214,

220-221, 232, 236, 242-243, 251, 255-256, 258, 272-273, 278-279, 282-283, 288, 304-305
External Evaluation People Pattern™, 345
facial expressions, 152, 214, 218, 429
far transfer learning, 286
fatigue, 117-118, 203, 207, 411
fault, 121, 137, 139, 211, 230
Fay, Dr. J. Michael, 380, 383, 385, 399, 410
Feels Right Decision People Pattern™, 356-358
Fleishmann, Dr., 88
Fleming, Howard A., 394
flip charts, 107, 223
Ford Foundation, 363, 372-374, 384
forgetting, 113, 122, 128-129, 234, 285
Foundation for Better Learning, 370
Franklin, Benjamin, 68
freedom of mind, viii, 9, 13, 21, 33, 38-40, 46, 48-49, 57-58, 295, 297, 311, 361, 370, 419
freeing minds, 7, 20
freeing minds one person at a time, 21, 38, 61, 92, 295, 377, 420
Freida, viii
French Resistance, 10, 26, 28, 324
Friedman, Dr. Steven S., 399

functional vocabulary, 34, 97-98, 192, 195, 234, 274, 287, 425
generalizations, 96, 159, 170, 181, 183, 194, 235, 249, 272, 287
George Washington Carver Junior High School, 379, 385, 399, 412
Gestapo, 11, 26-28, 352
gestures, 214-218, 429
getting to know me, 211-212 283, 326-327, 331-334, 346, 351, 359
Gibson, Mel, 34, 237
gift for languages, 82
global (perceptual filter), 353-355
Goldman, Daniel, 301
Goodled, Dr., 372-373
Goodman, Dr. Harold, 1
grammar, 34, 80, 94, 96-99, 101, 103, 141, 146-147, 149-150, 152-153, 155-160, 162-163, 168, 178, 180, 192, 195, 216-217, 219, 271-274, 277-278, 287, 338-339, 342, 354, 357, 401, 409, 425
Grammatical rules, 98, 131, 153, 158-159, 171, 183
grammatical terms, 98, 153-155
Griffith, Melanie, 34
ground rules, 101, 120, 236, 382
group dynamics, 96, 110, 221
Gruen, Victor, 366-368
guessing, 99, 117, 141, 154,

INDEX

156, 172-173, 208, 219, 278, 280, 282, 357
Gunsky, Frederic R., 397
Guri, 47, 70-74, 241
handles, 169, 179, 320
hatred, 53, 54, 68-69, 71-73
Hayden, Dr. Rose, 411
heuristics, 96, 170-174 176, 184, 195, 214, 220-221, 253, 258, 272, 341
Hirshhorn, Joseph, 364, 367
history (teaching), 237-246, 250
Hitler, Adolf, 51-54
homework, 4, 34, 68, 80, 99, 101, 103, 112-114, 143-144, 193, 236, 251, 257, 271, 302, 314, 386, 405
horizontal perspective, 237-239, 242
how to learn, 214, 261, 305-306, 310, 315
Hughes Aircraft Company, 397, 411
Hutchins, Dr. Robert, 363-364, 367-368
Idessa, viii, 24
imprint, 96, 123-124, 132-133, 143, 179, 201
incentive based learning, 96, 236, 348-349, 386
ineffective learning methods, 117
initial frames, 95, 96, 101-103, 115, 120, 145, 236, 255, 291, 391
innate drive for learning, 4, 13, 14, 19-20, 45, 64, 76-80, 91-92, 105, 118, 137, 140-141, 184, 201, 204,

257-258, 297, 301, 304-305, 310, 312, 349, 377, 385-386, 406, 417-418
inner potentials, 106
intangible (perceptual filter), 350-352, 355
interchange, 110
Internal Evaluation People Pattern™, 74, 345-347
in the now, 115, 124, 127
intuitor, 351
Jacquard, Mr., 401- 402
Jefferson, Thomas, 40, 68
Justice, Robbie, 411
Karthaus, Rob, 395, 414
Kasza, Mrs. 387
Keegan, Warren, 414
Kelly, Grace, 35, 364
Kelly, Janis, 414
Knittel, SS Major Gustav, 31
knowledge based on *understanding*, 126-127, 134-135, 232
La Chanson de Roland, 245
La Société d'Encouragement au Progrès, 378-379
Lange, Hope, 34
layering, 96, 143, 196-199, 210, 232, 235, 239, 248, 254
Le Carre, John, 23
learning by rote, 80, 101, 103, 117, 193
learning environment, 95, 96, 105-108, 110, 139, 207, 221-222,, 235, 256, 288, 308, 421
Learning How to Learn Technology™, 124, 308,

313, 436
learning potential, 35, 70, 76, 81, 105-107,138, 222, 303
learning process of the human mind, 33-35, 61, 90, 93, 107, 131, 133, 195, 261, 271, 322, 334, 357, 359
learning transfer, 267, 287
learning with *understanding*, 267
lectures, 109, 114, 193
lecturing, 65, 108-109, 114, 167, 228, 244, 251, 258, 302
L'Enfant Sauvage, 82
Levitte, Ambassador Jean Louis, 436
Lincoln, Abraham, 68
Lippman, Walter, 363
Locke, John, 246
long box, 159-163, 338-339
Looks Right Decision People Pattern™, 354-355
Los Angeles County Superintendent of Schools, 410
Lozanov, Georgi, 287-288
Mahl, Emil, 30
makes sense, 131, 134, 141, 159, 171-172, 177, 183, 231, 254, 279, 340,
Makes Sense Decision People Pattern™, 354-355
Mann, Katherine, 371-372, 397
Mansfield, Jayne, 34, 84
mantram, 63, 127, 141, 174, 327
Maritain, Jacques, 361
masses, 15, 38, 40, 41, 42, 43, 44, 45, 46, 48, 49, 50, 51, 52, 53, 54, 55, 56, 57, 61, 69, 75, 415, 417
mathematics (teaching), 246- 248
meaningful memory associations™, 96, 125, 146, 170-174, 176-178, 180-181, 184, 190-191, 194-195, 214, 232, 239, 254, 258, 272-274, 278-279, 282-283, 288, 305, 342
Meede, Ed, 373
memorization, 4, 86, 101, 104, 114, 116, 117, 122, 123, 126, 141, 146, 156, 159, 162, 163, 175, 176, 193, 194, 236, 244, 246, 248, 255, 275, 281, 285, 286, 300, 312, 315, 340, 341, 386, 408
memorizing, 80, 94, 98, 103, 112, 113, 115, 123, 131, 133, 135, 164, 172, 239, 243, 244, 247, 248, 267, 268, 271, 273, 281, 284, 286, 304, 312, 313, 354, 407, 413
memory, 96, 124-126, 133-134, 163, 177-178, 206, 247, 255, 271-274, 285-287, 313, 315
memory mechanisms™, 96, 120, 123-124, 274, 305, 315
Mencken, H.L., 44

mentally reaching, 228
meta-cognition, 183, 212 230-231, 240, 267, 280-283, 285, 287, 324, 327, 329, 332-333, 428
method (definition), 94
method elements, 96
Michel look, 10, 11, 28, 40, 224, 381
Michel Thomas Method, 4, 6, 13-16, 23, 37, 38, 43, 67, 70, 90-93, 110, 120, 125, 134, 148, 176, 193, 262-264, 267, 289, 297, 310, 318, 331, 336, 404-405, 416, 427
Milice, 28
Mind Prison™, 39, 48, 61-62, 66-69, 75-76, 80-81, 85-86, 91-92, 100-101, 107, 112, 141, 150, 175, 191, 196, 200-201, 203, 205, 213, 236, 251, 253, 289, 297, 301-302, 309-311, 313-314, 316, 344, 354, 417, 419
Mishie, 47, 69-70, 74
mismatcher, 323, 344
mistakes, 69-70, 99, 121, 136-137, 152, 156-157, 165-168, 211, 213, 230-234, 251, 275-280, 282, 288, 291, 331-332, 348, 425, 427-428
misunderstanding, 218-219
model of the world, 5, 221, 237, 270, 283, 297, 318, 319, 325, 332, 342, 343, 417, 422-423
model school, 34, 302, 361-363, 370-374
Moniek Kroskof, 23
Montand, Yves, 34, 150, 215-217
Morris, Dean Herbert, 400, 403-404, 410
Motivation People Pattern™, 319, 347-349
motivation for learning, 78-79
move away from (perceptual filter), 347-349, 386
move toward (perceptual filter), 347-350, 386
multi-tracking, 198
Murray, Bill, 34
myths of learning, 81
National Archives of the United States, 30
National Education Association (NEA), 399-400, 409-410, 412
National Research Council, 264, 268-270, 275
native speakers, 147, 425
Nazis, 11, 24, 52, 71-72, 336-337
near transfer learning, 286
neuroscience, 265
new school, 5, 126, 212, 268, 270, 272-274, 286, 428
no *trying*, 114, 123, 172
not being understood, 218
notes, 34, 99, 101, 103-104, 107, 114, 236, 250, 255, 407, 425
old school, 267, 270, 274, 284, 286, 289, 311, 315
Operation Paper Clip, 337

Oppenheimer, Jesse, 363
overview of method elements, 96
paradox of *trying*, 115
parent-centered teaching, 308
parents (what to do), 307-311, 418-419
Parsons, Louella, 368
patterns, 45, 67, 119, 143, 159, 162, 176, 183-184, 187, 258, 269, 271-272, 305, 309, 319, 342, 344
pedagogical principles, 5, 261, 288, 295
People Patterns™, iv, 74, 176, 191, 258, 318-320, 322-325, 327, 331-333, 336-337, 344-355, 357, 359, 438
Perceptual Source People Pattern™, 350-352
physics (teaching)
polarity responder, 322-323
politicians, 55, 65, 75-76, 261, 267, 270, 297-298, 300, 303, 310-311, 373
Polyglot Institute, 33, 431
Posvar, Wesley, 395, 413
practice, 97-98, 116, 131-132, 135, 189, 201-202, 254, 261-264, 265, 270-272, 285, 287-288, 291, 295, 425
practitioners, 262, 289
pre-existing knowledge, 267, 274, 280, 287
Preminger, Otto, 217
Presidio, 392, 394
Presley, Priscilla, 34

press, 4, 55, 75, 202, 218, 368, 378, 407
pressure, 66, 129, 135-137, 144, 156, 233, 256-257, 275, 299-300, 310
Preston, Kelly, 34
Prince Rainier, 35, 364-369
Princess Grace, 365, 368-369
qualified difference (perceptual filter), 321-322
qualified sameness (perceptual filter), 321, 343
Rabi, Isador, 363
Rand Corporation, 373, 398
rapport, 185
real learning, 20, 77, 116, 142, 184, 203, 258, 405
real teaching, 80, 108-110, 114, 167, 186, 248, 251, 382
Reed, Joseph Verner (UN Undersecretary General), 413
Reiners, The Carl, 34
relax, 111, 114-116, 121, 191, 193, 218, 230, 290-291, 410
relaxation, 111-113, 115, 289, 291
remembering, 67, 94, 102-104, 110-112, 119-124, 126-128, 130, 132, 136-137, 145, 172, 178, 213, 236, 251, 255, 258, 271-274, 278, 288, 291, 349, 386
research on memory, 125, 177

responsibility, 66, 67, 70, 72-74, 94, 102-104, 111-112, 115, 119-122, 124, 136-137, 140, 211, 213, 233, 236, 251, 258, 271-272, 274, 279, 288, 291, 300, 304-307, 313, 349, 355, 383, 386, 405, 418
responsibility for learning, 66, 136, 213, 251, 288, 349, 386, 405
responsibility for remembering, 67, 112, 119, 122, 124, 274
Robbins, Christopher, 23
Roberts, Hayden, 395
Ross, Diana, 34
rote learning, 115, 122-123, 205, 252, 270, 272, 407
Sadler, William, 414
sameness (perceptual filter), 297, 320-322, 332-333, 338-339, 343, 401
Sameness People Pattern™, 176
San Antonio Texas School District, 412
San Fernando Valley State College, 394
Sberro, Michel, 27
school boards, 75, 297-298, 311, 418
science (teaching), 246-252
scientific, 261-263, 286, 364
second mother, 89
secret of remembering, 120
self-confidence, 83, 85, 100, 138, 310, 347, 349, 377, 383, 398, 410, 429
self-correcting, 96, 231, 279, 332
sequencing, 95-96, 191-192, 235, 252
Seventh Annual International Bilingual Bi-cultural Education in San Juan, Puerto Rico, 389, 429
sharpened awareness of one's own language, 96, 146, 149-151, 169-170
Sheldon, Steven, 402
Sherman, Joan, 413
short box, 160-163, 340-341
Silver Star, 29, 436
Simon, Herbert, 267
Smith, Sharon P., 413
social psychology, 265
Sorbonne, 33, 87, 90, 365
Sorenson, Garth, 402, 410
Sounds Right Decision People Pattern™, 356-357
specific (perceptual filter), 353-355
standardized tests, 253, 267, 270, 275, 299-300
starting vocabulary, 147
Stein, Jules, 362
St. John, Jill, 34
Streisand, Barbra, 34
structure, 80, 96-99, 101, 103, 105, 142, 149, 153, 168, 171-172, 175, 178, 185, 188, 191, 193-194, 216, 219, 234- 236, 244, 254, 271, 278, 332, 338-340, 354, 357, 390, 398, 400, 410, 412
students (what to do), 312-

316
subconscious, 116, 128-129
suggestology, 289
suggestopedia, 289
supra-national university, 34, 361-363, 365, 368, 419
Sutherland, Donald, 34
tapes 98, 143, 187, 202, 277, 292-293, 373, 389, 392-393, 416, 426-429
teachers (what to do), 303-305,
tenses, 34, 80, 96, 99, 101, 103, 112, 153, 155-157, 163, 168- 169, 175, 192, 216-217, 274, 287, 338-339, 357, 389,425
tension, 66, 81, 86, 91-92, 103-105, 107, 110-122, 124, 128, 134-139, 144-145, 152, 156, 168, 178, 182, 194, 206-207, 209, 210, 213, 222, 231, 233, 236, 252, 255, 273-274, 279, 288, 291, 302, 304, 310, 348-350, 377, 386, 393
textbooks, 80, 94, 101, 103-104, 114, 158, 163, 193-194, 236, 251, 255, 257, 344, 408, 411
The Children of Light and Wisdom Foundation, Inc., 17
The CLWF Institute for Global Leadership, 17, 302, 438
The Test of Courage, 23
theory, 126, 167, 248, 261-265, 269, 295, 421
thinking it out, 99, 208, 272, 282
thinking out, 115, 208-209, 282, 288
think it out, 99, 137, 141, 205, 234, 272, 278, 282, 288
Thompson, Emma, 34, 121, 409
thought control, 13, 16, 18-19, 38, 48-49, 54, 295, 415
Thunderbirds, 29
Tillich, Paul, 363
tools of the language, 94, 96, 425
traditional belief systems, 107, 113
traditional classroom, 106, 107, 200, 229, 236
traditional demands of learning, 113
train course, 406
transfer problem, 284
Truffaut, François, 34, 82, 83, 409
truth about memory, 124
try to remember, 103, 111, 120, 123, 128, 132-134, 136, 255
trying to remember, 4, 101, 103, 111, 122-123, 129, 133-134, 172, 271-272, 274, 410
Twelfth Commandment, 75, 328, 329
two mothers, viii, 11, 24, 325, 329
unconscious competency, 5,

420
understanding, 96, 126-131, 146, 211, 232, 273, 357-359
United Teacher, 378, 400, 412
United Teachers Los Angeles (UTLA), 397, 400, 410, 412
Universalist, 11, 70, 73
University of Alberta, 395
University of Bordeaux, 24, 87, 90, 336
University of Calgary, 394
University of California's School of Law and of Journalism at Berkeley, 30
University of Lethbridge, 395
University of Pittsburgh, 395-396, 413
University of Southern California, 401
unlearn, 165, 187, 276-277
unteach, 157, 187
Venge, 75, 328-330, 334, 347, 380, 382
vertical perspective, 238
Victor Gruen Associates, 366
violence, 64, 65, 204, 205, 302, 405
Voltaire, 246
Warner, Senator John, 436
Washington, George, 68
Welds, M.W., 397
Welsh, Raquel, 34, 409
wings, 174
wisdom of practice, 5, 6, 20, 36, 265, 271, 273, 280
Wolfe, Robert, 30
Wood, Natalie, 34
work hard, 66, 112, 135, 313, 349

Made in the USA
Charleston, SC
28 February 2010